Actors and Systems

**Michel Crozier
and Erhard Friedberg**

Translated by Arthur Goldhammer

Actors and Systems

The Politics of Collective Action

The University of Chicago Press

Chicago and London

Originally published as *L'acteur et le système*,
© 1977 by Editions Seuil

The University of Chicago Press, Chicago 60637
The University of Chicago Press, Ltd., London

87 86 85 84 83 82 81 80   54321

Library of Congress Cataloging in Publication Data

Crozier, Michel.
  Actors and systems.

  Translation of L' acteur et le système.
  Bibliography: p.
  Includes index.
  1. Organizational behavior.   2. Organization.
I. Friedberg, Erhard, joint author.   II. Title.
HD58.7.C7613   302.3′5   80–13803
ISBN 0–226–12183–6

MICHEL CROZIER is the director of the Centre
de Sociologie des Organisations de Paris and the
former president of the French Association of
Sociology. He is coauthor of *The Crisis of
Democracy* and author of *The Stalled Society,* as
well as the author of *The Bureaucratic
Phenomenon* and *The World of the Office Worker,*
both published by the University of Chicago
Press. ERHARD FRIEDBERG, a fellow of the
International Institute of Management in Berlin
from 1973 to 1976 is assistant director of the
Centre de Sociologie des Organisations de Paris.

Contents

Acknowledgments

This work is the fruit of extensive labors carried out at the Centre de Sociologie des Organisations in Paris, at Harvard University in the United States, at the Center for Science in West Berlin, and at the advanced sociology seminar of Paris's Institut d'études politiques. We would like to thank all our colleagues—faculty, researchers, and students—at these various institutions for their helpful comments and criticisms.

In addition, both of us have benefited greatly from assistance generously provided by several research foundations, which has made our work far easier. Work on the book was begun while one of us was guest scholar at the Center for Advanced Studies in the Behavioral Sciences at Stanford. The other was supported throughout the period during which this work was written by the Internationales Institut für Management und Verwaltung of the West Berlin Center for Science, and particularly by its director, Professor Fritz W. Scharpf. Finally, both of us were guests of the Rockefeller Foundation at the Villa Serbelloni, where we were able to complete the writing of the book together. We would like to take this opportunity to express our deepest gratitude to these institutions and their directors.

Even a theoretical work in sociology cannot do without a considerable fund of empirical research from which to draw material for reflection. We hope that officials of the various French research agencies, as well as of the Ford Foundation in the United States, whose financial support made this work possible, will accept this expression of our thanks. Last but not least, we want to thank all those who participated in these studies, particularly those in the French governmental agencies, firms, and political and social organizations that we have investigated, for having been kind enough to answer our questions and thereby further our research efforts.

Michel Crozier
Erhard Friedberg

Introduction

This book was written for a French audience. Given the usual transatlantic misunderstandings, the English-language edition requires a special Introduction. Our intellectual trajectory is very different from that of our American colleagues. We started from the American organization theories of the fifties and in the course of trying to apply them in the interpretation of French realities, came to realize that we needed new theories. The limitations of the old paradigms were apparent in their inability to account for conditions in France, but the significance of this failure was even more profound. We came to believe that it revealed the fundamental inadequacy not only of the original models of organizations and systems theory but also of that of their contemporary American successors.

Despite its past glories, French sociology had subsided into a major lull from the twenties to the fifties. It began to flourish again in the fifties and caught up with the American-dominated international quantitative mode only in the mid sixties. In the field of organizational study there were two starting points: the Merton-Gouldner-Selznick sociological model, and the Michigan psycho-sociological model. But French researchers working from these models faced very specific cultural constraints. Trade unions, for example, were much more resistant to sociological surveys whose claims to neutrality remained to be demonstrated. More important was the tremendous gap within French management between theory—which tended more and more to be that of the American business schools—and actual practice. Under these circumstances the American paradigms could not be successfully applied. As usual in new scientific fields, misunderstanding and failure were strong incentives to break new ground. The elaboration of new paradigms led once again to major differences between European and American approaches. The issue, however, is not only one of European versus American sociology but of alternative approaches to the study of organization. This book presents one such approach developed in the course of twenty years of field research in France.

During most of this period the dominant Anglo-Saxon mode has been theoretical regarding the aims, quantitative regarding the methods.[1] Sociologists, particularly Americans, had become confident enough to believe that they could build theory or present theoretical propositions of universal value by comparing quantitative results derived from statistically significant variance of crucial indicators within samples of organizations. These theories, even when they were more sophisticated than the very crude first organizational laws proposed in the late sixties,[2] could not be applied to the French case. Viewed from France, even the dominant structural-contingency theories which appeared later were unduly deterministic.[3] To account for French empirical evidence and to obtain significant data, one had to develop a very different research strategy, one that led gradually to the elaboration of new paradigms and to the questioning of the American paradigms for the American context.

We believe that the social sciences have not progressed sufficiently in this field to make it possible to use such sophisticated instruments as our American colleagues use despite the poor quality of the very fuzzy indicators they are able to define. In our view research strategy should focus on organizations as distinct autonomous phenomena, but without treating them as quantitative units. We also believe that ethnomethodologists, even when they use the same empirical evidence as we do, do not provide a satisfactory alternative. They tend to extrapolate from the description of primary face-to-face encounters to generalized propositions about global society. Not only do they ignore the goals and results of human action, but they bypass the complex interrelations at the organizational or at the organized-systems level—market or institution—which do influence and give meaning to individual interaction.[4] For us, organizations and organized systems have enough au-

1. There had been, however, a timely warning against this trend, especially in B. G. Glaser and A. L. Strauss, *The Discovery of Grounded Theory* (London: Weidenfeld & Nicolson, 1968).

2. As in P. M. Blau and R. Schoenherr, *The Structure of Organizations* (New York: Basic Books, 1971). The vitality of Blau's flimsy model, even after the sharp and pertinent rebuke of Chris Argyris (1972), is attested to by the recurrent publication of laborously sophisticated articles in the *Administrative Science Quarterly*. See for example Robert Dewan and Gerald Hage, "Size, Technology and Structural Differentiation: Towards Theoretical Synthesis," *Administrative Science Quarterly*, March 1978, and Janice Beyer and Harrison M. Trice, "A Reexamination of Relations between Size and Various Components of Organizational Complexity," *Administrative Science Quarterly*, March 1979.

3. As shown by Paul Lawrence and Jay Lorsch, *Organizations and Environment* (Cambridge, Mass.: Harvard University Press, 1967), and John Child, "Strategies of Control and Organizational Behavior," *Administrative Science Quarterly*, March 1973.

4. Not only H. Garfinkel, *Studies in Ethnomethodology* (Englewood Cliffs, N.J.: Prentis Hall, 1967), and A. V. Cicourel, *Method and Measurement in Sociology* (New York: Free Press, 1964), but also E. Goffman, *Asylums* (Chicago: Aldine, 1961), and Howard Becker, ed., *The Other Side: Perspectives in Deviance* (New York: Free Press, 1964).

tonomy to make it impossible to understand their functioning either from a deterministic standpoint or as an extrapolation from primary group interaction. Our research strategy therefore consists, first of all, in using individual behavorial data. These indicators are the only reliable evidence for understanding not only the cultural or psychological forces but the specific "human construct" which our interviewees confront daily, namely, a single organization or a broader organized system. Instead of considering organizations as neutral transmission belts of human wishes, we assume that such transmission belts are more important than their motors. Our focal point is what Chandler has very aptly called the *management of the throughput* between the technological input and the economic results.[5] This may seem to bring us back to an earlier period when case studies were basic research strategy. Although we do appreciate and revere such works of the fifties as those of Gouldner, Selznick, and Whyte, we nevertheless have quite different concepts and methods.

The new paradigms we shall present and subsequently test on specific cases in this book can better be understood by examining our basic concepts: collective action, games, uncertainty, and power.

The concept of collective action is not original, of course, especially for organization theory. Nevertheless, its full implications have not been explored in the sociological literature.[6] It seems crucial to return to them in the present circumstances for one basic reason: when one begins from the collective-action standpoint, human behavior appears as neither a logical or necessary outcome of social interaction nor a result of the structures of the problems to be solved. The means and devices by which collective action is brought about can therefore no longer be considered as something obvious or natural (in the sense of "the nature of things"). It becomes a problem for research and explanation.[7]

Organizations are not "natural" beasts whose existence is a given of nature. They are "human constructs" developed half consciously, half

5. Alfred D. Chandler, Jr., *The Visible Hand: The Managerial Revolution in American Business* (Cambridge, Mass.: Belknap Press, 1977).

6. As a matter of fact, it is only during the last years that the basic paradigm of Mancur Olson (*The Logic of Collective Action* [Cambridge, Mass.: Harvard University Press, 1965]) has begun to be used seriously by young American sociologists. See for example the seminal article by Mark Granovetter, "Threshold Models of Collective Behavior," *American Journal of Sociology*, vol. 83, no. 6 (1978), and the excellent case study by Gerald Maxwell and Ruth Ames, "Experiments on the Provisions of Public Goods: Resources, Interest, Group Size, and the Free Rider Problem," American Journal of Sociology, vol. 84, no. 6 (1979). In both cases it is characteristic, however, that the references are only to economics and that the reasoning does not account for the organizational or even social construct.

7. Here our debt to Herbert Simon is great. We feel much closer to some American political scientists and economists (such as Herbert Simon, James G. March, Tom Schelling, and Graham Allison) than to most of our fellow organizational sociologists.

unconsciously, by man to solve problems of collective action, and above all the most basic of these—cooperation for the production of some collective good by relatively autonomous social actors pursuing diverse and always, in a certain sense, conflicting interests. The most urgent question posed by the existence of organizations, therefore, is not what kind of formal and structural regularities exist in organizations. A basic paradox of collective action, the counter-intuitive effect, may be presently considered, in that respect, the first useful paradigm of organization and system theory.

The counter-intuitive effect arises from the logical structure of the problem. If one looks further, however, it is also, and may be principally, an organizational or systemic effect. When results of collective action are the opposite of what individual actors wished, it is never merely because of the properties of the problem. It is always also the result of the human structuration of the field of action, that is, because of the characteristics of the organization or of the system in which the actors interact and to which they are committed.

Moreover, the real advantage of organizations and organized systems may lie in their ability to offer a more reliable and more useful way to structure the human field of participants, actors, and clients than that offered in a nonorganized field. In other words, organizations control the counter-intuitive effects inherent in problems. But when organizations regulate these first-order distortions, they produce second-order distortions of their own, which are those we usually discover first in practice.

For the creators of the concept of collective action, the counter-intuitive paradox was only logical. We believe it has a sociological, that is, a "human construct" dimension—not because management problems would tend to be strongly influenced by "natural sociological"[8] determinants, but because very often it has become a social or organizational paradox. We therefore use the concept of collective action as yet another device to help people—and many an organizational sociologist as well—understand that organizations are extraordinarily binding human constructs, but that they are also contingent. In them there never was and never will be either one best way or the best contingent solution. Men build organizations to solve problems otherwise intractable. Before measuring the instrument or even trying to improve it, one should consider the actual problem to be solved.

But sociology has yet another contribution to offer. Organizations pro-

---

8. The two words should of course be antinomic, but we think that in many of our present trade discussions they are almost equivalent: God-given facts man has to cope with. The same remark is made by Andrew Van de Ven in his extremely pertinent critique of Howard Aldrich's book, *Organizations and Environments* (Englewood Cliffs, N.J.: Prentice Hall, 1979).

vide a crucial area in which the link between material results and human wishes may best be studied.

Let us recall, for the sake of clarity, the dilemma faced by two criminals arrested for the same crime but with no material evidence against them other than what might be elicited by the one's informing against the other. In this situation, each of the two prisoners has only two strategies for extricating himself: to deny the facts, or to incriminate the other. If both deny the facts, the police have no proof for their charges; all they can do is get the defendants convicted of lesser charges and sentenced to a year in prison. If one of the defendants agrees to turn state's evidence by informing on the other, the informer goes free, while the other is sentenced to twenty years in prison.

Aware of these consequences, each prisoner knows that the success of his own strategy will depend upon the strategy adopted by his accomplice. But since they are held in different jails, they have no opportunity of communicating and cooperating with each other. The logical structure of the problem is such that if they act "rationally," that is, serving their individual interests, each will betray his accomplice and both will find themselves back in prison for ten years. It should be emphasized that no judgment on "human nature" is implied here; it is merely assumed that each defendant will try to win and will place his own interests above those of his accomplice. Knowing the result makes no difference; both are caught in an "infernal logic" that leads them inevitably to defeat and is a consequence of the structure of the problem.

Only one thing can free people from the dilemma: the capacity to trust one another. Although this presents an ethical dimension, ethics here, as is often the case, is a result of a "social construct." The unwritten laws of the underworld are a good example. The law of silence may be subsumed, as it is in many romantic movies and thrillers, as an ethical principle; it is first of all a human construct achieved by training and sanction. What seems simply affective retaliation has become an organizing principle which is manipulated by the leaders of the underworld and which will be the cornerstone of whatever organization may be developed around these activities.

The free-rider problem can be analyzed in an analogous way. As trade unions everywhere well know, organization is the only way to force free-riders to pay for their benefits.[9] More generally, organization is a way of dealing with the otherwise insoluble problem of aggregating interests whose contradictory pursiut would otherwise frustrate all participants.

9. See the whole discussion of public goods in modern economics and especially G. Hardin, "The Tragedy of the Commons," *Science,* December 1968, p. 1243, and Gerald Maxwell and Ruth Ames, "Experiments on the Provision of Public Goods," *American Journal of Sociology* 84, no. 6 (1979):1335.

The trade union is, for example, built on such unnatural social behavior as trust, loyalty, accountability, responsibility, and so forth, all qualities whose social character is suggested by the sacred aura they still had in the early Middle Ages and by the very strong moral—that is, nonrational—connotation they retain now.

How is it done? Not by using these emotional moral feelings directly. These are indispensable props that make it possible for people to interact and cooperate, but they do not dictate behavior. They are merely the consequences of organizational life and, conversely, the condition for its development. They certainly do not integrate the conflicting strategies of the actors involved. This is accomplished through the creation and use of *structured games,* which must be considered as the real discovery of man as an organizational animal.

To engage in collective action, people pursuing contradictory interests have either to be coerced (or manipulated ideologically or affectively) or to bargain. Bargaining, first of all, is itself unnatural, and people do not engage in it without protective devices. Its possibility hinges upon the existence of those unnatural "moral" feelings we have just mentioned, and even then, it always means facing up to power relationships and to the constraining consequences of one's own course of action. Bargaining, moreover, is threatening, as its dynamics can operate in such a way that all parties involved may suffer.[10]

A good game is the real organizational trick. Suppose the field is structured and the problem redefined so that people can still pursue their own interests, while their winning and losing will not alter the collective good—will, in fact, improve it. We then avoid any kind of prisoner's dilemma; cooperation is achieved without suppressing people's freedom, that is, their right to pursue antagonistic interests.

One may object that reality is not so simple. Fair enough; this is why organizations, when considered as a human construct, appear such difficult, fragile, and almost impossible endeavors. Considering the context not only of bounded rationality, but also of bounded legitimacy (incomplete normative integration of members) and of bounded interdependence (incomplete functional integration of members), it is a miracle that organizations exist at all. Indeed, one could say that they do exist not so much because, but in spite of, the strategies of their members. The solution to this apparent paradox—and also a key to an understanding of an organization—lies in the analysis of the different power games which indirectly structure the strategies of the actors involved and constrain their freedom of choice.

10. Collective bargaining in many Western countries is a good current example. It can very well be understood as a mild prisoner's dilemma whose German or Swedish solution of complicity seems to be giving better results than working-class purity (and bourgeois egoism) of Italian or English partners.

When thinking about games, however, people have been too obsessed by the problems of the rules. Rules are necessary to maintain the game, to make it possible for people to be sure that no cheating will jeopardize their stakes, but they do not command behavior.[11] People are channeled, oriented, and led not by the rules but by the structure of the game, which determines a range of possible strategies and results. The game remains open, and several strategies remain possible, among which the players must and will indeed choose. Moreover, a player can even—if his resources allow it—accept initial losses in the hope of a later reversal of the game which will be profitable to him. In any case, the constraint here is always of an indirect nature; it is the result of the simple fact that so long as a player wishes to continue to play, and in order for his participation in the game to be profitable to him, he must adopt some strategy whereby he will contribute to the continuation of the game and thus, nolens volens, to the production of the collective good.

What about coercion or ideological or affective manipulation? We do not deny that they exist and constitute a means to enforce the rules and to command behavior, but we rather analyze them as another kind of game, a very poor one indeed, which is at best a zero-sum game and which may indeed have negative results.

Now let us examine the paradox with which we began. Organization is a human construct with which people hope to solve the problems that remain intractable so long as one is limited to the singular logic of collective action. With the help of such a construct, people do not get rid of counter-intuitive effects, but replace one kind of negative counter-intuitive effect with another, more positive, kind.

Two questions then arise. First, what kind of a link exists between the logical and the organizational structure? Second, what about the new counter-intuitive effects?

The first question brings us back to the results of organizational analysis. We propose *uncertainty* as the key concept of the logical structure of the problem to be dealt with and *power* as the key concept for the human construct that will have to deal with it.

There are no social problems without uncertainty, none which do not, in other words, leave the actors with a substantial margin of liberty in the choice and implementation of practical solutions. Problems without uncertainty are not really human problems. They can be dealt with by automatic or cybernetic (in the sense of self-regulating) devices.[12]

11. Cheating may be understood as another free-rider problem, but as a matter of fact, it may be and usually is organized in another kind of game.

12. This seems to us the basic fallacy of the cybernetic analogies that seem to gain ground in social science and in systems theory; it is based on the assumption that human systems can be compared to systems controlled and governed by self-regulating services.

Uncertainty, however, is the basic resource in any kind of bargaining.[13]

Here we can find the basic link between the two structures. People are unequal before the uncertainties of the problem. Those who can cope with them because of their situation, their resources, or their competence have an advantage.

The logical structure of the problems as embodied by individual or collective actors thus unavoidably becomes a structured field. This means that real solutions will develop along three possible lines:

1. No bargain can be struck; the logical structure cannot be dealt with by the concerned players as they can presently organize; the problem will be ignored.
2. Bargaining will develop empirically along lines corresponding to the structure of the problem and to the personal and social strengths and capacities of the players.
3. An organization already in charge will handle uncertainty according to its own capacities; it will, that is, develop a game that will be its contingent solution.

The third eventuality is, of course, the crucial one for the discussion of formal organizations. Organizational games are built around logical, "objective" uncertainties, those of the techniques, of the markets, of the different constraints which are, at least for the short-run, stable, unshakable givens.[14] Those who get the upper hand in the game are those who control most of the crucial uncertainties. But the way the game is structured and the stakes determined will reduce the possible gains and losses to acceptable proportions. Artificial uncertainties such as authority distribution, information channels, and legal constraints, can, on the other hand, counterbalance the "objective" ones. Indeed, the creation of such "artificial" uncertainties will be a precondition for the establishment of a game. In any case, this means that to be processed, problems will have to be redefined either to fit prevailing games or at least to allow for the creation of some artificial uncertainties without which no bargain can be struck. Finally, most formal organizations cannot be understood on the basis of one game that explains them entirely. There are many games and layers of games. Part 1 and 2 of this book will deal with formal organization games. Part 3 will deal with organized systems which correspond to the second eventuality.[15]

13. This mode of reasoning was first tried by March and Simon in a logical, nonsociological way. Crozier used it first in an article published in French in 1962 (De la bureaucratie comme système d'organisation. Archives Européennes de Sociologie, 1, no. 2: 18–52). Crozier developed it substantially as a sociological concept in *The Bureaucratic Phenomenon*. Many Anglo-Saxon sociologists have since used it: D. Hickson and Ch. Perrow in the late 60s; more recently P. Abell (1975) and G. Benveniste (1977).

14. Ultimately, all constraints, even technical ones, are amenable to change and can also be considered for the long run as a human construct.

One last point: what is uncertainty in the logic of the "objective" problem is also *power* from the point of view of the actors and for the organization. Organization as a human construct deals basically with power.[16] It is organizing, regularizing, taming power that makes it possible for men to cooperate. Organizing, however, is a difficult endeavor: if it goes too far in trying to suppress empirical "natural" power, it will risk raising artificial power to an unbearable degree; if it does not try hard enough, a growing maze of privileges will develop.[17]

This leads us to the problem of the counter-intuitive effects of the organizational construct. They are the immediate consequence of the course taken. Each organizational solution, because it deals directly with the most threatening element of human interaction, power, raises problems of communication and commitment. Because power is involved, threatening information will not be processed. Bureaucratic dysfunctions will develop. Vicious circles of low commitment, poor communications, and inadequate performances will develop. Efforts to shake them will bring back privileges and will initiate other vicious circles. New games will emerge, games of privilege and cheating. We will then have a real organization, the human construct of the practitioner, not the one with which the theoretician is familiar.

From this standpoint organizations and organized systems can be considered as, at the same time, the necessary means and the basic operational constraints of collective action.

Now we come to the second question: What about the new counter-intuitive effect? Organizations and organized systems generally appear to be the basic operational constraints of collective action. From a short-run perspective, at least, collective action takes place only through already

15. In this part we will join a growing and more promising trend in American sociology: networks, interorganizational systems. See especially J. K. Benson, "The Interorganizational Network as a Political Economy," *Administrative Science Quarterly,* June 1975; William Evan, *Organizational Theory* (1976); and Herman Turk,*Organizations in Modern Life: Cities and other Large Networks* (San Francisco: Jossey-Bass, 1977).

16. American organizational sociologists never seemed to understand this point. American sociology in any case did not face up to the problem of power, except for the recent Marxian treatment, which was more emotional than reasoned. Europeans have been more open to this new paradigm. See for example David Hickson et al., "Grounds for Comparative Organization Theory: Quicksand or Hard-Core?" in C. J. Lammers and David Hickson, eds., *Organizations Alike and Unlike: Towards a Comparative Sociology of Organizations* (London: Routledge and Kegan Paul, 1979); Mauk Moulder, *The Daily Power Game* (The Hague: Martinus Nijhoff, 1977); and Peter Abell, ed., *Organizations as Bargaining and Influence Systems* (New York: Halsted Press, 1975).

17. This too sketchy presentation could give the impression that we pretend this is a black-and-white or zero-sum game proposition, which it is not. The capacity of people to play more sophisticated games of conflict and cooperation must be added as a necessary third dimension. Developing this capacity is the only alternative to the increase of "artificial" bureaucratic power. We deal with those problems specifically in part 1 of the book.

existing organizations, or at least through stable organized systems, the underlying games of which mediate between the means and the ends of collective action. Substitutions among these organized structures are possible, but on the whole there is not much possibility of selection. We are in a sellers' market: many problems and few solutions, which in turn implies that, in the short run at least, means have more importance than ends. Ends are chosen to a surprising degree because of the availability of means. Very often means command over ends.

Of course, new organizations can be built; new systems to regulate cooperation and conflict can be achieved; even new markets can be developed. But it takes time. Achieving flexibility through all-purpose or very malleable organizations can be hoped for, and there is certainly a good deal of progress in that direction. But we generally remain within the domain where constraints prevail.

In the past, the counter-intuitive dimension of organizational life was obscured behind religious, moral, and patriotic taboos. People played games, of course, but they would not admit this. The gradual disappearance of the aura of "natural law" which hung over this order of things, which we now begin to think of as a construct, has led to an intellectual as well as a moral crisis. While the contingent, that is, man-made, nature of existing arrangements becomes more visible and thus more difficult to legitimize, our intellectual tools—and above all the still dominant mode of reasoning from ends to means—become more inadequate to deal with our difficulties.[18]

Behind this crisis and the revival of half-baked utopias such as the transparent society, the self-management society, the relational society, as well as such scientific naiveties as cybernetic models,[19] there lies a real organizational crisis, for conditions of organizational life are in the process of radical transformation. The basic game patterns we had been accustomed to and which were, to some extent, self-perpetuating, have been upset. New patterns do not emerge easily. Our capacity to handle problems decreases, while the pressure for solving the ever increasing number of them rises considerably. The main reason for this new course can be traced back to the impact of the very success of economic development and the rapid increase in human interactions and communications which that development brought about, on the basic bargaining relationship of the individual with an organization or with any established authority. In this respect, one can never emphasize enough the funda-

18. Here again we recognize the influence of Herbert Simon and James G. March, whose concept of bounded rationality helped us immeasurably. We discuss the problems of rationality in part 4, "Decision Making."

19. Their common characteristic being the absence of any thinking about power and the problem of power as an unavoidable ingredient to any human interaction.

mental changes that take place when the existence of real alternatives allows the individual to take risks, for as soon as the freedom of choice of the individual has passed a certain threshold, the structure of the games changes. Once the individual can choose effectively, once he has alternatives, he can and will bargain differently. Not only can he compare overall alternatives, but he can bargain on a day-by-day basis. Government by fragmentation, isolation, and control of possible alternatives will give way. To give but one example: once the parish priest can really opt out of his institution without being sanctioned for his deviant behavior, as he traditionally would have been, the ecclesiastical authority of the bishop lost much of its power, and the traditional game between the two changed. Value changes may eventually follow these more basic changes. But in this case, as in many others one could think of, traditional authority disintegrates not so much because of value changes as because of the changing structure of the conventional game.

This development forces upon organizations an enormous and hardly manageable increase in complexity in two ways. Those who can choose among several games are much less predictable and therefore cannot be led as easily. Moreover, when a choice exists, the structure of the problem itself becomes more complex. The communication explosion, which can be viewed as a consequence of freedom and complexity and which feeds back on both, has also had its own special impact. It helps change the balance of the bargaining, since communication is a basic resource of the power play. But it also invariably changes the problem itself; and by forcing the counter-intuitive effects into the open, it is at the root of the intellectual and moral paradox which we have presented and which brings another form of pressure upon the traditional order of things.

All these converging pressures and the vicious circles that tend to disintegrate old forms of organizational games can thus be viewed as the results of an irrevocable trend toward more complex and more open kinds of collective action. This should be considered with hope, or at least with equanimity. Man will be forced to invent new games and more flexible organizations and organized systems. He is gradually liberating himself from the constraint of the means, of which he had been a prisoner. The accompanying moral crisis, the exaggerated hopes and fears we are suffering, may be simply episodes of false consciousness that were to be expected.[20]

This may be true in the long run, but one ought to beware in the short

---

20. This has been discussed at length in the European section of a Trilateral Commission report by Michael Crozier, Samuel Huntington, and Joji Watanuki, published in English as *The Crisis of Democracy: Report on the Governability of Democracies to the Trilateral Commission* (New York: New York University Press, 1975).

run of the sheer limits of the problem structure and the extreme difficulties one meets in developing these exceptional human constructs: new games, new organizational forms, more sophisticated organized systems. Here, we feel, we converge very much with the seminal work of Argyris and Schon on double-loop learning which, for us,[21] revives the best tradition of American pragmatism. The salience of the problem does not make it easier to tackle. We will discuss in the last part of this book the problem of change[22] and the contribution the sociology of organizations could make and should make to it. Two preliminary remarks seem pertinent here.

Present circumstances increase the relevance of organizational analysis and at the same time make it more difficult. The disappearance of ritual forms and traditional smoke screens has eliminated a great many of the old taboos. Authority, especially, has been exposed in a ruthless way; it has become quite easy to get at it, now that it has lost all its earlier paraphernalia. But a last taboo remains: power, a taboo which indeed is most stifling for the analysis of organized action.

Some people, including many an American sociologist, may be puzzled by this proposition, since they implicitly equate power with established authority. But this is exactly what has to be questioned. Power relations and the problems they raise are not merely the result of superimposed authority structures, be they organizational or social, that is, the expression of patterns of social domination. They are a basic and ever-present ingredient in any kind of social relation which can always be analyzed as an embryo of collective action involving power and influence bargaining.[23] There is no getting around it: any attempt at defining away the phenomenon by labelling it differently (as, say, influence) and by subordinating it (that is, making it a function of some superordinate mode of domination)[24] does not change this basic fact: power and its hidden counterparts, manipulation and blackmail, are unavoidable components of any collective endeavor. As such, they raise concrete problems that have to be handled. However critical we must be of the traditional and present hierarchical structures built to deal with these problems, getting rid of the former will not be enough to bring about a solution for the latter. To solve these, men will have to find new ways, develop new games, to handle power. And the first way in which social science might make a real contribution is to break the taboo of power by dealing with it in a more

21. Chris Argyris and Donald A. Schon, *Organizational Learning: A Theory of Action Perspective* (Reading, Mass.: Addison-Wesley, 1978).

22. See part 5, "Change."

23. Among many others, this has been shown very forcefully by the work of Ronald Laing. This has at last been recognized by Michel Foucault, *Discipline and Punish: The Birth of the Prison*, trans. Alan Sheridan (New York: Pantheon, 1978).

24. As for example Stuart Clegg, *Power, Rule, and Domination* (London: Routledge and Kegan Paul, 1975).

detached and scientific way, and thus to train people to face the problem by themselves.

This brings us to our second remark concerning the methodology of organizational research. When considering the problem as it has been outlined, especially in view of the strength of the power taboo among politically progressive people as well as among conservatives, we believe that the basic strategy of organizational research should revolve around organizational analysis understood in an empirical way.[25]

It seems obvious that we should first of all try to understand present power arrangements as the key to these contingent constructs we call organizations. Though this should be simple enough, it seems to present some difficulties. When one realizes that few organizational papers published in American journals have been written by people who have had personal contact with the organization studied, and that few of the remaining articles have dealt with any kind of power issue, one can understand why American sociology has lost so much ground and why a change of paradigm in Kuhn's sense is strongly need.[26]

In a very provocative recent book Roberts, Hulin, and Rousseau[27] discuss the "sense of discouragement" with which one confronts the present state of knowledge in the field of organizational theory. "The continued emphasis on narrower and narrower views of responses made by individuals in organizations, concentration on individual differences to the exclusion of environmental effects or concentration on organizational variables to the exclusion of individual differences or societal variables will generate more precise knowledge about increasingly trivial matters."[28]

In this book we seek to establish a high priority for empirical analysis over any kind of hypothetico-deductive theory. This does not mean discarding theory but using it to enable us to get at the facts and question them in a more sophisticated manner. This means that we are trying to elaborate a new paradigm which should help overcome the present complacency and discouragement so prevalent in the American sociological milieu.

This of course is only a first attempt and cannot be a refined intellectual system. But in the present state of the art, we believe that explorations are more useful than formal coherent theories.[29]

25. This point is developed in the Appendix.
26. European sociology seems much more lively by comparison. Works of young Englishmen like Peter Abell, of Swedes like Eric Rhenman and Richard Normann, of Germans like Niklas Luhmann, not to mention one's own countrymen, testify to Europe's presently greater creativity.
27. Karlene Roberts, Charles Hulin, and Denise Rousseau, *Developing an Interdisciplinary Science of Organizations* (San Francisco: Jossey Bass, 1978).
28. Ibid., p. 136.
29. This is what Roberts, Hulin, and Rousseau call a Dionysian strategy as against an Apollonian one.

One   **The Organization as Problem**

1

The Actor and His Strategy

The Actor's Margin of Liberty

A completely inaccurate image of organized action is generally accepted. We overestimate by far the degree of rationality that operates in organizations. We are thus led, on the one hand, to admire their effectiveness uncritically—or at least to assume that it requires no explanation. On the other hand, we exhibit greatly exaggerated fears for the oppressive threat to mankind which organizations supposedly represent. A mechanical analogy comes to mind. "Organization" evokes, first of all, a complex set of gears perfectly fitted to one another. Such a clockwork mechanism seems admirable as long as it is examined solely from the aspect of the desired result, the end product. Its significance changes radically when it is realized that the cogs are in reality men. It then becomes the nightmare of "modern times."

Despite the tenacious efforts of certain visionaries to achieve their technocratic dreams, reality has never even remotely approached this fictional view. Every minimally serious analysis of the real life of an organization has shown the degree to which the human behavior within its framework can remain complex and escape the confines of a simplistic model of mechanical interconnection or simple determinism.[1]

The first explanation of such a gap between theory and reality is that, even in extreme situations, men hold on to a minimum of freedom which they cannot refrain from using to "beat the system."[2]

True, it is possible, while admitting the existence of such practices, to consider them as exceptions which the system can tolerate because they do not call its effectiveness into question and only marginally weaken its oppressive character. Such a facile explanation does not really withstand scrutiny. If men are capable of beating the system in the most extreme situations, how does it come about that they allow themselves to be dominated in less constraining circumstances? Can it be seriously maintained that manipulation and conditioning are more powerful influences than constraints? On the contrary, research confirms what common sense suggests: namely, that conditioning has a real impact only in conjunction with constraint. The former cannot be substituted for the latter.

At least in nontotalitarian systems, actors make such extensive use of their margins of liberty that it is impossible to consider their special arrangements simply as so many exceptions to the rational model. To take just one very simple example, an individual's conduct with regard to his superiors within an organizational hierarchy in no way corresponds to a simple model of obedience and conformism, even if such a model is modified to allow for passive resistance. Such conduct is at once the result of and part of a negotiation. Of course, the subordinate's autonomy in his work, along with the technical and social traditions of his profession, largely determines the possibility not only of his replacement but also of his knowledge, and therefore of his control, of the precise nature of the problems to be solved. These factors, therefore, define in relatively rigorous manner the agenda of such a negotiation. The subordinate's conduct, however, will also be a function of opportunities to form coalitions with his colleagues and thereby mobilize their support. It will depend as well upon his capacity to exploit these various elements and, particularly, upon his capacity to withstand the psychological tensions inherent in every risk of conflict. Finally, and most importantly, his conduct will depend upon the choice he makes of the best course of action, a choice which will be based upon an intuitive understanding of all these factors.

Even in such situations of dependence and constraint, men do not adapt themselves passively to circumstances. What is more, they are able to deal with such circumstances and to make active use of them far more frequently than is generally believed. Thus some regulation or formal procedure, which appears at first sight as a constraint, can be diverted from its original intention and used as a protective device against the superior. An "aggressive" angry behavior, for example, which may appear to be the impulsive expression of an emotional instinct in the individual, can be used as an instrument to win himself respect and to impose his point of view in an unstructured and potentially conflictual situation. The superiors, for their part, will also make use of whatever resources the context offers them, along with any skills they have been able to develop. In addition, the behavior of the partners will profoundly influence one another, depending on what course the negotiations take. Therefore, it will be conceded that there is in truth a much more complex as well as contingent reality behind the deterministic clockwork with which we began.

Of course, the official prescriptive model is not uninfluential. It largely determines the context of the action and hence the resources of the actors. It can certainly be stated that the actors are never totally free and are to a certain extent "co-opted" by the official system. Nevertheless, this is true only if we recognize that the system is equally influenced and even corrupted by the pressures and manipulations of the actors. Instead of considering informal practices solely as exceptions or accommodations within the traditional logic, we should change our perspective and try to understand the official system itself on the basis of a more realistic analysis of the difficulties it encounters. To pursue this point further, we may even regard the formal system as a response to such informal practices and a solution to the problems which they pose.

The same remarks apply to any deterministic theory of intra-organizational behavior. Instead of regarding unforeseen behaviors as exceptions, is it not ultimately more fruitful to use them as points of departure for understanding the limits and the real significance of constraints and conditioning?

We ourselves have stressed in a previous work the fact that, in an organization, man cannot be considered merely *as a hand,* as the Taylorist model of organization assumed, or even as a *hand and a heart,* as the advocates of the human-relations movement would have it. We pointed out that both these camps neglect the fact that man is first and foremost a *head,* or, in other words, that he can exercise his *freedom,* which in more concrete terms means that he is an autonomous agent capable of calculation and manipulation, who can adapt himself and invent responses depending on the circumstances and the maneuvers of his partners.[3]

Consequently, an organization cannot be analyzed as the transparent entity which its leaders often wish it were. It operates in the realm of power relationships, of influence, of bargaining, and of calculation. On the other hand, it is not the instrument of oppression which its detractors take it to be, because its conflictual relationships are not ordered according to an integrated logical schema. Within the framework of such relationships, innumerable actors can find the means to make their wishes felt and to influence the system and their partners, even if such means are distributed quite unequally.[4]

It is important that we state emphatically, contrary to the illusions harbored by the theoreticians of domination and conditioning, but also contrary to the fantasies of omnipotence and the simplistic views which are prevalent among men of action, that human conduct may in no way be assimilated to mechanical obedience or to the pressure of structural givens. Human behavior is always the expression and consequence of freedom, no matter how minimal that freedom may be.[5] It reflects choices made by the actor in order to take advantage of available opportunities within the framework of constraints imposed upon him.[6] For this reason, behavior is never entirely predictable, since it is not determined but, on the contrary, always contingent.[7]

The Limits of A Priori Reasoning

If one assumes that, in every organization, the individual actor retains an irreducible margin of liberty in his ordinary activity, then it is illusory to seek an explanation of empirically observable behavior in an organization's rationality, objectives, functions, or structures. These are not just so many given conditions to which individuals can do no more than adapt themselves or which they can internalize in order to regulate their conduct. There is thus a great temptation to proceed in an altogether opposite direction, starting not from the organization but from the actor himself. The relationship between the individual and the organization can be explained on the basis of an analysis of the actor, his objectives, and the logic of his action.

As attractive as such a procedure might appear at first sight, in practice—as we hope to show now—it runs into difficulties similar to those which plagued the rational mode. Reasoning in a general, not to say universal, manner, about an actor posited in an abstract way and isolated from his context, the models we have in mind are forced, in order to cap their speculations with concrete propositions, to have recourse to a set of *a priori* postulates concerning human behavior. Such postulates are no more than simplistic devices which hardly withstand serious empirical analysis.

The early work of Chris Argyris is a good example of the first kind of simplification. He sought to show that behind apparent conflicts among partners and their rational objectives, a necessary negotiation took place between the individual and the organization at a more fundamental level. This negotiation could be understood by means of an investigation not only of the material but especially of the psychological needs of individuals, and of the laws governing the emergence and evolution of such needs.[8]

Inspired by Maslow's motivational theory,[9] Argyris diagnoses a hierarchy of psychological needs which an individual seeks to satisfy by participating in an organization. He proposes that the developmental stages, dysfunctions, and conflicts of the organization be understood by analyzing the ways in which it is or is not able to satisfy the needs of individuals. Central to such a viewpoint is the normative precept that there is a "fit" between organizational structures and the psychological needs of individuals, all of which must be treated as independent variables.

Such a model clearly gives undue priority to the individual relationship between the actor and the organization, and sees the latter as a totally abstract entity detached from the actors who make it up. Furthermore, it leads to a reification of the psychological needs of individuals with respect to a normative hypothesis which is difficult to accept: namely, that there exists for individuals, and consequently for organizations, an ideal model of psychological and moral health. This leads to interpreting the entire organizational game solely in psychological and moral terms.[10] As a practical consequence of these defects, this model can give no better an account than the rational model of the complexity of human behavior within an organization, a complexity which always confounds the most ingenious *a priori* motivational theories.[11]

A second simplification, of an abstract sort, has seen more widespread use. It involves studying the interaction between the individual and the organization no longer on the basis of the individual's theoretical needs, but rather by analogy with an economic market model. It is assumed that the individual will always seek to obtain a return equivalent to his real contribution.[12] His negotiation with the organization takes place within the limits prescribed by this fundamental equation. The fact that the actors will make different estimates of their investments and returns introduces a considerable complication, which can be resolved by invoking the theory of the frame of reference: the criteria by which a given actor will make such estimates depend only on his individual frame of reference, which has to do with the group to which he naturally belongs (objective determinant) and the environment that shapes his choice of objectives (subjective determinant). The reductionist model permits the individual's current objectives to be taken into account and inserted into a simple model of negotiation, which serves as a common denominator for all the complex relationships which are the fabric of the organization's life.

Unfortunately, such a model, like the preceding *a priori* one, does not seem to be based on any sort of empirical foundation. Whenever observations are made of the actor in his actual situation, as we shall see in what follows, it appears that he does not base his behavior on any sort of balance sheet of investments and returns, but rather on what opportunities he is able to discern in the situation and on his capacity to comprehend them. There is no such thing as a fair return or a fair price from the standpoint of the actor's objectives. Even if he often uses this sort of argument, it is the possibility of obtaining a profit, a raise, a promotion, or a moral or material advantage which is crucial. The arguments which justify such demands are generally discovered in the process of decision or even after the fact.

Due to their very methodology, finally, both these models tend to neglect or overlook the autonomous constraint imposed by the organizational context. This context is neither neutral nor transparent with respect to the actors' needs or objectives—factors which do influence individual behavior, but are not significant in determining the organization's functioning.[13] The actors, faced with the organization's inherent opacity and "weight," are obliged to make compromises and to digress from pursuit of their own ends, which ultimately may lead them to betray their own objectives or evade the "needs" of their personalities.

Hence neither model is capable of explaining the existence of groups within an organization. In the first case, we have pointed out that the model is centered on the individual and hence neglects the existence of groups. The second model would appear to allow these to be taken into account. In fact, it has for the most part inspired studies which are in reality examinations of group behavior, where the groups in question are defined by demographic or ecological variables exterior to the organization, by their frames of reference, objectives, etc. (depending on the case). Such groups are consequently treated as natural phenomena needing no explanation.

This procedure, however, does not make it possible to explain the origin and existence of groups, since it does not distinguish between abstract categories of personnel and concrete groups of persons. As we shall have occasion to demonstrate, a group, just as much as an organization, is a human construct, meaningless apart from its relationship to its members. To speak of the objectives of an abstract category—e.g., the category of those who desire a promotion—seems to us a dangerous oversimplification, because the members of such a category, while they may behave similarly in regard to a given issue, have no capacity or desire to act as a group.

Even where a specific set of people are associated in direct contact, the existence of a group with the capacity and desire to act jointly is not self-evident and must be demonstrated. If we try to understand how and why groups form, we notice that similar grievances or shared objectives are less decisive than the presence of a common opportunity, together with a sufficient interactive or cooperative capacity for action which is bent on making the most of that opportunity.

The results of a study of the behavior of certain groups within a large American corporation are extremely enlightening in this respect.[14] There are great differences among these groups, which do not seem to relate either to the ratio of investment to return or to the members' frame of reference. Some of the groups are completely passive. They do not occupy a favorable position within the production process. They control nothing of importance in the life of the factory, and they have been unable to discover or create the least opportunity for themselves. Against this background it is shown that they have failed to develop any cooperative capacity. In fact, they have no concrete existence as groups.

On the other hand, other groups, called by the author *strategic* in certain cases and *conservative* in others, possess a good communications network, are capable of coordinated action, and play a crucial role in the life of the factory.[15] Between these two types of groups are the so-called *erratic* groups, which are capable of action, even of vigorous action, but only intermittently and in short bursts.

These behavioral differences appear relatively rational if three elements are taken into account: the strategic location within the production circuit; the degree of professional qualification, at least insofar as this variable controls liberty and autonomy on the job; and, finally, the degree of interaction among members of the group. If qualification is considered as a given, and the strategic situation as an opportunity, the problem becomes one of the use made of this opportunity. The degree of interaction can then be interpreted as an indicator of the collective capacity of the group.

In this perspective, the essential problem is to show how this human construct is created. Two preconditions of its development are the existence of (1) an *opportunity* and (2) a *capacity*. Passive groups have neither. Erratic groups have opportunities but have a great deal of trouble taking advantage of them, because their membership is too large and the characteristics of the relationships among the members are such as to make the establishment of continuous, organized coalitions very difficult.[16] Strategic and conservative groups, on the other hand, with relatively fewer members and relatively greater capacities for taking an active role, are able over a period of time to acquire considerable capacities. They are not only capable of taking advantage of existing opportunities but may also succeed in creating new ones. Erratic groups may eventually, however, learn how to organize themselves so as to make better use of their opportunities.[17] Even passive groups may, by developing a capacity, discover opportunities, or, conversely, may develop capacities by discovering an opportunity. Here nothing is predetermined for all time.[18]

The Strategic Method

With perspective, two related explanations emerge for the fact that all such analytic models regularly lead to insuperable difficulties, even though they are based on the same principle of the actor's freedom, which is the basis of our own model. The fact is that while focused on the actors' freedom, such models fail to recognize the necessarily contingent character of their behavior. On the one hand, by isolating the actors, such schemes endow them with unlimited liberty and rationality and treat them as sovereign, rational agents freely negotiating over the conditions of their cooperation.[19] On the other hand, in order to deal with the resulting complexity, such theories introduce a reduction by way of an *a priori* model: norms of health applicable to individuals and organizations alike; economic models of negotiations; social models involving groups and categories.

The difficulty is that this arbitrarily introduced reduction in no way corresponds to the reduction which is inherent in the actual situation. The organization, as we have already said, can and should be considered as a collection of reductive mechanisms which greatly limit the actors' possibilities for negotiation, and which thereby allow the problems arising from cooperative activity to be solved. Instead of exaggerating the actor's freedom and rationality at the beginning, only to be obliged later to impose arbitrary restrictions, wouldn't it be more effective, as well as more realistic, to turn the method around by trying to reconstruct the actor's freedom and rationality, limited and contingent as they always are, by linking his conduct to the context in which he is observed? On this basis, it would be possible to formulate an interpretation of the concrete reductive mechanisms, themselves always contingent, by which the organization is integrated as a unit.

March and Simon long ago proposed a model of rationality which permits this reversal of viewpoint to be effected. According to them, we customarily reason with the aid of an *a priori* logic which presumes that man seeks the best solution to every problem from a synoptic point of view. Such reasoning is both quite cumbersome and totally incorrect. The human being is incapable of optimization. The freedom and information at his disposal are too limited to enable him to succeed in such procedure. Instead, in a context of *bounded rationality*, he makes decisions sequentially, choosing for each problem facing him the first solution which corresponds to a minimum threshold of satisfaction.[20]

In light of this general model of the decision-making process, the terms of the discussion change. Each actor's freedom is limited, and he is capable, correspondingly, of only a limited rationality. In other words, the actors—their freedom and rationality, their objectives and "needs," or, if you will, their affectivity—are social constructs rather than abstract entities.[21] From this viewpoint, the problem is no longer to choose an explanatory model, but to elaborate a *research methodology* that will reveal the material, structural, and human conditions of the context which limit and define the actor's freedom and rationality. Then the meaning of his empirically observable behavior can be determined.

This methodology, whose initial steps have already appeared in the foregoing discussion, can be defined in terms of the central concept of *strategy*. To understand this concept and the use we make of it, one should begin from the following empirical observations:

1. The actor rarely has clear objectives and, even more rarely, coherent projects. His objectives are diverse, more or less ambiguous, more or less

explicit, and more or less contradictory. Some will be changed in the course of action, some rejected, others discovered during the process or even after the fact, if only because the unforeseen and unforeseeable consequences of his action require him to "reconsider his position" and "readjust his aim." What is a "means" at one moment will be an "end" at another, and vice versa. It follows that it would be illusory to regard such behavior as deliberate and reasoned, i.e., mediated by a lucid subject calculating his moves as a function of objectives established at the outset.

2. The individual's behavior is nevertheless *active*. While he is always constrained and limited, his behavior is never directly determined. Even passivity is always in a sense the result of a choice.

3. The behavior in question is always meaningful; the fact that it cannot be related to clear objectives does not signify that it cannot be rational—quite the contrary. Instead of being rational with respect to objectives, it is rational, on the one hand, with respect to opportunities and through them to their defining context, and, on the other hand, with respect to the behavior of the other actors—to the decisions which they make, and to the game which is thus established among them.

4. This behavior always has two aspects: one offensive, involving making use of opportunities with a view to improving the actor's situation; the other defensive, involving the maintenance and broadening of his margin of liberty and, therefore, his capacity to act. This opposition does not imply any necessary equivalence of the time frames involved (short-term gains against investment, for example), the important thing being the duality and not the signification of the terms.

5. Therefore, there is no longer any such thing as irrational behavior. The very usefulness of the concept of strategy is that it applies equally to behaviors which seem the most rational and to those which appear completely erratic.[22] Behind the moods and emotional reactions which determine behavior from day to day, the analyst can discover *regularities,* which make sense only relative to a *strategy.* This strategy, therefore, is nothing other than the *inferred basis,* ex post facto, for the *empirically observed regularities of behavior.* It follows that such a "strategy" is in no way synonymous with willed behavior, any more than it is necessarily conscious. To take an extreme case, it would be possible to speak in these terms of the "rational strategy" of a schizophrenic who, in the face of the extreme pressures confronting him, "adopts" a schizophrenic behavior, "choosing" schizophrenia to "solve his problems."[23] Or again, to paraphrase Sartre, it might be said that a person who faints with fear in the face of an imminent and unavoidable danger has chosen a "strategy." Since the threatening world cannot be changed, he has instead opted to change his consciousness of the world by fainting.[24]

It is not enough, however, to consider the actor alone, since his behavior cannot be conceived apart from the context from which, as we have seen, he derives his rationality. Strategy's great virtue as a concept is that it necessitates transcending the sterile dichotomy between actors and objectives, and at the same time it makes it possible to do so. While a study of objectives tends to isolate the actor from the organization by opposing them, a study of strategies insures that the actor's rationality will be sought in the organizational context and that in turn the organizational construct will be understood through the actor's experience.[25]

Strategy and Power

How can we best approach what we are calling, in an imprecise way, depending on which point of view we adopt, the organizational context (passive viewpoint) or the organizational construct (active viewpoint)? What is needed is an additional concept, the concept of *power*. It will enable us to shed new light on the actor and his strategy, thus rounding out, from a practical empirical standpoint, the strategic method.

To put what is at issue here in concrete terms, let us reexamine the by now well-known case of the shops of the Industrial Monopoly.[26]

Recall, if you will, the features of the organizational context of the Monopoly's production shops. Three categories of personnel are involved: the *shop foremen*, responsible for general supervision in the shops; the *production workers*, relatively unskilled, assigned to the machines; and the *maintenance workers*, a dozen per shop, highly skilled, each responsible for regular maintenance and minor repairs of three to six machines assigned to him personally on a fixed basis. .

These three categories are sharply distinguished. Each one has a clear function, quite distinct from the others, involving neither exchange nor cooperation with the other groups. These circumstances are reinforced by the fact that no one in a given category can either hope for or fear promotion or demotion, as the case may be, to one of the others.

The technical organization of the shops contributes to the impression of a static and impersonal structural context. Rationalization and specialization of tasks are highly advanced. Production norms—established in an "objective" manner—and bonuses regulate the manufacturing process. Each worker is specialized and knows what he has to do and how to do it. Most importantly, nothing in the shop is left to chance or to individual choice: impersonal rules establish in advance a solution to every problem that might arise.[27]

Nothing, in short, is supposed to be left to individual choice and interpersonal negotiation. There is presumably no cause for tension or conflict, since every eventuality has been foreseen and each man assigned to his proper place.

The organizational context of the shops cannot be completely described, however, as a set of formal arrangements or technical and structural conditions. It also, indeed primarily, involves a set of relationships among the actors. Through these relationships, the actors reveal the strategies they choose in the course of mutual interaction within the given context. These relationships are indicative of the power relationships on which the shop organization is based. It will be useful, therefore, to review the data collected during the investigation concerning the actors' attitudes and behaviors.

First, *the relations between production workers and shop foremen* are minimal and given little weight. The production workers, who feel very little involved either emotionally or psychologically in their relations with their foremen, show little deference or respect for their nominal superiors, whose role is actually marginal. On the whole, however, these relations are rather good and devoid of serious troubles. On both sides, the dominant impression is one of peacefulness. Interpersonal relations are cordial and tolerant, but neither workers nor foremen ultimately place much importance on them.

The *relations between production and maintenance workers,* on the other hand, are characterized by a tense and conflict-ridden climate. Psychologically and emotionally, the production workers seem deeply involved in these relationships, which reveal an undercurrent of hostility that would more likely have been expected in their relations with their foremen. They see little agreement between themselves and the maintenance workers. The latter group, for its part, sees the production workers as its subordinates and doesn't hesitate to interfere frequently with their work. The maintenance workers take a deeply paternalistic attitude toward these "subordinates." In this respect, they resemble the foremen. They find the production workers negligent, lacking in their comprehension of technical requirements, and unlikely to do as much work as they should.

These tensions are not easily expressed openly, nor are they personalized. The production workers judge the maintenance staff in general much more severely than their individual maintenance worker with whom they work closely. The same is true for the maintenance workers: they tend to recognize difficulties when speaking of their colleagues' relations with the production crew, but they minimize them in speaking of their relations with their *own* production workers.

Finally, the *relations between maintenance workers and foremen* are openly hostile and conflictual and involve a strong emotional component on both sides. The maintenance workers are severely critical of the foremen's competence and deny that they have any importance in the shops. The foremen, while perhaps equally critical of the maintenance workers, show some embarrassment in their answers, as if they were hesitant to venture onto this terrain. In passing, we observe that the more aggressive the maintenance workers are toward the foremen, the more they seem satisfied with their work and their personal situation. The foremen, on the other hand, seem more satisfied with their personal situation to the degree that they are resigned in other respects to the general state of affairs.

These findings can be given sense and coherence if we recall that the maintenance workers occupy a dominant position and are the real "bosses" of the shops. By bringing to light the power structure in the shops and the opportunities and constraints that it either imposes upon or offers to the different categories of personnel, we are able to understand the rationality of the main strategies discernible in each category.

First, the structure of power enables us to understand the "rational" significance of the aggressiveness shown by all the maintenance workers, independently of their personalities, in their remarks on the foremen. To be sure, they occupy a very favorable position with respect to their competitors, but their privilege is in some sense "usurped" because their "power" is illegitimate, and is not recognized in the official hierarchy. Their aggressiveness toward the foremen, coupled with their methods for assuring themselves a monopoly of the skills necessary for making repairs, can be analyzed as a strategy aimed at keeping the foremen in an inferior position in order to forestall any potential contest. From this standpoint, it is also clear why their satisfaction should increase along with their aggressiveness: aggressiveness is not only responsible for their success, but is also in fact a sign of it.

The *foremen,* on the other hand, are in a relatively defenseless position. They have no real means of exercising the authority conferred on them by the organization chart. Unless they leave the organization, the best they can do is to accept their inferior situation by reducing their involvement and resigning themselves to their lot. Their resignation and "apathetic participation" can thus also be understood as a strategy whose "rationality" becomes evident when it is related to the structure of power.

The *production workers,* finally, are in a situation of direct, personal dependence on the maintenance workers, whose good will is indispensable to them. The maintenance workers thus dominate the production workers at every turn, even in the union, whose leaders are drawn from the ranks of the former.[28] The production workers are careful to keep on good terms with these superiors, at least openly. But in a covert and astute way, they make their hostilities felt, and as we have seen, the maintenance workers are certainly aware of them.[29] When situated within the power alignments of the Monopoly's shops, such "ambivalent" or "hypocritical" attitudes and behaviors make good sense: they are excellent means by which the production workers can maintain good relations with the maintenance workers while putting pressure on them to insure that they will not abuse their power in the situation.

Thus, in spite of an altogether exceptional organizational model, in theory quite close to the model of the rational organization, the empirical analysis of the experience of the actors brings to light an autonomous, stable, and well-defined dominant strategy in each personnel category, which could not have been foreseen by the planners charged with drawing up the organization chart.

The case of the shops of the Industrial Monopoly, thanks to the very clarity and simplicity of the data, lends itself to an analysis of the development of an organizational construct which virtually serves as an experiment. This construct is based on the establishment of relations of power where there had appeared to be merely technical relationships. Such a construct, then, corresponds to a certain power structure among the parties involved, which is characterized by the superiority of the maintenance workers, who determine the frequency and duration of machine stoppages by their monopoly of maintenance and repair skills and hence control the degree of inconvenience occasioned by such stoppages which must be endured by the production workers. The strategies involved are comprehensible only by reference to the power structure. In turn, the strategies condition this structure.[30]

To understand the dynamic of organizational life, therefore, we must analyze this phenomenon and its inherent logic. This will be the object of the next chapter.

2

Power as the Basis
of Organized Action

We have stated above that contexts and constructs are
primarily relations. From the strategic point of view we have adopted,
these relations involve power. Since the organizational construct is revealed only through the actor's experience, our method can begin only
with the actor's strategic choices. It is the study of power which will
enable us to analyze this construct, because power, as a fundamental
stabilizing mechanism in human behavior, is at the root of the collection
of relations which constitute it.[1]

Our approach to power will be to continue our study of strategy, beginning with a consideration of power from the actors' point of view.[2]

Power from the Actors' Point of View

The phenomenon of power is simple and universal, but the
concept of power is elusive and complex. Therefore, we will begin with a
simple formulation of what in some sense represents the common denominator in all manifestations of power: whatever its "type"—meaning
its sources, objectives, degree of legitimacy, or means of exercise—
power, on the most general level, always implies that certain individuals
or groups are able to act on other individuals or groups.[3]

As vague as it is, such a formulation has the advantages of not taking
for granted a theory of the essence of power, of being applicable to any
form of power, and, especially, of drawing attention to what we consider
the essential point: the relational character of power. To act upon
another, in fact, is to enter into a relation with him,[4] and it is within this
relation that the power of person A over person B develops.

Thus power is a relation and not an attribute of the actors. It can
appear, and consequently become constraining for one of the parties involved, only by being introduced into a relation[5] which confronts two or
more actors dependent on one another[6] for the achievement of a common
objective which modifies their personal objectives. More precisely, it can
develop only through *exchange* among the actors involved in a given

relation. To the extent that every relation between two parties pre-supposes exchange and reciprocal adaptation between them, power is indissolubly linked to negotiation: *it is a relation of exchange, therefore of negotiation,* in which at least two persons are involved.

Several remarks deriving from this fact will help to make the nature of the relation more precise.

First, it is an *instrumental relation.* This is not to deny that its existence always entails a series of very powerful affective phenomena which pro-foundly condition its development.[7] Nor does it signify that all the conse-quences and effects of a relation of power are necessarily conscious or intentional. To take D. Wrong's example,[8] it is surely not part of the intention of an overprotective and domineering mother to "feminize" her son's character. In this and other instances, purposeful action by individ-uals entails its portion of unforeseeable, unexpected, and "dysfunc-tional" consequences. Furthermore, we do not thus exclude from the anlaysis the forms of social domination and control which, when inter-nalized by the various actors, give rise to the phenomena known as "def-erential adjustment" or "anticipatory adjustment"[9] and which no longer require a conscious commitment of resources on the part of any of the actors.[10] To say that every relation of power is instrumental is merely to underscore the fact that, like every relation of negotiation, power is con-ceivable only from the standpoint of an aim which, in the context of an instrumental logic, motivates the actors' commitments of their resources.

Second, the *relation of power is a nontransitive relation:* while person A can readily get person B to perform action X, and B can elicit the same from C, it may nevertheless be true that A is incapable of obtaining X from C. Moreover, if power is thus inseparable from the actors engaged in a relation, it is also inseparable from the actions demanded. Each of these represents a specific stake around which a particular relation of power is erected. Thus A might be able to obtain X from B quite easily, Y might be a little more difficult to get accomplished, and Z, impossible, while, on the other hand, C might be able to obtain Z from B without difficulty.

Finally, *power is a reciprocal, but unbalanced, relation.* Its reciprocity derives from the fact that negotiation always involves exchange. If one of the two parties involved has no further resources to commit to the re-lationship, it no longer has anything to exchange; hence it cannot enter into what may properly be called a relation of power. In other words, if B can no longer bargain over his willingness to do what A is asking, there is no longer any question of a relation of power between them, because B has now ceased to be an autonomous actor with regard to A, since he has been reduced to the status of an object.[11] In addition to being reciprocal, however, the relation in question is unbalanced. If A and B have equal advantages in the relationship, so that the exchange between them is on equal terms, then there is no reason to consider that one of them has power over the other. But once the exchange becomes unbalanced in one or the other's favor, where this inequality reflects the respective situations of the two parties, then it is legitimate to speak of a relation of power.[12]

It then becomes permissible to redefine power as a relation of exchange, hence a reciprocal relation, but one in which the terms of exchange favor one of the parties involved. *It is a relation of force from which one party can obtain more than the other, yet in which neither party is totally defenseless.* To paraphrase R. Dahl's previously cited definition, it may be said that the power of A over B corresponds to A's capacity to obtain favorable terms of trade in his negotiations with B.[13]

What is the basis of power? What is its source? The answer to these questions seems obvious: the advantages, resources, and forces of each of the parties involved—or, in short, their respective strengths—determine the result of a relation of power. What is meant by "strength," however, needs to be made more explicit. What is actually exchanged in a relation of power? The answer is that it is not so much the forces or the strengths of the different parties involved as it is their *possibilities for action.* A does not enter into a relation of power with B solely in order to test his strength against B's. He has a more definite objective: to obtain from B a behavior on which his own capacity to act depends. In other words, B in some sense controls, by means of his own behavior, A's capacity to achieve his objectives. The more B can bargain over his willingness to do what A wants, and the more his available resources allow him to keep his future behavior from becoming perfectly predictable for A, then the more power he will have over A in this particular relation. *Power, therefore, lies in the margin of liberty available to each partner in a relation of power.* In other words, the more one partner is free to refuse what the other asks of him, the more power he has. Force, wealth, prestige, authority—all the resources, in short, which any one of the parties may claim—play a role only to the extent that they provide a greater freedom of action.

At this point, it might be useful to digress a bit in order to confront Schelling's argument, apparently in contradiction with the above, which can be found in a remarkable book cited previously.[14] In rich, stimulating, and frequently amusing analyses, the author offers numerous examples of situations—or rather of games and game structures[15]—in which the *"winner"* is not the one who manages to maintain his margin for maneuver by keeping his future behavior unpredictable, but rather the one who does the opposite by tying his hands and reducing his maneuverability to zero, *thus making his future behavior completely predictable.* His is the power of the weak, of the player without alternatives, who, having "burned all his bridges," finds himself with his "back to the wall." Schelling gives the example of the striking railwaymen who succeed in halting a "strike-breaking" train by chaining themselves to the rails.

In our opinion, Schelling somewhat overestimates the generality and universality of the situations he studies. His games have special structural conditions and dynamics.[16] A closer examination reveals that they are games in which each of the adversaries/partners has a more or less urgent but always imperative need to arrange and settle things with the other, and, moreover, in which this other cannot be chosen but has been part of the game from the outset. The fundamental logic of such games is that of the *bilateral monopoly*, a structure which already limits drastically the margin for maneuver of each partner/adversary. In the author's example, chaining oneself to the rails makes sense only because there *are* rails, structures which drastically limit the other's freedom of action: the train's engineer can choose only between surrender and massacre.

Such structural conditions are found, though rarely, in reality.[17] It should be noted, however, that in the actual cases familiar to us, the fact of making one's future behavior perfectly predictable has significance and consequences which extend beyond the confines of the game itself. To do so always amounts to *changing the nature of the game,* or to *displacing the stakes and the zones of uncertainty,* in order to take advantage of circumstances to force one's adversary onto less favorable terrain or into a position where he must yield. In the case of the railway strikers, the stakes are not the stoppage of the train or even the continuation of the strike. *Human lives are at stake.* With these new stakes, *the strikers as a group* (hence indirectly the men chained to the rails) take control of a new zone of uncertainty, involving the future behavior of their group and allied groups in the event that the train runs over the strikers. In short, by chaining themselves to the rails, the strikers place the train's engineer, and particularly the company which chartered the strikebreaking train, in the position of having to choose between the relatively predictable consequences of stopping the train and the less predictable, indeed incalculable, consequences (riots, mass movements, etc.) of the death of the strikers. This explains why it is probable that the train will stop.

If, however, the conditions of the expanded game introduced by the strikers are changed—for example, by the supposition of a lack of solidarity among the railway workers or of a society in which the value of human lives, or simply of the strikers' lives, is nil—a different "solution" to the conflct may be anticipated. The consequences of a fatal accident being negligible, the zone of uncertainty controlled by the chained strikers will not be relevant. The train will continue on its way. The weak will remain weak.

The power of an individual or group, or social actor, is thus a function of the size of the *zone of uncertainty* that the unpredictability of the actor's conduct enables him to control vis-à-vis his partners. We have already explained that not every zone of uncertainty is important. It must be relevant to the problem at hand and in relation to the parties involved. It must be a zone of uncertainty whose existence and control condition the capacity of these parties to act. The strategy of each of the partners/adversaries will then naturally take the form of *manipulation of the predictability* of his own and others' behavior, either directly or indirectly, by means of judicious modification of the structural conditions and "rules" regulating his interactions with others.[18] In other words, each actor will seek to widen his own margin of liberty as much as he can in order to maintain as broad as possible a range of behavior, while trying at the same time to limit his partner/adversary's range and to shackle him with such constraints as to make his behavior foreseeable.

An example will help to review and clarify the argument. We have deliberately chosen one whose simple, if not simplistic, character will aid in pinning down our ideas, which we will then be able to broaden as the analysis proceeds.

Mr. Dupont, a prominent and well-to-do resident of a small provincial city, asks Mr. Durand, a craftsman with a small business, to make some repairs on his house. Thus, by this request, a relation of power is established between them. The price which Dupont will ultimately agree to pay will be a function of the balance of power which prevails.[19] If Durand is the only one in town capable of undertaking the necessary repairs, if he has all the work he needs, and if, for various reasons, Dupont cannot take his business out of town, the zone of uncertainty which Durand controls by his behavior alone is maximal: his client has, in fact, no choice. The balance of power is clearly tilted in his favor. Dupont, however, is not completely empty-handed. He can, in fact, refuse to have the repairs done at all if Durand's conditions seem exorbitant. He can even tip the balance in his own favor if he is able to call on competing craftsmen. This is true, at least, unless these competitors can agree among themselves and thus eliminate Dupont's freedom to choose, which would put us back, *mutatis mutandis,* in the original situation.

To analyze a relation of power, then, *two series of questions* must be answered. First, what resources are available to each partner, and what are the *advantages* by which, in a given situation, each might enlarge his margin of liberty? Second, what criteria define the *relevance* of these resources and determine their *degree of mobilizability;* or, to put it another way, what are the *stakes* involved in the relation, and what *structural constraints* does it exhibit?

The first of these questions involves us with every sort of resource (individual, cultural, economic, and social) which an actor may have at hand by virtue of his over-all social situation. These define the *social, spatial, and temporal framework* in which his strategy is set. Such an inventory allows inequalities among the actors to be introduced explicitly into the analysis. These inequalities depend on the relative positions of the actors within a structured social field.

Knowledge of an actor's social situation allows us to understand how he *might diversify his investment,* or, in other words, how he might become involved in several power relationships at once.[20] The multiplicity of an actor's commitments offers him a considerable advantage from two points of view. On the one hand, such multiplicity protects him against the risks and losses inherent in relations of power insofar as he can thereby distribute his investments and thus avoid "putting all his eggs in one basket." On the other hand, he can strengthen his ability to play offensive games. By his involvement in several relations of power, an actor can parlay the resources accruing to him from other commitments and invest heavily in a specific relation in order to reinforce his position.

We will illustrate this statement by expanding our earlier example. Dupont, as a prominent member of the community, is on the best of terms with the local tax collector. He is therefore in a position to intervene judiciously at the right moment in order to smoothe Durand's periodic negotiations with the authorities over the size of his tax bill. In addition, Dupont's profession is that of estate administrator. As a result, he controls a large amount of business which Durand might well be interested in obtaining, and for which his particular skills might not in all cases be as indispensable as they are in relation to the repairs on Dupont's house. As thus redefined, the situation is rife with important advantages for Dupont which allow him to "open" the game up and put the relation on a new footing, even if *a priori* the balance of power was not in his favor.

The social situation of the actors also makes it possible to understand how each actor can make use of the *time factor* in relations of power. It is even conceivable that the temporal dimension is essential for a relation of power to develop, since it is a source, and sometimes the only one, of diversification of investments. In fact, an actor can accept loss in the short term only if this loss seems temporary, and he can hope subsequently to win. Above all, time is a dimension of an actor's margin for maneuver. As a result, the capacity to adopt a more distant temporal horizon in a power relationship becomes an important advantage.[21] To return to our example, if Durand urgently needs the money from the repairs on Dupont's house, and if Dupont is not in a similar hurry to have the repairs done— either because the problem is a minor one or because he has other places to live—then Durand's negotiating margin, "cornered" in the short term, will be weakened with respect to Dupont, who can "wait and see."

Taking the respective resources of the actors in a power relationship into account thus complicates the initial design considerably. It becomes clear that, faced with the same power relationship, different actors do not share similar alternatives or temporal horizons. In short, their capacity to *proportion their commitment* or adjust their investment, thereby limiting the risks to themselves which inevitably accompany relations of power, is not the same.[22] By dint of their social situation, actors have different "strategic capacities."[23]

By situating the actors in a structured social field, and by showing how their strategic capacities are limited by their position therein, this type of analysis allows us to give more operational definitions of such notions as "social power," "strength," and "social ascendancy." These can now be defined in terms of a player's capacity[24] to extend the area over which power is exercised so as to move the relation onto terrain where the balance of power becomes favorable to himself. Such an analysis also allows social inequalities among the actors to be integrated into the discussion. Clearly, it is these very inequalities that are responsible for the fact that, from the outset, certain actors will be more likely to occupy dominant positions than others. To return once more to our example, in spite of his weakness in one particular relation, the likelihood is great that Dupont will win in the end: his more numerous involvements allow him to expand the game until the balance of power becomes favorable to himself.

While it is *probable* that this will be the actual course that events will follow, it is not *necessarily* so. While economic and social inequalities among actors are fundamental factors in understanding the development of a given power relationship, only rarely are these inequalities reflected mechanically and without modification. The special structural constraints of a definite situation can attenuate or cancel out such inequalities. This is because it is insufficient to look only at the actors' resources. These must be *mobilizable* in the specific relation, and they must be relevant to the objectives of the partners. In the example, if the tax authorities refuse to tolerate any interference in the assessments on tradesmen, and if the sort of work which Dupont, as estate administrator, controls does not fall into Durand's province, then Dupont's particular resources lose much of their relevance and are no longer mobilizable in the relation. Thanks to these specific structural constraints, which at least at a given moment apply to both actors, the balance of power may shift toward the "weaker" partner, Durand.[25]

Now that we have examined power relations from the point of view of the actors involved, it is useful to change our perspective and investigate the *structural constraints* characteristic of a given negotiating situation. Through structural analysis of the constraints imposed on all the actors in a given relation of power, we will be able to answer the second question raised above, namely, what resources can an actor actually mobilize in a relation of power, and how *relevant* are they?

Power and Organization

This is the level at which the structural characteristics of an organization come into play. They establish and limit the range of power relationships among the members of an organization and thus define the conditions for negotiation. They are constraints imposed on all participants.

First, the organization makes the development of continuous relations of power possible. Power, we have seen, does not exist in itself. It can be exercised only in a relation in which two actors are willing to engage, or are forced to engage, for the purpose of accomplishing a given task. Thus, temporarily, at least, they become part of an organized structure.

Power and organization are thus inextricably interwoven. Social actors can attain their objectives only by exercising power. At the same time, however, they can exercise power over one another only in connection with the pursuit of collective objectives whose constraints very directly condition their negotiations.[26]

Second, the structures and rules governing the official functioning of an organization determine where relations of power may develop. These structures and rules, by defining some sectors in which action is more predictable than in others and by setting up fairly easily mastered procedures, create and circumscribe *organizational zones of uncertainty*. Individuals or groups will attempt to gain control of these zones in pursuing their own strategies, and as a result power relations will grow up around them. The power and capacity for action of an individual or group within an organization depend, in the final analysis, on the control which can be exercised over a source of uncertainty affecting the organization's capacity to attain its objectives, as well as on the importance and relevance of this source of uncertainty to the other members. Thus the more *crucial* the zone of uncertainty controlled by an individual or group, the more power he or it will command.[27]

Finally, the *organization regularizes the development of relations of power*. Its formal hierarchy and internal regulations place constraints on what individuals and groups within it may do, which fundamentally influence their strategic orientation and content. This imposes a certain minimum predictability on all behavior within the organization in two ways. First, the organization affects each member's *capacity* to play by determining what resources may be employed in power relationships. Second, it influences the members' *willingness* to make use of these resources in their strategic choices, by setting the *stakes* which each member can hope to win by committing resources to a particular power relation.

Not all the resources available to an actor are equally *relevant* or *mobilizable* within a given organization. The organization's objectives and the types of activities they determine encourage the use of some resources and rule out others. The ability to play the violin is of no use in a machine shop. If you are, on the other hand, one of the few people familiar with the mysteries of an extremely complex machine on which the smooth running of this same shop depends, your negotiating position will be enhanced and your power increased as a result. Furthermore, the organization establishes channels of communication among its members and so defines the opportunities for access to information which the actors may need for carrying out their respective strategies. The organization also invests certain of its members with a legitimate authority over others, or, in other words, with special punitive or recompensatory powers. The members thus favored obtain advantages which may give them a greater weight in negotiations. In our example, it is not a matter of indifference whether the person who knows the machine in question inside and out is the chief official in the shop or an ordinary workman without formal prerogatives. The strategy and hence the behavior of this person, as well as of all the others in the shop, will be fundamentally affected by the circumstance.

To possess *advantages,* however, is not enough. The members of the organization must also be willing to use these advantages in particular relations of power. Insofar as the organization is always just one area of strategic investment among others for its members, this commitment is in no way automatic, as we have previously emphasized. They will agree to mobilize their resources and take the inherent risks only if the organization offers *sufficiently relevant stakes* with respect to their advantages and objectives, and stakes that are of *sufficient importance* to justify their mobilization.[28] At this level, again, the organization has a role to play. For example, by the way it organizes promotion internally, by the number and importance of the zones of uncertainty which are left to be read between the lines of the regulations, by the prerequisites established for this or that post and the prerogatives and advantages attached to it, the organization eliminates certain individuals or groups from competition for a given source of power by defining their respective potentials for gain. Not all the organizational zones of uncertainty are stakes for all members of the organization. Competition is organized around intermediate stakes or objectives.[29] Take, for instance, the maintenance function in a production shop. To the extent that the satisfactory performance of the shop depends on maintaining the machines in good working order, the person responsible for this maintenance derives power from his role and obtains advantages which he would like to hold on to. As a result, this function can become a stake for anyone who has the technical qualifications to exercise it. Such a person might attempt to use this position for his own strategic purposes by mobilizing whatever resources he can. Suppose, however, that a rule is put in force prohibiting access to this job to all bachelors, and that all the potential candidates happen to be single. The job will cease to represent a stake for them. The outcome is determined in advance; there is nothing to win. They will therefore invest their resources elsewhere.

Types of Power Produced by the Organization

The concrete relations of power which form within an organization, it follows, are never merely carbon copies of the balance of power and modes of domination found in the ambient social structure, nor do they simply reflect the relations of production and the derivative technical and social division of labor. This does not mean, as S. Clegg seems to believe, that the structural inequalities which characterize the action potential of the various "players" within an organization are neglected.[30] Negotiations among these players are, of course, overdetermined by these inequalities, and the outcome of such negotiations is by itself incapable of abolishing them. To use Clegg's example, borrowed from chess: in the organizational game, the queen (the general manager, roughly speaking) usually occupies a position of considerable and often insuperable privilege as compared to a simple pawn (the worker), since a certain number of nonnegotiable cultural and legal rules bestow a greater possibility for action on one player than on the other. Similarly, the queen (the manager) clearly cannot act with an altogether free hand: just as the unalterable rules limit the queen's freedom to maneuver, a business manager's choice of policies is constrained by the logic and rationality of the dominant mode of production and exchange.

Accepting this point, however, in no way helps to account for peculiarities in the functioning of an organization: the same logic of action, as can be observed every day, may be adapted to a wide variety of situations and embodied in quite different policies. As far as organizational analyses are concerned, it is this diversity which interests the investigator and which he has to attempt to understand and explain. This is possible only if the development of relations of power within an organization is related to the relatively autonomous structural constraints associated with that organization. For it is within the constraints discussed above, and around its formal hierarchy and official rules, that the organization produces its own sources of power, about which a little must now be said.

As a first approximation, four broad sources of power can be distinguished, each corresponding to different sources of uncertainty particularly relevant for organizations. First, there are sources of power which derive from special skills and from functional specialization.[31] Second, there are those connected with the relations between an organization and its environment, or, more precisely, its several environments. Third, there are sources of power engendered by control of communication and information. Finally, there are sources of power in the existence of general organizational rules.

Before developing these points, however, the limits of any typological classification should be stressed. Clearly, its only purpose is to clarify the ideas involved and to illustrate concretely a mode of argument. As with all resources which actors employ in their strategies, organizational sources of uncertainty are not objective and unequivocal facts.[32] While rooted, certainly, in the exigencies of certain technologies or production processes, as well as in the characteristics and particularities of the formal structure of a given organization—all of which may summarily be referred to as the "objective" factors of a situation—they are simultaneously integrating elements in the human system which underlies the organization, a response to its essential problems, and, as such, human constructs. They should therefore be analyzed as artifacts, as so many props which the actors in the organization "put together" out of their material and cultural resources to support and sustain their exchanges.

It is therefore imperative to avoid arguments of the following type: such and such a group is in possession of such and such a structural, "objective" source of uncertainty; hence it has a certain power; hence it exhibits such and such a behavior or strategy. The nature of the subject precludes any simple determinism. Here, as elsewhere, a source of uncertainty exists and becomes significant for organizational processes only when it is understood and invested in by actors pursuing their own strategies.[33] The "objective" existence of a source of uncertainty tells us nothing about the willingness or even the capacity of actors to use the opportunity it represents. This explains how, as in the case of the Industrial Monopoly treated above, a single source of uncertainty of an apparently technical nature either could become an important source of power profoundly influential in the operation of the organization, or else could remain a relatively minor and unexploited circumstance in another situation, even though the same technology was involved in both cases.

Let us now say a few words about the first important source of power. In fact, we have already had a good deal to say about this factor, as it was the most apparent of the four. Recall that we are speaking of the source of power which has to do with the possession of a special skill or functional specialization for which no ready substitute is available. The expert is the only person with the competence, knowledge, and experience of the situation needed for solving certain problems crucial to the organization. He therefore occupies an advantageous position in negotiation both with the organization and with his colleagues. When the smooth operation of an activity depends on his services, he can negotiate for advantages and privileges in return for them. The mechanism is well known, and there are few exceptions. Take, for instance, the privileged situation of maintenance services in most shops, or the advantages in the hands of the technocrats in France. Or consider the evolution of the power structure in large business or industrial groups where power has passed from the hands of bourgeois families to managers capable of controlling the great uncertainties within these still poorly integrated amalgams.

What is properly called "expertise" is relatively limited. Few persons in a society as complex as ours are really the only ones capable of solving a problem within a given setting. Yet a great many people enjoy a de facto monopoly because it would be too difficult or costly to replace them, in view of their having succeeded, generally by way of organizing as a group, in making or keeping esoteric and inaccessible what special experience and knowledge they possess. In the strict sense, every person within an organization possesses a minimum "expertise" of which advantage can be taken in negotiations, in the sense that it is difficult to find a replacement (because of the costs of advertising, training, etc.).

The second major source of power found in the organization has to do with the uncertainties which arise in connection with the organization's relations to its environment. It is rather similar to the previous source since control of the environment may be considered a form of "expertise." No organization can exist without establishing relations with its environment or environments.[34] The organization depends on its environments in two ways: first, as the source of the human and material resources necessary to its functioning (supplies, personnel, etc.); and, second, as the outlet for its product, be it a material good or something intangible. Consequently, an organization's *relevant environments*, the sectors of society with which it thus enters into relation, always represent a source of potential disturbance of its internal functioning and hence a major and unavoidable source of uncertainty. Individuals and groups capable, by means of their manifold connections with one or more sectors of the environment, of at least partially controlling this zone of uncertainty, and of turning it to the organization's use and profit, will enjoy a considerable power within that organization as a result. This sort of power has been called boundary spanning,[35] since it is possessed by an actor participating in several related systems of action. As a result, he can play the indispensable role of intermediary and interpreter between different and even contradictory logics of action. The sales representative, with his wealth of outside relations, as well as the worker who is an official of his union and who may be instrumental in triggering a strike, are two examples, among others.

Power does not, however, derive solely from the "objective" factors inherent in the technique, the job, and the manifold problems created by relations with the outside world.[36] It comes, too, from the active use to which the actors put their positions within the organization.

The organization creates power merely by the way in which it organizes *communication and information flow* among its subunits and members. To perform adequately the task or function assigned to him, an actor needs information that is in the possession of other individuals who occupy different positions within the work process. If, for a variety of reasons, he cannot short-circuit or forgo their cooperation, such individuals will have power over him, inasmuch as the manner of their transmission of information (with longer or shorter delays, withholding or "doctoring" of pertinent data, more or less, etc.)[37] will have a profound impact on the recipient's capacities for action. No regulation can do any good in this respect. The recipient can defend himself in such a situation only if he in turn possesses information (or controls another source of uncertainty) affecting his counterparts' capacity to play. The same process of extortion and counterextortion, of negotiation and bargaining, will then develop around the control and transmission of information relevant to each involved party.[38] A good example is provided by the strategy of lower-level supervisory personnel in the clerical agency analyzed by Michel Crozier.[39] To make his decisions, their superior in this organization needs information concerning detailed work situations which these lower-level personnel are responsible for furnishing. As a result, they enjoy a power over their superior which they use to influence his decisions, by biasing the information so as to favor their own interests. This state of affairs is the natural and systematic consequence of their position within the organization, which puts these personnel in competition with one another and leaves them *no other* means of influencing their superior's decision, on which their own capacity to maintain a suitable working environment within their respective sections depends. They cannot push this procedure too far, however, as it is the superior who ultimately makes the decisions. If they were to provide information too obviously erroneous or biased, he might be prompted to investigate the actual underlying situation for himself, thus sapping the source of their power. These considerations may not always be explicitly present in the minds of the lower-level supervisors. Nevertheless, it is easy to imagine that their real strategy will be quite subtle, quite unlike the conventional image according to which information moves up or down as dictated by the rational criteria embodied in the rules and structure of the organization.

The fourth source of power which we have singled out is the *utilization of organizational rules*. We take it up last because, to a greater extent than its predecessors, it is a construct, and can be understood as a managerial response to the problem posed by the existence of the three other sources of power. We saw previously, in the discussion of power deriving from the control of information, that managerial authority is able to adapt the circuits of information necessary for internal cooperation for its own purposes. An analogous problem arises here. In principle, the rules are supposed to suppress sources of uncertainty. What is paradoxical is that not only are these rules unsuccessful in completely doing away with such sources of uncertainty, but they also create new uncertainties which can be capitalized on by the very person whom the rules sought to constrain and whose behavior they were supposed to regularize.

The negotiation and bargaining which follows in the wake of a rule's application provides the best example. It is generally thought that a rule is a device by which a superior obliges his subordinates to behave as prescribed. By making this prescription precise, the rule reduces the subordinates' margin of liberty, hence increasing the superior's power.

Another analysis is possible, however, which shows that the rule's rationalizing effect is not one-way. If it limits the subordinates' margin of liberty, it does as much for the margin of choice of the superior. For example, the latter can no longer exercise his power of sanction apart from certain explicit circumstances. Similarly, the rule becomes a protective device behind which the subordinates can take refuge from their superior. By knowing how to apply the rule, they can disarm the superior so far as they are concerned. Since it is usually the case that the smooth functioning of an operation requires more than the rule prescribes, and since the superior is himself judged on the results of the operation, he is placed in a position of weakness, having no way of compelling his subordinates to do more than the rule prescribes.

How can the superior regain control of the situation? Usually, he will have not just one but several rules at his disposal. By allowing his subordinates to flout some of these, he gives himself a way to put pressure on them, as he can always threaten to end this indulgence and return to a strict regime, and can thereby extract a special effort when necessary. Yet he is aware that he cannot go too far, for then the subordinates would take him at his word and apply the strict letter of the rules, turning the tables on him by taking shelter behind them.[40]

Thus, while reducing one uncertainty as to the subordinates' behavior, the rule creates another uncertainty, since the extent of the use they will make of the rule as a protection against the superior's arbitrariness is indeterminate. Hence the power potential in the rule is not so much in its imposition of definite prescriptions as in the possibilities for pressure and negotiation which it creates. The superior's power is the power to create rules which he can use to obtain the desired behavior from his subordinates.

When an organization is studied from the point of view of the relations of power by means of which the actors continually use the available zones of uncertainty to negotiate over the implementation of their respective strategies, what emerges is a second power structure, parallel to the one codified and legitimated in the official organization chart. Bringing this parallel structure into the discussion allows the real extent of the official authority conferred by the formal organization to be ascertained, and the real margin for maneuver of the various actors to be measured. In short, such a study can shed light on the "anomalies" and "disparities" which never fail to exist between an organization's official façade and its actual functioning. This parallel power structure, which completes, modifies, and even nullifies the formal plan, is in fact the real chart of the organization. The strategies of all parties are shaped and guided by their relationship to this shadow organizational structure.

3

The Game as an Instrument or Organized Action

Let us sum up the preceding. *A given organizational situation never completely constrains an actor.* He always retains a margin of liberty and negotiation. This *margin of liberty* (signifying a source of uncertainty for his partners as well as for the organization as a whole) *endows each actor with power over the others,* which increases with the relevance for these others of the source of uncertainty controlled by the actor. This relevance is to be understood as the extent to which the source of uncertainty affects the capacity of the other actors to play according to their own strategies. An actor's behavior can and should be analyzed as the expression of a rational strategy whose aim is the use of power to increase his "winnings" through participation in the organization. In other words, the actor will always try to profit from his margin of liberty by *negotiating his participation* and by seeking to "manipulate" his partners and the organization as a whole so as to make his participation "pay."

The employment of such strategies, as we have said, always involves two contradictory and complementary aspects. Each actor will seek to *constrain the other members* of the organization to satisfy his own requirements (offensive strategy)[1] and, at the same time, to *escape the constraints which they would impose on him* by taking advantage of the systematic protection offered by his own margin of liberty and maneuver (defensive strategy). Of course, the relative importance of these two strategic orientations will vary in space and time as a function of each actor's own advantages and situation. Both will coexist, however, in every strategy of action. Their employment will involve the innumerable relations of power and bargaining linking the various actors. Together with these relations, the strategies form the functional backbone of the organization by providing the necessary common mediation of the divergent objectives of its various members.

The vision of the organization which emerges from this reasoning is far more complex, "incoherent," and conflictual than what appears in the "spontaneous" view of the phenomenon. Clearly, the functioning of an

45

organization no longer corresponds to the Taylorist image of an arrangement of cogs set in motion by a single rationality. Nor can it be understood as the expression of impersonal mechanisms or functional requirements which are supposed to assure the "spontaneous" satisfaction of the "needs" of integration and adaptation of a system whose structure is given at the outset. In the present view, the organization is in the end nothing more than a universe of conflict, and its functioning is seen as the outcome of confrontation between contingent, multiple, and divergent rationalities employed by relatively free actors using the sources of power available to them. The resulting conflicts of interest, incoherencies, and "structural inertia" are not manifestations of some sort of "organizational dysfunction." They are rather the price which an organization must pay for its existence, the condition of its being able to mobilize the contributions of its members and to obtain their "good will," without which it could not function properly.

Thus we are led to question the notion of "common objectives," which is too facilely assumed. There can be shared objectives. There is not, and cannot be, a unique objective within an organization—for two reasons. First, because the division of labor inherent in all organized activity gives each member of the organization, according to his structural position and function, a special and "distorted" view of its objectives.[2] There is little prospect that this view will be corrected, since it will generally be in the interest of each member to consider the limited and intermediate objective assigned to himself as the principal one.[3] Each member will construct, therefore, a different hierarchy of the organization's objectives and will consequently align his action[4] in accord with a general plan. In a universe of scarcity, where the benefits and advantages due to the organization are limited, individuals and groups clearly must compete among themselves for their distribution.

Therefore, we cannot speak of an organization's rationality and objectives as though they existed in themselves, apart from and above the individuals and groups who embody them in their strategies and behavior. Strictly speaking, the organization itself exists only by virtue of the *partial* objectives and rationalities of its component groups.

If it is true that an organization is a theater of confrontation and conflict such as we have described, then its very existence as a setting for collective action becomes precarious and problematic. Contrary to what certain proponents of "systems analysis" seem to believe when they abusively compare organizations to self-regulated "organic" or "cybernetic" systems, neither the integration, the cohesion, nor, *a fortiori*, the endurance of an organization comes about naturally and automatically.

In fact, the organization's stability is under constant threat from the centrifugal tendencies stemming from the deliberate actions of its members. In pursuing their personal strategies—always divergent, if not contradictory—the members of the organization naturally seek to protect or perhaps to enlarge their zones of freedom by reducing their dependence on others, or, in other words, by *limiting their interdependent relationship to the other parties involved.*[5] It might even be said that an organization exists not so much because of as in spite of the action of its members.

Let us pause for a moment over this point. When we say that the organization—and, more generally, any structure of collective action—is constantly threatened with disintegration because its participants are pursuing their personal strategies and because no absolute rationality[6] or unchallenged legitimacy exists to counter them, we do not mean to ignore or deny the fact that most organizations do manage to remain in existence and continue to function. We intend merely to introduce the idea that the organization constitutes a problem whose nature we should like to make precise, in order to understand what difficulties men must overcome in order to form and maintain it.

This problem includes not only the integration of the various activities essential to a result but also the integration of the relations of power and the strategies of the actors which assure the execution of these activities. This formulation may appear quite simple. Yet it counters, in fact, the reasoning underlying most theories of organization.

Those writers, on the one hand, who remain faithful to the classical rational model evade the problem altogether or, if you prefer, consider it solved. Since they believe that all rationalities can be hierarchized and integrated in a single rationality, the organization can perfectly well be defined by its objectives and technological, ecological, and economic characteristics, which are considered as so many constraints. From this standpoint human factors are seen as just one more constraint, more difficult perhaps, requiring accommodations and exceptions, but, within certain limits, tolerable. In general, the contract offers the best method for treating this constraint.

This view comes apart only when it can be demonstrated (as we believe we have been successful in doing) that there is no dichotomy between an omnipotent organization, in a sense a perfect incarnation of rationality, and the individual actor who remains a negligible quantity for want of a viable alternative to adjusting to this rationality. On the one hand, the organization is human and therefore incapable of transcending the limited rationality which is all the human mind can claim.[7] On the other hand, the individual actor is a free agent who retains his capacity of calculation and choice, not merely at the outset, at the moment of commitment, but as long as he remains actively engaged: he never relinquishes his capacity to elaborate strategies which, from his point of view, are rational.

In this respect the analysis of the complexities of relations of power leaves us in no doubt. Appearances to the contrary, the relative order imposed by the leaders on a complex collection of interactions is never preestablished. It is influenced by the pressure exerted by each partner and is constantly under examination.

Paradoxically, the problem is eluded just as much, but in a different way, by the various interactionist, Goffmannian, and ethnomethodological currents in sociology.[8] Having discovered the complex game in which the interpersonal strategies of actors in their situations are involved, the writers in question have focused on these strategies to the point of forgetting the organization entirely. Their point of view is too one-sidedly phenomenological and leaves untouched the central question of how regulatory mechanisms integrate behavior within collective structures. This leads to two types of explanations, which, in spite of being contradictory, both elude the problem raised above. The first, to which a good number of the Goffmannian analyses correspond, bases integration on a mutual adjustment among the actors, using a sort of market model of interactions and significations.[9] The other explanation, involving the omnipresence and universality of domination,[10] sees integration as based on the wider social and cultural relationships of power, which are held to be reproduced unchanged in interactions within the organization. In other words, the same phenomena of domination which are the essence of social interaction are experienced as such throughout the social organism; and in order to understand their character there is no need to refer to the intermediary institutions which embody them. In a sense, these institutions are considered as neutral transmission belts, which modify nothing of the essential.

Thus, in a curious way, there is a certain parallelism between the two positions. In neither case is the organization a problem; on the one hand it is too perfect, on the other it is transparent.[11]

Similarly, a difficulty in comprehending the organizational phenomenon as something completely autonomous and artificial, whose existence requires explanation as a contingent construct rather than as a consequence of general laws, also characterizes, though in a less obvious way, yet another attempt to establish a theory of organizations. We are thinking of the group of writers, for the most part English-speaking, as it happens, who have sought to base their theory on a structuro-functionalist approach.[12]

The two classical notions which they employ—normative integration of action and the concept of roles—do provide a preliminary level of understanding which was useful in its time for going beyond the mechanistic interpretation of the rational model.

From a narrow perspective of socialization, it is clear how individuals may be fashioned by the norms of their roles, reinforced by their partners' expectations, and supported by integrative values. In the more complex perspective which is introduced by the concept of relations of power within an organization, however, such a conceptual apparatus does not adequately account for the strategies of free actors, as distinct from the isolated behavior of passive actors.

The insuperable flaw in the structuro-functionalist theory is its overly rational conceptualization of mutually interdependent roles elaborated by a *deus ex machina* within a coherent structure. Even leaving aside the problem of the genesis of these roles, our analyses still contradict the essential hypothesis of the theory: namely, the supposition that the occupant of a given organizational role naturally conforms to his partners' expectations of his role. In the game of power, as a matter of fact, the ability to depart from the expectations and norms associated with one's "role" is an advantage and a source of power "opening" the possibility of bargaining. Conversely, to be confined within a "role" is a clearly inferior position for an actor who, when perfectly predictable, has nothing left to bargain with.

This explains why analysis always reveals in conjunction with and, if you will, underlying, the game of socialization, an instinctive and more or less conscious tendency on the part of all the actors to modify their assigned functions so as to elude the expectations and pressures of their partners in order to maintain or enlarge their margin of liberty. There are, to be sure, considerable differences in this respect within the organization. Yet everyone seems capable of profiting from the ambiguities, incoherencies, and contradictions inherent in his role.[13]

The best exponents of the structuro-functionalist approach, such as Robert Kahn[14] and his colleagues, are prevented by their theory from recognizing this fact. As faithful adherents of the clarity and coherence of roles, they diagnose situations of role conflict as "abnormal," if not pathological. For them, role conflicts and ambiguities are instances of *stress* and hence appear as important sources of modern anxieties. They fail to notice that the pathological cases who experience these ambiguities and contradictions are always persons who are in an inferior position, as distinct from the winners or stronger opponents.

If we are correct in the above, it is difficult to see how a theory of the formation and maintenance of an organization can be based on a collection of roles together with the normative integration of the action which goes along with them. We do not claim that there can never be normative integration of values, functional principles, and ritual; nor do we claim that the individual is not often subjected to the pressure imposed on him by the sum of his partners' expectations. Still, the inadequacy of this line of argument, which would make the actor respond passively to normative injunctions, is signaled by the fact that to a greater or lesser degree the individual always escapes these pressures and manages somehow to exercise his freedom.[15]

Many investigators have leveled similar criticisms at this apparently static model, which is incapable of accounting for organizational change. Nevertheless, it seems difficult to find a substitute for it. The critique can be pushed farther, as David Silverman has done,[16] but then, as we have seen, the problem of integration tends to be overlooked. Or else, from any overly facile "systems" point of view, one can concentrate on the needs and functional imperatives of the system, with the resulting tendency to neglect or ignore the actors, their strategies, and their freedom. This is the case with Amitai Etzioni,[17] whose work, in spite of a good many extremely acute detailed observations, does not give rise to a model substantially different from that of the structuro-functionalist. Similarly, the theoreticians of the "structural contingencies" school, such as Charles Perrow, J. O. Thompson, or David Hickson, make the rational model more flexible at the upper echelon, but do not recognize the actor's strategic freedom and so fall back into a normative economic or technical determinism equivalent to role theory.[18]

The interesting attempt by a German theoretician, N. Luhmann, who has been cited in the Introduction, to escape from the dilemma by radicalizing and "phenomenologizing" the structuro-functionalist theory does not seem to us any more conclusive in this regard.[19]

Luhmann's analyses try to answer the ancillary question concerning the genesis of role structures (what is the *deus ex machina?*), as well as the question of the system's capacity to motivate its members in spite of their divergent initial orientations, which make every hypothesis of a total normative integration illusory. To the first of these questions, he answers by radicalizing and, if you will, phenomenologizing the functionalist approach. In his view, social systems and their structures and processes must be understood on the basis of their *function,* which is to reduce the otherwise intolerable complexity of the world. Without "strategies" of selection and determination of meanings, anything would be possible, which is to say that nothing would be.[20] He answers the second question by a theory of the formalization of social systems, which he analyzes in terms of the process of differentiation which creates for each position in the system's structure a minimum *role* as *member.* This role is the official expression of the minimum expectations of behavior necessary to the survival of the whole which each actor accepts once and for all upon entering the system.[21] In short, legitimated by their function as sources of order in a complex world, systems can motivate their members by creating "member roles" whose freely accepted content assures the minimum integration of actors necessary to the survival of the system.[22]

Luhmann's analyses are not wanting in ingenuity. After frequently tortuous detours, however, they end by rediscovering a well-known conceptual framework, the engineers' classical rational model, complemented by the liberal contractual model.[23] The two are simply made rather "problematic," the first thanks to the use of cybernetic systems theory, the second by use of the theory of members' roles. Despite the contributions of phenomenological analyses, the organization continues to be regarded as a fact of nature rather than a contingent human construct. The free and inventive character of human behavior disappears altogether, since it is assumed that the actor accepts all the functional cybernetic constraints of the system when he assumes his role as a member.

While Luhmann is correct in stressing that participants need not subscribe to an organization's objectives to insure its survival, his analytic framework does not allow him to treat the problem thus raised. Avoiding the political dimension which is part and parcel of all organized action is not the way to explain the fundamental problem we have brought to light: how can the autonomous strategies of free members of an organization be integrated? Nor is the explanation to be found either in the structure as such—men must adapt themselves to roles defined by a structure, itself defined by other men—or in the structure as function—men must adapt themselves to the minimal roles that a structure, itself a necessary response to the problem of the order of the world, imposes on them.

The failure of these successive attempts is, we think, due to the fact that the *how* of integration has not hitherto been sufficiently penetrated with analytical tools. If a caricatural comparison is not out of place, we may say that the ethnomethodologists have a tool for understanding interactions, and the functionalists have revealed a problem. The tool should be used to understand not the problem in general, but rather the specific and contingent solutions which men have given it through their interactions.

We do not intend to work with the ethnomethodological tool, however. Instead we shall adopt the strategic approach outlined in the previous chapter.

The Role of the Formal Structure

We will now proceed to reformulate the problem in terms of the actor rather than the "system" or its structure. Instead of asking how the organization motivates its members, let us ask why the latter do not profit more from their potentially superior situation. In this connection, we need to reconsider the dynamic aspect of power relations.

The expert who controls a source of uncertainty crucial to certain others will naturally make use of his power to increase his advantage over them, perhaps at their expense. He will be able to do so, however, *only in a certain way and within certain limits,* because to maintain his power, he has to "keep the game going." He can do so only by satisfying at least in part the others' expectations of him, by controlling, partially at any rate, "his" source of uncertainty. It is tit for tat. An actor can exercise power over others and "manipulate" them to his profit only by letting himself be "manipulated" in turn and by allowing the others some power over him.[24]

To return to the example of the Industrial Monopoly, it is clear that while machine breakdowns are the maintenance workers' primary strategic advantage, breakdowns cannot be allowed to become so frequent as to threaten a halt to production. To put it in the extreme, the maintenance workers face the following *dilemma:* how should the machines be maintained so as to work well enough not to compromise production, while at the same time presenting enough problems to keep maintenance a crucial source of uncertainty?[25]

There is good reason to object that this formulation is extreme and valid only "in the last resort," and that many other factors prevent the maintenance workers from exploiting their privileged situation.[26] The objection falls flat, however, to the extent that the very importance of these other constraints is based on this same fundamental limitation of power which no actor can avoid without risk to his personal strategy, indeed to his continued existence as a factor which the others must take into account.[27] To have power with regard to others, an actor must *partially* satisfy their expectations of him, and, consequently, *they become a constraint* for him. This also explains why to some extent he must accept the precise number of "rules of the game" which will insure that relations will continue and play not cease. The rules accomplish this by effectively limiting each actor's choice and by structuring his negotiations with the others.[28]

On another level, the organization's need to survive imposes limits and constraints analogous to those inherent in all power relations. Ultimately, the whole collection of rules—whether they are formal or informal matters little here—which regulate and structure the course of conflicts and bargaining among the various participants is based on this need. All the participants desire the organization's survival in order to achieve mutual objectives. Hence the organizational "rules of the game"[29] become constraining for all participants, since these rules are based on a source of uncertainty commonly imposed on all of them: namely, the question of the organization's survival and, with it, their capacities to play.[30]

In the final analysis, an organization's leaders, as well as the possessors of capital, whatever may be said, derive their actual power from control of this source of uncertainty. There should be no misunderstanding. This uncertainty is fundamental but vague and even abstract for most purposes. The whole problem for the leader or leaders who control it is to find ways to use this power of dissuasion, which is difficult, and to transform it into a limited but concrete source of influence. From a certain point of view, they are no different from the Industrial Monopoly's maintenance workers. They might find it temporarily useful to have the problem of survival, like the problem of breakdowns, arise often, but this usefulness is limited to the short term, and becomes threatening in the long run. On the other hand, at the inception of the organization as well as at certain crucial times when its survival may have been in question, they undoubtedly exerted a considerable influence on the organization of structures and rules. As a result, they obtained control of artificial sources of uncertainty quite a bit more practical to manage than the threat of catastrophe.[31]

Looked at in this way, structures and rules have two contradictory aspects. In one sense, at any given moment they are constraints upon all the members of an organization, including the leaders who created them, while in another sense they are themselves the product of relations of force and of prior bargaining. They are *provisional, always contingent institutionalizations*[32] of the solution to the problem of cooperation[33] among relatively free actors. This solution is given by the actors themselves, in light of the constraints, resources, and negotiating capacities of the moment. As such, rules and structures are neither neutral nor uncontested.

They are not neutral because, in structuring the negotiating field, they give advantages to certain actors in preference to others, and because the actors use the artificial zones of uncertainty thus created both as tools and as defenses in pursuing their own strategies. As a result, the codification of such structures and rules will be a major stake in the conflicts between members of an organization.[34]

Nor are rules and structures uncontested. Depending on what new advantages become available, each member or group involved will try to modify in his or its own favor the balance of power in some sense "institutionalized" by these structures and rules, by depriving them as much as possible of their substance—i.e., their constraining character—thereby hoping to regain a degree of freedom. This means that the rules themselves embody relations of power, without which they would be lifeless and pliable.

The example offered by the phenomena of power grafted onto relations of authority is striking in this respect. The superior, as we have seen, can actually exercise his formal authority only by using extortion against his subordinates. Only by tolerating certain of their transgressions of the existing rules can he obtain in return the cooperation he needs to accomplish his own tasks. Without this possibility of extortion, his authority runs the risk of becoming a merely formal, theoretical attribute.

Such a view, it should be pointed out, has profound repercussions on the status of the whole formal structure of an organization. In effect, this formal structure has no rationality of its own. The operational significance of the formal structure derives from its relation to the power structure and to the rules of the organizational game. Ultimately, it is merely a provisional, contingent, and, above all, partial *codification* (formalization) of the rules of the game which prevail in the system of action underlying the organization. While it indicates to us that such a system of action exists,[35] it does not by itself permit us to discover either the extent or empirical configuration of this system,[36] or the characteristics and rules of the games being played in such a system, or the modes of regulation which assure the harmonious interdependence of these games. Although the formal structure clearly fulfills "functions" connected with these games and with the fundamental problem of the cooperation of relatively autonomous actors, no *a priori* logic can tell us what those functions are and what they signify.

It follows that the study of organizational functioning cannot be done in the abstract or on the basis of any *a priori* rationality, even one based on systems. What is essential is the observation and determination of the attitudes, behaviors, and strategies of the members, and the evaluation of their specific resources as well as of the various types of constraints limiting their margins for maneuver and influencing their strategies. Such an approach is a necessary preliminary to understanding the rationality of these attitudes, behaviors, and strategies in terms of the structures, nature, and rules of the games played by the members.[37]

A case-by-case approach is thus called for. This is at once a modest and an ambitious procedure. An experimental and inductive approach, it is modest insofar as it aspires to be a *method of analysis* of social reality and eschews the elaboration of a "theory of organizations" or of "laws" or general precepts which would define *a priori* what the "good" organization should be. It is ambitious because it explains the organization's functioning on the basis of its members' strategies—that is, it analyzes the organization as a system of action reflecting the individuals or groups which make it up. It thus goes far beyond its initial domain to approach the questions of how organized human action develops and what are its intrinsic constraints. We are concerned not with a sociology of organizations, but with a sociology of organized action.

The Game as an Instrument of Organized Action

The preceding analyses, which place the accent on the contingency of the structural data in any organizational situation and on the preponderant position to be assigned to the various strategies of the actors concerned, are as yet incomplete. While the idea they emphasize—the struggle of man against man—is well adapted to moments of organizational crisis in which the power inherent in systems of action takes a cruder and more brutal form than usual,[38] these analyses leave aside the phenomena of socialization and "structural inertia" which ordinarily, and rountinely, occupy such an important place not only in organizations but throughout social life. Organizations, however, are very far from being constantly in crisis, any more than individuals daily challenge the rules which, as we know, underlie and channel social interaction. Without stumbling into the impasses brought out and criticized above, a faithful and complete analysis of organizational life should incorporate these aspects as well.

We are not denying the existence of constraints, without which no structure of collective action could exist. We all know from experience how certain organizational situations or positions constrain the behavior of the person occupying them. The problem is to understand how this constraint operates and how it can be integrated into the analysis.

In this connection, it seems to us that to use the notion of role other than as a mere linguistic convention (which offers both the advantage and the disadvantage of evoking an image)[39] is a way of resolving the issue. In choosing the system with its "needs" and "necessities" as the point of departure for research, with all the dangers of reification and determinism which such a choice entails, one must simply take the constraint for granted. The almost inevitable result is that one finds determinism where there is only constraint and conditioning where there is actually choice. Exactly what is meant when one says that the role of a certain actor is to do a certain thing? One of two things. Either one understands what the actor *ought* to do, in which case no reference is made to his real behavior; (thus one does no more than describe the formal prescriptions which determine his position), or one merely specifies the normative requirements determined by the functional imperatives of over-all survival and adaptation. Or else the term "role" denotes the actor's empirically observable behavior, in which case this behavior is reduced—implicitly or explicitly—to the prescriptions and expectations associated with his position.

This is the essential limitation of every organizational analysis in terms of role: *the analysis is based on the univocal problematic of adaptation.*

Unless one is willing to accept a theory limited to purely formal and/or normative propositions,[40] in fact, one is obliged to reduce individual behaviors to what is expected in terms of role, and to consider the individual as locked in—even if by choice—to positions where conduct is predetermined. From that point on, behavior can only be *adaptive* and *passive*. Individuals support structures and are conditioned by their role.[41] "Deviance" in all its forms is abnormal, indeed pathological, stemming from a poor perception or comprehension of role,[42] or, in short, from functional defeats in the organization: conditioning is the rule.

To avoid the difficulties implicit in such a mode of argument, and to restore individuals to the status of autonomous actors whose conduct is the expression of their freedom, as minimal as it may be, the problematic must be changed.

The new problematic we suggest is based on the *game concept*. This is not merely a matter of a new vocabulary, but of a change of logic. Instead of concentrating on a series of well-delimited concepts—structure, role, person—which are insufficient for comprehending the phenomena we consider essential, including relations, negotiations, power, and interdependence, we focus on the mechanisms for integrating these phenomena. For us the game is much more than an image; it is a concrete mechanism which men use to structure and regularize their power relations, while leaving these relations—and themselves—free.

Men have developed the game as an instrument to regulate their cooperation. It is the essential instrument of organized action. The game reconciles freedom and constraint. The player remains free but must, if he wants to win, adopt a rational strategy which conforms to the nature of the game, whose rules he must respect. This means that, to further his interests, he must accept the constraints imposed on him. If the game is one of cooperation, as it always is within an organization, its outcome will be the result sought by the organization.[43] This result will not have been obtained directly and intentionally by the participants, but rather by the orientation each of them will derive from the nature and rules of the games in play, in which each seeks his own interest. So defined, the game is a human construct. It is linked to a society's cultural models and to the capacities of the players, but like every construct, it remains contingent. The structure is nothing other than a collection of games. The strategy or strategies of the participants are nothing but the tactics they employ in the game, and the nature of the game makes these strategies rational.

In other words, instead of considering the functioning of an organization as the result of various adaptive processes in which a collection of individuals or groups with their own motivations adjust to the procedures and "roles" laid down in advance by the organization, we propose to consider it as the result of a series of games participated in by the various organizational actors. By defining the possibilities for gain and loss, the formal and informal rules of these games delimit a range of rational, or "winning," strategies, which the actors can adopt if they wish their involvement with the organization to serve, or, at least, not to disserve, their personal aspirations. When the organization is conceptualized as a collection of interdependent games,[44] the properly sociological phenomenon of the integration of the actors' conduct is not interpreted as the direct result of learning a set of interdependent behaviors together with their corresponding norms and values. Instead, it is analyzed as the *indirect* consequence of the fundamental constraint obliging each participant, provided he wishes to continue to play and to insure that his involvement "pay" or, at least, not "cost" him too dearly, to take account of the requirements and rules prevailing in the games played in the organization, and so to contribute *nolens volens* to the accomplishment of the organization's objectives.

To say that the players play games in no way implies that there is any initial equality whatsoever among them,[45] or that there is any consensus as to the rules of the game.[46] It is certainly probable that socialization processes will become established around relatively stable game structures. But they are in no way necessary to the game's continuance, for the constraint imposed by the game does not determine behavior, but rather a range of possible strategies among which the actor chooses. Such choices can bring about a modification of the game itself. The game always remains open.

Let us return once more for purposes of illustration to the example of the Industrial Monopoly's shops. The system of action examined there can be readily conceptualized as a three-actor game, and, what is more, a zero-sum game: what is won by one player is lost by the others.[47] This characteristic makes the game particularly constraining for the participants. This constraining character does not, however, arise from any consensus among the actors; it is due simply to the fact that as long as they want to continue to play, there is no possible rational (or winning) strategy which does not oblige each player to behave in a way which contributes to achievement of the over-all objective and to the maintenance of the game itself.[48] Of course, they can choose to lose. Normally, however, they must win or at least avoid losing. In short, in order to "get out of the situation as much as they possibly can,"[49] they will be led to adopt such winning strategies. Thus the constraint[50] and also the persistence of the game.

We have already alluded to the fundamental dilemma of the maintenance workers, who are the really privileged participants in this game. We can show that a similar situation exists for the production workers: given the structure of the game that confronts them when they enter the organization (which they can escape only by leaving it), they cannot place themselves on a "bad footing" with the maintenance workers without risking the potential profits from their involvement in the Monopoly. They will therefore treat the latter with caution while attempting—through the roundabout means we have already seen—to exert indirect emotional pressure on them. The effect of such a strategy is clear: it reinforces the position of the maintenance workers while keeping them in line so that they don't overly neglect their "official" mission of repairing mechanical breakdowns. The least that can be said is that such a strategy does not contribute to breaking up the operation of the shops. The shop foremen's case is similar. Given their "losing" situation, their only option is to cut their losses by minimizing their involvement. How constraining this type of game can be is evident in the sanction meted out to the shop foreman who wanted to get involved with machine repairs. Ultimately, he was forced to leave the organization, because he had refused to "play the game."[51]

Learning the constraints of the game is likely to lead to acquisition of a system of norms and values corresponding to the rational strategy adopted. Clearly, however, the process in this case has a different status and meaning: it is no longer prior, but rather subsequent to the game, and it is not an automatic or even necessary condition for the game's maintenance. The extreme case of behavior which is apparently schizophrenic and/or perfectly cynical and in flagrant and permanent contradiction to the norms and values accepted and/or professed by a given actor, is not ruled out by this point of view, even if it remains rather implausible empirically. In sum, socialization can no longer be considered as the product of a passive adaptation, determined in advance. Since it always involves a relatively free actor, the process is *a priori* relatively open, always full of surprises.[52]

We should point out that such a perspective does not eliminate the actors' freedom of choice. In the first place, an actor may restructure his strategic field to reduce his vulnerability, and hence his potential loses, within a given game as far as possible. Conversely, he may seek to restructure the game in order to make other available resources relevant and mobilizable.[53] Failing this, he may, for reasons that in each instance are susceptible of empirical analysis, accept greater risks in the hope of a change of the game in his favor; and he may persist in this strategy in spite of initial losses. To give a vivid illustration: an actor remains free to ignore the lessons of experience by beating his head continually against a wall in the hope, perhaps illusory, that one day the wall will give way. And it may actually come to pass that, against all expectation, the wall *will* give way, which would mean, in game terms, that a new winning strategy will have become substitutable for the hitherto dominant strategies, since the nature of the game will have changed.

Depending on the diversity of strategies "authorized" by a game, a whole range of situations is imaginable, from the single-strategy, hence closed, game, to very open games, including the possibility most typical of organizations, that the game has only a limited number of "winning" strategies. Clearly, from this viewpoint, a game defining a unique strategy—hence a single "role behavior"—is an exceptional case which must in its turn be explained and which can have pathological consequences.[54] In the great majority of cases, on the other hand, a margin of liberty remains, and the actors will profit from it when *chooosing their strategies*—or their "role behaviors"—by taking into account such characteristics of the game as they can perceive with their own affective, cognitive, and cultural capacities.[55]

Depending on the actors' intrinsic capacities,[56] on the particular configuration of their respective strategic fields, and on the "rule" structure of the games in which they participate in the organization, strategies can vary a good deal, and may be more or less risky, more or less aggressive, or, conversely, more or less defensive. In any case, the ones chosen are not necessarily the only possible ones.[57] To speak of role in such a context takes on an entirely new significance. The relative homogeneity and stability of choices, and hence of strategies, which underlie this notion will then no longer imply a unique mode of behavior, but rather the existence of a *structured set of possible strategies* within a given situation and game. The "role" as understood by classical analysis might thus be reconceptualized as a relatively stable equilibrium state between a *dominant majority strategy,* on the one hand, and one or more minority strategies on the other. This state of equilibrium is defined by a threshold beyond which a shift might take place, and thus a new dominant strategy would take the place of the old one, with all the consequences which that would entail for the game, and, consequently, for the organization.

Such a viewpoint makes classical analysis in terms of roles much richer and much more flexible, if it doesn't destroy it altogether. For the behavior of the actors called upon to play certain roles influences the stability and persistence of the organization, as it is here defined, only indirectly. Instead, the dividing up of a number of possible strategies, a dividing up which the actors must respect if they wish the game to remain stable, but within which they can also *experiment* with other "role behaviors" without immediately incurring sanctions for "deviance," is what conditions over-all stability.[58]

From the point of view of research methodology, this explains why deviations and irregularities are as important, if not more important, for the analysis than regularities and dominant behavioral modes. The existence of these "minorities" (in a given "role") shows that choice exists, and not just constraint, and that other strategies are possible which would provide the same or eventually larger "compensation," even though a path different from that of the majority is followed. The very success of such minority strategies, moreover, by bringing about a restructuring of the diverse strategies coexisting within a given role, can in the long run result in a transformation of the game itself.[59]

This viewpoint, by forcing the investigator to consider the margin of liberty and, consequently, the possibilities for experimentation, invention, and discovery available to individuals occupying given "roles," makes it easier to explain both the changing and the permanent selections the individual actor will make among the potentially contradictory roles which his simultaneous participation in different structured groupings and games leads him to take up. Secondly, and more importantly, this perspective makes it possible to understand the origin of change in the interaction itself, without reference to the "needs" or "functional imperatives" of the system or group. Starting from the characteristics and rules of the game in which the individuals participate, and from the resources at their disposal, for example, one can analyze what modifications in the arrangement of their advantages will allow one or more of them to "discover" or even create new opportunities for action within a "role," together with appropriate new strategies, which—by triggering a restructuring of the various possible strategies within a given role—can result in a total transformation of the game.

The primary interest and advantage of an analysis in terms of "strategies" and "games" is that it opens an avenue of research capable of explaining the constraining and prestructured character of collective action, while treating human behavior as it is, as the exercise and expression of *choice* within a range of possibilities. The conduct of the actors is considered as the expression of a *rational strategy associated with a game to be discovered,* which leads the investigator to reconstruct this game from observable behavior. In so doing, he discovers the kinds and extent of constraints involved, along with the processes by which these constraints become operational. In sum, the procedure emphasizes that every structure of collective action is a social construct, maintained by social action. Rules of the games do, of course, direct individual choices, but, in return, these choices condition the manner in which the structure is maintained. This does not eliminate the possibility that relatively stable and constraining "roles" or "sets of strategies" may exist. A stable balance of power between two or more actors may well lead to equally stable reciprocal dominant strategies. Such stability, however, depends neither on mutual role expectations nor on the common values or functional imperatives of the system which supposedly underlie such expectations, but rather on the balance of power established by the actors in the situation. This balance is reflected in the characteristics and rules of the games from which the actors cannot abstain. Their participation further serves to stabilize the situation.

Management Revisited

In the light of the foregoing, we can clarify the definition given above of the formal structure as a provisional codification of a state of equilibrium among opposing strategies of power. It is clear that just as with the rules of the game, this codification involves something much more vague, indistinct, and indirect than a simple set of rules prescribing or proscribing certain actions. Such rules surely do exist and play a certain role, but the essential mechanisms of regulation lie elsewhere. What is codified is not the type of conduct allowed, but rather the type of game. This, in turn, makes certain kinds of behavior and certain strategies more probable than others.

With such a view, we can point out, first, that if there is constraint in organizations, there cannot be determinism. Structure in a situation does not preclude freedom for the actors.[60] In the second place, our viewpoint enables us to take a more realistic look at the possibilities for change and for operational intervention in organizations. At the same time, we are able to put in perspective the often exaggerated role attributed to the leaders in this connection.

What is the actual position of the leaders? What inherent advantages do they have? To answer these questions, one should begin with the zone of power under leadership control, which determines the meaning and significance of their authority and formal prerogatives. This power derives from the fact that they most powerfully and directly[61] control the survival of the organization and, with it, the stability of the rules of the game which are fundamental to play. They are expected to insure continuity. In a manner of speaking, they thus find themselves in the position of the dealer or, better still, the croupier who distributes the stakes and turns the wheel in roulette: all the participants must, in a sense, play against the leader, but also with him.[62]

Thus placed in a predominant position, the leaders will naturally attempt to exploit their advantages in order to structure the game to their own benefit, in favor of their own objectives and/or the organization's. Yet their margin for maneuver and potential for action are not in this respect unlimited.

First, they are constrained by the environment and the sanctions that it can impose upon the organization, to the extent that actors located outside the zone directly controlled by the leaders can behave in ways threatening to its survival and success. The extent of constraint effected by these sanctions increases with the existence of more effective techniques for measuring "performance" and results, both within the organization and in its environment.[63]

Second, since the leaders, too, depend on the survival and success of the organization,[64] their situation is comparable, making all due allowances, to that of any expert, whose dilemma is exemplified by the case of the maintenance workers of the Industrial Monopoly. Their power to intervene and their means of action are thus basically limited. To channel and structure the organizational games for their own profit (and/or for the benefit of the organization's objectives), they certainly can and actually do make use of whatever concrete levers are at hand—such as, for instance, information, channels of communication and interaction, creation or distribution of organizational stakes through personnel policies, organization of careers, choices of investment, etc. Yet in all these areas their actions are necessarily confined within limits narrower than one would think at first glance. Thus, for example, by intelligently combining secrecy and openness, every leader will try to use his control of information to create artificial zones of uncertainty for the other personnel and so exert pressure on the orientation of their strategies. He will withhold certain information, divulge other bits, and quite generally slant and manipulate the information's content in transmitting it to his collaborators. If he were to manipulate it excessively, however, he would ultimately remove all significance from the information transmitted, which would inevitably have repercussions on the information he receives, which is a basic element of his own task.[65] Similarly, issuing organizational rules in order to change the structure of the games in play always cuts two ways: as we have previously shown, such rules tie the hands of their promulgators as much as those of the subordinates they aim to regulate. Moreover, while the confusion engendered by the absence of rules decreases the number of opportunities for the leaders to intervene, the proliferation of rules reduces their potential to exert influence. Like the foreman who insists on formal rules while tolerating infractions of them by "his" workers, the leaders can make the best of their lot and achieve their ends only by doing two contradictory things simultaneously, and assuming the consequences of the contradictions: their "duplicity" is in a certain sense dictated by the objective situation.

Finally, and partially in consequence of the foregoing, leaders are constrained by the inevitable incompleteness and indirectness of their intervention in the system's operation. Exceptional situations and serious crises apart, they do not create games *ex nihilo,* nor can they radically change existing ones. Games are already in progress, and, as political and cultural constructs, they enjoy a certain autonomy and permanence. By restructuring the stakes as far as possible, and by changing the relative advantages of the players, their channels and circuits of interaction, and their various possibilities for coalition, etc., the leaders can certainly influence and redirect the evolution and the outcome of these games. Since they do not control all the parameters, however, their efforts in this direction are always incomplete. They are indirect as well, because the intrinsic logic and regulations of prior and ongoing games influence their character and mediate their effect.

No technical recipe can change this state of affairs. Rationalizing structures, developing more liberal and participatory climates, asserting a charismatic and personalized leadership—any, in short, of the "classical" means and instruments of action—can be used to good effect and even produce measurable results, creating games more open and more satisfying to all the participants. Because existing games always exert a fundamental influence on the use of such instruments, however, each of them can bring about unexpected and frequently unpredictable consequences which are contrary to the desired ends. To name just one such example, there are the well-known vicious circles of regulation and control which grow up around rationalization, or those of loyalty, deference, and passivity which develop around a charismatic leadership or a policy of integration. Hence such instruments should not be considered as absolutes but rather have to be put in perspective among the many possible, indeed parallel, alternatives for altering the games and influencing their development. The instruments must be evaluated in light of their intrinsic risks and limitations.

Two   The Organization and the Environment

4

The Limits of a Theory of Structural Contingency

Thus far, the essential part of our analysis has treated what might be called the *internal system of action* of an organization. Admittedly, the logic of the strategic method took us beyond this deliberately restricted framework and led us to introduce the innumerable unavoidable interferences which arise between this "internal system of action" and its technical, economic, social, and cultural context. In showing, first, that an actor's strategy within an organization can be understood only within the total context comprised of all the games in which he is simultaneously a participant, and, second, in identifying the control of relations with sectors of the environment as a source of power within the organization, we have (at least implicitly) brought out the *porosity* and *fluidity* of the "organizational frontiers" and the difficulty, if not the impossibility, of determining once and for all a clear and precise line of demarcation between what is "internal" and what "external." The time has now come to go beyond this simplification of reality, justifiable only as an analytical convenience, and to focus, in this part of the book, on the organization's relationships with its environment.

Need we remind the reader that no organization exists in the abstract? It is part of a given society which has attained a certain level of technical, economic, and cultural development, which is characterized by a certain social structure, and which inculcates certain values to which its members are particularly attached. These factors establish and impose a series of conditions and requirements on the organization's structures and functions. Organizations, whatever their manifest and/or latent objectives, cannot escape these conditions as long as they depend in two ways upon their environment for satisfactory operation. First, the environment supplies the organization with resources of every variety. Second, the environment must absorb whatever "products" the organization fabricates. Through this twofold dependency (which can be infinitely subdivided, since neither the required resources nor the products are unique but rather manifold and diversified), the environment's capacity to impose sanctions on the organization is, in one way or another, established. This explains why the technical, economic, social, and cultural conditions prevailing in the environment become constraining for the organization, whose success, and even survival, depend on them.[1]

The analysis of this dependence is the unifying theme of a whole current of research, with a "structural" orientation, which grew progressively throughout the sixties,[2] notably in reaction to an approach to organizational analysis which concentrated too exclusively on internal processes by way of qualitative and quasi-ethnological case studies.[3] Better known as the *theory of structural contingency,* this current of research sought to establish what the main dimensions of this dependency were, and to measure, with the help of exhaustive statistical analyses of samples of organizations, their respective importance and impact on organizational structure and function.[4] Two basic sets of questions characterize the procedure. What types of variables affect the characteristics (usually structural) of organizations, and to what extent? What is the influence of these characteristics on the level of performance of the organization?

Focused first on organizations as structural entities, considered by these theorists as the only appropriate object for analytic treatment,[5] such a "quantitative" and apparently more scientific approach to the organizational phenomenon allowed a useful stress to be placed on the importance of the organization's environment and context (especially the technological context) for the comprehension of their internal processes. Their research broadened the traditional analyses to include problems which in the past had too often been ignored. Their treatment, however, of the relationship of organization to situation as a simple unilateral dependence is indicative of a mode of argument whose technological reductionism and determinist bias lead to denial of the autonomy of the human construct underlying every organization. By means of a critical analysis of the most representative works in this current of research, we would like to show that this is the case. Then, in the following chapters, we will go on to examine the basis, limits, and significance of the autonomy of the organizational phenomenon as a political, hence cultural,[6] construct, whose purpose is to integrate the divergent strategies of the actor-participants.[7]

Technology, or the Temptations of a Technological Determinism

Of all the "contextual" factors (such as the origin and history of an organization, its size, its technology, its localization, etc.), technology was the first to be made the object of an in-depth empirical study in the pioneering research of Joan Woodward in England.[8] Based on a very broad and complete sampling of industrial enterprises in Essex, this work was the first probing empirical study of the influence of technology on organizational structures and on business performance.[9] Woodward introduces the complexity and predictability of the production techniques employed as criteria in her work. At the extreme end of the scale is *unitary production* (for example, the fabrication of a prototype or of small-volume items required by specific orders), which is characterized by lack of complexity and unpredictability. At the other extreme is *continuous production* (for example, the production of chemical products in a multifunctional enterprise); between the two is *mass production* (for example, the assembly line).[10] Woodward's study brings out statistical correlations among these technological types and the organizational structures of the firms studied: the number of hierarchical levels and the proportion of management personnel increase with the degree of complexity/predictability. These results correspond to the initial hypotheses. Other results, however, are unexpected: it is in the middle of the scale, not in those industries with the most sophisticated technologies, that the distinctions of specialization between functional management ("experts") and hierarchical management ("administrators") are most pronounced, and it is here as well that the bureaucratization of structures is greatest.

To explain these surprising results, Woodward suggests considering what she calls the "essential problem" of a technological system for organizational structure. She concludes that there are no organizational structures good in themselves; rather, structures are *adapted* to the problems raised, or to the constraints imposed, by a given technology. She shows that the companies in her sample which are unsuccessful in the sense that their rate of profit is below average for their technological category are also the ones whose structural characteristics are least typical of this category, and vice versa.

This empirical relativization of the *one best way* of the classical theory (*one* optimal organization model regardless of the situation) as a function of the technological variable (*several* optimal models depending on the technology employed) remains open to criticism in more than one respect. Without lingering unduly over the gaps and inadequacies in Woodward's proposed conceptualization of technology,[11] let us merely underscore the dangers of a technological determinism to which a simplistic interpretation of these results can too easily lead. According to this sort of approach, the requirements of a technology, *via* the constraint of performance, determine the organizational structures.[12] Such a "technological imperialism"[13] is contradicted by Woodward's own research results. In fact, there are a relatively large number of companies which, despite their below average rate of success in relation to their category, continue to operate even with their atypical structures. The mere existence of such "aberrations" suffices to show that the market is not some sort of Darwinian universe where only the fittest survive;[14] hence the performance constraint is less strong—and thus the real margin for maneuver left by the technology is broader—than postulated by such an interpretation.[15]

Although essentially theoretical and nonempirical, much of C. Perrow's work[16] has a similar orientation. Starting with a more properly sociological conceptualization of technology, he has proposed a comparative framework for the study of organizations, based on a typology of the links existing between production techniques (understood in the broadest sense) and organizational modes of operation.

In his work, the technology(ies) utilized in a given organization can be conceptualized as processes in which the *various inputs* (raw materials—whether in the form of stock, as in an industrial enterprise, or of human services, as in the case of a school, psychiatric hospital, etc.) are *transformed* by an appropriate processing, which it is up to the members of the organization to *seek*. Two key variables, therefore, define the nature of a technology. The first has to do with *the nature of the raw material itself,* essentially with its *variability,* which can be expressed in operational terms by the number and frequency of exceptions which the organization, or the individual in charge of the operation, must anticipate. The second relates to the *nature of the search* in which the members of the organization must engage in order to find an appropriate solution to the problems posed by the transformation of the raw material.[17] By then crossing these two variables after distinguishing them (as "inputs" involving *few* or *many* exceptions to the rule; as search behaviors either *analyzable* or *nonanalyzable*),[18] Perrow obtains four broad classes of technology.

Limiting his analysis to companies in a single sector (production) and to only two groups within this sector (middle and top management), Perrow then shows that each of these four types involves very precise consequences in terms of four major organizational dimensions: the margin for maneuver left to each of the two groups, their power, the coordination processes employed within them, and their degree of interdependence. In short, each type corresponds to a certain organizational structure and entails determined modes of behavior.

The obvious interest of such an original conceptualization of technology should not conceal the limits of the model Perrow proposes. First, it involves a series of simplifications which significantly restrict its operational validity. It is conceivable, for instance, that several types of technology usually coexist within a given organization. How, then, can their respective influence be determined? Moreover, what is even more important, the dichotomization of two principal variables defining a technology can be misleading. In reality two continuums are involved whose combination would in fact give rise to an infinity of possible structural variants which the model does not account for or interpret.

Furthermore, by defining technology on the basis of a set of variables implicitly considered as objective facts imposed on actors having no control over them, such a model assumes a static standpoint and takes for granted the solution of the very problem which needs to be understood and explicated: *why, how, and within what limits* do technological characteristics become constraining for the actors, and, conversely, to what extent can they "play" with such constraints? Quite plainly, neither the "variability" of the raw material nor the "analyzable" or "nonanalyzable" character of a search behavior is an immutable or intangible factor to which the actors can only adjust passively. These two dimensions are themselves stakes in the negotiations and bargaining among the organizational actors concerned, and as such reflect in part the "rules of the game" prevailing in the systems of action which underlie an organization or its subunits. The previously analyzed example of the Industrial Monopoly illustrates this point clearly. As has been shown by other investigations conducted in comparable companies, using the same technology in Perrow's sense, and even the same machine, the strategic importance of breakdowns is not merely or even primarily a technical matter.[19] Its importance comes from the attitude of the maintenance workers, who hide machine diagrams and maintenance instructions and, as we have seen, guard jealously their monopoly of maintenance, etc. Quite as much as they are technical matters, these breakdowns also have *human implications,* which are indissolubly linked to the modes of negotiation between groups and to the types of games prevailing in the Monopoly.

It is because he has misunderstood this essential aspect in his technological model that Perrow does not really succeed in integrating change into his analysis, other than in the form of a general postulate according to which, for the sake of efficiency, organizations attempt, consciously or unconsciously, to adjust as well as possible their structures to their technologies.[20] Immediately, one detects the determinist odor and the dangers of reification involved in such a recourse to the *deus ex machina* of "needs" or "wills" of organizations conceptualized as natural systems.[21] Let us make what we mean clear. Either the use of the word "attempt" implies that the organizations will not be able to succeed in making an adjustment, in which case it is not clear what the hypothesis adds to the schema or why one bothers to offer it. Or else the word indicates causal determination, in which case the dangers noted above are quite real, and the model's underlying reasoning becomes subject to the same critiques which were leveled at Woodward.[22]

The "Organizational Context," or the Dangers of Multivariate Determinism

The influence of other contextual factors, especially *organizational size,* is the primary focus of the work of Peter M. Blau, who has turned, after quite different early work on bureaucracy,[23] to this sort of structural approach. A number of other English-speaking authors, such as Richard H. Hall,[24] Derek Pugh, and David J. Hickson, among others, have also paid particular attention to the organizational context.

But Peter Blau presents what is probably the most elaborate and ambitious case for the structural effects of organizational size.[25] On the basis of a quantitative study of all the employment agencies and their branch offices in the United States, he proposes a formal[26] and deductive theory concerning the structural differentiation of organizations from a point of view which is spatial, functional, hierarchical, and occupational. His conclusions—relatively simple—may be summarized as follows: with declining intensity and effect, growth of organization size entails greater structural differentiation. This has a twofold effect: first, a saving of administrative personnel, to the extent that a greater homogeneity of tasks within a unit facilitates the control function; second, an increase in administrative personnel, to the extent that greater differentiation requires more coordination. Self-regulatory mechanisms exist which moderate the effect of structural differentiation by limiting organizational size, thereby avoiding a situation where the benefits of a great differentiation are compensated for, or possibly overcompensated for, by an increase in the costs of administrative coordination.

We will not renew here the fierce, and unfortunately justified, criticisms which C. Argyris has brought against Blau's most recent work.[27] In our own opinion, this work seems a particularly vivid illustration of the formalist traps which constantly menace organizational research based on structural premises. One cannot fail to be struck by the disproportion between the magnitude of the means employed by Blau[28] and the relative inconsequence, not to say banality, of his results, which hardly go beyond what was already taught by the classical theory of organizations,[29] and which remain in more than one respect open to criticism, even if one accepts this very limited viewpoint.[30]

Although the size factor is equally important, if not preeminent, in the results of D. S. Pugh, D. J. Hickson, et. al., they refuse to grant it this central position at the outset. Criticizing what they call a unitary or one-dimensional approach, which *a priori* gives priority to one contextual variable (the technology, size, objectives, etc., of an organization) at the expense of all the others, they plead for a multidimensional approach to understanding the influence of the context on organizational structures.[31]

In their research on a sample of "work organizations" in the English Midlands around Birmingham, seven contextual factors (origin and history of the organization, type of appropriation and control, size, "charter,"[32] technology, localization, and dependence on the exterior)[33] have been employed as independent variables in a multivariate regression analysis aimed at predicting three main structural variables previously established empirically: "activity structuration," "concentration of authority," and "line of control of work flow."[34] From the results of this analysis, the authors show that organizational structure is an essentially multidimensional phenomenon and, consequently, that a unitary concept like bureaucracy has no more than a limited utility, since organizational structures can vary along each of these dimensions.[35] Similarly, they modify and complete Woodward's conclusions by showing that technology's only direct and important effect is on the structural variables directly connected with the work flow. The smaller the organization is, the broader are the structural effects of technology; but the larger it is, the greater will be the total effect of other factors such as size and dependency, and the more limited will be the effects due to technology alone.[36]

This review, not exhaustive, of a few particularly significant works relevant to this line of research clearly indicates the general problem which underlies all these efforts: what is involved is the systematic, and if possible statistical, study of relationships among the various contextual factors (especially organization size) and organizational structures, in order to develop empirically observable causal laws.

At the outset, let us say that the contributions made by such analyses have certainly not been negligible. They have contributed especially to an understanding of the multiplicity of ways in which "context" influences organizational structure, to more precise measurement of the complexity of such influence, and thus to relativizing an approach which focuses too exclusively on constraints imposed by technology.[37] It must be noted, however, that their results remain incomplete (after all, even multivariate analyses leave an appreciable part of any structure unexplained), and their explanatory value remains dubious and fragile, and even dangerously fallacious.

In the first place, these limitations are related to the *formalist character* of this research. In fact, because it is satisfied with demonstrating statistical correlations between structural and contextual variables in formal development models of organizational structures, this work assumes that the characteristics of the formal structure which lend themselves most easily to quantitative study are the only mediation between the "contextual" variables and organizational performance. It is taken for granted that such formal characteristics have a special, if not exclusive, explanatory value.[38] Clearly, it is excessive to assume that the organization will in reality conform to the model envisioned in the formal structure (in the broadest sense); such a hypothesis will not withstand even superficial empirical investigation. Such an investigation would show, on the contrary, the importance of the informal processes which develop precisely because the formal structure does not regulate everything. Actors are always free to maneuver and use this freedom to interpret, manipulate, and sidestep what the structure prescribes. This problem has been amply treated in the preceding portion of this book, and there is no point in dwelling further on it.

The point is important, however. For uncertainty as to the precise status and impact of the phenomena measured leads legitimately to doubts about the meaning of the measurements proposed and the models based on them. For example, what exactly is being measured by a "formalization score" established by counting number of documents written within a given organization?[39] Or what is the significance of a "specialization score" defined by the number of specialized services in each of sixteen categories of organizational operation, or of a "centralization score" determined by analyzing the various hierarchic levels on which nearly forty typical decisions may be taken?[39] What do these measurements tell us about the relational models and operational modes characteristic of these organizations? How, then, is one to interpret the results of an international comparative study done by Hickson et al.,[40] in which the authors conclude that the context of organizations is *culture-free*, imposing constraints which operate similarly regardless of the particular cultures in which the organizations are located? In the light of the foregoing, are we not entitled to believe that the uniformity discovered is ultimately rather insignificant, and that the international, if not universal, validity of the relationships established by the model merely reflects its formalism?[41]

The virtually exclusive concern with formal organizational characteristics explains why this type of research can scarcely hope to get beyond a *static description* of reality. At best, it is limited to developing statistical correlations between organizational structures (treated as dependent variables) and contextual factors, correlations which tell us almost nothing about the only question that matters: namely, *under what conditions* and through *what mediating mechanisms* do these contextual factors affect and modify (and in what sense) the *rules of the game* governing interactions in the system of action underlying the organization. At worst, such research, in interpreting correlations as causal relations, leads to an extremely mechanistic and deterministic conception of organizational change. The attempt by D. S. Pugh et al. to construct, from the results of their factor analyses, a *causal sequence* for organizational development illustrates this manner of proceeding, the problems it raises, and the stumbling blocks it faces.[42] On the one hand, as the authors themselves insist,[43] the connections which they establish, and the classification which they propose, are purely descriptive and in no way explain organizational development. This would be possible only if one understood the underlying processes in a qualitative way. Statistical correlations are not helpful in this regard.[44] On the other hand, though—and in this respect the ambiguity which the authors leave lurking is significant—their attempt clearly indicates the risk inherent in such research of falling into a relatively simplistic determinism[45] of the following type: given a certain contextual factor, a definite organizational structure follows.[46] In this connection, the use of multivariate procedures only extends the range of determinants counted and analyzed; it does not change the mode of reasoning. Quite clearly, this method is insufficient for understanding social phenomena as complex as organizations. Not that the context does not represent a constraint. It is precisely because it is just that—in other words, a set of factors limiting, but never completely eliminating, the capacity of the actors within the organization to choose—that we have no right to assume that the context can determine organizational structures or operational modes.

External Constraints: The Adaptation of Organizations to the Requirements of Their Environments

We are next going to consider research that has been centered on the types of equilibriums which are established between organizational structures and their internal operational modes, on the one hand, and their social and economic environments, on the other. More generally, this research looks at the constraints deriving from the necessities and difficulties imposed by the environment.[47]

In one of the first studies devoted to these problems, Burns and Stalker[48] investigated the degree of adaptation of more or less bureaucratic organizational structures to their social and economic environment. On the basis of a study of twenty-one British firms operating in different types of markets, they elaborated two ideal-typical models of organization, representing different types of social and economic adaptation.

In the first place, they describe what they call the *mechanical model* of organization, which is characterized by a very elaborate and rigid organizational chart, very little communication, and a great deal of centralization of decision-making at the top. The *organic model* of organization is contrasted point by point.[49] The authors show that the mechanical model tends to appear in situations characterized by a stable environment (little technological innovation, regular market), while the organic model is a possible (or necessary?) response to a turbulent socioeconomic environment.[50]

Following a similar procedure, but more intent on formalization and conceptualization, Emery and Trist[51] stress the causal interrelations of elements in the environment. They distinguish four types of environment according to their rates of change and the predictability of their orientations: "placid random," "placid clustered," "disturbed reactive," and, finally, "turbulent." Each environment roughly corresponds to an economic structure of the market and constitutes a causal web for the structure of the organization and the type of relation it establishes with the "exterior." Thus the environment itself becomes an "organizational matrix" whose own regulations govern the interactions among the organizations involved.[52]

Taking a different point of departure, Paul R. Lawrence and Jay Lorsch reach comparable conclusions.[53] They begin by considering the fundamental contradiction between the importance of organizational differentiation, in the broad sense of the word,[54] in dealing effectively with a fragmented environment, and the importance of organizational integration, i.e., of procedures for controlling centrifugal tendencies and resolving conflicts due to differentiation. Lawrence and Lorsch arrive at a simple conclusion: there is a fundamental relationship among (a) external variables (the uncertainty, diversity, and kind of environmental constraints); (b) internal states of differentiation and integration; and (c) procedures for resolution of conflicts. The more a firm's organizational structures and procedures take account of this relationship, the higher its performance level will be.[55] In other words, the material situation dictates no single recipe: the "right" dose of integration and differentiation depends on the characteristics of the environment and the problems it poses to the organization.[56]

This research, indicative of the growing acceptance and usefulness of an "open systems" approach in organizational studies, has considerably advanced our comprehension. It remains, however, a captive of a conception which sees the environment in terms of impersonal "factors" whose "objective" characteristics are somehow imposed automatically upon organizations from the outset. From this derives a *unilateral* conception of environmental influences, which neglects or ignores the fact that the organization can "play" with the "requirements" and constraints imposed by the environment, and even manipulate them in its turn. The more or less explicit result of this approach is to single out the processes of organizational adaptation to the environment as the ultimate explanatory factors.

Quite clearly, the environment should not be regarded as unified and homogeneous. It is made up of numerous fragmentary segments, possibly enclosed in separate compartments, each of which impose fluctuating, ambiguous, and frequently divergent or even contradictory requirements. This is one reason that there is indeterminacy and hence *freedom* and *choice* in the relationship between an organization and its environment, as J. Child has rightly stressed in an excellent critique of the structural contingency model.[57] It is important, however, to go further and examine this relationship itself. Environmental "requirements" are not disembodied "factors" imposed on the organization by impersonal or automatic mechanisms. They become constraints on the organization—and, strictly speaking, exist—[58] only when certain individuals or groups, social actors located inside or outside the organization, incorporate these requirements in their personal strategies and use them in their game plans.

This point has already been sufficiently stressed by Chandler[59] in the conclusions drawn from his study of the institutional history of several giant firms in the United States (Du Pont de Nemours, General Motors, Standard Oil of New Jersey, and Sears, Roebuck). Chandler shows that a firm's strategy over a period of time determines its structure, and that this strategy in turn should be analyzed by looking at the firm's willingness to make the best use of its resources as a function of market possibilities.[60] Of course, he repeatedly emphasizes the importance of changes in the environment for making new strategic choices and, indeed, regards such changes as a key factor in the choice of new structures. Bringing in the intermediate variable of strategy, however, he points out that external influences are *mediated:* in fact, he holds that environmental "requirements" influence organizational structures only insofar as they are incorporated in organizational strategies formulated by the leadership, or, to borrow the formulation of Cyert and March, by the "dominant coalitions" within the organization.[61]

A series of results from the previously cited studies of Burns and Stalker, which tend to contradict their initial hypotheses, are open to similar interpretation. In their sample, they actually found instances where changes in a firm's environment not only did not bring on the organizational modifications one might have expected, but rather accentuated all the features of the mechanical model in spite of the fact, or perhaps because, their environment became much less stable and predictable than it had been. Their attempt to explain these surprising discrepancies through analysis of the power and prestige systems underlying the operation of these organizations[62] is indirect evidence for the "political" character of relations with the environment and for the existence of elements of freedom and autonomy in the organization's dealings with external "requirements."[63]

The Organization and Its Constraints:
Unilateral Adaptation or Interstructuralization?

To sum up, there can be no doubt that the "theory of structural contingency" has contributed importantly to a conceptual and, above all, practical renewal of organizational studies.[64] We think nonetheless that on another plane it reproduces what might be called the *technological bias* of the classical theory of organizations. Of course, the procedure followed and the means employed are more complex. Instead of applying *a priori* principles, one aims to give a detailed empirical evaluation of the situation in order to identify the problems which require development of new, more adequate organizational structures. In more sophisticated terms, such an approach considers the problems only on an economico-technical basis and more or less explicitly gives primary importance to the structural aspects of organizational operation, but refuses to consider another very basic set of factors: we are thinking of the actors who must confront and resolve these problems in a concrete sense. We also have in mind the relationships, negotiations, and games through which this confrontation must take place, all of which will impose constraints that will inevitably condition the potential solutions. As before, the perspective remains too narrowly economic and technical. Organizational efficiency is seen as a simple function of the more or less optimal equivalence of structures to objective situational characteristics.[65]

Failing to recognize the autonomy of the human construct underlying an organization, and, hence, the constraints it imposes,[66] such a "technician's" view is intimately connected with a line of argument whose underlying deterministic presuppositions ultimately reduce organizational change to a quasi-mechanical process of unilateral adaptation. In fact, starting with a finding that the degree of adaptation of an organization's structure to technical or economic factors indeed determines its capacity to attain the performance and efficiency levels necessary to survive and compete successfully, one argues that the organization can survive in a changed environment only by changing its structure. From this preliminary proposition, the conclusion inevitably follows[67] that, unless a decreased performance level and the eventuality of ruin in the more or less long term are tolerable, an organization must invariably seek to optimize its structure's adaptation to the requirements imposed by its technology or environment. In other words, organizational change is a response to functional imperatives arising out of the "needs" to survive and to operate efficiently which organizations, conceived as natural systems, are supposed to experience.

As attractive as it may be at first sight, such reasoning is based on two largely implicit assumptions. The first holds that the market, as the environment's mechanism for applying sanction, allows only the fittest organizations to survive, and that, as a consequence, in a basically hostile environment, an organization's threshold of survival is more or less identical with its threshold of success.[68] The second supposes that structural arrangements have a decisive influence on an organization's performance level. Neither of these assumptions withstands empirical verification.

First, success is neither as imperious nor as narrowly defined a constraint as theoreticians of this school seem to think. On the contrary, as shown by the presence in Woodward's or Lawrence and Lorsch's sample of companies functioning in atypical modes at reduced performance levels, the difference may be great between the performance level necessary for an organization's success and that indispensable to its survival. This difference defines the environment's area of tolerance, i.e., the margin for maneuver within which an organization is relatively free to set its own objectives and performance norms, which will most frequently correspond to an efficiency level merely satisfactory and not optimal.[69]

Second, empirical research shows precisely that structural arrangements ultimately have only minor and indirect influence on an organization's level of success. This is what seems to emerge from R. E. Caves's work on "success" factors in English industry.[70] Similarly, later work of Lawrence and Lorsch seems to indicate that the "right" dose of integration and differentiation is obtainable throughout a relatively wide range of structural arrangements.[71] Even more striking, J. Pennings's research[72] suggests that organizations "nonadapted" to the objective factors of their situation succeed quite well, so that the model's normative prescriptions cannot rest on any empirical determinism.[73]

One must yield to the evidence: in this area, there is no determinism; nothing follows automatically. The structured complex of human relations, which underlies the organization and is the source of its life, is not a passive product of situational constraints. It conforms to a logic and rationality of its own. For it corresponds to a collection of relations of power distributed in various games, within whose framework relatively autonomous actors pursue their divergent interests and negotiate the conditions of their participation in the group. Depending on their functions and on the sources of power they control, these actors will naturally be led to act in such a way that the solutions adopted to problems posed by technology, the environment—in short, by the situation—will be compatible with the preservation of their own capacity to negotiate within the organization, at least. In other words, problems will be perceived and responded to in response to the actors' strategies in intra- and extra-organizational games.[74]

In fact, what is involved here is something quite different from a unilateral adaptation of the organization to the constraints of its situation. As in every concrete process of interaction, we find mechanisms of exchange and reciprocal influence[75] through which the organization structures its situation (in the broadest sense) quite as much as it is structured by it.

We should point out that stating the problem in this way in no sense denies that situational constraints dominate an organization's system of action. We are merely integrating these constraints in a wider investigative context in which they can assume their real status. They are constraints limiting the actors' rationality and freedom of choice, but not eliminating them. The question, then, is to understand more concretely how, under what conditions, and within what limits the kind of solution given to the problems posed by the situation affects the negotiating capacities and game positions of the different actors within the organization, and, *conversely,* how and within what limits the logic of organizational games determines reactions and responses to the constraints of the situation, and, indeed, these constraints themselves. Like the internal procedures of an organization, the solutions given to problems posed by the environment in the broad sense are *political and cultural constructs* and should be analyzed as such.[76]

To leave the confines of the narrow scientistic perspective of structural contingency theory, and to escape the deterministic implications which such an approach entails, in terms of both the structure and over-all development of the organization, we must change our focus of study. Instead of looking at the internal system of action, we should focus on the *mechanisms of regulation governing the whole organization-environment system.* Here we find a structure of networks of power and exchange tying together the various actors involved, which we can analyze in terms of the actors' power and strategies, as we have already done in the case of an organization's "internal" system of action.[77]

5

The Organization and Its Environment
Transactions at the Frontier

The environment is not a set of independent variables: it is a collection of differently structured systems or subsystems and consequently poses a number of specific problems which each organizational actor has to solve. He can successfully accomplish this only by entering into relations of power and exchange with other actors both inside and outside the organization proper. By virtue of their own regulations, these outside relations define "environmental" requirements and determine how the organizational actors must respond to them.

In other words, just as an organization's "internal" operation should be conceptualized as the product of a collection of interdependent games whose rules constrain the actors participating in them and which integrate their divergent strategies, relations to the environment may be considered as products of games which reach beyond the formal frontiers of the organization. The logic and rules of these games determine the possibilities and capacities for action and thus become the basic device for mediating the influencing of the environment.

To understand the dynamic relationship between an organization and its environment and to grasp the reciprocal processes of exchange and influence involved, we have to analyze how such games originate and are maintained and regulated. We also have to look at their interrelations with intraorganizational games. We intend to take these problems up next, using the same concepts and the same strategic approach in this broadened context as we used for studying an organization's "internal" system of action.

The Structuration of the Environment:
"Organizational Gatekeepers"

In pursuing its objectives, as we have said, every organization must negotiate with *its environment*.[1] In terms of strategic analysis, this means that different actors in an organization's *relevant environment*[2] invariably control major sources of uncertainty for the organization. The organization must constantly seek to control and dominate these uncertainties to protect itself and to foster its development. It must attempt to *stabilize* and *personalize* these external sources of uncertainty in order to control them. One possible way to do this would be to create specialized departments within the organization relating to specific sectors of the environment. These departments would be responsible for keeping in touch with the problems and trends in their special sectors. They would keep the organization posted on these developments, and would also take charge of formulating adequate strategies for responding to whatever eventuality might arise in their particular sector.

This raises the problem analyzed by Lawrence and Lorsch in their previously cited work[3]—the internal differentiation of organizations brought about by the necessity of relations with the environment. In carrying out their missions, in fact, the actors with posts in these specialized departments will almost inevitably be led to identify with the needs, problems, and even "mentalities" prevailing in the particular sectors of the environment with which they have to maintain good contacts. Thus they may come to give these things more importance than the requirements or success of their own organization demand.

The Concept of Gatekeeper

Internal structural differentiation of organizations in response to the necessity to "organize" relations with their relevant environments is only a part of the answer.[4] The specialized departments mentioned above cannot conceivably fulfill their purpose of making contact with a particular sector of the environment without elaborating fairly permanent networks, structured around certain privileged interlocutors, or *gatekeepers*, who thus become indispensable to their work.[5]

These gatekeepers may be of various kinds. In a commercial enterprise, they will be suppliers, bankers, subcontractors, manual-labor brokers, labor unions, sales networks, and retailers. In the case of a private school they might include parent-teacher associations or banks. In a public-administration setting, they might be political officials, professional organizations, or, more generally, any group of persons falling under the administration's jurisdiction. Whatever their nature, their role with respect to the organization always has two aspects.

First, the gatekeepers are supposed to *represent the sector of the environment* on which the attention of all or part of the organization is focused. They keep the organization abreast of the situation in their respective sectors and of the implications of that situation for the organization. Thus they contribute to the organization's operation, either by facilitating the mobilization of necessary resources, or by improving the prospects for distributing products by making these more suitable for the requirements of the sector which they represent. They can play this part of their role only by establishing certain rules between themselves and the organization's representatives. These rules may be more or less explicit and formal, depending on the case; they relate to the general conditions for obtaining resources or distributing products, thus serving to regulate and normalize exchanges between the organization and its environment.

Through this process, their "role" is reflected in a second dimension which is, in some sense, the mirror image of the first: they must command respect for the rules established by the organization. Serving to extend the reach of the environment into the organization itself, the gatekeepers cannot help being the organization's agents. Because the two aspects of the role are complementary, they are inseparable. You can't have one without the other: structurally, the gatekeepers have a dual function and must live with the resulting contradictions.[6]

The gatekeepers' ambivalent situation and the constraints on their action which derive from it enable us to understand the extent of the power they control relative to the organization. We can also describe the type and logic of the game that all the participants must play.

Insofar as they are successful in reconciling the contradictory functions of their role, the gatekeepers occupy a position of strength relative to the organization, for which they become indispensable as *reducers of uncertainty*.[7] Their situation gives them a significant extortive power which they will naturally use against the organization to obtain desired advantages in return for their favors.[8] In other words, like the members of the organization itself, *they will always negotiate–implicitly or explicitly–by exploiting their capacity to reduce uncertainty*. Their power in this respect is not unlimited, however: the relation of dependence is reciprocal. Though indispensable to the organization, they are nevertheless dependent on it, since a fairly significant part of their own power and capacity to act (and hence to pursue their personal objectives) is linked to their gatekeeper function and thus indirectly to the existence of the organization. They therefore become the organization's allies, to some degree at least.[9] The balance of power which will prevail in such negotiations will in turn be a function of the way in which each partner/adversary handles his situational constraints and plays his trump cards. It will also depend on his capacity to mobilize these advantages effectively in a given relation, and, in particular, to make the organization pay for its willingness to continue the relation.[10]

The Structuration of the Game between Organizational Sectors and Gatekeepers: The Logic of Monopoly

In analyzing these relations, it is important not to lose sight of one of the essential characteristics which distinguish them sharply from the games prevailing between an organization and its members: the theoretically greater liberty of each of the partner/adversaries to leave the relationship.

This means that the replaceability of each partner/adversary becomes one of the stakes—if not the central one—in every relation of this type. We think this is the best point of view from which to give a coherent interpretation of the mechanisms and functional principles shown by empirical analysis to underlie the extremely diverse forms of power equilibriums which exist between organizations and their gatekeepers. We believe that it is legitimate to make the hypothesis that behind the diversity of particular configurations, a single logic is at work, structuring the strategies of the various actors and, consequently, conditioning the games they are involved in. This logic, paradoxically for a society known as liberal or even "advanced liberal," is a logic of monopoly.

Not that there are no situations where it would be in the interest of each partner/adversary—for reasons to be specified in each case—to play a game of differentiation rather than monopoly. Not that it is impossible for the gatekeeper to pressure the organization without exercising a monopoly, or for the organization to manipulate its gatekeepers without having established itself as the only acceptable interlocutor. Other games can be imagined in which it would be possible to occupy a position of power, not in the role of an intermediary, but rather as an informant or regulator in an open competition.[11] Yet while potentialities of this type may exist, the predominant game is one in which each player seeks to set himself up before the other as the only possible interlocutor, while trying to arrange for himself substitute solutions and partners.

In the framework of the simplest power relation, of the sort we have found in every organizational situation, we showed that negotiation could be reconstructed logically on the basis of a discussion of predictability. Each participant seeks to confine the others to predictable positions, while remaining at liberty himself. The winner, the one who can manipulate the other and hence orient the relationship to his own advantage, is the one who possesses the greatest margin for maneuver. It is as if there were an equivalence between predictability and inferiority.

It is no different in the relationship between an organization and its gatekeepers. What is the problem? For each partner, it is a matter of monopolizing a certain social function in a relatively unstructured set (where "structured" has the sense of "consciously organized"). Because it is unstructured, the set is quite opaque and difficult to understand and, *a fortiori*, to transform. In the case of the gatekeeper, this social function is to represent a social demand, i.e., to give it form and order and to render it operational by becoming its representative. In the case of the organization, it is to satisfy an existing social demand, which originally it helped to create (although that matters little here). If the gatekeeper is independent and there are substitute interlocutors available, if he can become involved with several different organizations, and if the organization must go through him in order to reach its clients, he is in a position of strength. If, on the other hand, the organization has succeeded in establishing itself as the sole interlocutor because it alone is capable of responding to the demand expressed through the gatekeeper, he is in practice integrated into the organization, hence dependent, hence in an inferior situation.

Of course, the game is not over when the gatekeeper is integrated into the organization. With control of organizational zones of uncertainty, the gatekeeper may recover the means to play with a more diversified group of interlocutors within the organization. Integration, however, is a sort of "return to the ranks" for the gatekeeper which fundamentally changes the nature of the game. Of course, integrated gatekeepers retain a good deal more autonomy than is afforded the organizational actor in the usual sort of analysis. After integration, however, they are obliged to obey rules over which their influence is limited, and the games in which they become involved are more formalized and constraining. Above all, it is much more difficult for them to transform such games. Individually, they can always quit the organization, but it is much less easy to take with them the cells they control. Thus their power of direct negotiation has been greatly diminished.[12]

Using the degree of monopoly[13] exercised by each partner relative to the other as an analytic dimension, the range of situations and potential equilibriums of power can be laid out along a continuum. At one extreme is a system of negotiations biased in the organization's favor insofar as it occupies a monopoly situation, so that the environment is relatively incapable of imposing sanctions on it. In the extreme case, what results is a *colonization of the gatekeepers* by the internal requirements of the organization.[14] One concrete example[15] of this situation is given by the subcontractor relationship which links a large company with many small suppliers who work only for it. Another example is offered by the relations established between a highly ideological and centralized political party and its elected officeholders, who, under an electoral system of voting by party list, depend on the party and its fortunes in order to be elected.

At the other end of the continuum, we find a constellation of one or more gatekeepers who face a number of organizations fulfilling similar social functions, hence in competition with one another. In one way or another, all these gatekeepers have succeeded in establishing a monopoly over the representation of a particular sector of the environment whose cooperation is indispensable for the survival of these organizations. Since, in this case, the organizations have few means of pressuring the "gatekeepers," the balance of power shifts in favor of the latter. The extreme, but not atypical, case may also be observed, that of a *colonization of the organization* by its gatekeepers and the external requirements which they represent or convey. Various examples come to mind to illustrate this case. Consider, for instance, a company forced into reorganization by a variety of difficulties of all kinds, which compel it to accede to the demands of its bankers. In another sphere, there is the example of certain American cities where the political "machine," originally created to insure victory in the local elections, ultimately took complete control and exerted a pervasive influence on the policies of the elected government. Finally, the insurance profession, with the unstable situation it has occupied and for the moment continues to occupy in France, offers a whole range of intermediate cases along this continuum, from the free agent who retains a fairly wide range of choice, to the salesman at the mercy of the company.[16]

Autonomization of Relations between Organizational Sectors and Gatekeepers

Whatever the composition of the ring of gatekeepers surrounding the organization, however, and whatever the prevailing type of equilibrium, the systems of negotiation and power thus created will enjoy a certain permanence.

There are two complementary reasons for this. First, such negotiations are never "one-shot" events. Deriving from an organization's functional requirements, they form part of a lasting exchange process. As a result, the relational systems which mediate them will tend to endure. Second, it is in each partner's interest to maintain a minimum of stability, insofar as each one draws from such a relation a specific power which increases his own capacity to pursue his objectives. Indeed, the more stable their relations with their gatekeepers in the environment, the more the actors in the corresponding organizational sector will depend on these relations and gatekeepers to strengthen their hands in intraorganizational strategies.[17] A reciprocal situation obtains for the gatekeepers: the more stable the relations permitting them access to the organization and influence over its product, the more power they can derive with respect to the "clientele" which they represent. In short, each of the two partners must satisfy the other in order to increase his own capacity for action.[18] The stakes are interdependent.

Until now, we have stressed a logic involving a search for a "monopoly" relation underlying the transactions between organizational sectors and their respective gatekeepers. We are now in a position to explain why this logic is the one which is constantly operationalized. The primary reason is that each partner can insure stability in the relationship by establishing himself as the only possible interlocutor for his counter-parts.[19] Empirically, this is reflected in the establishment of private preserves from which intruders are forbidden, as well as in the use of the threat of "bypassing" in order to extort certain advantages.[20]

Usually, this involves a process of cumulative reinforcement of the power of the respective actors, regardless of how little they may care to "play the game." What happens is that an embryonic system of action crystallizes around the binary relationship between an organizational sector and "its" gatekeeper(s). This system has its own characteristics, which are intended precisely to insure that each partner maintains his possibility to negotiate and act. In short, this is a relatively *autonomous* system of action whose logic is irreducible to the original purposes and instrumental rationality in effect at its inception.

It seems to us that this description corresponds well to the general dynamic underlying the transactions between an organization and its relevant environment. Still, it is, of course, true that factors appropriate to each situation will impose more or less narrow limits on the development of this dynamic. Put differently, the more a given situation insures the stability of these systems of relation, *the greater will be their autonomization*. This depends in part on the structural factors themselves, which determine how easy it is for an actor to replace his partner(s) with others. The introduction of competition in this sense, however, will have real impact only if there is concurrently available a measuring technique accepted by the parties involved which allows their respective "performances" to be evaluated.[21]

In other words, the gatekeepers may succeed in keeping the manner and degree of their control over a given environmental sector secret, thus making it difficult to judge how representative they are. Or, conversely, the "requirements" of a particular organizational sector may be ambiguous, diffuse, relatively inarticulate or unintelligible, so that it may be difficult to evaluate the organization's capacity to respond. In that case, it is left largely to the organization to define the "social demand."[22] In either case, the possibility of changing partners loses much of its attractiveness for both sides and will usually occur only in exceptional circumstances. The autonomy of the system of relation linking an organizational sector to its gatekeepers will thus be reinforced.

We may conceive of a theoretical case which would illustrate, in some sense, a minimal degree of autonomy. Suppose that both the organization and its gatekeepers are involved in situations of perfect competition, and that there exists a measuring technique by which the performance of both may be evaluated. Then *the actors' game of power is rigorously subject to a rational method of evaluation*. The organization will be able to pressure its gatekeepers only insofar as its services are "effective" and actually respond to "external demands." Conversely, the gatekeepers will be able to obtain power over the organization only if they continue to be representative and are thus "useful" to the organization. With each partner, then, constrained by the "requirements" of his "role," the system of relation will have little autonomy.

At the opposite extreme, we may conceive of a second case which would maximize this autonomy. Indeed, if both organization and gatekeepers exercise monopolies with respect to one another, and if performance can scarcely be measured in either case, *the stability of the game will in some sense be dictated by the facts of the situation.* Unless the given conditions are radically altered, each partner must avail himself of the other's services and cooperate with him, regardless of the real satisfactions he obtains. In this case, we observe an extremely integrated autonomous system in which phenomena of identification, complicity, and even symbiosis among the actors are free to develop. The system will consequently tend to endure well beyond the conditions which brought it into being. Shoulder to shoulder, *organizational sectors and gatekeepers will complement each other.*[23]

Regardless of the relative independence of their instrumental purposes, it is clear that such systems of relation will always represent a constraint on the internal operation of an organization, as well as on its capacity to develop and change. The organization of relations to the environment will not, then, merely transmit external influences to the "internal system," but may become an *additional factor of rigidity.* In fact, even if they are not totally assimilated by their gatekeepers, the various actors in the organization cannot act without their cooperation. It follows that these actors can redefine their objectives, and consequently, their strategies, only if they change the balance of their relation to the gatekeepers, or else build up new networks of external alliances.[24]

In this, however, they are not free to act as they might like, because they will usually encounter resistance from the existing gatekeepers. The power of the latter actually depends, as we have shown, on the stability of the structures to which they have access. They will therefore do whatever they can to safeguard this stability. What is more, because the legitimacy of their roles, and, consequently, their power as gatekeepers, is connected in part to the objectives and functions of the organization, little by little the gatekeepers become the guarantors of these objectives and functions. They will attempt to screen those forces which come from outside the organization, especially those which would challenge their representativeness and thus their capacity for action as gatekeepers.[25] As a result, the organization will be protected from overly violent upheavals, but its structural rigidity will in turn have been increased.

Clearly, the relation to the environment cannot be reduced to a mere unilateral adaptation to an exterior influence. It is actually a permanent process of exchange through which an organization opens itself selectively, so to speak, to the broader system of power in which it participates. Because it does participate, it integrates parts of that system in a fairly permanent way into its own system of action, for the purpose of *adapting the broader system* to its own requirements.[26]

The consequences of this approach for organizational analysis are important. In this perspective, the extent and limits of the system of action which underlies an organization and, in the final analysis, conditions its members' capacity for action cannot be defined *a priori* in terms of the organization's official frontiers or by formal criteria such as belonging or nonbelonging. *Organizational limits themselves become a problem for research.*[27] We will be in a position to determine them only at the end of our search, after we have mapped the organization's *jurisdiction,* i.e., once we know the "extent and nature of the individual or group population which is affected by the organization's action and responsive to it." We must also analyze its "elasticity," i.e., the means and processes available for "mobilizing and demobilizing the members within its province."[28] Thus we shall find that certain actors, though they are not properly speaking members of the organization, maintain such constant and "regular" relations with it, implicitly if not explicitly, that there remains practically nothing to distinguish them from its formal members. We shall also discover that the real frontiers of the relevant system of action are fluctuating; they move as circumstances dictate and in response to the problems with which the organization must deal and to the field in which it is operating.[29] In any case, it is this broader system of action which must be delimited and analyzed in order to understand the mechanisms of regulation which occur within the organization.[30]

Finally, and more generally, it is clear that this approach enables us to relativize the status of the formalized organization as a primary object of research. Depending on the objectives and interests of the investigator, the organization may either be studied for itself or used as an introduction to another subject. In the latter case, we regard the organization as a particularly prominent, formalized, and conscious sector of a broad system of action. For these reasons, it is more accessible to empirical analysis, which should make it possible to discover and analyze the mechanisms which are applicable to a broader system. The organization is regarded merely as an index of the existence of such a system, and its analysis is merely a way of imposing a hypothetical structure on the broader field of study.[31] In other words, a change in research priorities can contribute to the development of a fruitful heuristic device, which uses the strategic analysis of organizations in order to get at those more diffuse systems of action which structure man's collective action at every level.[32]

An Example of a "Nonorganization": The Case of the Ministry of Industry

To make the approach we have just described concrete, we have chosen an administrative organization, the French Ministry of Industry, as an example. This ministry is actually a special case—in some respects, a limiting case[33]—which brings the observer to the point of shelving the notion of organization altogether. To account for the observed facts, one has no choice but to broaden the field of investigation from the outset. The causes of phenomena occurring within this organization must be sought outside. The ministry is then reduced to no more than the apparent site of organizational integration. It is not an organ of the state capable of bringing about an autonomous mediation between the means and ends of industrial action; it is not even the site where such mediation could take place.

Formal Structures and Informal Phenomena

Simplifying somewhat, we may say that at the time of the investigation[34] the Ministry of Industry was composed of several *vertical directorates,* each of which corresponded to a major industrial sector or sectors,[35] and of one *horizontal directorate,* which was in charge of the internal coordination of the ministry and was also responsible for representing the ministry's interests to other administrative departments. As interfaces between state and industrial interests, the vertical directorates had a twofold mission. On a day-to-day basis, they were responsible for following and analyzing developments and problems in their particular industrial sectors in order to keep the appropriate administrative bodies informed. They also proposed suitable actions or responses.[36] At the same time, they were charged with implementing the state's industrial policies and initiatives within their jurisdiction. The role of the horizontal directorate was more narrowly administrative. It was created as a result of a desire to unify the initiatives of the vertical directorates in order to strengthen the ministry's negotiating position with respect to outside interests. In particular, this was to have been accomplished by "elaborating a stockpile of information and knowledge"[37] which was to have made it possible to define an integrated, hierarchized strategy of industrial development. The whole structure, finally, was capped by the minister and his cabinet, a sort of private council which consisted of fifteen members drawn from the ranks of high ministry officials and, not least important, from other administrations.[38]

This summary description of the formal structure, which, all in all, is not very remarkable, should be complemented with two further remarks. The first of these relates to the particular character of the decision-making systems in the French state concerned with industry, and to the Ministry of Industry's position within them. In point of fact, this ministry possessed few resources of its own. State action in this area was actually within the jurisdiction of a much broader decision-making system, distributed throughout the administrative and para-administrative apparatus. Each participant in this system pursued his own objectives in his own particular sphere of interest with relative autonomy, relatively isolated from the other participants.[39] Consequently, on most important decisions the Ministry of Industry could not act alone but needed to convince and involve at least one if not several other actors within the administration.[40] In short, its capacity for action depended largely on its capacity to persuade and influence other administrative units.[41]

The second remark concerns the more "informal" characteristics of the ministry, which had a profound influence on its formal modes of operation. In the first place, its predominantly "vertical" organization, as described above, should be noted. It resulted in a fragmentation of the ministry into a series of vertical directorates, each of which was jealous of its prerogatives, isolated from the others, and involved in some sense in a "closed-circuit" relationship with "its" industrial sectors. This mode of operation was firmly rooted and highly resistant to change, as attested by the blatant failure of repeated attempts to create a horizontal directorate capable of integrating the ministry and effectively coordinating the disparate initiatives of its directorates.[42] Secondly, certain directorates were favored by an imbalance of influence and power which existed within the ministry. This inequality between vertical directorates was, of course, in contradiction with the formal equality of the organization chart and seems, moreover, to have been more marked than similar imbalances in other administrative departments. All aspects of the ministry's organizational existence were affected, and a veritable abyss developed between "strong" and "weak" directorates, between those which were prestigious and those which were not.

To understand how the ministry functioned and what constrained its capacity to act and to change, we must explain these two phenomena. We shall treat the second first. Its analysis will help us to comprehend the first and explain its significance.

It would no doubt be possible to bring in "objective" structural or contextual factors at once in order to explain the disparity in the power and prestige of the vertical directorates. For instance, it is true that the 'strong" directorates could rely on a certain number of direct means of intervention which the "weak" ones lacked. The "strong" directorates, moreover, were responsible for the highly structured oligopolistic sectors of industry, while the "weak" ones were confronted with much more heterogeneous industrial structures. But other factors operated in the opposite direction. Thus the state's intervention in the electronic, electrical, and mechanical industries (domain of a weak directorate) was not at all comparable with its intervention in the nonferrous metals industry (domain of a strong directorate). Similarly, the strategic importance of various industrial sectors for the economic and technological development of the country did not correspond to the hierarchy among directorates: sectors such as machine tools and electronics (under weak directorates) were as "important" and central in this respect, if not more so, than the nonferrous-metals industry already mentioned.

It is probably pointless to extend this list further. The explanation at this level remained partial, if not frankly contradictory. Things became clearer, by contrast, when the analysis was focused not on the structures of the ministerial services or on certain characteristics of their environments, but rather on the *problem* with which each department was confronted when it was considered as an actor in the state decision-making system on industrial policy. This new outlook also took in the range of resources and constraints which determined each department's margin for maneuver in this enlarged context.

The Hierarchy among Directorates and Systems of Action

If we simplify the analysis a bit, we may say that the problem for each department was to develop its own "expertise" for the purpose of acquiring some influence both with the industrial interests in their jurisdiction and with their administrative counterparts in other ministries and departments. If we look at the specific configurations of the systems of action with which each department became involved in the process of acquiring this expertise, we will then be in a position to understand how the hierarchization of the ministry developed and why its fragmented and compartmentalized vertical structured persisted.

What was responsible for the greater influence and power of the "strong" directorates? We have already mentioned the more favorable context which certainly contributed to their success. But beyond this, their power and influence seems to have been directly related to their capacity to mobilize the manipulate networks of outside relationships and gatekeepers. This capacity was due to the presence within the ministry (and especially in the minister's cabinet), in the various administrative decision-making centers, and in the appropriate industrial sectors, of a leadership group linked together by a common training and career background. We are thinking of members of the Corps of Mines.[43]

In the first place, certain advantages derived from the fact that engineers from the Corps of Mines headed companies under the jurisdiction of the strong directorates. As a result of their common schooling and early career experience, leaders on both sides of the fence spoke the same language and were joined by interpersonal bonds which were often quite close. Officials in these directorates, therefore, had more ready access to necessary information and were in a better position to elaborate a coherent industrial strategy for their sectors—and usually, moreover, in collaboration with the companies involved.

This "vertical" network was supplemented by a second, horizontal network within the state apparatus itself. In fact, the strong directorates were in contact with gatekeepers, who were members of the Corps of Mines, in all the important centers of decision. In addition, they made use of members of the other *Grands Corps,*[44] who were usually given the task of managing relations with the administrative sectors from which they came. In this way, the strong directorates were able to maintain informal and continuous relations with the other administrative departments involved in their problems, which enabled them to keep informed of the activities, preoccupations, and projects of these units.

The strong directorates thus were at the center of networks of information and interpersonal relations. This enabled them, at least partially, to control their environments. The result was a cumulative reinforcement of their strength. Owing to their close contacts with high management in industry, the strong directorates enhanced their reputations for expertise. This made them sought after as middle man by other departments, and consequently they were able to get their points of view across more effectively in the interministerial negotiations on which most decisions concerning industrial policy depended. Hence they acquired a greater weight in political and administrative decision-making systems, which strengthened their hand vis-à-vis "their" industrialists, for whom it became a matter of "good policy" to turn to the directorates in question and to supply them with the requested information. This, in turn, reinforced their position as experts, and so on.

As an exclusive and homogeneous group of high civil servants, the Corps of Mines clearly played an absolutely central role in enabling these networks of information and interpersonal relations to come into being and operate effectively.[45] The corps was well equipped to play this role by virtue of several advantages which it enjoyed, whose total effect was to enable it to implement an independent and deliberate personnel policy. In the first place, it controlled its own school and thus dominated the training of its members, shaping them to conform to the needs of the moment. Secondly, it controlled its own independent financial resources which were diversified in many outside services which it could manage and appropriate as it saw fit.[46] Finally, thanks to both formal and informal prerogatives and to its gatekeepers and connections in both the administration and industry, the corps could promote individual careers in a way that would gratify and bring prestige to itself as much as to its favored members. These could be tailored to the individual and professional profile of each "corpsman."[47]

The corps could thus offer its members extraordinary opportunities to participate in its business affairs.[48] The sum of these factors created strong bonds of camaraderie and allegiance which cemented a system of action, which, though outside and independent of the Ministry of Industry,[49] was nonetheless essential for understanding not only the predominant role of the strong directorates, but the limits imposed on their potential actions.[50]

To explain why the weak directorates grew progressively more feeble, one also has to look at the quality and configuration of their networks of gatekeepers. Because they lacked the same formal prerogatives available to the strong directorates, their potential influence both within the administration and in industry was even more dependent on possession of independent information relative to the industrial sectors under their jurisdiction. As it happens, however, the kind of gatekeepers they were able to use to build their relations with industry made it extremely difficult to develop, exploit, and shape such information. This, in turn, largely determined their internal organization, as we shall show.

Each of these directorates was divided into a certain number of departments, each of which in turn specialized in a product and/or manufacturing technique. These departments were highly compartmentalized and functioned in isolation.[51] Yet they were in close contact with the trade associations in their respective branches. In a sense, they considered these trade associations as their extensions in industry. Indeed, the structure of the directorates reflected the structure of these managerial organizations, which were also specialized according to product or manufacturing technique. Little by little, extremely stable systems of relations crystallized between the various departments of the weak directorates on the one hand and the trade associations on the other. The permanency of these systems was predicated upon an incessant exchange of information legitimacy. Each partner found the profit it was seeking: the civil servants found information relative to the branches in their charge, a way to maintain contact with a diverse environment, and, thanks to the support of the associations, a way to legitimize state measures;[52] the trade associations also obtained information, support, and administrative legitimacy, which strengthened their positions with respect to the companies falling under the purview.[53] Finally, each side found in the existence of the other a justification for maintaining the status quo and an effective obstacle to the slightest desire, much less to more serious initiatives, for change.

Whatever the reasons for the preservation of such balances of power, the fact of which we can in the present context do no more than note,[54] their persistence entailed direct consequences for the capacity of the weak directorates to act, by profoundly affecting the type of knowledge and competence which they could develop.

The screen which such systems placed between the companies and the respective departments of the directorates made the latter largely dependent on the trade associations for gathering and elaborating the required information. But these associations were clearly not neutral transmitters of information but autonomous actors with strategies and objectives of their own. The possession of information relative to their branch of industry was an important advantage, and sometimes the only advantage, which the trade associations could exploit in their dealings with the ministerial departments. The information actually transmitted was therefore colored and biased by their preoccupations and by the constraints of their situation.[55] As a general rule, it projected a rather pallid image of the branch, one which did not question the balances of power prevailing within it, and which did not make it possible to identify the companies' concrete problems. Nor did it shed much light on the actual performances of the various firms, which varied widely.

This state of affairs was exacerbated still further by the fact that the relationships in question did not reflect the unity of the institutions in their charge, but rather fragmented them on the basis of product, raw material, or manufacturing technique. This eliminated the company as economic actor. While such a structure may have been perfectly adapted to the distribution and rationing requirements of the immediate postwar period, when the ministry's action was necessarily oriented toward the product, such a structure was made increasingly obsolete by economic and industrial development.

As a result, the weak directorates were largely ignorant of the fundamental economic forces at work and usually had only fragmentary, incomplete, and biased information concerning the problems of their branches. Thus they proved increasingly incapable of guiding the State's interventions in the industrial sectors for which they were responsible. The long-term consequence of this was a loss of confidence on the part of the other centers of administrative decision-making, and a concomitant dimunition of the weak directorates' capacity to win acceptance for their proposals in interministerial negotiations. To compensate for this loss of power, they tended to make thorough use of the remaining regulations and procedures[56] and to take great pains with their relations with the trade associations, whose contacts and confidence grew to be indispensable. This only accentuated the irrelevance of the policies to actual industrial conditions, which in turn weakened them still further.

The Organization of Systems of Action

Cumulative reinforcement in one case, cumulative weakening in the other: both processes can be understood only by grasping the contours and rules of the game prevailing in the systems of relation and exchange between organizational sectors and certain actors in their environments. The balance of power in these games, and their specific logic and constraints, conditioned the capacity for action and change on both sides.

From this standpoint, the difficulties encountered by the horizontal directorates and their inability to unify ministry policy and coordinate disparate initiatives from the vertical directorates cannot be surprising. Far from having only interorganizational repercussions, every attempt on the part of any of the several successive horizontal directorates to impose "coordination" affected—if it was effective—the negotiating capacity of the various organizational sectors of the ministry relative to their partners in the environment, thus attacking the very basis of their capacity to fulfill their missions.

Our model is clearly quite different from one in which changes within the environment bring about corresponding changes within the organization. If adaptation takes place, it is neither automatic, nor uniform, nor unilateral. The impact of the ministry's diminishing influence in the wake of an over-all growth in the state's role in industry was cushioned by the strong directorates.[57] Their systems of action provided resources which enabled them to adapt to the new conditions. On the other hand, a regressive process was triggered in the weak directorates, as shown by the persistence of their increasingly anachronistic and "dysfunctional" systems of relation with the trade associations. In the end, this led to the progressive and *mutual* ossification of both partners. We are also far from a model in which the type of structure exerts a direct influence on the type of operation and the level of performance of an organization. In this respect, the differences between strong and weak directorates on the level of formal structure are totally disproportionate to their respective "performance" and "success."

The structural factors must therefore be seen against a wider backdrop. The organization as it first appears, with its hierarchies, coordination procedures, and apparent unity and integration, must give way to the analysis of the manifold systems of action which surround it, but which always transcend it. These constitute the constraining framework within which the actors may develop their strategies.

6

Organization and Culture

Our analyses have led us repeatedly to emphasize the contingency of observed phenomena, and the relative but irreducible indeterminacy of individual behavior and action—in short, the *autonomy of the organizational phenomenon* as an integrating process of the strategic behavior of relatively independent social actors. It remains to investigate, in this chapter, the basis and significance of this autonomy.

The Problem: Organizational Mode and Culture

To give a clear exposition of the problem we are going to raise, it is perhaps best to return to the method of strategic analysis, in order to show how it leads to a new point of view and hence to a new interpretation of the observed data. The strategic method is one which takes the strategies of the actors to be rational. "Irrational" results and "dysfunctions" originate in the structures of the games which induce and regulate these strategies. These games are arbitrary. The problem then becomes one of understanding why such structures have been chosen and instituted, and why they are maintained.

This type of analysis shows that, in the final analysis, the *organizational phenomenon is a political and cultural[1] construct*. It is the instrument which the· social actors forge in order to "govern" their interactions in such a way as to obtain the minimum cooperation necessary to the pursuit of collective objectives, while preserving their autonomy as relatively free agents. Clearly, then, in this realm there is neither simple determinism, nor a universal solution, nor a generalized "one best way." For collective action is, after all, a problem of relation, or, rather, of the *organization of human relationships*. Its fundamental dilemma does not admit solutions reducible to a simple economo-technical logic. The constraints deriving from a given situation do condition these solutions, but they do not mechanically determine them. The solutions adopted also reflect the *relational, i.e., cultural capacities of individuals,* which derive from their

97

learning experiences in family and society. These capacities are supplemented by others acquired and, indeed, created, in the games in which the individuals participate within structures of collective action.

If we think of organizations as game constructs which develop in time in such a way as to conform with the capacities of their members to forge relationships,[2] then we are led to discover the *cultural element* which is of the first importance in organizational phenomena. The autonomy of each member depends on this element, which is the subject of this chapter.

To be specific, and to illustrate our mode of argument, we shall use the example of "French-style bureaucracy," a well-known model devised by one of us and developed in a whole series of investigations focused particularly, but not exclusively, on French public administration.[3]

This model is distinguished from others by four basic features which insure its coherence: *impersonal rules,* which largely prescribe, often in great detail, organizational tasks and positions, and specify how each member should behave;[4] *highly intensive centralization* of the decision-making power, which places great distance between those who decide and those who are affected by their decisions; *stratification* of individuals in homogeneous groups, separated from one another by often insuperable barriers;[5] and, finally, the development of *parallel power relationships* around zones of uncertainty unforeseen, and as a result uncodified and unregulated, in the organization chart and formal guidelines.

Mutually supporting and reinforcing one another, these characteristics, it will be recalled, tend to perpetuate themselves through a series of vicious circles. From one point of view, centralization may be analyzed as a "functional" response to the rigidities and difficulties of communication created by the extension of impersonal rules and the assignment of individuals to more or less rigid strata. In return, however, centralization reinforces these characteristics. In fact, the central decision-makers, who alone are in a position to make the necessary changes, can hardly attack the real problems. Owing to their distance from the operational level, they are scarcely aware of them. The only weapon they wield is that of further refining the rules and formal directives, which in the long run increases the previous difficulties, and so on. The same holds true for the development of *parallel power relationships.* In one sense, it is clear that these are the indispensable safety valves which alone make it possible to make the partial adjustments necessary to the over-all operation of the organization, which would otherwise run the risk of being paralyzed by its impersonal mechanisms. Yet their clandestine and illegitimate character, combined with their relative scarcity, makes it difficult for individuals to hold their own by playing competing powers off against one another. These zones of special power and privilege become bones of permanent and pronounced contention and are sources of frustration and discontent.

Quite naturally, attempts will be made to do away with them, by increasing rules and impersonalism.[6]

Clearly, one is dealing with a structure whose elements are coherent and which possesses its own logic. It is a *logic of impersonalism and individual isolation*. If we try to understand the game which underlies such a structure, and the rules which govern it, we find that its basic characteristic is the nonexistence—or at least the signal weakness—of the informal group as a framework for action.[7] Rather than join informal groups, individuals tend, on the contrary, to use the *formal group* to protect and defend their autonomy and capacity for action. These strategies, combining defensive aspects on the level of the formal group with offensive aspects on the plane of individual action, indicate the existence of a certain number of *implicit rules* governing the group's operation.[8] These rules insure that nothing can be accomplished on the informal group level, so that, quite "rationally," individuals seek to make private arrangements behind the protection of the formal and abstract group[9] of peers, whose pressure, similarly impersonal, is also one of the primary means of integration.[10] Of course, it bears repeating that within the framework of these rules, several strategies will always be possible; but if the individuals—even "deviant" ones—wish to win, or at least to avoid losing insofar as their involvement is concerned, they are obliged in one way or another to respect the rules.

Though we can only briefly outline the steps in such an interpretive procedure here, strategic analysis can explain the rules of the game with respect to which the observed individual strategies recover their rationality. The procedure remains incomplete, however. As it stands, in fact, it relies on a universal argument based on a general naturalism; the implication is that since all organized actions require rules, their content and significance must always be the same. Even a superficial comparative analysis is sufficient to show that this is not the case. Put differently, every mode of social action may infallibly give rise to unanticipated consequences or "perverse effects," which in the long run reinforce the need to apply these very same modes of action. Organizational "dysfunctions" and the vicious circles which result from them seem, therefore, to be universal mechanisms and processes.[11] Nevertheless, their precise local form and character depends upon a relatively open range of concrete situations; fundamental differences in types of game and models of relation may be masked.

To give a first illustration of such differences, we may turn to the development of bureaucracy in American organizations. In the well-known studies by Gouldner and Selznick,[12] the development of impersonal rules does not have the same significance as in the French case. For Gouldner, the rules define tasks and specify precise methods for evaluating work results. For Selznick, they lay out the manner in which authority is delegated to decentralized groups. In both cases, then, the significance of the rules is different from the French case: they are used not so much to eliminate the arbitrary personal authority of the superior as to limit the extent and sphere of his influence, and to lay down precise procedures for the resolution of conflicts.[13] Such processes, with the particular vicious circles they entail, mask particular strategies and types of games. Schematically, we may say that instead of games of avoidance in which isolated individuals protect themselves from an overly powerful central authority by using the formal group as a way of maintaining distance from the decision-making power, these processes involve games of interaction and even confrontation in which individuals are supported by their informal groups.[14] Abuses are limited because authority is parceled out, and because there is a set of procedures for resolving eventual conflicts.

Japanese organizations provide another illustration, perhaps even more striking, of the differences in the implicit rules which, in apparently similar contexts, structure the games by which individuals regulate their cooperation. Growing numbers of observers of the Japanese scene[15] seem to be in agreement that Japanese organizations[16] are based on a very old model of relations which has been adapted and improved for modern use. Based on a high degree of individual involvement and participation[17] in the life of their primary group, this model emphasizes a vertical tie[18] of loyalty which makes it possible to temper authority and dependence relations by subjecting superiors and subordinates alike to a complex, constraining network of reciprocal obligations. The persistence of this model and its present predominance indicate that it cannot be reduced to a mere residue of a bygone feudal and paternalistic era. It is rather a particular mode of management of human relations. Without underestimating the idyllic nature of such a model or hiding the difficulties which it cannot fail to entail,[20] it must be said that it does offer an original solution to the problems of integration implicit in every collective action. The particularities and paradoxes[21] of this solution, no less than its successes, can be useful reminders of the relativity of our own experiences.

Let there be no mistake about the scope of these few examples. Given the present stage of comparative studies of organizations, and the fragmentary and still frequently impressionistic character of the available data in this area, the above and similar comparisons[22] cannot claim to be laying the foundations of national models of organization. They have a more modest goal. Comparative study calls attention to the ever-present danger of organizational ethnocentrism, which often leads to a quite unjustified universalism.

Once we have accepted diversity, we must then go on to investigate why certain rules, relational arrangements, and game constructs are in force rather than others. Cultural analysis is an answer to this question.

To avoid any possible misunderstanding, it is important to point out that we have no intention of introducing another determinism to replace the ones we endeavored to refute in the preceding chapters. To say that collective action and its concomitant integration mechanisms are cultural constructs does not mean that organizational structure or function is determined by a society's basic cultural traits and values.

In this connection, it is essential to beware of the traps and pitfalls involved in a certain type of cultural analysis. Using attitude studies and in-depth interviews, this type of analysis is aimed at bringing to light the basic national values and cultural traits which are supposed to determine the behavior of members of a given society. This is supposed to make it possible to describe the specific features of the manner in which that society's institutions operate. Not that these values or cultural traits are nonexistent or negligible. Not that it is not possible to observe differences of a cultural order in the styles of action of individuals, social groups, or even whole societies.[23] Thus it is not the principle of such work which must be challenged, but rather an argument which underlies much of it, which we may roughly summarize as follows. The cultural traits, attitudes, norms, and characteristic values of a given cultural universe are supposed to constitute the beginning of a causal chain. Individuals accept and internalize these attitudes and values upon entering the cultural universe in question. This subsequently determines their perceptions of reality and even their emotional reactions to it, thus guiding their choice of objectives and means of action.[24]

We have already implicitly criticized the static character of such a deterministic view by proposing an interpretation of human behavior as expressive of a strategy in a game, within a set of constraints to be discovered. Because this form of determinism emphasizes coherence, passive adaptation, and conditioning, it is powerless to treat the fundamental problem of change (organizational, social). This it can explain only as a moral persuasion and/or an impersonal evolution whose roots remain, to say the least, mysterious. At this point, we can make this critique somewhat more explicit and systematic. Such a schema does not withstand empirical scrutiny, in our view. When individuals are called upon to act, they do not passively reflect values accepted and internalized at the outset. As we have tried to show in the preceding chapters, it is imperative to take a more realistic and fruitful view of human action, which should be regarded as an *active process* in which individuals respond to the most pressing needs in order to overcome the difficulties which arise in the course of action. It should be thought of as a process in which individuals are continually *learning* to use the material and *cultural instruments* (it is the latter which interest us here) available to them in a manner suited to the constraints and opportunities of the situation.[25] It is true that pre-existing game rules do structure individual notions of "rationality" and so determine an initial spectrum of possible "rational" solutions. Yet the process is nonetheless an active one: several strategies are always possible, and the choice among them will depend on individual capacities and resources. Here, as elsewhere, it is necessary to reject any deterministic view of human conduct in favor of a view emphasizing relative indeterminacy and freedom. This means that *the process must be analyzed as the reflection of a choice requiring certain capacities on the part of the person (s) who make (s) it.*

Consider for a moment the results of a study by W. Schonfeld on authority relations in French schools.[26] Using this work, we can make our argument more precise and concrete. Analyzing a comprehensive sample of the various types of secondary schools in France, the author first demonstrates the ubiquity of a phenomenon well-known to the French, called the *chahut*.[27] This is a type of relationship which arises between students and certain professors, precisely those in whom the students do not recognize what Schonfeld calls a "Caesaristic legitimacy."[28] The results of the survey are strikingly consistent: whatever the social origin of the students, and regardless of the type, structure, or orientation of the schools, between 20 and 25 percent of the teachers confront pronounced forms of *chahut*,[29] i.e., organized and permanent insubordination in their classes. The one exception—also general—to this widespread phenomenon is in the preparatory classes for the *baccalaureat* degree.[30] There, another style of relationship replaces the alternative between the "authority-laden syndrome"[31] and the complementary model of the *chahut*. Schonfeld calls this new style the model of "assumed coverage." In this case, students are obedient to an "internalized" set of directives which they have in fact learned from their prior experience,[32] but which they nevertheless perceive as being imposed on them by their teachers. On the whole, relations between teachers and students are the same here as in the case of the "authority-laden syndrome," and, in particular, the behavior of the students is similar; the only difference is that the teachers in the baccalaureate classes ultimately issue very few orders.

Schonfeld proposes the following interpretation for this surprising and widespread phenomenon. He begins with the dilemma which confronts students in the senior classes of the *lycée*. To succeed in their final examinations, they must avoid provoking *chahuts* against the teachers. The students, however, have not learned how to set limits on their own behavior. Control has to be imposed by an external authority if it is to exist. Certain teachers, because of their "weak" personalities, will not be capable of imposing this necessary control and so run the risk of having to face *chahuts,* even if their subject is important for the examinations. This means that the students must solve the following problem: how can submission to the authority of the teachers be legitimized and solidly established without reference to the individual personalities of the teachers?

This solution is provided by the model of "assumed coverage." In this model, students are not obeying the directives of this or that particular teacher. They are actually submitting to teachers they have had in the past, in whom they recognized (and continue to recognize) the necessary legitimacy. As a result, the particular personality of each individual teacher loses its importance: *submission is depersonalized.*

It is easy to reformulate this interpretation in the terms of our earlier argument. It is possible to consider the process we observe here as one in which the students acquire a special capacity to structure their relationships with their teachers in such a way as to allow both students and teachers to tolerate one another and get on with the common task of preparation for the examination. In other words, the "depersonalization of submission" described by Schonfeld, or, if you prefer, the emergence of a *"bureaucratic"* game between teachers and students, may be interpreted as the development of a *relational capacity,* that of constructing and coexisting with avoidance relations.

In such a relational capacity, something quite different from individual motivations, values, or objectives is hidden. It is not something which can be understood by asking what the students think they want to do. Nor is it reducible to individual personalities: in Schonfeld's example there is no reason to believe that all the students have personality structures consistent with the "bureaucratic" behavior they exhibit; the contrary is certainly nearer the truth. In this context, when one speaks of capacities, one is actually incorporating a more dynamic dimension in the argument, which aims at another level of analysis. The point is to discover what individuals *are capable* of doing, what kind of relations they will be *capable of organizing,* what opportunities they will be able to take advantage of as a result, and how and when they may acquire or develop new capacities which would make other games possible, other problems soluble, or other opportunities available.[33]

It should be noted that if one adopts this point of view, one is essentially broadening the use of the term *culture* and assigning it a new place and status in the analysis. No longer is culture seen as residing in an unalterable set of norms and values which ultimately determine observed behavior. Instead, it is now viewed as an *instrument* consisting of affective, cognitive, intellectual, and relational components from the mental and psychic domain. It is a *capacity* acquired, used, and transformed by individuals in the course of establishing and conducting their relations and exchanges with others. Values, norms, and attitudes are a part of this collection, but their status is changed. They are now merely elements which structure individual and group capacities in a way which conditions but never determines their strategies.[34]

There are two advantages, in our view, to redefining the object of research in this way. First, the analysis may now be focused on the fundamental sociological phenomenon of collective action. We are thinking of the cultural construct composed of those games which indirectly regulate the conduct and relations of the actors in the course of the action which they make possible. Second, our redefinition provides a more operational formulation for the purpose of studying the links between modes of collective action, institutional development, and cultural context. Our formulation involves the capacities of individuals, groups, and organizations: *individuals,* insofar as they depend on instruments acquired and developed in various areas of socialization and learning, with the associated national, professional, etc., cultural milieus; *groups and organizations,* to the extent that these structures provide certain instruments and delineate specific areas of experimentation.

Culture as Capacity

As we have noted several times, all other things being equal, several rational strategies are possible in a given situation. An individual will choose among them in part according to his own objectives, but also, and perhaps not least, on the basis of his resources and in particular his capacity (1) to *discover* the available opportunities which may be more or less evident in a given situation; and (b) to tolerate the difficulties and risks inherent in each strategy. The first point is related to the psychological and/or structural factors described and formalized by March and Simon, in their concept of bounded rationality. The second has to do with *relational capacities,* the degree to which individuals are capable of organizing their exchanges with others.

To understand clearly what is at issue here, let us consider *the affective problem posed by a relationship with another person, insofar as such a relationship involves power and the risk of dependence.* Indeed, as a social being, every individual *depends,* at least in part, on others, and on the perceptions and definitions of himself which he receives from the outside and uses to establish and maintain his own identity. From this it follows that every relationship with another person is profoundly ambivalent and will always be experienced as such by the individual: while such relationships are at least partially the basis of an individual's identity—hence of his capacity and potential to *exist* in the true and strict sense of the word—they may also disrupt his integrity and psychic equilibrium, in that they convey disparate and potentially contradictory perceptions which the individual must confront.[35]

This means that total communication is impossible. To enter into relation with another, seek him out, and open oneself up to him is at the same time to hide and protect oneself against his encroachments, and to resist him. In short, *every relationship with another person is strategic and involves a component of power, however repressed or sublimated.* By its very structure, the relationship is conflictual and sets in motion extremely deep-rooted and powerful affective mechanisms, since the stakes are ultimately the very identity of one or the other, or, if you prefer, the destruction, as autonomous actor, of one by the other.[36]

This problem is amplified in structures of collective action. Each individual has a different potential for controlling sources of uncertainty crucial to the pursuit and success of common activities. Such structures give rise to relations of power and therefore continually subject the individual to situations of dependence and domination which accentuate and intensify the potentially threatening character of interpersonal relationships.[37]

It is here that the individual's "culture," in the sense given the term above, plays a role. This central phenomenon of affective and social existence profoundly influences each individual's learning experiences in family and society. Through such experiences, the person acquires and develops cultural equipment and frames of reference: the cultural tools, in short, with which he constructs his relations with others and with the world and controls their affective consequences. As a result, individuals are not equally capable of withstanding the situations of dependence, conflict, and tension which are implicit in the very fabric of collective action, and of accepting the risk inherent in compulsory games of power.

That such relational capacities exist, that they differ from one individual to the next, and that they influence choices of strategy are facts known from everyday experience. It is possible, however, to pursue this point further. As we tried to show in a few comparisons above, differences also exist among national cultures and among the cultures of professional groups and social classes or categories within a given society. These differences structure learning patterns and individual opportunities for experimentation. In return, such structuring tends to perpetuate the differences, which then indirectly condition individual capacities, at least in terms of the integrative processes involved in fostering cooperation.

We must not, therefore, be too quick to "generalize" and "psychologize" about these capacities. It is important that they not be used as "all-purpose" explanations, as it were. These capacities are a factor in a certain phase of the analysis, and they do correspond to an irreducible part of the individual personality, a sort of personal capacity to support conflict and tension which becomes established very early in the form of certain traits of personality; still, we are now concentrating on something rather different. The focus is on the way in which such capacities are acquired and developed through action and experience, and are analyzed as a sequence of problem-solving processes. This implies that these capacities are to be related to different modes of individual participation in social and organized groups; to opportunities for access to various sources of power and for distributing investments in order to minimize risk; and to opportunities to comprehend what power and resources others possess. In short, we hope to relate these capacities to the whole range of material, structural, and social constraints which limit individual choices of strategy in games inside and outside organizations. These constraints and rules can, on the one hand, inhibit or even prevent—and on the other hand, encourage and facilitate—the acquisition of necessary relational capacities (even on the level of individual psychology).[38]

It is therefore imperative that individual relational capacities not be reduced to simple components of psychology or personality. Acquired and developed through and for action, these capacities are inseparable from the structures within which social action must unfold. A system is comprised of two mutually conditioning elements.

Furthermore, we may analyze these structures themselves as collective capacities which supersede the individual capacities which they condition, in that they constrain individual action and experience and oblige the individual to take part in preexisting relational models. Thus we cannot be satisfied with an analysis confined to the individual level, for relational capacities exist as well on the level of the group, the organization, and even the system.

It cannot be sufficiently stressed that a collection of individuals in similar situations and even with similar, if not identical, objectives, does not necessarily form a group capable of action as such. In other words, a group's existence may not be taken to be a self-evident fact of nature, any more than an organization's may. A group is always a social construct. It exists through time only to the extent that it is supported by mechanisms which make it possible to integrate the different strategies and outlooks of its members, and thus to regulate their conduct and interaction. These mechanisms—or, if you prefer, constructs—constitute the *group's collective capacity*. Like the situational factors, this capacity influences the group's behavior by restricting or enlarging the range of possible choices.

This conclusion was among those we drew from our discussion of the main results of L. Sayles's classic study on the behavior of work groups in industry.[39] We showed that the type of strategy adopted by the groups was influenced not only by their own objectives and resources but also by their capacity to organize and even, in the final analysis, to find an identity and give coherence to their existence.

Here we touch on an important element in the existence of groups which is all too often neglected: the cultural instruments which are the means by which the group constitutes itself. With these instruments, it must resolve not only the problem of aggregation but also that of mobilizing divergent, if not contradictory, skills, knowledge, and interests among relatively autonomous actors (its members). It must also manage the affective consequences of the process. To take just one example, consider groups which have learned through action (i.e., subject to the organizational and social constraints characteristic of their situations) to manage and in some sense domesticate, rather than stifle, the conflicts, tensions, and power phenomena which inevitably arise. As a result, these groups have *acquired a collective capacity* of their own which exceeds the capacities of their individual members. With this capacity, they can organize themselves more effectively; they are more capable of defining and controlling their action, and they have a greater margin for maneuver than other groups which for various reasons have been unable to develop such cohesiveness.

Using the results of D. Kergoat's analyses of the development and effects of a strike in an industrial plant during the May–June 1968 crisis in France,[40] we can make the foregoing discussion somewhat more concrete. She shows that during the strike, the worker group in this factory first went through a phase of fragmentation which saw a good deal of internal conflict and even splits among various factions. As a result of the conditions created by the strike, which made the power structure of the firm more transparent, the various components of the worker groups[41] discovered their own distinctive resources and interests, and hence became conscious of what separated them from the others. The experiences of the various groups during this phase were, of course, not identical and were differently timed. But that this self-consciousness constituted an identifiable phase in the strike is perhaps best illustrated by the behavior of the group of assembly-line workers[42] who, at a decisive moment and against the advice of the union delegates who had largely directed the development of the strike to that point, imposed a halt to the experiment in self-management then under way in order to force the hand of the plant management and oblige it to begin serious negotiations. This first phase was followed by the restructuring of the worker group as a whole. There was a new, more self-conscious solidarity and a more "strategic" alliance among the various components, each of which had become more coherent and homogeneous. This was confirmed one year later by a second strike which was touched off by a subgroup, the drivers, who were pressing demands of their own, but who were actively supported by the line workers, who, at a decisive moment, staged a walkout in solidarity which shifted the balance of power in favor of the drivers. In short, this process of destructuring/restructuring had led to a *collective learning experience,* because the unusually open conditions created by the crisis and strike had made it impossible to suppress conflicts, antagonisms, and divergent interests. Instead, these had to be taken up and overcome, which in the long run increased the capacity of the workers as a group to act.

Like groups, organizations, as formalized systems of action, possess many such collective capacities. The choices they are capable of making as to development policies, relations with the environment, etc., are conditioned by the cultural characteristics (in the sense we have given the term here) of their structures and of the various games which integrate the divergent strategies of member individuals and groups. A "rigid" organization, which is governed by means of hierarchy, secrecy, rules, distance, and compartmentalization, and whose dominant games are games of protection (of the minimax type), *will simply not be capable* (in the short term, at least) of adopting a decentralized structure in order to increase the effectiveness of its control and management of the conflicts and problems engendered by relations with a "turbulent" environment. From a more normative standpoint, it is certainly possible to advise such an organization to undertake a significant, long-range effort to develop other capacities. In the short term, however, it may be in the organization's interest to strengthen its lines of communication in order to permit its strong echelons to respond more rapidly to the demands of the environment.

If we take a closer look at the situation, we can see that this is what normally happens, moreover, usually in quasi-spontaneous fashion, as the work of Burns and Stalker, in particular, shows.[43] In response to threats emanating from a turbulent environment, several companies in their sample in fact reacted by reinforcing the principal characteristics of their modes of organization, even though these characteristics were no longer adapted to the "objective conditions."[44]

Such phenomena may readily be understood if one is willing to accept the fact, amply stressed above,[45] that the human constructs which underlie organizations are not mechanically determined by the "objective" constraints imposed by the context and environment.

Within the organization, there are preexisting game models which represent responses to the specific problem of integrating a number of autonomous actors within a purposeful body. Certain types of regulations are set forth in order to insure the harmonious interdependence of these games, and these inevitably impose constraints on the members of the organization. Consequently, one may analyze these regulations as an *organizational collective capacity* which establishes a certain kind of rationality and provides, indeed imposes, certain instruments of action with which the members of the organization may build their relationships and interactions. Other conceivable instruments are at the same time excluded. This collective capacity, therefore, has two contradictory aspects. On the one hand, it allows the members of the organization to "function," i.e., to cooperate and resolve in their fashion the "objective" problems encountered in the environment. On the other hand, it is at the same time a cognitive barrier, an obstacle to individual as well as collective learning, insofar as it conditions the capacities of the members to invent new relational modes, new game rules, and the like, when and if "objective" changes in the situation require it.[46]

Of course, the significance of this organizational capacity will not be the same for all member of the organization. One may conceive of a curve which illustrates how central to each actor's strategy the organizational games are—i.e., of the relative weight of organizational resources and constraints in the respective strategic fields of the various actors. At one end of the scale would be actors for whom the most important resources came from the organization itself. At the other end, one would find the so-called boundary spanners whose basic resources are relatively independent of the particular organization in which they work. Although we cannot make the assertion *a priori*,[47] it is possible that the relatively greater independence of the latter as compared with the former affords them a margin for maneuver and, in particular, for experimentation within the framework of preexisting games, if only because the supreme sanction, exclusion from the organization, is a less effective threat against them.[48]

Regardless of the empirical content of the strategies of the various organizational actors, their ability to experiment and learn will always be limited by their belonging to the organization, and by the constraints and "rationality" of existing games. This means, conversely, that the organization may be analyzed as a system of action whose mechanisms of integration will tend to endure and to *reproduce themselves through certain processes of self-maintenance.*

To illustrate our assertions, let us consider the two ideal-typical models of Burns and Stalker already mentioned. There can be no doubt that the characteristics of the "mechanical model" lead to formal games in which *use of the rules* is one of the essential instruments of action. In fact, not to use the rules, even if only to evade or undermine them (in letter if not in spirit),[49] not to take account of the formal limits they establish, would be to forgo an important advantage without deriving the least assurance that this is a viable choice. Of course, the rules can be interpreted in a variety of ways and can lend themselves to diverse uses. They can be exploited defensively as well as offensively, in games "with the system" or in games "against the system." Quite different behavioral models can, therefore, coexist within a given rule structure. Such diversity may even be a necessity, lest the whole structure collapse under the weight of its own rigidity. Individuals will always attempt to use the rules in support of their action. This in turn tends to perpetuate the rules and even to increase their effectiveness in regulating interaction.

The "organic model" may be analyzed in a similar way, insofar as the processes envisioned are concerned. This model defines a relatively unformalized context which has a very high "integrative capacity" in that the disparate initiatives of the various actors can easily be incorporated by the group. Strategies of isolation, noncommunication, distance, and retreat behind the screen of authoritarian rules are therefore hardly likely to "pay" here; on the contrary, it is rather by establishing interpersonal bonds, taking initiatives, and asserting competence that the various players find a "rational" employment of their resources, together with a regulatory principle to govern their interaction, with its attendant conflicts over jurisdictions, specializations, professionalization, etc.

Clearly, each of these two models defines a different "market" in which transactions between an organization and its members take place. Each offers different guarantees and protections to member individuals and groups. Each provides different instruments for comprehending and solving problems. Each requires the actors to play different sorts of games. Different capacities for organizing relations are developed in each case. A particular model structures the field of rationality in a certain way and favors certain instruments of action.[50] In this way, certain processes are selected out which reproduce the essential characteristics of that model. Certain vicious circles (centered, for example, on regulation and control in the case of the "mechanical model," or on delegation of authority and specialization in the "organic model") will insure that both models will continue to function well after they have ceased to be adapted to the environmental conditions.

Cultural Analysis: An Opening

Cultural analysis begins with the problems and difficulties of collective action. These are necessarily related to power and dependence relations which require the actors to have certain relational capacities. The analysis reveals a new functional logic. This is a logic of an affective and cultural order which underlies, in the final analysis, the autonomy of the organizational phenomenon as a process for integrating human conduct. In this way, we can understand the formal and/or informal rules which govern relations between individuals and groups. These are seen to be political, hence cultural,[51] constructs, invented by the actors in view of the specific capacities and resources in order to contain the risks implicit in unrestrained tensions. This makes cooperation for the achievement of certain ends possible.

It is no doubt unnecessary to point out that the autonomy of such constructs is, of course, far from being total. For their development is neither free nor gratuitous. They are coalitions of men against nature formed with a view to performing certain actions and to obtaining certain results. In short, they are *instruments* whose development is constrained by the characteristics of the situation in which they are employed.

At this point, we again encounter the weight of the argument, particularly relating to technology in the broadest sense of the term, which we have seen was analyzed by the theoreticians of "structural contingency." Technologies, of course, are themselves mediated, changing, and contingent and may in their turn be analyzed as products of as well as stakes in the power struggle, both from the point of view of society as a whole and of the organization.[52] In the short term, however, they impose themselves as "objective" constraints which focus on a certain number of limited problems which must be resolved by organizations with given sets of objectives and at certain stages of technical development. These technologies also impose certain kinds of relations in a relatively strict way.

This is also the point at which we encounter the still more important constraint represented by the evaluation of results, which largely determines the environment's capacity to impose sanctions on the organization. We have already had occasion to allude to this factor in connection with our analyses of the relationship between the organization and its environment in the previous chapter. This argument may be carried further: the more difficult it is to measure the results of action by evaluating them in relation to the means necessary to obtain them, the more "political" will be the human constructs underlying the organization ("political" in the sense of "reflecting the problems and difficulties intrinsic to the organization of relations of power and dependence").

Even though these constraints may limit the autonomy of the organizational phenomenon, this autonomy never disappears. For it is the expression of a certain state of affairs which, despite its obviousness, not to say banality, too many analyses are too prone to neglect:[53] namely, that an organization is also a totality of human relations, and hence of power relations problematic in their own right and deserving of a separate analysis. To solve the problems inherent in power relations, which is a basic requirement of collective action, specific capacities are needed, capacities which are produced in the course of action and which always profoundly influence the outcome.

These capacities, and the manner in which they develop, are the object of cultural analysis, which may be regarded as complementary to strategic analysis. Its task is to enable us to understand how the actors can make effective use of the opportunities implicit in a given situation, and how, in doing so, they impart a particular structure to the contextual problems. This is a field in which research is indispensable if we are to appreciate the possibilities for organizational change which do exist, as a prerequisite to the formulation of normative precepts applicable to such change.

Three The Systems Phenomenon

7

From the Organization to the System

The Lesson of Organizational Analysis

Now that we have made a preliminary survey, to the extent permitted by the present state of our knowledge, of what might be called the organizational phenomenon as autonomous entity, it is time to step back a bit in order to ask ourselves whether the arguments elaborated in this very special setting might have more general application, insofar as the problem to which they apply transcends this special case.

Let us return for a moment to our point of departure. We began with the observation that "perverse" or counterintuitive effects were a general characteristic of human affairs. Insofar as such counterintuitive effects are products of a system, it is also possible to analyze them as "systems effects," where, by "system," we understand a structured (i.e., non-neutral) field, whose various elements behave in a coordinated and interdependent manner.[1]

We have devoted as much attention as we have to organizations because we believe that organizational analysis is crucial from this standpoint. In our view, the organization represents a sort of experimental model of the systems effect. It is a special case which is both more formalized and more artificial than the general case, but which involves the same basic problems of cooperation and interdependence. One might think of its artificial character and constraints as experimental conditions in a certain sense: they eliminate outside interference and background noise, as it were.

We are next going to attempt to turn our methods around. Having concentrated on the special case for experimental purposes, we will now attempt to reason from it to the general case, from the organization to the "system."

Are we justified in this? To understand the problem implicit in such a generalization, we must reexamine the method we used to analyze organizations. Our argument has consistently been that the organizational phenomenon was a constructed rather than a natural one. Many theories

115

of organization take a naturalistic point of view and hold that there are general, universal laws which men are bound to observe in forming and maintaining organizations. We, on the contrary, have always argued that the coordination and structuring of human activities were a problem to be resolved and not the consequence of a natural order of things. It is true that men solve this problem on the basis of certain data which are given to them at the outset and over which they have relatively little influence. But these data are themselves constructs, repertoires of solutions among which the actors may choose and to which they are free to add others.[2]

Now we are going to turn to a discussion of systems, which are also constructs, but nonformalized ones, with entirely empirical rules. The actors, while more or less conscious of the results, are totally ignorant of the mechanisms and thus are incapable of influencing, much less controlling, them.

The organization, then, may be regarded as a special case in which an artificial machine was constructed in order to provide a solution for a problem which had previously been resolved by what appeared to be a "natural" empiricism, but which in fact was another, older construct which had been "naturalized" over the course of time.[3]

Thus we may justify our generalization in the following way. Organizations may be considered not as different, less complex instances of a general phenomenon which has yet to be defined—the phenomenon of human systems—but rather as deliberately fabricated special cases. Our procedure is legitimate: it does not involve reasoning from the less complex to the more complex, nor is it a matter of reducing a complex phenomenon to a simpler one without having understood the nature of its complexity. Instead, we learn what lessons we can by analyzing a given problem in special experimental cases, in order to prepare ourselves to state and solve the same problem in terms of more general cases.

In this sense, what we are dealing with is a transposition of the argument, which we separate out from the contingencies of the situation in which it was first elaborated. Our procedure is not merely to extrapolate a descriptive law of organizations to a law which one would then claim to be applicable to more complex, or in any case different, systems. Instead, we take an argument which was worked out to solve a problem in one context, and apply it to the solution of the same problem in another, effectively more difficult context.

In order to explain the significance and legitimacy of the transposition we are proposing, it will be useful to consider the characteristics of the two arguments we have identified above in greater detail. We must show how they are effectively independent of the contingencies of the organization, which we are now regarding as our artificial and experimental system.

The Two Complementary Modes of Argument in
Organizational Analysis

The analyses we have hitherto carried out are consistent with two modes of argument which are at once complementary, contradictory, and convergent: the *strategic* argument and the *systemic* argument.

The strategic argument starts with the actor and proceeds to discover the system, without whose constraints it would be impossible to explain the apparent irrationalities in the actor's behavior. The systemic argument begins with the system and proceeds to discover the actor as the source of the contingent, arbitrary, nonnatural dimension of its constructed order.

The *strategic argument* may be analyzed in the following way:

1. The participants in an organization are each actors equipped with personal strategies. The rationality of these strategies cannot be understood solely in terms of the preferences and motivations of the actors, or in terms of the results of their actions. In fact, the behavior of the actors may appear to be irrational from either of these points of view. The significance of any particular behavior emerges only when it is related to the opportunities for profit and loss inherent in the game(s) in which the actors were participating.

2. If we know the strategy of each actor, as well as the objective constraints imposed on the actors by the uncertainties of technology and the market, for example, then we may reconstruct the game in relation to which the various strategies may all be viewed as rational. Since it is possible to make reasonable approximations to these strategies on the basis of the attitudes expressed by each actor,[4] it is thus possible to determine what games condition the behavior of the actors in an organization by analyzing their experience.

3. In the organizational setting, the integration of behavior, which is the basic sociological phenomenon, may thus be analyzed as an indirect process which constrains the actors to adopt a "winning," i.e., rational, strategy in the game, if they wish to win or at least minimize their losses. The investigator thus obtains access to the constraints imposed by the game through the strategy. Regardless of the actors' original motivations, it is rational for them to accede to the game's requirements, and so they come, in the end, to cooperate in the common purposes.

4. The organization as sociological phenomenon is therefore a cultural construct which enables men to orient their behavior so as to achieve the minimum degree of cooperation which is necessary and which will also permit them to maintain their autonomy as free agents.

The strategic argument is a *heuristic device* which can help us to formulate hypotheses of increasing generality regarding the characteristics of a social group, beginning with the problems encountered by individuals participating in it. Its use entails a risk, in that it leads to an overly hasty extrapolation from the actors' experience. It was this risk which proved fatal to one after another of the exponents of the various models of interactionism which have been developed over the last thirty years, not only the classical interactionism of the forties and fifties such as it has been practiced by the Harvard school and systematized by George Homans, but also the phenomenological and ethnomethodological analyses and even symbolic interactionism developed by Mead or Goffman.[5] None of these interpretive and analytical models of behavior really treats the sociological problem of integration. Although one might expect a discussion of actual experience to contribute notably to our understanding, in fact the sociological dimension is reached only at the price of an extrapolation which is difficult to accept. The field is always treated as though it were neutral, or as though the participants had effectively internalized the affective burden of structuring it. This is in plain contradiction to the lessons of experience and leads to unjustifiable assertions of the following sort: "domination is an inevitable and constant experience of life inside an organization"; or to equally regrettable oversimplifications: "domination which is not experienced does not exist."

To avoid the danger of accepting a model as simple and inadequate as the market model or the model of universal domination in order to account for the great variety of possible forms of interaction, our procedure has been to develop the heuristic features of the strategic method, rather than simply to use it for purposes of interpretation. We have also complemented it by degrees with an additional argument which takes its point of departure from the game rather than the actor. Of course, it is by application of the heuristic features of the strategic argument that this game will have been brought to light. We call this complementary argument the *systemic argument*.

The latter is actually already implicit in the logic of the strategic method, if we are careful to distinguish strategy on the one hand from the game or system on the other, though we must always be careful to note the necessary relationship between them. It should be noted, furthermore, that we are speaking of a type of reasoning which is systemic in two senses: clearly because it relates to a system in the empirical sense of the word, but more significantly because it rests on a systemic rather than a linear type of causality.

Perhaps we should explain what we mean. By linear causality, we understand a simple mode of causation in which we explain an effect by a cause, or, to complicate the picture a bit, by the conjunction of several independent causes. Systemic causality, on the other hand, means that we think of causes and effects as being interdependent within a system whose properties (modes of regulation or government, predominant types of games) make it possible to understand and predict the results which are to be explained. This distinction between the systemic and the most common sort of linear argument may be pursued somewhat further; where linear causality implies that one ought to look for a guilty party or parties, or find a structural or functional vice, systemic causation, by contrast, makes it imperative to arrive at a diagnosis of the system whereby the sense in which the incriminated behavior or mechanism is actually rational within the given system can be understood.[6]

This distinction is not merely a matter of form or philosophical subtlety. To demonstrate its practical consequences, we will discuss a simple example, drawn from an actual case.[7]

In the case in question, we find that the introduction of a computerized system of integrated management failed to resolve a serious problem in the relationship between the sales and production departments in a firm whose survival was at stake. The technical rationality and financial utility of this system had been satisfactorily demonstrated, and the practical applicability of the procedures had been strenuously tested with complete success. Yet ultimately the system had to be withdrawn in the face of an undercurrent of opposition on the part of the personnel and management in the main plant of the firm in question.

Rather than limit ourselves to a straightforward examination in supposedly realistic and concrete terms of the opposition to the reform which led to its eventual failure, we propose to employ the systems argument in order to understand the problems raised by the introduction of the computer. When we do this, a totally new set of problems and solutions emerges.

From this standpoint, we can see that the information gathering which is necessary for the installation of computerized management actually has a fragmenting effect. If the information required by the machine were to become common knowledge, it would be necessary to give official recognition to the wide latitude afforded the workers by the foremen in connection with the time allowed for performing their functions; this latitude is such that by indulging in a little deception, the workers can increase their earnings by more than a third. From a "rational" point of view, however, it seems that it would have been in the firm's interest to increase the rates in such a way as to allow the personnel not only to maintain but even to increase their over-all remuneration. The gains to be expected from the integrated management system would have more than compensated for this traditional "slippage."

This leads one to wonder why a compromise solution could not be found—why, indeed, one was not even sought. It then becomes possible to discover that this firm is in fact a "system" characterized by the fact that the negotiations between employer and wage earner take place in a gray area, which makes it possible for foremen and worker representatives to make use of a margin of liberty which is not recognized by the formal organization structure.

If we look into the significance of this margin of liberty, we will ultimately discover a five-partner game. The participants are (1) workers, (2) representatives, (3) foremen, (4) management, (5) unions. The formal provisions of management-union agreements are not applicable without the aid of representatives and foremen. Neither management nor union can implement the necessary arrangements or monitor their consequences. The intermediaries, however, exploit their indispensable role for their own purposes. By controlling a crucial zone of uncertainty, they acquire power which enables them to offer a variety of services to their common constituency, the workers. In turn, the workers can play each of their partners against the other and thus acquire a zone of liberty and a capacity for action. On this level, we obtain the results of strategic analysis.[8]

We do not conclude by designating the guilty parties and indicating how they ought to be forced to make amends. Nor do we merely propose a structural reform designed to enforce the clarity and "rationality" which ought to assure efficient application of the new system. Instead, our viewpoint leads us to investigate the properties and characteristics of the system of action implicit in the firm, in view of which the game we have discovered is in fact reasonable and useful. We are also interested in how such a game could have developed in such ubiquitous form.[9]

We hope that this example will have clarified three sets of ideas:

1. First, there exists a possible causal logic different from the classical logic used to analyze human activity.

2. This systemic logic is not an abstract logic: it depends on knowing how systems of action influence actors by limiting the objectives which they may reasonably set for themselves.

3. If one hopes to foster individual development, to enrich individual activity, or to improve the climate or over-all performance of an organization or system, one has to proceed by transforming the system in question.

The argument in terms of the properties of a system has something in common, of course, with Gestalt thought, whose revitalizing force, relatively exhausted in psychology, has found a new vigor in the sciences of action. This comes in the wake of a reaction against the dominant analytical tradition, which aimed to reduce each problem to the point at which it became susceptible of mathematical solution.[10]

The danger in this sort of argument is that one is likely to forget the freedom of the actors. This may occur because one does not take the trouble to make a strategic analysis, settling instead for a general description of the games and their structure. Or it may be that even after making a strategic analysis, one neglects the artificial, hence contingent, character of the system. There is also a tendency to explain or justify the relationships which are observed in actual games as fulfilling stable functions that have a logic of their own.

The Problem of Transposing the Organizational Argument

Perhaps it would be worthwhile to contrast the two modes of argument which we are proposing to use in organizational analysis in the form of a caricature: to understand the same crime, one begins, on the one hand, with the guilty party and the logic of his relations with the various principals in the case, and, on the other hand, with the situation in the guise of a system which conditioned these relations and therefore determined the possibility of the crime.

The two procedures, as we have seen, are difficult to distinguish. Without the systems argument, strategic analysis does not go beyond phenomenological interpretation. Without confirmation in terms of strategy, systems analysis remains speculative; it needs the stimulus of the strategic argument to keep from becoming deterministic.

In a certain sense, two contrasting logics underlie these arguments: one is inductive, based on a model of negotiation and calculation; the other deductive, deriving from hypotheses as to the coherence and purposes of the system. In the first place, one seeks to know how each actor calculates his own interest in the course of the negotiations in which he must engage with his partners. In the second, the inquiry aims to discover what overall coherence and hierarchy of purposes are likely to be established as a result of the games which the actor is obliged to play.

If the two logics are employed separately, divergent results are obtained. One leads to a market or mutual-adjustment model, even if the inevitable inequalities are projected onto an internalized constraint originating outside the system. The other offers no escape from a mechanistic model of functional determinism.

But it is not easy to combine the two logics, even if constant borrowing and reference from one to the other are inevitable. To integrate them, we have had to rely on another concept, the game. Ultimately, this calls for yet another logic and another behavioral model. As we have used it, the game concept is basically a model of behavioral integration which assumes a dualistic vision and is not integrated in the field of social relations. Both the private strategy of the actor and the system's coherence of purpose remain in evidence, without reconciliation, as contradictory orientations. One is applicable to the behavior of the actors in the game, the other to the outcome of that game. Only the game as integrative social mechanism succeeds in transcending both.

The transposition we have been referring to may be made on the basis of this model, but *not* simply on the basis of one or the other of the two arguments, or a confusion of both.

The systemic logic is applicable to the problem of interpreting an organization as a structured and constraining entity. A coherent goal structure can impose its logic only if it operates within a hierarchical and strongly integrated organization. One may think of the organization as an obligatory constraint for the achievement of certain goals. But the model clearly cannot be extrapolated to less structured situations.

It may appear that interactionist logic is better suited to the task of analyzing such "nonstructured" fields. But our fundamental axiom is that no nonstructured field exists; we shall attempt to demonstrate this below through empirical analysis.[11] Even if the degree of structuration is small and relatively incoherent, it will always be sufficient to cause trouble for any simple interactionist logic. The latter, moreover, is easily transformed from a logic of anomic liberty to one of total conditioning; this is because it can take its point of departure in a concept according to which the actor is conditioned by the system, of which he is reduced to no more than a structural support. It is then supposed to be possible to analyze the actor's calculations in order to discover the logic of the system which conditioned him or which was internalized by him; in essence, one ends by assimilating social entities to hierarchized organizations in a still more abusive, though hidden, manner.

There is a tendency to make things in one way or another more black and white than they really are by opposing a notion of absolute constraint corresponding to a totalitarian picture of the organization, on the one hand, to an utter absence of organization corresponding either to the theoretically free egalitarian market or to general deterministic theories of social constraint on the other.

Suppose, however, that we start with the axiom that no situation is either black or white in this respect; that every group of human beings is structured, but only partially; that, moreover, its structuration is contingent; and that not even the most highly integrated organization is governed by the systemic logic of integration, as we have shown above; then the difference between the case of the organization and more general cases is much less marked. This means that it is possible to make the transposition discussed above. This should be done by combining the two logics which emerged in our discussion of the game model, which is by far the most economical description of the situation.

Does the game really exist outside the formalized organizational situation? Once this problem is formulated, it is actually easy to find numerous examples of such games. At the same time, we discover that the differences between what happens within an organization and what happens outside are much less great than we might have thought.

Take the example of relations between employers and wage earners. This is not a question only, or even primarily, of conflict between management and unions. It is better to describe it as a complex game involving several players, which resembles the intraorganizational model discussed earlier in connection with the introduction of the computerized management system much more closely than it does a formal model of bilateral negotiation in a nonstructured field, or a hierarchized deterministic model based on the principle of the class struggle. The importance of this system, as well as its contingent character, emerged clearly in the breakdown of normal relations which occurred in France in May 1968. The collapse of the game which had previously predominated created a highly erratic situation which took months, if not years, of effort to regularize with the formation of a new game. This effort bore mainly on the crucial problem of confidence, not between unions and bosses, but within the various echelons of the union hierarchy. In other words, the problem was basically the same as in the case of the computer system: it took the form of persistent failure to communicate and concealment of information between the partner/adversaries involved.

We may apply the same analysis to less overtly material phenomena, such as fashions in clothing or intellectual fads. In these cases, one never finds a situation where equal and independent actors are offering innovations to a group of theoretically interchangeable consumers. Supply and demand are subject to structures which, though they do not imply conditioning in any sense, do involve a game which is at once constraining and contingent. Even family situations, according to the conceptual model elaborated by Caplow on the basis of the potential games implicit in triads,[12] may be clarified significantly with the application of this schema.[13]

Intuitively, then, it is clear that one may use the game concept and model in order to transpose the lessons learned from organizational analysis to the whole range of human activities and social situations.

Such a game model is not all-embracing, however. The problem is that it takes for granted that other elements in the system will play the role that the organization played in the formalized experimental cases. The idea of the game presupposes certain limits, inclusions, and exclusions. Generally, moreover, there is not a single game but rather a whole collection of more or less tightly integrated games. These are in any case mutually interdependent and presuppose some sort of general regulation. But this implies that there must be some sort of *concrete system* in which the regulatory mechanism which guarantees this interdependence resides.

This notion may be somewhat problematic. We are used to an abstract notion of the term *system*, as implicit, for example, in the idea behind the systemic argument, or, alternatively, in the terms *social system* and *subsystem* which are familiar to the functionalists.

To be more precise, we suggest that *concrete system of action* be used to refer to the new object whose existence must be assumed if we are to transpose the lessons drawn from organizational analysis to social situations in general.

Cybernetic Servo-Systems or Open Systems of Action: The Problem of Constituting a New Object

Unfortunately, the notion of system is a particularly ambiguous one. For sociologists it generally evokes functionalist models of what are usually quite large groups; it refers to either a whole society or a domain of particular activities within a society, such as social or political systems. These models envisage systems as consisting of a variety of interdependent functions, together with mechanisms of a homeostatic type which insure the performance of these functions and the maintenance of their equilibrium.

This relatively ambiguous notion is at once abstract and concrete. Abstract, since it is the construction of an observer and not verifiable in reality: there is no question of isolating the system of values or, to speak in Parsonian terms, the function of maintaining norms; concrete, on the other hand, insofar as it claims to account for the persistence and development of a definite social organization.

There is an uncertainty hovering about the epistemological status of this notion which makes it very susceptible to the sort of distortion that one notices when an analogy is made with the notion of cybernetic system, which supposedly contrasts with the "simplicity" of functionalism. The cybernetic analogy is drawn from a general model which is found in increasingly widespread applications in the natural sciences. It is a model of a concrete system functioning in a very specific way within the framework of a highly constraining model of regulation.

The *concrete system of action*, the new object we have postulated, should be distinguished from both the cybernetic system and the system of the functionalists. The formulation and use of this notion require that we combine the strategic and systemic arguments identified above within a single methodology. It is to be a concrete object and not merely a philosophic construct.

Let us pause for a moment to discuss this last point, which may appear out of place to many readers. Have we not made a rather dubious epistemological leap in postulating the existence of a concrete system in order to give a coherent interpretation whose main interest is to be economical and satisfying to the mind? In other words, in taking our own abstract construct for a real object because our demonstration requires it, are we not laying ourselves open to the same critique of reification that we have previously leveled at superficial funtionalist analyses of organizations conceptualized as "natural" systems with their own "needs" and "requirements"?

This would in fact be the case if the model of inference and proof employed were a structuro-functionalist one. This would mean that the investigator's mental model would actually be projected onto reality. As we have seen, the logic of the structuro-functionalist argument in the manner of Parsons in sociology or Easton in political science[14] begins with the functions indispensable to every social (or political) system, and deduces from them the mechanisms and properties of the concrete groups to which the model is applied. The investigator's problem is, then, to discover how these functions are accomplished and internalized, and to interpret the observed phenomena in the terms provided by the model. In this way, he will tend to ascribe any failures of the system to its inadequate response to one or more of the intrinsic needs hypothesized at the outset.[15] Should such be the case, it would be justifiable to say at this point that the analyst was guilty of reification in the sense of Berger and Luckmann, in that he has allowed his abstract interpretive schema to become a "natural" model enforcing certain requirements which, if not met, result in the application of sanctions.[16]

The *concrete system of action* involves no such risk. In this case the system is not an *a priori* schema but rather an attempt to assemble a description of a human construct useful for the achievement of common social goals. In asserting this system's existence, our underlying assumption is that there must be a *game* which allows the different strategies of the partners in the relationship to be coordinated. In other words, there must be a *containing* system within which this game takes place, and which makes it possible for the necessary conflicts, negotiations, alliances, and interactions to occur. This philosophical hypothesis is in the first place an assumption in a program of research and includes no substantive postulates as to the "nature" of the system, its properties, or its "needs." We are merely assuming that the existence of regulated games and hence of concrete systems of action can be demonstrated. For instance, when we speak of the employer-employee relations in a branch of industry in a given country, we are referring to a concrete system of action which has come into being at a certain moment and has undergone a certain course of evolution. It can be shown to have certain contingent, nonuniversal properties,[17] and these serve to manage and reproduce the whole set of relations among the partners, which conditions their action.

In a certain sense, one may regard this postulate of the existence of concrete systems of action as a reformulation of the hypothesis that there is no nonstructured field. This, in turn, was based on the finding that there is no social action without power and that all power at once presupposes and constitutes a structuration of the field.

Yet when all is said and done, it is the invasive image of the cybernetic model which represents the most serious risk of misunderstanding.[18] In simple terms, the fascination of cybernetic models is due to the prestige of their supposed universality. They give the impression of providing a foundation in exact science for an interpretation of human behavior. Indeed, once one eliminates the contingency of regulatory mechanisms, which is concealed in formulations of the cybernetic model, then everything can be made simple and coherent.

This fascination is particularly dangerous because the cybernetic model is totally unsuited to the application. It is of course useful and even stimulating as a source of analogies; but as soon as one moves beyond this point, serious errors result. By its very nature, a cybernetic system is a servo system. According to the original definition, a cybernetic system consists of a regulating mechanism and a regulated device. Here, regulation is understood to mean action ordered or sustained by an automatic control device. The system is called a "servo system" because its adaptive range is limited to a repertoire of solutions or "system states" somehow stored in the regulating device or implicit in a control parameter, which is ultimately its fundamental feature.[19] To take the image of a thermostat—rather simplistic, of course, but nevertheless frequently used by the cyberneticians themselves—a heating system regulated in this way will be able to adapt only to environmental conditions "foreseen" by the control parameter, to which a limited number of "states" correspond.

Clearly, no human system can fit this description, which is only slightly caricatural. The model underlying the analogy with cybernetics[20] neglects the strategic dimension (it being wholly unpredictable) of human behavior. If strategy were taken into account, it would rule out any regulatory mechanism based on direct control of the regulated phenomenon, which in the present instance is human behavior. The cyberneticians, of course, are not dealing with men but with information circuits, functions, relations, and the like. But the cybernetic model cannot distinguish between the command and requirements of abstract functions on the one hand, and concrete human actors on the other. This confusion lies at the root of the proposal to employ in an analysis of the vicissitudes of history a servo system model which would pretend to be scientific. In the hands of imaginative political scientists, the use of this model often results in contradictory assertions, ultradeterminist on the one hand, ultravoluntarist on the other; both camps nevertheless share a total lack of realism.[21]

The concrete system of action may be contrasted with the cybernetic as

much as with the structuro-functionalist model. It is an empirically verifiable, concrete phenomenon and not an abstract system; it is a constructed, i.e., contingent system, not a natural one. Let us define regulation as the collection of mechanisms by which this system maintains
itself;[22] we find then that this regulation is due to the structure of the
games which predetermine what rational strategies exist for each actor.
The type of game and the rules condition the actors' strategies, but are in
return conditioned by them. It is rare that an actor will have only one
possible strategy. The game may be transformed by the pressure of the
actors; it is not rigid, insofar as it is possible to adopt strategies which "go
against" it, or even aim consciously or unconsciously to change it. There
are, of course, many "natural" elements in the game, in the sense that
they are relatively stable and out of the actors' reach, at least in the short
term. This is true to the extent that the negotiating strength of the various
actors is determined by sources of uncertainty which, at the outset, are of
an objective order, "natural" or "technical." Though the game and the
system construct may be based on specific features of the natural and
historical context, they are entirely artificial in themselves. Their existence presupposes a redefinition of preexisting problems and a redisposi-
tion of the "material" sources of uncertainty aimed at establishing new
"artificial" sources, without which no game would be possible.

Strategic Analysis of Concrete Systems of Action as a Sociological Method

The justification of the foregoing discussion lies ultimately
in its capacity to serve as the foundation of a fruitful empirical analysis.
    Earlier, we tried to cut down to reasonable proportions the outsized
amibitions of a general (or special) theory of organizations. Our hope was
to shed some light on the *organizational phenomenon* and to give an
epistemological grounding for its analysis. By the same token, we are
aware that we have begun once more to plead the case against all general
systems theory and for empirical analysis of the *systems phenomenon* as a
priority.
    It would clearly be premature to try to establish general rules. Instead,
we think that research ought to focus on the problem of defining the object
in question. Here, we find that the use of arguments transposed from the
context of strategic and systemic analysis of organizations is essential.
Thanks to a firmly grounded methodology, it has been possible to express
these arguments in a concrete form and to prove the existence of *concrete
systems of action*. We are now in a position to formulate certain initial
problems relating to the nature of this object; at the same time, we shall
try to give partial solutions to these problems.[23]
    In studying a given organization, we must first try to identify stable

strategies. Then we may look for games, their rules, and the mechanisms of regulation which insure their interdependence; the games in question are those in relation to which the strategies we have identified become rational. If we succeed in this, then we have effectively proved that it is legitimate to consider the organization as a system. We will also have obtained specific information regarding its mode of government.

The problem is less simple than it may appear, however. We must be careful to take account of the risk of reification. There is a danger of arbitrarily limiting the analysis to the categories chosen at the outset simply because they happened to fit or to correspond to certain accepted notions. That it is easy and almost inevitable to do so only increases the danger.

We can call upon the methods of organizational analysis, however, for help in meeting this objection, in particular by relying on the initial, inductive phase of the strategic argument. If we can isolate sufficiently noteworthy power relationships among the actors, we may infer that relatively stable strategies must be present. From these strategies, we can derive hypotheses concerning the games with respect to which they may be regarded as rational; in addition, we may formulate hypotheses regarding the system that contains such games. This gives us some hold on the configuration of the system most likely, in empirical terms, to exhibit such regulatory mechanisms. We may then test the usefulness and probability of our hypotheses on concrete cases. It is therefore imperative to determine that power relationships exist before making a "diagnosis" of the system. To justify our argument, of course, we are implicitly assuming that power implies structure, and that structure presupposes regulation—in other words, that we are faced with a concrete system of action.[24]

At this point in the argument, it should be noted that it would be possible and useful to undertake a comparative study of various systems of action, which would aid us in understanding the true significance of their various characteristics.

Without pretending to be exhaustive, we think it would be useful to mention a few of these characteristics. First, one may classify systems of action according to the degree of fragmentation and compartmentalization which they exhibit. This is an essential feature of the system's mode of regulation. Distance, for example, enters into the mode of government in ways to which we have already alluded. It favors those who occupy the system's critical junctures and thus plays a special role in the regulatory process.

Next, we might think of categorizing systems of action on the basis of which mode (or modes) of communication is (are) dominant. Many concrete systems of action are, in fact, based on secrecy, on the impossibility of communication. Every system restricts communication in some way, whether formally or by the imposition of de facto limitations. The influence of any mode of communication is never homogeneous, however. A given mode may facilitate lateral communication and impede vertical, for instance, or favor contacts between certain actors while segregating others. It is particularly enlightening to look at employer-employee relations from this point of view.

A third property of systems is the degree of structuration, in the sense of conscious organization. It is important to understand the structure of the various games, as well as the ways in which they interact with or depend on one another.

Finally, and perhaps the most difficult of all the characteristics to analyze, is the problem of the limits of a system. This is related to the even more complex problem of analyzing the interaction of several different systems of action, which might also be conceptualized as the application of several types of regulation to a given situation. Every concrete system of action is an open system. Systems may be distinguished according to their degree of openness, both internal and external. This influences the possibility that a system will incorporate outside actors, where "outside" is defined in terms of the limits of the system as it exists at a particular moment. This flexibility has an impact on the ability of actors within the system to take up different positions in the game structure or to move from one game to another. Here the problems are much more ambiguous than they were in the case of the organization itself. Now we are in the realm of contingency. The emergence of a particular problem may give rise to temporary but highly active systems of action.[25] On the other hand, a change in the configuration of the problems may lead to the obsolescence of a system of action on which a good many actors had been counting. Regardless of the diligence of their efforts, they will no longer be able to accomplish anything because the system of action which circumscribes their participation has ceased to be relevant.

These questions are all of decisive importance. Hence it is easy to accept that the first goal of analysis must be to explain the nature and limits of concrete systems of action. We make no effort to hide the fact that our approximations are still crude; but such approximations are more consequential and more immediately useful than more elegant formulations adapted to mathematical techniques of measurements, which nevertheless remain abstract and irrelevant (e.g., theories of communications flow).[26]

With these preliminary results, analyses, and remarks, it should now be possible to formulate in a precise way the problem of the mode of regulation or government of the concrete system of action whose existence we have just demonstrated. For the actors, this mode has certain properties which entail quite practical consequences, imposing limits on their behavior and determining what range of activities is possible or proscribed. Furthermore, we might try to anticipate the outcome likely to be produced by the divergent activities subsumed under a given system of action.

At this point in our argument, however, we will not try to develop these somewhat overly programmatic points. In the following chapter, we will give an empirical analysis which will help to make them concrete.

8

Strategic Analysis of Systems of Action as a Sociological Method

The Significance of Analysis as a Research Method

In our method, analysis takes precedence over theory, as we have already pointed out several times. It should be noted, however, that we do not intend to oppose analysis to synthesis. The point is not to decompose a concrete problem into a series of simpler problems through a process which reduces the original question to unintelligibility. By contrast, we hope to understand how the simple elements are integrated in such a way as to produce a universal phenomenon which incorporates them. When we contrast analysis with theory, our point is to oppose a procedure whose primary objective is to establish the existence of a new phenomenon and to understand its logic, to one which tries to deduce universal laws from general principles in order to subject some class of phenomena to a comprehensive determinism.

Our choice is based on a judgment of the state of our knowledge and the research strategy best suited to it. We do not think it possible at present to elaborate a general theory of social systems. To our knowledge, all such theories are interesting only as stimuli to reflection and analysis. There is a risk, however, that the facile and unverifiable interpretations to which they give rise will turn our attention from the necessary confrontation with the empirical data.

This does not mean that we reject theory. The reader has no doubt noticed that we rely on a certain number of theoretical postulates which we seek to submit to the test of the facts. In our view, however, theory is only the foundation of the method employed in our analytic work. The precedence we have given to the analysis thus means also that we grant priority to discussion of the research procedure.

In this chapter, therefore, it is natural that we should try to apply our general discussion to a concrete example. Then, in the following chapter, we will go on to draw some provisional conclusions regarding the "concrete system of action" phenomenon.

131

The Case of the Politico-Administrative System
in a French *Département*
The Problem

A *département* in France is, as most readers will know, an administrative unit, and in a certain limited sense, also a political unit (in some respects comparable to an American state, in others quite different). Along with a prefect appointed by the national government in Paris, a general council sits whose members are elected by the people of the *département*. In the political and administrative sense, as well as from the point of view of collective decision-making, a *département* is a complex assemblage of independent administrative units, cooperatives, groups, and associations. These include the general council, the prefecture, elements of the national bureaucracy, municipalities, chambers of commerce, agricultural and professional bodies, federations of workers' and farmers' unions, employer groups, etc.

May we regard such a complex entity as a system of action? From the standpoint of administrative logic, this is not so obvious. The coordinating measures regularly resorted to are not very effective, and there is general complaint concerning the jealous isolation of the component bodies, the compartmentalization and lack of comprehensive communication. Yet if we approach the problem through the descriptions given of the workings of the *département* by the actors involved in it, we see that the various units and their members behave interdependently, as though they were involved in a common game. Although the game may ostensibly be one of mutual protection and noncommunication, it nevertheless unites all the players. Coordination from above may meet with resistance, not because the actors are isolated, but rather because they are parts of a system in which other forms of coordination are at work. That these may be semiconscious only serves to make them all the more effective.

Demonstration of the Existence of the System

The way to identifying this system was prepared by Jean-Pierre Worms's discovery of the "couple phenomenon" in his noteworthy analysis of the relations between prefects and mayors in small and medium-sized towns.[1] The apparent hostility of the mayors toward *their* prefect, and the criticisms leveled by the prefect at *his* mayors, hide a very profound complicity: a good prefect knows how to listen to *his* mayors, and a good mayor naturally has the ear of his prefect. There is a connection between their activities, which may be understood only if we consider them as a couple consisting of two partners. It may be up to the mayor to take the initiative, but he allows the prefect to suggest the most desirable alternative, provided that the prefect sees to it that the mayor will derive some profit and provided also that the mayor's desires and needs are taken into account. The relationship is clearly a subtle one which may give rise to misunderstandings and run into impediments to communication; it is not suitable for working out the sort of coordination which the technocrats would like to see installed. There is nevertheless interdependence; to understand the outcome of common action, it is more important to understand how the couple functions than to fix one's attention on the *a priori* preferences of the "responsible officials," much less the needs and rules of the organizations for which the prefect and the mayor are respectively responsible.

The case of the prefect and his notables is not an isolated one. The deputy administrator of the Ministry of Equipment also has his notables, as does the tax collector. The general councillor has his bureaucrats, as has the member of the National Assembly. As Pierre Grémion has shown, communications flow more easily between bureaucrats and notables than among bureaucrats or technicians within a given hierarchical pyramid. Pressure arising within the system of action is therefore stronger, in certain cases, than pressure stemming from within the official administrative organization. The difference between notables and bureaucrats is much less great than it appears. The *départemental* bureaucrat is in many ways a notable. As for the notable, he is frequently more of an expert in "bureaucracy" than his bureaucratic confrere. Between bureaucrats and notables, there is a complicity based on shared experience, complementary interests, and identical norms. It is a strong bond which can stand up under stress.[2]

Primary Characteristics of the System

That the actors in the system are interdependent is indicated first of all by the fact that no actor can make any decision unilaterally: an acceptable compromise must be struck as an indispensable prerequisite to any action.

This rather general proposition is reinforced by a second fact which we consider quite characteristic of this particular "system": it seems impossible for a compromise to be negotiated directly by the parties involved. It appears that the negotiations are always conducted with the aid of some other authority. This explains why the processes of coordination and integration are so important: it is through these that compromises—hence decisions—may be obtained.

Integration and coordination are always accomplished by a person whose activity and source of legitimacy are of a different order from those of the parties being integrated and coordinated. It is even likely that the coordinator will impose a preconceived solution which takes account of the interests involved, but which is imposed without open negotiation.

The success of this tactic is often increased by the fact that the imposed solution is likely to have been elaborated under the cover of another type of rationality: technical imperatives, "local traditions," the public interest.

In general, each unit in this system acts solely through the channels which are open to it, without communicating with or showing much concern for its neighbors (and sometimes even in concealment from them). There is no effort to create a common front. As a rule, cooperation between units of similar type is avoided. Each one seeks to settle its own affairs directly with the higher echelons. The intervention of an outside body is therefore crucial, both for coordinating the units among themselves and for providing means of access to the center. The system is based on oblique rather than purely vertical or horizontal interdependence. This is reflected in the very strict compartmentalization which separates the various vertical channels from one another.

Finally, it should be noted that there are many individual exceptions to the general rules we have just described. These are likely to be persons who occupy advantageous positions, in particular those who accumulate several posts, such as mayor, general councillor, deputy, or president of the general council. Though their case is somewhat different, mayors of large cities must also be considered exceptions, because of their more immediate access to the central authorities in Paris.

The Model of Power Relations Underlying These Characteristics

At this point, it will be useful to try to understand the system's characteristics in a more concrete way. We may do this by calling attention to the power relations which underlie the general features revealed by the analysis. To simplify matters, we shall consider the example of a rural commune or small town, in which the mayor is the central figure. The model we are going to construct is based on a systematic comparative study of interviews with a sample of fifty-five mayors in three *départements* and with all of their administrative and political interlocutors (527 notables were interviewed in the three *départements*).[3]

The mayor enjoys an exceptional position of power due to the fact that he is the only person in the commune who performs the tasks of integration and coordination. This power is not inherent in the office in a direct sense, but rather derives from the fact that the various special interests in the town find it difficult to arrange compromises among themselves, even if they are represented on the municipal council. Instead, the mayor conveys the notion that he represents the public interest, and makes independent judgments on matters of general concern. In practice, moreover, he is more responsible for choosing the municipal council than vice versa. He holds hostage the representatives of the various interest groups whom he has been careful to seat there. No outside force or interest can effectively organize a coalition against him. The "interests" do, of course, exert their influence, but, though they may exert pressure on the mayor, they find it difficult to manipulate their clients on the council against him. Should they succeed at this, disorder reigns and the town is torn apart.

Yet even so powerful a mayor lacks the means necessary to act positively. His financial resources are limited, and there is no independent source of technical expertise on which he can rely. To obtain good loan terms, he must have a subsidy, and to obtain a subsidy, his proposals must have sound technical documentation. In practice, this means, for instance, that he must turn to the deputy administrator of the *Corps des Ponts et Chausées* (Department of Bridges and Highways).[4] The technical specialists of this bureaucracy monopolize the expertise necessary for construction, maintenance, repair, and "public works" projects. Their experience makes them the best counselors in such undertakings.[5] Then, too, the *percepteur*,[6] or local tax collector is crucial, since only he is capable of drawing up a "good" budget or of giving advice concerning loans.

The nature of French economic development over the past twenty years has made investments necessary in a wide variety of areas, which has left the mayor largely dependent on local-level bureaucrats, without whose aid he can accomplish nothing. Thus the mayor's public-works policy is actually determined by the deputy administrator of *Ponts et Chaussées* under the watchful eye of the *percepteur*, who monitors the town's indebtedness. In return, the mayor obtains the benefits of "sound" management. Municipal planning policy is a technical affair. For his part, the deputy administrator finds good reason to promote a policy of his own, thanks to the incentive offered by the "honorarium principle."[7] This produces a revenue for his Corps when he assumes responsibility for the technical management of local projects. If the town is a fairly large one, it is not unusual for the deputy administrator to become the town's chief of technical services as well.[8]

The system is not closed, however. Local-level bureaucrats do not arbitrarily decide what projects to undertake. Indeed, the facts offer a striking contrast with the usual image of a "hierarchical" and "centralized" administration.[9] Only to a very limited degree are local bureaucratic officials responsive to the wishes of their superiors in the *départemental* directorate of their particular agency or in the central administration in Paris.[10] They are more directly influenced by pressures stemming from local politics. Though they dominate each mayor individually, these bureaucrats are at the same time prisoners of the clientele of elected officials whom they must serve and whom they cannot irritate without risking loss of their potential effectiveness. In practice, their attitude will be "political"; they will cultivate the most powerful politicians, and will respond to the influence of a group which in certain respects they control. Hence there is no surprise in the fact that mayors refute the conventional view and actually feel that the local bureaucrats defend their interests against the central administration. This contrasts with the usual assertion that the bureaucracy exercises an anonymous and insupportable tutelage over local government. The most influential notables, moreover, play a direct role in the coordination and integration of local-level bureaucrats; this means that higher echelons of the bureaucracy can intervene in local affairs only by going through political channels.

A traditional sort of "political" argument, however, is quite as inadequate as a bureaucratic argument. Local decisions are even less conditioned by politics than by bureaucracy. Political organs never negotiate with administrative bodies. We find political parties as such completely absent from the game.[11] In addition to this, it seems that from the point of view of the system, the mayor's political coloration is irrelevant. Politics, in the sense of the partisan battle for office, is important; but, while political considerations may determine certain key players in the system, they do not directly affect its operation.

One point to which we shall have occasion to return should be clarified: political differences between elected officials do have some influence on decisions, although they must be coupled with personality differences that are at least as strong. Nevertheless, this influence does not change the system's operation. It does affect the system's product, insofar as a given system of regulation can adjust, within certain limits, to a rather broad range of potential "products." On the other hand, there are certain "products" which are considered totally unacceptable. Knowledge of the system enables one to predict the spectrum of possibilities facing the decision-maker, but not the decision itself.

Let us return to the question of power and the decision-making process. Contrary to common stereotypes, the dominant model is neither hierarchical nor democratic nor contractual. Instead, it is based on a zigzag process particularly well adapted to the avoidance of responsibility. Deeply rooted in social life, this model extends its influence over the *départemental* system. We have have already observed that the relationship of the general councillors to the prefect and his principal officials is similar to the relationship among the mayors and the local-level bureaucrats. The game is the same in the following sense: the policy decisions of the general council are in fact elaborated by representatives of the State. But the State's representatives still must take politics into account. In particular, they are strongly influenced by the most important local notables, who are capable of using the compartmentalization separating the various bureaucracies, of exploiting their role as coordinators, and of setting themselves up as necessary intermediaries between the *département* and the ministries in Paris. As a general rule, vertical communication in such a system of zigzags is quite poor. Deputy administrators and *départemental* directors are scarcely in communication, and the same is true of mayors and general councillors. Each functional group (i.e., elected officials and bureaucrats) must appeal to the expert advice of someone belonging to the other group; it is this fact which regulates the system's operation.

The Crisscross Model of Regulation

Elective channel   Bureaucratic Channel

president ————————————————————————→ministry of finance
(prime minister)

national political figures←————————————————————other ministries
(legislators, etc.)

département notables←————————————————→prefects and principal
(general councilors, etc.)   *département* directors

mayors←————————————————————————→local-level bureaucrats
  ↓
municipal councillors

Plurality of Offices as an exception to the Model and Regulatory Principle of the System

One of the essential characteristics of this system, which transcends political differences and regional variations, is the widespread practice of accumulating a plurality of functions. A small number of mayors and notables gain control of other offices, such as a seat in the General Council, Senate, or Chamber of Deputies. Indeed, it is rare to find a national political figure who is not also a mayor, whether he began his rise as mayor or had himself elected to a mayoralty in the process. Multiple roles, it seems, are absolutely essential for a successful political career. Mayors who have managed to accumulate several other offices quite naturally assume informal leadership roles. The mere fact of holding several offices makes them notables, and even rather important ones. The political interpretations of this phenomenon are too facile. The reasons for the mechanism's ubiquitous recurrence must be sought in the system's functional principles.

If a local politician comes to occupy three or four offices which normally are separated by barriers to communication, then he will be in a very favorable position. He will be able to play several games at once and will be certain to win at every turn insofar as these games are interdependent, enabling him to put knowledge obtained in one to use in the others.

The elected official who holds several offices can use his position in his negotiations with ministers, *départemental* directors, and local bureaucrats. He will have an advantage over his partners, who can communicate with one another only by applying indirect pressure on their intermediaries.

Thus equipped, a politician is in a position to use his influence in a more socially acceptable, less threatening manner. He can lend his friends a hand without inflicting overly severe damages on his enemies or antagonizing the public. He will obtain what he wants almost without asking for it. Effortlessly, he will have become a powerful integrative force. As one consequence of this situation, intermediaries assume a very important role because favors are essential to the system, even though, culturally, favoritism elicits very strong disapproval.

The elected official who accumulates several offices does not thereby become an adversary of the administration, however. On the contrary, his influence depends largely on the fact that he has the prefect's ear or claims to have an "in" with a ministry in Paris. In a sense, he becomes an accomplice of the bureaucracy; he is acutely aware of the degree to which the local bureaucrats are responsive to the wishes and influence of officials like himself. This is one result which emerges clearly from our interviews with the mayors. Those politicians who have accumulated several offices are especially convinced that the local bureaucrats represent the *département*'s interests in their dealings with Paris.[12]

The System's Mode of Operation

The network of units involved in the regional management of public affairs thus constitutes a system of action. This system is structured by the interrelationships between the bodies and hierarchies responsible for the various traditional functions (administrative, political, economic, etc.). Civil servants, mayors and other elected officials, and economic units are profoundly interdependent. Each vertical channel participates in the regulation of the others, and in turn is regulated by them. Among the different organs at each hierarchical level, communication and integration proceed by a crisscrossing process: one might think of a honeycomb as an image for the process. Hierarchy and leadership are never direct. Substitution is essential in this system of crossfertilization.

Its corollary is compartmentalization. Kept in place by the pressure of the system, each unit has no interest in any of the others. Communication between neighboring units is reduced to a minimum, since they are regarded as competitors. Similarly, communication with superior units in the vertical chain of command is also reduced, since this involves a risk of dependence. Instead, each unit tries to press its advantages by skillfully manipulating the crisscrossed mechanism. Here, there can be bargaining over the use of a unit's influence. In this manner, face-to-face encounters can be avoided. On the surface, relations appear to be good; this is because important affairs are kept quiet and managed privately. Isolation and atomization of the political process are the consequences.

From another standpoint, one could say that such a system encourages and even requires a high concentration of power and privilege. Since impediments to communication are everywhere, the small number of persons occupying crucial positions in the network derive immense profit from their positions. Influence and initiative are concentrated in a few hands: the mayor in the town, the notable who has managed to acquire several offices, the prefect and the president of the General Council in the *département*, and a few national political figures in Paris.[13] The game is closed and secret. The system is exclusive. Public noninvolvement is so deeply rooted in the psychology of the leaders that it becomes incorporated in their game. The system functions in the shadows. Public opinion frightens the leadership, and they flee from it.[14] Mayors, general councillors, and administrative officials all believe that the public is incapable of managing its own affairs, except in terms of irresponsibly advancing some particular private interest.[15] To safeguard the public interest, an outsider must dictate the correct solution at each level of the system.

The system is centralized, but not in the generally understood sense. Paris does exercise an inordinate power, but its decisions must be consistent with the constraints imposed by the system it governs. Consequently, the central leadership is also the prisoner of the system. In general, one may say that the system is characterized more by interdependence and ambiguity of function than by hierarchy. Centralization has a different significance. A centralized organization puts considerable distance between the decision-makers and those affected by the decision. Decisions are conceived and executed by those who have access and are in on the secret; that this group is considerably removed from the groups affected by their decisions is a general over-all principle of the honeycomb. As a result, the circulation of information is limited. It is always mediated by third parties. The information which reaches the decision-makers is consequently inadequate and distorted. Those who possess the vital data have no access to decision-making circles.[16]

Finally, we may turn to the role of the local authorities, elected and bureaucratic. This involves the mediation and defense of local interests, not decision-making. The primary function of *départemental* leaders, for instance, is to put pressure on Paris.[17] Similarly, in the eyes of his constituency, the mayor is the highest-ranking official who is responsible for promoting the interests of the town. Hence the best mayor is not the one who might accomplish the most or who is politically most attractive, but rather the one who has the best network of contacts with the people who count in the *département* and in Paris. The honeycomb system also functions as a structure providing access to the top. Crisscross regulation plays the role of gatekeeper, by channeling demands and pressures from base to summit.[18] The dependence of lower authorities on notables and regulatory bodies does not derive from a formal hierarchy; it is rather that the interests of the lower authorities can be promoted in high places in no other way. There is no subterfuge in such a mechanism. The regulatory authority actually identifies with the interests it controls. The local echelons of the bureaucracy are regarded by both elected officials and bureaucrats as advocates of local interests no less than as representatives of the central authority.[19] Through a paradoxical twist, power is exercised by the very same officials who represent the interests of the units they dominate. It must be borne in mind, however, that this representation of interests always proceeds in a crisscross manner from one channel to the other; the gatekeeper demands a stiff price for mediating between the worlds of practice and decision. At every step of the way, his power depends upon this position. The mayor takes personal charge of the chore of looking after relations with bureaucratic notables.[20] The prefect jealously watches over his "personal" contacts in Paris; similarly, the three or four other people who "count" in the *département* are powerful only because they monopolize access to the national political sphere.

Advantages of the System for the Individual and for Over-all Stability

As presented here, the French *départemental* system may appear oppressive and irrational. It does in fact give rise to considerable frustration and cause difficulties which have frequently been denounced. It nevertheless continues to exist and to function. To try to explain why, we must turn to the behavior and attitudes of individuals and groups as they are manifested in the day-to-day operation of the system. If we do this, we find that the system actually provides a less rigid and more humane form of government than first appears. Furthermore, although it is characterized by favoritism and lack of participation, it does maintain a relatively high level of equality and a certain independence. What is more, the system is perpetuated in part by pressures exerted by individuals themselves.

The system is oppressive and authoritarian. Yet at the same time the oppression is anonymous and the authority impersonal. One or two individuals cannot dominate and manipulate the entire system.[21] The collective game operates without reference to individual personalities. The system imposes general rules and norms on all individuals, even the most powerful. Regulation derives from the whole set of relations and is not imposed by the arbitrary orders of a few. The oppression is therefore much more diffuse, hence more easily tolerated. Meanwhile, it is possible for emotional relationships to develop between individuals who do not share identical opinions. The conflict is one of functions; individuals are not prevented from communicating on other planes.

Similarly, though the system may be based on dependence and passivity, there is a compensating advantage. Crisscross regulation insures that an upper echelon in a given channel will not have to bear the brunt of direct pressure from its lower echelons, and, conversely, that a lower echelon can escape the overbearing domination of its superior. The intervention of third parties who are experts in a different kind of "technique," as it were, makes it possible to avoid the sources of conflict and tension occasioned by direct negotiation. Everyone is protected against loss, even if an error should be committed. No sanctions are possible, because responsibilities are neither visible nor direct. The fault lies with the system. No one person bears responsibility; all are autonomous and protected. What is more, every minor notable is guaranteed a certain degree of success, even if he accomplishes nothing. Success is highly personalized, and the circumstances create individual charisma. It is possible to operate outside the system and its crisscross pattern of regulation, but there are considerable risks in doing so. Anyone who does may enjoy a greater freedom of initiative, but must assume personal responsibility without a shred of protection; it should be borne in mind also that he would then be put in a position where he would be identified as not having "played the game." The individual's best strategy, therefore, is to do as little as possible. The late starter has the advantage over a player with initiative. The race is won by the slowest runner. Apathy and nonparticipation are elements of a rational strategy. Notables will mobilize only after the system has given them the green light. Once started, however, they are hard to stop.[22]

In addition, the system is exclusive and engenders favoritism. The main purpose of the rules is to invite exceptions. These, in turn, confer benefits which arouse jealousy. Everyone manages to obtain some exception to the rules which is applicable to his own case. It would almost be possible to say that the system exists in order to dispense exceptions to its own rules.[23] In the long run, everyone obtains some sort of favor, but, by the same token, there is no one who is not to some degree excluded. In short, the system is a machine for manufacturing exclusions and privileges—which creates discontentment and malaise; but it is also a distribution mechanism, which spreads its favors around in such a way as to keep complaints below the danger level.

Finally, we may say that even centralization can develop only by the grace of the very groups which are thereby deprived of the power to make decisions. The town, for instance, is willing to invest all power in one man—the mayor—because this is the best way to promote its own interests in high places; at the same time, the mayor protects his citizens from outside pressure.

At this point, we are able to understand how the model of the all-powerful mayor could have developed and endured. The power of the mayor is in fact only the counterpart of the weakness of the unit he represents and the difficulty of communication with the higher authorities on whose decisions prosperity depends.

The prefect is perceived by the local officials not as the administration's man but rather as a resource for the *département*. His preeminence is officially sanctioned, hence indisputable. It is therefore hoped that he may use his role as chief executive of the *département* to pressure Paris to look after local interests.

Each actor jealously guards the gatekeepers useful to himself. In this connection, the higher the level of access provided by a given gatekeeper, the more valuable a resource he becomes. The ideal is direct access to Paris. Local interests are better "defended" by involving Paris in their management. Paris's intervention is not merely requested, but required. The complaint commonly heard is not that Paris should leave more initiative to local authorities, but that it should become more involved in their affairs. The "mobilization" of the center is not a threat but an advantage eagerly sought. The game is won by the player with greatest access to the highest possible level. Not to wield good gatekeepers and committed agents is a major handicap. The only remaining alternative in that case is to "politicize" the problem by appealing to public pressure at the grass roots in the hope of being heard at the summit. This is a dangerous game, however, and the chances of success are most uncertain. The honeycomb is safer and surer.

Thus the French *départemental* system is apparently quite stable. Though all are its prisoner, each gains something in return. Its advantages are practical; they are also symbolic and emotional. The stakes are wholly conditioned by these factors; hence if each player plays to win in his own private game, the over-all model is preserved.

Some Possible Conclusions of the Analysis

Unfortunately, we have had to abbreviate this analysis,[24] but several conclusions have already become clear:

Underlying the contradictory relations, pressures, conflicts, and alliances which divide or rally notables and bureaucrats in each decision affecting the *département*, there exists a concrete system of action whose regulations constrain all the parties.

We have been unable to treat in adequate detail the problem of how conscious the actors are of the existence of this system. We may, however, hypothesize that many of them have at least an intuitive notion of it and wisely consider the constraints it imposes and the limits which must not be exceeded in order to operate effectively within it. Most of them, in any case, are acutely aware of the requirements of the game(s) in which they participate. Their answers bear eloquent witness to this.

The system's most singular feature is its mode of regulation, which has a variety of characteristics: on the one hand, direct regulation is provided by the crisscrossed control of the disparate units, where communication in a vertical direction is impeded but where mutual influence and constraint can be exercised laterally, in conformity with a regular model; on the other hand, indirect regulation is applied by the activity of plural officeholders, whose exceptional situation gives them clear advantages over their colleagues. In general, we may say that this is a model in which regulation is by exception.

There is more than an academic interest in the fact that this system exists and structures in a comprehensive way the power relations within the *département*. In a very practical sense, we are now in a position to understand which decisions can be made in such a system and which cannot. In particular, one can show how useless or even harmful many reforms would be. Rather than eliminate the heaviness and rigidity of the system in order to make it more dynamic, they would only load it down with new burdens.

Other factors naturally influence the performance of the system. These include the tactical requirements of action itself, economic and financial opportunities, national political choices, and the politics and personalities of the various actors. The effect of all of these is mediated by the system's characteristics and regulations, however. Of course, neither the quantity nor the quality of the results obtained can be "explained" as direct effects of the model. But we can indicate the limits of potential performance which may be anticipated. We can also show that the existence of the system entails constraints on certain kinds of performance; this makes it possible to predict what the chances for improving that particular performance are.

Finally, there is one further contribution which the analysis we have set forth can make. One can use it as a basis for formulating the problem of how to change the system itself. In the most immediate sense, this means that it can be used as the basis of a critique of all the solutions currently being discussed in the political arena. This is of particular importance at present, since it does not seem likely that the *départemental* system of action will gradually adapt to changed conditions, because of both its primary characteristics and its mode of regulation. Its typical response to outside pressure is to withdraw. The larger cities have long since ceased to be controlled by it, although in theory they continue to be a part of the institutional framework of the *département*. Many other interest groups are now embarking on the same path, even if their success to date has been much less. Yet the system seems magically to reconstitute itself without the least sign of movement. It is not difficult, in these circumstances, to envision an eventual crisis which only a fundamental recasting of the structure would help to avoid.[25]

Renal-Dialysis Services in a Hospital

We have gone into considerable detail in setting out the high points of what has been our most elaborate research effort to date. Our purpose was to demonstrate the procedure by which we were able to prove the existence of a concrete system of action. We hope that the example has illustrated the usefulness of our method. In the process, we have pointed out how such an analysis can contribute to a new logic of action. We have also considered what practical consequences might derive from this new view in evaluating the costs and prospects connected with a potential reform of the processes of collective action.

For our first case study, we chose an example taken from the supra-organizational, or, if you prefer, interorganizational, context. There is no reason, however, to suppose that one could not also find a strongly marked system of action on an infraorganizational level. In fact, Olgierd Kuty's research offers a striking example of such a system. His work treats four artificial-kidney services in two Belgian and two French hospitals.[26] The official organization which embraced these services, the hospital, was not referred to in the research, which ultimately demonstrated the existence of a concrete system of action, much more limited than the hospital in its personnel structure, but much broader in its decisional jurisdiction.

What is the problem? We have four operational units which use the same technology and infrastructure, but which are organized in quite different and contradictory ways. Two of the four units are characterized by sharp and clear-cut distinctions between "roles," strict hierarchy (with deference to the technical competence of the doctors), privacy and relative difficulty of communication, and lastly, passivity of the patients, who exhibit characteristic psychosomatic complaints. The two remaining units, on the contrary, are marked by relatively ambiguous delegation of responsibilities, complex interpersonal relationships which in part bypass the hierarchy, active participation of the patients in these relationships (some of them being quite influential), a good deal of publicity and ease of communication, and a clear decrease in the number of psychosomatic complaints.

Through the analysis, one can show that these two modes of operation reflect two different responses to the problems posed by a particularly distressing struggle against death, one in which the technology happens to be quite effective in keeping the patient alive but incapable of curing him. In this struggle the source of uncertainty very quickly moves from the machine, whose use soon becomes routine, to the patient, whose physical and psychic qualities determine his chances of survival because they enter into the decision as to whether an organ transplant may or may not be envisaged.

Thus one is apparently faced with a choice which is ethical as well as structural: on one hand, hierarchy, order, and traditional science; on the other, democracy, cooperation, and freedom of communication.

In reality, the choice is much less simple, for there is a question as to whether the patients are capable of tolerating a level of participation which forces them to face the risk of death directly. Although the key decisions regarding the "style" of these units may have been influenced by ethical considerations, in fact something rather different is involved: a choice had to be made which would determine the boundaries of the system within which the problem would be formulated. The traditional "hierarchical" units had chosen from the beginning to implement a policy of open admissions, accepting any patient who sought help without distinctions. The "democratic" units had chosen, on the contrary, to be very selective, accepting only patients likely to succeed physically, and also, and not least, psychologically, in facing the risks of an organ transplant.

In the first case, it is not difficult to see that a policy of open communication would have involved risks; since the chances of survival of the various patients varied widely, it would have been difficult for them to accept open discussion of their cases. In the second example, on the other hand, not only was discussion possible, since none of the patients present was a bad risk, but it was even of considerable comfort, since it created a warmly supportive environment for each patient by involving the entire group in a common struggle against the same dangers.

The artificial-kidney service is merely a part of the hospital organization, within which, it is apparent, different choices of concrete systems of action can be made. Who will be part of the system? How is one admitted to it? What are its limits? These choices must be considered along with the other objectives,[27] as must the choice of a mode of government.

What more general lesson may we draw from this analysis, particularly in comparing it to the *départemental* politico-administrative system? We believe that it is important to call attention to the fact that the character of the system of action is *highly contingent* (i.e., radically indeterminate and arbitrary).

We have four services and two systems with contrasting limits and rules, which determine the admission or exclusion of patients and the priority of purpose accorded either the dialysis or the transplant. What is quite evident is that, even after the technology is selected, the particular system which results is not predetermined but the result of a choice. With the same technology, we find that two contrasting choices were possible.[28]

The initial objective situation did not determine a *natural system* which would have developed in a logical manner that could be adapted to the given conditions; instead we find that a choice was made which determined the boundaries of the system which was to be constituted. In two of the four services, this choice resulted in limiting access and instituting a process of selection of the patients to be treated. These two cases may be further distinguished according to additional objectives which differed in other respects: in one case, the choice of system was designed to favor a regulatory mode in which open communication and democratic decision-making were desired goals; in the other, the choice of system was intended to facilitate the transplant, which was the end result desired.[29] In the two remaining cases, finally, the choice was to maintain the traditional open-admission system. Therefore, there was no attempt to achieve other kinds of performance or other regulatory modes.

The choice of system of action, then, also implied other choices: of limits, admissions policies, and strategies which, in this particular example, had effects which reached beyond the constraining organization which contained the kidney services. Of course, these choices did have to be compatible with the hospital rules and with the system of power in force within that organization. But this compatibility was largely dependent on the characteristics of the supraorganizational system of action which contained the hospital organizations themselves: the French and Belgian medical professions, with their contrasting forms of relationship with patients, public, and authorities.[30]

What we are dealing with, then, is a multiple-input system of action involving technology, performance, mode of regulation at different levels (between doctors, between doctors and nurses, and among doctors, nurses, and patients); several combinations are possible. A system of action may be chosen in order to achieve a particular kind of performance, or, conversely, the performance may be chosen in view of the constraints imposed by the system of action. The choice of system may be decided on the basis of a choice of mode of communication or regulation, or, conversely, the latter may be selected because of its greater compatibility with a particular choice of system.

It should be noted, moreover, that the value judgment implicit in the choice of a "democratic" mode of regulation is not necessarily reflected in the decision to implement the system of action which that choice implies. When viewed in the context of the more comprehensive system of action represented by French medicine as a whole, the decision which instituted more democratic regulation may be regarded as one of an elitist type; it gives the doctor arbitrary power over admission, which arouses controversy.[31]

Two points may be made which complement the conclusions drawn from the case of the politico-administrative system. First, what appears *natural* to us in a system of action may actually be contingent, even if we are unable to affect it. Second, the relation among the various contingent choices which affect the constitution of a system is often described as a relation of values; this is inaccurate. One cannot ignore the perverse effect which is an inevitable part of every system of action; no universal logic of values, attitudes, and behaviors is sufficient to determine the outcome.

9
Concrete Systems of Action
and Sociological Analysis

We would now like to consider what the significance of this new notion of a concrete system of action is, and how it might contribute to sociological analysis.

The first major idea to emerge from our general discussion and case studies is that a system of action is not a natural given, but rather a contingent construct.

The Constructed and Contingent Character of
Concrete Systems of Action

The idea that a concrete system of action, like an organization, is not a natural given may at first sight be shocking. All too often we tend to regard abstract categories as data derived from experience. The primary group and the community appear to be natural units. Students of social class and organization view the entities they are studying in the same way. Of course, many analysts of class challenge the idea of the organization as autonomous system, and certain analysts of organizations challenge the idea of class. Yet each thinks of the phenomenon which draws his attention as a natural one. This is at least partly due to the mode of argument employed, whose main priority is to discover universal laws which presuppose a natural order which may perhaps evolve but which in the short run, at least, is stable and universal.

By contrast, our argument casts doubt on both the universality of the laws and the natural character of the phenomenon. Even in the case of a primary group, apparently the simplest phenomenon, it is not obvious that a group exists merely because a certain number of persons are gathered together; the very existence of the group may be problematic, and the diversity of groups as collections of structured relations suggests the relativity of the universal laws.

When we are dealing with a more complex unit like a concrete system of action, the problem becomes crucial. Take an example which *a priori* may not seem very promising: the village. Most investigators analyze and

148

compare villages without posing the prior question of their existence as systems of action. But one may question precisely this point, at least in the present state of French society. This is what emerges, in any case, from Wylie's research on Chanzeaux.[1] There is hardly any respect in which it is possible to regard the village as a system of action, unless it is in the area of municipal management, whose importance is limited, however. From the social point of view, in terms of human relationships, as well as from the patrimonial and professional standpoints, there is no village system; instead, we find other, distinct systems of action. The village may be a convenient setting for study, but this does not mean that it is automatically a system of action.

Similarly, if we look at a particular profession within a given geographical area, we may find a system of action, but this is not absolutely self-evident. Even the existence of a formal association only proves the existence of a core leadership group, which constitutes a small system of action.

We have already pointed out that even an organization may not always coincide with the concrete system of action most relevant to its problems. The case of the French Ministry of Industry was a good example of this. Similarly, Olgierd Kuty's treatment of the renal-dialysis services showed that these, too, depended on systems of action which did not coincide with the hospital organizations of which they were a part.

Since the existence of systems of action is problematic, and in each case, sufficient evidence of interdependence must be established, it is easy to see that research which seeks to discover supposedly universal laws governing their operation is a waste of time. Despite their protestations to the contrary, the theoreticians furnish a formal framework or "taxonomy" more than genuine laws; this does provide certain points of reference which may be useful. Yet the deduction of the universal properties of social systems from a set of axioms à la Parsons, or systems references (*Systemreferenzen*) à la Luhmann,[2] does not enable us to decide whether a system in fact exists, much less to understand its modes of regulation, their properties, and the accompanying constraints. There is nothing to prevent one from extrapolating the various functions or systems references implicit in the chosen approach or theory onto any social grouping, with the blessing of tradition and conventional wisdom.

It is important that we make clear the implications of our approach—with its stress on the nonnatural character of concrete systems—for further research. Our method contrasts with the functional approach that we have just criticized in that we do not seek to discover or "test" universal and substantive laws or propositions theoretically implicit in the nature of systems, together with the contingent conditions imposed by external data. In the strategic approach we advocate, the first problem is to give an empirical demonstration of the existence of the phenomenon in question. Not being given in nature, its properties are contingent and must be ferreted out by the investigator; they can never be known in advance.[3]

Because the system of action is not given in nature, it follows immediately that such a system must be a construct. It is not, however, our intention to propose another general theory, although a theory concerned with the origin of concrete systems of action is more readily attainable and likely to prove more fruitful than the search for universal laws. We merely wish to emphasize the contingency of the phenomenon. Nothing given in nature enforces conformity with universal institutional models. It is true that traditions and constraints do exist which cannot easily be eradicated. It is also true that usually there are but a limited number of programs and solutions which can be called upon in order to solve a particular problem, and these are consistent, in general, with the dominant models. But the constitution of the system of action begins with an analysis of the problem to be solved. It is not modeled on a general institutional evolutionary schema of some sort. Of course, there may be a failure to recognize a problem or a refusal to act. It is more likely that a choice will be made to solve problems for which solutions exist. Still, there will be times when an attempt will be made to lay out a new program or to find a new model, in order to confront a problem for which no solution is known.

The analysis of systems of action designed to make use of dialysis technology revealed how wide a margin of liberty can exist. The lessons of that analysis may be transposed. The French *départemental* politico-administrative system, though deeply rooted and stable, is nevertheless contingent. The problems whose solution it represents might equally well be solved in other ways, and in societies in many respects similar to the French such is the case. To say that a system of action is a construct does not mean that is a necessary response to a problem, any more than that it is the inevitable consequence of an evolutionary process. Being a human creation and invention, it is not governed by any general determinism. There is no universal or even relative "one best way." Of course, it may bear repeating that constraints, even very strong constraints, do exist. Insofar as we are incapable of grasping the complexity of a system which will never change by itself, such constraints are apparently all the more difficult to overcome. History shows, however, that profound changes have already taken place, and, moreover, that such transformations could come in rather brief periods of time. We shall return to this question when we discuss change. For the moment, it is important to focus on the system of action as a nonnatural construct, an always precarious and problematic structure imposed on human action in the form of a mode of rationality and social control.[4] This structure is reinforced by a particular context, which adds constraints of its own. The system requires certain capacities and relational models which, in turn, impose limits on its developmental possibilities. Nevertheless, it remains fundamentally contingent, i.e., irreducibly indeterminate, hence "arbitrary."

To say that a human system is contingent is merely to say that it is not a servo-mechanism, that the actors are free. The rigidity and constraint associated with systems of action is due precisely to this freedom; constraint is not imposed from without.[5] It is a problem associated with change and with the difficulty of taking arbitrary decisions and making them effective in combinations of structured games. But no social action is possible apart from such games; man has no other opportunity to assert his freedom.

Regulation and System

At this point, we are going to try to give a preliminary definition of a concrete system of action. We shall begin with the general idea that a system is a unity, all of whose parts are interdependent. It is therefore endowed with a certain degree of structure, which distinguishes it from a simple aggregate, and at the same time it is provided with mechanisms to maintain this structure, which we will call mechanisms of regulation. This rather broad definition is applicable to human as well as physical systems. When we attempt to refine the definition further, however, the distinction between the two becomes immediately apparent.

For a human system, general propositions concerning interdependence and homeostasis are true only within certain limits. Human systems do have a certain continuity, but they also undergo transformation, in particular by adaptation. Though one may speak of regulation in connection with a human system, such regulation is not of the same type as cybernetic regulation, as we saw previously. The quite specific properties associated with self-adjusting mechanism do not apply to human systems. Insofar as a human system tends to return, over relatively long periods, to the state of equilibrium implicit in its structure, one may think of it as regulated. It therefore has homeostatic properties; nevertheless, it is not a servo-mechanism.

What, then, is the nature of its regulation? This is the central problem that we face. Two broad types of mechanisms come readily to mind, each associated with a type of constraint observed in all human societies. First, the actors in a system are subject to a certain number of customs which appear over the course of time. Transgression of customary limits may be met with formal or informal sanctions. Eventually, specialized organs may come into being in order to impose sanctions designed to keep behavior within acceptable limits. In this way, the effect of each actor's efforts is guided, regardless of his particular objectives, in such a way as to produce a common result, which may in time come to be internalized and discussed as a common goal or purpose.[6]

One may think of customs in a sense as "rules of the game"; mechanisms of mutual adjustment then determine the outcome of the game. Though these primary mechanisms frequently come to be joined by violent, coercive, or manipulative practices, and even supplanted by the latter, they are never entirely effaced. The game may be rigged, but it endures.

From this standpoint, we are in a position to draw one basic conclusion from our case studies. This is that the human systems we are calling concrete systems of action are regulated not by a specific organ, or by the effect of a constraint, even unconscious, or by automatic mechanisms of mutual adjustment, but rather by means of the games which integrate the "strategic" calculations of the actors according to a structured model. Structure and regulation apply not to men but to the games in which they play. A concrete system of action is ultimately no more than a group of structured games.

We do, of course, find that constraint has a role to play, in punishing infractions of the rules of the game; still, the constraint does not determine behavior directly, but rather insures the continuance of the game which guides it. The misconception that constraint can be substituted for the game, or that a desired result may be obtained by issuing supposedly constraining orders, leads to the danger of ineffective action without eliminating the game, but only transforming the presuppositions which it incorporates.

Automatic market mechanisms, moreover, are only special cases of a nonstructured game. Clearly, it may happen that a game involves relations among its players analogous to the mutual adjustment model which describes behavior in a free market. But if we compare the two models, we see that the essential elements of a concrete system of action are its structure and the nature of the game(s) played within it. We may regard an economic market as a concrete system of action, of course. Inequalities between the actors are reflected in the structure and interrelationships of the games in a system, yet this does not deprive the actors of the opportunity to try their luck.[7] Once the nature of a game becomes known, of course, it is susceptible to a mathematical solution which in some sense expresses the necessary character of the outcome or the result of mutual adjustment. But it was the choice of game models which determined the mode of regulation characteristic of the system. The pure and transparent market does not exist, except in the special case of a nonstructured game.

It is useful to make the distinction between a concrete system of action and what is usually called a social system more precise. Insofar as the mechanisms which regulate a social system elude explanation, there is a tendency to look upon that system as objectively, if not naturally, pre-determined. One can of course speculate as to the nature of these mechanisms, but the hypotheses advanced are inevitably incomplete and are usually projections of *a priori* models onto reality.

A concrete system of action, by contrast, is a system whose existence and mode of regulation can be empirically demonstrated. Insofar as it may be considered a solution to the problems of collective action, such as interdependence, cooperation, and conflict, we may apply the term "system of action."

Finally, then, we may define a concrete system of action as *a structured human ensemble which employs relatively stable game mechanisms to coordinate the actions of its participants. It furthermore maintains its structure, i.e., the stability of its games and the relationships among them, by means of mechanisms of regulation. These, in turn, form the content of still other games.*

We have already noted that organizations fit this definition quite well. As a first approximation, then, we may say, oversimplifying somewhat, that organizations represent a particular class of concrete systems of action with certain special characteristics. These include a more marked structure, the existence of more clearly defined aims, formalization of the games in view of these aims, conscious awareness of the goals by the participants, and partial assumption of responsibility, at least by the leaders, for certain of the regulations.

Regardless of their concreteness, such characteristics must remain relatively vague. This is difficult to remedy, unless we apply criteria of judgment relative to one particular aspect only—namely, formalization.

From this standpoint, it seems that organizations are located at one end of a scale of concrete systems of action. If we invoke the criteria of formalization, structuration, consciousness, and deliberately assumed responsibility, we find a range which runs from such unconscious regulatory mechanisms as that of the system of action which produces, say, a fashion in clothing, to the conscious regulation of a perfectly rationalized organization.

Few organizations attain this extreme degree of rationalization. In other types of concrete systems of action, we find examples which cover a wide spectrum: systems where regulation is unconscious, others where it is conscious; systems whose participants accept responsibility for internal government, and systems where there is a formalization of consciousness and responsibility around clearly defined goals.

It is possible that the difficulty of the problem is related to the ambiguous distinction between goals and results. Every concrete system of action, no matter what its degree of organization, obtains results, if only to maintain itself as a system within which it continues to be possible for the members to interact.[8] To the degree that the results produced by the system are a matter of public knowledge, perceptible if not measurable, they become an object on which the participants will try to act, whether by regarding such results as stakes in a new game, or by internalizing them as goals for future action. From this standpoint, one might regard the transition from the system of action to the formalized organization as a passage from mere consciousness of a result to its measurement; the result becomes a matter for debate and is transformed to a goal which structures the group of games.

Yet the distinction remains rather unclear, even though it has allowed us to move forward in our interpretation. The fact is that an organization is always both a concrete system of action with semi-conscious regulations *and* a structured, purposive, "rational" whole. Indeed, because its regulations are more constraining, the organization insures that cooperation will continue to be possible and contributes to prediction and measurement of results; at the same time, the participants remain free to pursue their personal goals by choosing their strategies in the games imposed on them by the organization. On the other hand, in concrete systems in the process of "finalization," i.e., of acquiring a conscious structure of goals, we often find that the discovery of results attributable to the existence of the system is related to the presence of more powerful constraints.

These distinctions are not merely academic. It is possible, in fact, to verify that there is a twofold process in progress in contemporary societies which tends to lessen the difference between concrete systems of action evolving toward formal organizations and organizations which are already highly formalized. First, there is a tendency for the actors in a system of action to become increasingly conscious of how the system is regulated, and to take responsibility for such regulation. Second, organizations are becoming increasingly tolerant; in recognizing that they are purposive systems of action, their leaders become aware that they can improve the effectiveness of their goal-directed activity by adjusting their action to the characteristics of the underlying concrete system of action.

Concrete Systems of Action and Organization Theory

The analysis of concrete systems of action has forced us to reformulate the problem of regulation of an organized group in more concrete terms. This has enabled us to gain some perspective on organizational analysis, which is useful in helping us to look at our problems in a more penetrating way.

Let us return to the example of the *départemental* politico-administrative system of action in order to apply some of these lessons.

This system was characterized, as we have seen, by a structure of crisscrossed relations and by a mode of government based on the institutionalization of exceptions. It may be that these are not singular characteristics, but rather point the way to envisaging a number of different phenomena, both within organizations and in the more general setting of concrete systems of action.

First, we shall look at the problem of crisscrossed control. The various successive theories of organization have all to one degree or another emphasized hierarchical relations, which are regarded as the central phenomenon. In the light of our systems analyses, it is possible to question this assumption. There has been a tendency to be blinded by the ideology of hierarchy and to assume *a priori* that hierarchical authority and social control are perfectly equivalent. All things considered, however, it seems quite possible that a nonnegligible, and perhaps even a preponderant, part of the control function, even in industrial organizations, is exercised throught the agency of crisscrossed relations; these make it possible to place tight constraints on the various players without subjecting them to situations of direct dependence.

A second phenomenon worthy of further consideration is regulation by exception. A system may be organized in such a way that if an actor manages to violate the rules which govern its fundamental games, then he can participate in the government of the system itself. This finding calls for a reconsideration of the relationship between the formal and the informal. The traditional argument is that the formal arrangements structure the field; informal arrangements then develop in the interstices of the formal structure as exceptions which are more or less tolerable. The theorists of the human-relations school advance a second argument according to which the informal relations represent the real vitality of the organization, while the formal arrangements are only a superstructure of minor importance. There is yet a third type of argument, which we ourselves have applied to organizational analysis. According to this argument, the formal structure is a response to the pressures of informal extortion. This provides a means of governing the system by structuring and stabilizing the games of power which come into being in a natural way when the uncertainties inherent in joint action are faced. According to the present analysis, this argument should be completed by introducing yet another distinction. To contrast formal and informal is inadequate; it would also be useful to distinguish between the regular game, which includes both a formal structure and informal tactics, and a second type of game. The latter would be a game for initiates which would develop from the regular game, or, in other words, it would be a game of exception. Through it, the very difficult problem of interdependence among the whole set of games could be resolved. In certain systems, in any case, it is the flaws in the "regular" structure that make it possible to achieve over-all government and resolve inherent contradictions.[9]

These remarks apply to concrete systems of action, but we see no reason why they should not be equally valid for classical organizations. It would be worthwhile to use this problematic for a study of large French industrial groups. We think it rather likely, in fact, that these enormous organizations are governed at their upper levels by a mode of regulation entirely different from those found in their constituent firms. This, of course, would contradict all the classical theories of organization, as well as the efforts of rationalizers such as MacKinsey. Indeed, it is likely that success at the top depends on the ability to make skillful, intuitive use of the second type of game we have described, the game of exceptions to the rules.

There are innumerable examples in which it would be possible to use the model of crisscrossed control rather than the hierarchical model. The game we have identified in the shops of the Industrial Monopoly, for instance, may in a sense be seen as corresponding to a model of criss-crossed control. To adopt this view is not merely a matter of rhetoric. From this standpoint, the system of relations in the shop appears much less aberrant a solution to the problems of integration and social control within a human ensemble. Fred Goldner's analyses of the operations of a large American firm provide another example: in this case, both union and production hierarchies were involved in a system of crisscrossed control which can be used to explain the apparently "abnormal" influence of a department of industrial relations over the effective power of decision.[10]

We will conclude with two final remarks:

Using the analysis of systems of action, we have the means to renew the discussion of closed versus open systems organization. This is not an ontological problem. We have already said that no organization can be totally open or totally closed. From a methodological point of view, there might be some interest in considering an organization as a closed system, but clearly this would mean limiting the interpretation of the organization's role in society. Conversely, it makes sense to speak of an organization as an open system only if the degree of autonomy, or nonopenness, can be measured. This is an essential feature of the system of action which consists of the organization and its relevant environments. Thus it would seem that the best instrument for understanding, and eventually measuring, this particular organizational degree of freedom is the analysis of systems of action.

Secondly, we think that it would be possible to shed a good deal of light on the categories used in sociological analysis by means of the systems-of-action concept. Even more than organizational analysis, the analysis of systems of action leads to a reexamination of the categorial taboos on which many of our sociological "explanations" are based, including such widespread notions as "class" or "function."

The heuristic aspect of the strategic argument, in particular, is a useful instrument *which requires the researcher to look for the real social groupings and cleavages and enables him to find them.* Factors such as class or socioprofessional category may not be the pertinent groups in a given question; whether they are or not is always problematic. The apparent institutional structures are less influential in such an analysis; a greater degree of abstraction is therefore possible. It then becomes possible to gain a better understanding of the particular features of the object under study—we would almost be tempted to say a truer understanding. This improvement is made possible by a conceptual advance: namely, the replacement of so-called sociological factors in the explanation with an argument based on the actors' strategies within games which one seeks to discover. In effect, a deterministic argument has been replaced by an argument which draws all the consequences from the radically indeterminate nature of social action and its context.

Concrete Systems of Action as Instruments of Social Control

We have hitherto neglected the problems of the over-all social system, because our desire to conduct a thorough empirical analysis made it necessary to assume that the phenomena under investigation were in some degree independent.

At this point, it would be useful to return to this problem of interdependence between society and organizations, from which we hope to derive the consequences relating to the operation of the social system. We are not yet in a position to do this, however. To analyze the problems of the social ensemble, a different procedure from the one we have been using is required, since, for the moment at least, we have no way of empirically studying the phenomena of structuration and integration which are essential to our view at the level of society as a whole. Consequently, we think it best to reserve this question of the relations between societies and organizations, since at present we could do no better than to contrast speculative propositions with generalizations of empirical results.

Nevertheless, the analysis of concrete systems of action does open an avenue of research which may be useful in preparing the way for a more objective and concrete study of such problems. Within the social ensemble, concrete systems of action are crucial instruments. As we have seen, they provide a means to describe the context within which organizations operate, and they are the concrete embodiment of a good part of the "social control" exercised within the over-all social system. Though they do not enable us to answer the comprehensive question which we have just declined to treat, we do find material here for embarking on a preliminary discussion of this question. It is to this discussion that we would now like to call the reader's attention.

Before we continue, however, one remark is called for and this requires a bit of backtracking. The problem we are in fact raising has to do with the relations between microsociology, which has an experimental, or at least empirical, orientation, and macrosociology, which is perforce given over to less rigorous modes of knowledge.

In our opinion, the problem is generally discussed either too narrowly or too broadly—in terms of method, on the one hand, or scientific philosophy on the other—whereas a much more fruitful approach would be to regard it as a problem of research strategy. What one ordinarily asks, for instance, is whether it is legitimate to ignore the macrosociological context in making experimental studies of a group: this is the form the problem takes when posed narrowly in terms of method. Or else, the question is put in the broader—far too broad—terms of scientific philosophy, which asks to what extent it is legitimate to extrapolate conclusions drawn from experiments with small groups to problems of social conduct in general. Thus stated, neither of these questions is, we think, answerable, and both are largely irrelevant. It is clear that it is not legitimate to extrapolate from the small group to the comprehensive social system, yet this will invariably be done, precisely because this is what is most interesting about studies of small groups. It is also clear that one reaps diminishing returns after a certain point from the precautions which one takes to insure that one's experiments are methodologically pure; in any case, such precautions are of no importance to the problem of generalization.

By contrast, two points should be made in connection with the point of view we are recommending, which stresses a research-strategy approach. First, in spite of the critiques which may be made of the scientific logic implicit in microsociological work, we believe that the importance of such work and its extrapolations has been crucial. Second, it is nonetheless true that microsociology may have lost a good deal of its interest for sociologists in general, since it no longer appears capable of teaching us more about the social system within the framework of the dominant paradigm.

Why? Hitherto, discoveries made in the experimental setting of the small group were useful in that they cast doubt upon the sort of reasoning by which the functioning of social institutions was explained. Once the problem has become the elaboration of a new mode of argument, however, the question of what extrapolation procedures are used assumes a crucial importance. Now it happens that such procedures have been based—and this is not the result of chance—on totally inadequate models.[11]

For the sake of concreteness, we will discuss one particular model, which has been quite widespread though generally implicit. This model has been the basis of attempts to generalize the intuitions and discoveries of Kurt Lewin and his associates and followers of the Michigan school in the area of permissive leadership, for example.[12] One might call this a homological model, since it includes the assumption that there is, or could be, or should be, homology between the leadership styles at every level of an organizational hierarchy, or in the various institutions of a society. With such an assumption, it was possible to generalize the proof that permissive leadership was superior so as to form the basis of a comprehensive social policy. Organizational and systems analysis raises basic doubts about this assumption, however. Not only is it possible for different leadership styles to coexist within the same system of action, but it seems that the differences and contrasts we do find did not develop accidentally but rather serve as instruments for governing the system. This does not mean that Lewin was wrong, but that his discovery has a limited range of validity. To put it somewhat differently, the generalization of his theorem raises problems which are not problems of method or logic. To be stated properly, these problems require a new kind of empirical knowledge relating to the modes of integration and regulation inherent in social ensembles.

George Homans, in a more deliberate effort at systematization, has proposed a more explicit model, the interactionist model. He holds that it is possible to reconstruct the whole social ensemble on the basis of extremely simple rules, which can be established by analyzing small groups and observing human interactions.[13] His construction is of some interest, but only insofar as it shows what paradoxes can result if one tries to reduce a complex phenomenon to a deductive system based on a few simple, apparently obvious principles. Not merely is the explanation not very satisfactory, but even in its poverty it results in propositions manifestly in contradiction with the facts.

We do not think that macrosociological research is any more promising, at least for the moment, from the point of view of developing an effective research strategy. Why? Because it, too, neglects the crucial problem of integration and regulation of conduct. Furthermore, it is incapable of exploiting the empirical results accumulated by microsociologists concerning individual attitudes and behavior in very large groups, including societies.

To make use of such knowledge, contemporary macrosociology is forced to have recourse to a deterministic argument. Though we may have grown used to it, this argument is, in fact, highly debatable. In the first place, it relies on abstract categories,[14] like socioprofessional classification, education, income, or age group; these are in reality much more contingent than they appear.[15] Secondly, it is not legitimate to infer a causal or even a merely predictive determinism from the finding of a statistical regularity. The determinisms in question are actually quite vague; they are accepted merely because it is assumed that the field is nonstructured, which implies that any observed correlation must be due to a direct causal link between phenomena.[16] The fact of the matter is that the causation in question is never direct; it is associated with, and mediated by, the specific structuration of the field, which cannot fail to influence the conduct of the actors, even if, as we have tried to show, this influence is not deterministic.

It should be noted, moreover, that, at this level of generalization, the critique of macrosociology is identical with the critique of microsociology which attacked the extrapolation of its results. It was the fact that the field was not neutral which prevented one from inferring a general theorem applicable to the government of human ensembles from the finding that permissive leadership was superior in small-group experiments. In the same way, it is not permissible to take such data as the finding that the higher socioprofessional categories exhibit more liberal attitudes or more conservative voting behavior and use it to infer that belonging to these categories "causes" the observed result or can be used to predict it. In itself, this is neither true nor false: everything depends on the structure of the field in question, i.e., on the nature and rules of the game in which the actors are involved.

The most important contribution which organizational and systems analysis has to offer sociological theory is the proof that every field is structured. With this fact, it becomes possible to challenge a conception of causality which is at once crude and vague. Its critical significance is, in the first instance, negative, in that it reveals the random and, in particular, the *mediated* character of such broadly general deterministic notions as "conditionings" and "weights," on which our arguments all too often depend. But our critique may also have a positive significance in making it possible to substitute a new notion of causality for the old. For the purposes of the present research strategy, this is of crucial importance, for it introduces a new element: the *integration* and *regulation* of human conduct and activity. The analysis of the associated problems relies on new instruments and on a new and effective mode of argument shaped by the limits of our present knowledge.

To avoid any possible misunderstanding, we should point out that our purpose is not to resort to a new reductionism of social relations in general to organizational or systems analysis. We are convinced that it is no more possible to extrapolate from the organization to society than from the group to the organization. What we wish to suggest is that at present, and for some time to come, organizations and systems of action are and will remain central objects of social-scientific research, insofar as one of the major problems confronting such research is that of how behavior is integrated. We believe that the best empirical approach to the problem of behavioral integration is through organizations and systems of action. The present situation is analogous to the rather long period of time during which research on the small group was considered to be the most innovative, since it was such work which had led to the discovery of the problem of relationships.[17]

At present, however, it is becoming possible to look to this new field of knowledge for more than analogies and problems. We are beginning to witness the emergence of definitive empirical results.

Perhaps we should explain what we mean. Understanding how men cooperate with one another inside an organization enables us to understand how problems of integration are solved in complex ensembles, and how such ensembles are regulated. These results yield enlightening and suggestive material for discussing social systems and society in general, but it is by no means permissible to extend or extrapolate them as general laws applicable to a larger framework. We have to make use of these results, and yet we must try to keep from making the sort of error into which the irresistible (and moreover natural) penchant of every investigator to generalize would lead us if we did not take care to guard against it. Yet beyond the "analogies" and "problems" raised by the new approach, we can begin to make out certain concrete processes of integration and regulation which are usually discussed in microsociological terms. Now, we are in a position to analyze these processes empirically in terms of concrete systems of action.

To take just one example, it seems somewhat pointless to discuss the role of elites and social stratification in terms of logical models and statistical data (such as the probability of holding certain posts as a function of social origin), when we can instead conduct an empirical study, using the concepts associated with concrete systems of action, of the problems connected with the origin of an elite group and the nature of its influence.

For example, we may consider a concrete system of action which is quite important in French society, the "Grandes Ecoles."[18] We have in mind not the individual schools as such, in their role as instruments for training and particularly selecting the elites of the future, but rather the broader "Grande Ecole" phenomenon, that is the multiform network of influence which surrounds these educational institutions. The notion in question is not a narrow one of mere reproduction,[19] but a process that involves the integration and regulation of certain activities crucial to the development of the society.[20] The "Grande Ecole" is a relatively effective and widely accepted instrument of *social control* in French society, and yet there is scarcely any equivalent in any other advanced society.[21]

It is true, of course, that the study of concrete systems of action is difficult and never-ending. We may anticipate finding no more than incomplete answers, moreover, to the very basic question of "social control," since other forms of control coexist with those we have been analyzing (the most immediately perceptible ones). We do not deny that other forms of pressure and constraint impinge on the members of a society: religious and moral prohibitions, the charisma of leaders and fashionable personages, habits and customs, traditional forms of argument and intellectual tools come to mind, among others. Social control exercised through concrete systems of action, therefore, is certainly not the only form of control. We are not even in a position to measure the relative effectiveness of this as compared with other forms with any precision. Yet we consider it to be of great importance that the mechanisms of this particular form of social control can be demonstrated. We believe that this type of analysis will facilitate the task of formulating in empirical terms the problem of other forms of social control, which act through concrete systems of action which we are not yet able to identify.

In spite of appearances, in other words, we believe that the explanation ought not to be sought in authority or influence, though that would seem to be the basic mechanism. Nor do we think that the answer is to be found in the final outcome, the social order. Instead, we think that research should concentrate on the middle ground—organizations and concrete systems of action. It is here that operational social control is exercised. It is possible to believe, as our empirical examples suggest, that organizations and concrete systems of action, as specific, relatively autonomous modes of regulation of collective activities, always *mediate*—i.e., tailor and modify—all other forms of rationality and social control. In so doing, they destroy the homogeneity of the social field by introducing ruptures, discontinuities, and incoherencies. This accounts for their crucial importance for research.

If we may revert for a moment to the image sometimes used to depict organizations as transmission belts linking the broader society to the primary group, our final conclusion would be that in social matters, the transmission belt is more important than the motor.

Relations between mayor and municipal counselors, for example, are extremely inegalitarian. This is not due primarily to law or even custom, nor is it a consequence of a supposed inability of the council to manage its own affairs. It is due rather to the structure of the field of relations with the *départemental* politico-administrative system, as our analysis has shown. The consequence of this structure is that the most rational strategy for mayor, council, and citizens of the town is for the mayor to take personal responsibility for relations between the town and other authorities, and for the council and citizens to acquiesce in this. This explains the unequal game which we observed in our study. A consequence of this game is the existence of relations of authority and dependence which must somehow be managed.

With an argument of this type, we are in a position to improve our understanding of the practical and theoretical difficulties associated with self-management. In its present, "vulgarized" form, the self-management movement relies on two arguments whose limitations have been demonstrated. First, there is the homological argument according to which whatever takes place in the basic unit of a system can be extrapolated to the whole. Second, the fundamentalist argument claims that the basic unit directs all the others. These two arguments come to grief because of the fundamental fact that the units are situated in a field which is not neutral, but structured. Furthermore, while one may change the structure, it is impossible to construct a field with *no* structure. From this structure derive the constraints and resources which the members of the nuclear group use to elaborate the game by which they are governed. Of course, the nature of this game will necessarily be profoundly influenced by differences among the participants stemming from their personal and social inequalities with respect to the general structure of the field. These inequalities may be partially offset by constraints of a different sort, but only at some cost. To be effective, moreover, such constraints must be associated with the structure itself. The transmission belt is actually the key component of the system.[22]

The Notion of System and the Problems of Decision and Change

In certain superficial and rather abstract views of sociological theories, there has been a tendency to contrast a systems orientation, based on analysis of the interdependencies and regulations which establish constraints at any given moment, with an evolutionary outlook that relies on the observation of change, the dynamics of social movements, and the analysis of crises.

Nothing could be farther from the truth. It is true that structuro-functionalist models have often led to exaggeratedly static views of society. Such is not the case, however, with the analysis of concrete systems of action, whose contingent, nonnatural character we have stressed. In fact, such analyses are indispensable prerequisites of any serious study of the problems of change, since one cannot speak of change without knowing precisely what it is that is changing. It is quite naturally change in the structure and mode of government of a social system which is of primary interest to the investigator, since these factors influence man's potential freedom and equality within the system. Only within a concrete system of action can one meaningfully speak of such change. It should be noted, furthermore, that such change can come about only with the intervention of another concrete system of action—a social movement, for example. The nature of a crisis is more readily understood if the system or systems in which it occurs have been clearly delineated, and if the ways in which these systems were regulated before the onset of the crisis are understood.

Thus the notion of a concrete system of action is useful for stating the problem of change in more realistic terms. In a similar way, we may use this notion to reformulate the practical and theoretical problems associated with decision in a more useful way.

A decision is, in fact, always the product of a concrete system of action, either an organization or an organized system, a stable system of action or a temporary one designed to meet a transient circumstance. No decision may be considered rational in itself, it can only be understood in relation to the system of action which produced it.[23] It should therefore be possible to contribute to the theory of decision as well as change by analyzing concrete systems of action. In return, we hope that a discussion of change and decision will enable us to gain a little perspective on our initial propositions. This should help us penetrate further into the heart of the matter.

The next and last two parts of this work will be devoted to this task.

Four   **The Problems of Decision**

10

The Problem of the Rationality of Decisions

Why Is There a Problem?

At first glance it may seem paradoxical that a pragmatic approach such as organizational or systems analysis should have attracted, among leaders who pride themselves on realism, so much smaller an audience than an approach such as decision theory, which is so abstract and difficult to apply to real-life situations.

Its psychological advantages may account for the success of the decisional approach, which takes the point of view of an actor free of the system's constraints and thus gives the illusion of liberty.[1] The systems approach, by contrast, is addressed to no one in particular, since no one, not even one of its leaders, can identify himself with the system. Decision theory, furthermore, has the merit of simplicity and great logical force, while systems analysis is prone to complexity and subtlety. Thus the decisional approach offers a convenient language which facilitates communication and yet ruffles no one's feelings and questions on no one's ulterior motives.

Yet, if applied exclusively for any length of time, decision theory, even in the hands of contemporary decision-makers, becomes enmeshed in a web of abstraction. It is a mode of argument which gives action precedence over understanding. Hence every potential explanatory factor is transformed into a tactical consideration. Each such factor must be detached from its place in the system and assigned an objective value before being reassembled and incorporated into a presumably more efficient combination. The calculations may be impeccable; but if the data employed are based on an inadequate analysis, the result can be disastrous.

As long as one's efforts are limited to a known and relatively stable domain, no problems arise, because the objective values assigned to the various factors can be directly calculated from parameters already "tested" in practice. Once one ventures onto new ground, however, or seeks to attack a highly complex entity, then relationships and systems effects become crucial problems. This explains the preponderance of so-called systems analysis in modern techniques such as PPBS or RCB.[2] The problem then becomes one of making the transition from the computational logic to the systemic reasoning on which it is based. Three solutions are possible.

The first is the most common and is wholly empirical. It consists in accepting the rational logic of decision, but recognizing limits to its validity. Adjustments are made within empirically determined tolerances, and any pressure from the environment which would contradict the assumed autonomy of the decision-maker is referred to the realm of values and objectives. One further assumes that innovation or extension of the field of decision is beyond the scope of the calculation. If the field should be extended, then the calculations will again be applicable once the new field has been ordered.

A second, more ambitious solution is exemplified by the new methods for analyzing options. The goal of these methods is to integrate the understanding of the problem and the calculation of the option. Systems analysis is employed to delineate the field and define the problem and its parameters. Once these preliminaries have been laid out, the over-all problem is segmented into programs and subprograms, which reduce the initial task to a series of simple problems whose parameters are measurable and whose solutions may be tested by cost-benefit measurements. The segmentation process, however, is difficult and open to discussion.

The unrealistic pretentions of these first two solutions have been criticized by Aaron Wildavsky, who has shown the nature of the reductionism which they invariably entail.[3] The danger of linking systems analysis and cost-benefit computations is that the solution of the problem is then made to turn on its most arbitrary step, the segmentation of the task into elementary action units. In general, moreover, such approaches use a nonsociological type of systems analysis which neglects the autonomy of the human actors and the contingent character of their games.

It should be possible, however, to offer a third solution to this problem, and it is this that we are going to attempt to explore. What is needed is a relativization of the decision, along with the myth of the decision-maker. Rational means must be found for making the transition from the rationality of the system to that of the actor.

These objectives call for a fresh consideration of rationality, and this is what we shall attempt to do, following the lead of the few authors who have directly treated this subject. It should be noted that none of them was originally a sociologist. Yet we believe that the problems involved are primarily sociological, and we would therefore like to conclude with a discussion of the contribution that a properly sociological approach might make to our understanding of them.

A priori Rationality and *A Posteriori* Rationality: The Critiques of Charles Lindblom

It was in connection with the discussion of public-policy problems that the first and most profound controversy provoked by decision theory arose. It is easy to see why! In the case of private decisions, it is not difficult, at least in the abstract, to conclude that the rationality of a decision should be judged in relation to the decision-maker's objectives. On the other hand, it is hard to argue that the value of a public policy should not depend on the public interest. Though an administrator or politician may have been given the ultimate responsibility of serving the public interest, it would not be up to him to decide what this interest is *a priori*. If the rationality of a decision is no longer clear or univocal, it is more difficult to argue in favor of the rational model.

Classical democratic theory provides one answer to this problem. The sovereign legislature is supposed to be responsible for asserting the general will, and it has the duty to determine the legitimacy and rationality of all public policy. Yet analysis of government and administrative practices shows us that this theory is not easy to apply in practice. Legislative acts are compromises whose interpretation may leave a great deal of latitude. The legislator's intentions may be open to discussion. In any given case, there are legitimate, legally sanctioned interests in direct or indirect conflict, which may cause administrative and legal blockages or disputes. This explains why public activity often gives the impression of irrationality.

Charles Lindblom's great contribution was to demonstrate that, behind this apparent irrationality, another logic was developing. Although public action seemed to consist of a congeries of administrative and political deals, Lindblom showed that these were actually subject to an *a posteriori* rationality which was ultimately more humane and effective than the exploded *a priori* logic.

As early as his celebrated article, "The Science of *Muddling Through*",[4] published in 1959, he showed:

1. *that no administrator can seriously apply the rational method which* [at the time] *was represented by operations research;*

2. that instead, he tends instinctively to practice a method of "comparison at the margin" between two empirical alternatives, not distinguishing ends from means;

3. that it is fortunate and sagacious that he act in this way, because such a method involves fewer risks and turns out to be much more enlightening than the rational method.

In a brief but exceptionally systematic work published in 1965, Lindblom broadened his discussion to the whole range of decision-making processes and applied himself to demonstrating the logical superiority of the model of *a posteriori* adjustment, which he calls "partisan mutual adjustment," over *a priori* rationality, which he refers to as the synoptic model.[5]

The synoptic model would, of course, be superior if all the required information and necessary resources were available, if there were no ambiguity in the objectives, and if all the participants shared the same values. Such, however, is not and can never be the case. First of all, it is impossible to gather all the information *a priori*. Even to attempt to do so is pointless, since much information emerges only in the course of action, as a result of the pressures and counterpressures released in the process of negotiation and partisan mutual adjustment. Because our world is a complex one whose problems involve a good many uncertain factors and contradictory interests, moreover, the objectives cannot but remain at least partially ambiguous.

Although it is difficult, therefore, to apply the synoptic model, the model of partisan mutual adjustment accommodates this condition without difficulty. The initial objectives of a policy may well be ambiguous, even contradictory. Agreement would be impossible if one were to attempt to clarify these objectives in advance. But once the policy is implemented, the necessary solutions may be discovered through experience. It is inevitable that the parties to any particular action will not share identical values, and yet it is imperative that these disparate values be respected. It follows that it will be easier to obtain agreement on pragmatic policies which do not challenge fundamental values than on the ultimate goals of social action. It is nevertheless possible to achieve progress in this way, because the process brings new means of action into existence and provides experience in using them. The supply of available resources is not stable; new resources may emerge in the course of action, while existing ones may become exhausted. Experimentation brings the problems more clearly into focus and allows useful resources to be discovered and applied to their solution. Mutual adjustment allows for experimentation, whereas the synoptic model does not.

In this complex and sophisticated argument, which we summarize only briefly, it is of course true that one finds a restatement of Adam Smith's fundamental contention that the market imposes a hidden hand which guides competitors toward the general interest though they believe they are merely engaged in pursuit of their particular gains. In contrast with the model of popular sovereignty (which is what the unattainable ideal of a rational logic assumes), Lindblom presents a market model for the management of collective action which incorporates and justifies the myriad complications and difficulties which make the administrator impatient.[6] It is a pluralistic democratic model, in which the governmental apparatus is present only to guarantee the rules necessary to insure the mutual adjustment of all the parties.

Lindblom's demonstration is impeccable. Yet it leaves one as uneasy as did the classical rational model. All his arguments must be taken into consideration, to be sure. In our view, however, neither the framework within which they are developed nor the objective for which they are used appears adequate.

For one thing, the range of Lindblom's critique is much broader than the realm of public policy. Its strictures are applicable to the whole spectrum of man's organized activities. The synoptic model is just as dubious when applied to the management of a company, the exploitation of a market, the management of a hospital, or the organization of a school. But for rare exceptions, however, neither the *a priori* synoptic model nor the *a posteriori* model of adjustment applies in pure form to any of these activities, including public policy-making. In most cases susceptible of analysis, we find a mixture, in which *a posteriori* rationality generally serves as a corrective for the errors which result from the synoptic model. On the other hand, an *a priori*, synoptic type of rationality seems to be an indispensable instrument for establishing or reestablishing order in the wake of the confusion, anarchy, and injustice which are usually found in organizations and systems which for too long a period of time have been dominated by a partisan mutual adjustment model of rationality.

That such mixtures exist may with good reason be cited against the dominant rational *credo;* there is no reason, however, why they may not also be used to criticize the invocation of the *a posteriori* model as an alternative *credo*. One has to wonder, furthermore, why the synoptic model, despite its alleged logical weakness, continues to exercise a universal attraction and even to conquer new ground in practical applications. It should be noted that it is not without irony that in the same year that Lindblom successfully demonstrated the superiority of the American model of pluralist democracy, the American administration made the decision to expand the use of PPBS, its most ambitious undertaking to date in rationalization of public policy-making according to a synoptic model.

It is worth pausing to consider this paradox. Lindblom's negative critique is perfectly valid against the rationalist illusions of the PPBS. Wildavsky pressed this point with still greater vigor. The justice of the critique is proven by the almost total failure of the experiment despite the considerable effort expended to insure its success. Yet we cannot explain why such a program was implemented merely by alluding to a supposed aberration of a few leaders fascinated by the mirage of an *a priori* rationality. Behind the American PPBS, the French RCB, and various other versions of the same techniques throughout the world, one does not have to look very far to find a deep-seated and perfectly justified desire to

reform a machine so weighed down by the complexity of mutual adjustment that it has become impossible to run. The PPBS, like many earlier
attempts at reform, largely failed to hit its mark. If judged by its intentions, it may be considered the most resounding of failures. If, instead,
we think of it as an attempt to make over a decision system which had
become unworkable, then we see that it was not without positive effects
which sometimes led to real reforms and frequently compelled a reexamination of the relationship between goals and information-processing
procedures.

In fact, Lindblom's alternative is just as abstract as the rational model
he is combatting. The shortcoming of his model is that, like other
economic-type approaches, it assumes that the actors are autonomous
and on an equal footing in entering into relationships and making their
mutual adjustments. The model allows for differences in values, but it
fails to take into account their relative influence and power within the
system of action of which they are a part. If it did so, then the market
would indeed be the best solution.

In reality, however, systems of action are dominated by structures of
influence. Whether the mutual adjustments which occur represent the
best solution or not is irrelevant, because these adjustments tend to reinforce the characteristics of the structure, and particularly its dysfunctions and inequalities. The *a posteriori* rationality is a static rationality of
vicious circles.

One may, of course, raise the ideal of pluralistic democratic rationality
against the injustice and ineffectiveness of such structures. Yet the access
mechanisms suggested by Lindblom,[7] who is not indifferent to the problem, are usually inoperative. Every attempt at reform inevitably encounters structural resistance. If we really want to see change, then we must
alter our thinking to challenge the logic of mutual adjustment. It is clear
that the synoptic model is far from satisfactory for this purpose. Yet as
long as our understanding of concrete systems remains no more advanced
than it is at present, and until our capacity to intervene in the operation of
such systems in order to reform or at least regulate them increases, a
model as abstract and unrealistic as the synoptic remains indispensable to
counteract the errors which inevitably result from partisan mutual
adjustment.

The Problem of the Decision-Maker and His Preferences

In spite of Lindblom's efforts to give a comprehensive
treatment, his critiques neglect an essential problem, which we have de-
ferred until now for the sake of clarity: the problem of the decision-maker.
What Lindblom does, in fact, is to demonstrate the logical impossibility of

applying the rational model by adopting the system's point of view. This makes it possible for him to avoid casting doubt on the rationality of the individuals or organizations who make decisions on the basis of goals and preferences which guide their action. It is true that his idea that the compromises made in actual experience in the course of working out mutual adjustments can bring with them the discovery of new values does indirectly represent a challenge to the theory of the rational decision-maker. Yet Lindblom does not press this point any farther.

To us, however, this problem seems central if we hope to move beyond the sterile opposition of synoptic and partisan and mutual-adjustment models, in order to reformulate the question of the relationship between rationality of the decision-maker and that of the system.

In our view, decisive critiques have been made of the rational model by Albert O. Hirschman and James G. March. Both begin with an examination of the problem of the decision-maker. If we may give a somewhat caricatural oversimplification, we can identify two themes present in the work of both men, though their proportions differ according to the case:

1. Men, and decision-makers in particular, never know very clearly what they want.

2. They discover their aims, which are frequently new to them, through experience, i.e., by making decisions.

Albert Hirschman, in a work that is precise, pertinent, and witty, has drawn his conclusions from looking at a series of large projects financed by the World Bank in underdeveloped countries.[8] These projects, whose costs and benefits had been studied with much care in the light of the rational model, would have to be considered failures from the standpoint of rational logic. Their cost turned out to be far greater than envisioned, and the hoped-for benefits did not materialize. Yet what had to be considered as a failure from the point of view of the logic of classical rationality could, on the other hand, be regarded as a success from the point of view of development. The difficult and potentially disastrous situation brought on by these miscalculations in fact led the officials in charge to discover new resources and relations which had been impossible to foresee and which ultimately made it possible to attain different objectives—equally interesting, if not more so—from the original goals. The most spectacular case involved a textile concern set up to process jute in a new region of Bengal, which found itself paralyzed when it was discovered that the raw material which the project had been designed to consume would be unusable for several years, because it happened to be the low period of a fifty-year biological cycle to which the particular plants in question are subject. To save the project, it was necessary to find other raw materials, and in the process new resources were discovered which made possible considerable progress.

Following Adam Smith, Hirschman suggests that man's action is not only guided by a "hidden hand," but that he also needs a "hiding hand" without which he would not succeed in launching large-scale undertakings and would learn nothing. To learn, it is necessary to act without prior knowledge, and therefore to take a risk that a close calculation of costs and benefits would make impossible. The rational model freezes action on the level of established knowledge. But this knowledge is, of course, far from perfect and can prevent man from discovering what is possible—in terms of both new means and new ends.

The difference between this and Lindblom's argument is clear. Here the rationality is again *a posteriori* in character; however, one no longer seeks to find it in the operation of the system, but rather after the fact, in action.

In James G. March's, view, the decision-maker initially has no particular preferences, or else relatively inconsistent ones, for his point of departure. Using an argument more psychological in nature, he arrives at views concerning individual behavior that are quite similar to those of Hirschman. In his discussion of the completely uncoordinated character of decisions made by a university administration,[9] he directly challenges the myth of the rational decision-maker from a normative as well as an empirical viewpoint.[10]

It is impossible for the decision-maker to implement his rational preferences. Instead he will choose the least harmful alternative and discover his preferences after the fact. Although these may be mere rationalizations, it is also possible that he has learned new values and goals. Through experience it becomes possible to discover the advantages of any particular policy. The good administrator is one who can profit from the experience imposed on him by circumstance.

March concludes from this that the theory implicitly used in educating children ought to be applied to adults. We assume that the child is unaware of his desires, or, if he thinks he knows what he wants, that he is likely to be mistaken, because his values are too circumscribed. The parents, of course, cannot substitute their personal desires for the child's, but it is their duty to provide him with the experience which will broaden his values and range of choice. Scientists, too, rather than focusing on the problem of determining the best way to attain certain goals, should investigate how such goals come into being and how men discover their objectives. Always directly or indirectly catalysts for action, they should suggest ways to make qualitative improvements in the outcome by seeking more interesting goals. In this sense, even jokes, foolishness, and play are invaluable intellectual tools which contribute not only to relaxation but also to the exploration of new modes of behavior and goals.

March's work, outwardly even more jocular than Hirschman's, reveals beneath its surface paradoxes a dimension of learning and change. His interest in human psychological development tends to be left out of account by both the synoptic and mutual-adjustment models.

If we pay close attention to both these authors, we find that they endeavor to show that man is not capable of every kind of undertaking or experience. It is, of course, possible that adults, no less than children, will fail to learn anything from experience. But in decision-making the part played by learning is no less worthy of serious consideration than questions of costs and benefits. Our understanding of systems of action (and, more precisely, their capacity to change) and human learning procedures should be enhanced by our discussion. In passing, it should be noted that it was the problem of learning which made it possible for psychologists to transcend the two classical models of conditioning and motivation. It remains for sociologists and political scientists to develop comparable models for systems of action.[11]

Before we take up this problem, however, it is important to try to understand the relationship between the rationality of the decision-maker and that of the system which circumscribes his action.

The Limits of Rationality: Herbert Simon's Model

For fifteen years there has existed a theory, or rather a conceptual model, which makes it possible to overcome the antinomies mentioned above. The theory we have in mind was put forward by Herbert Simon as early as 1958 and was formalized in the book *Organizations,* which he wrote with James G. March.[12]

This model entails a complete reversal of perspective. Instead of demonstrating the limits of the rational model yet again, Simon proposes that one begin with another model, the model of *bounded rationality.* The English-speaking intellectual world was at first impressed with the revolutionary character of this proposal. Yet it has not, in fact, had the influence one might have expected, because its implications were not perceived. It was generally regarded as a new and more sophisticated version of the rational model.[13]

Let us consider Simon's argument. He attacks the classical model by making certain criticisms which would later be taken up by Lindblom and which we have already summarized, but it is the cognitive aspect of the problem that especially concerns him. Man is incapable of conforming to a model of *absolute* rationality, such as that put forward by the classical theory, because he cannot apprehend all the possible choices, on the one hand, and because he reasons sequentially and not synoptically, on the other. Rather than doubt the rationality of the decision-maker, however, Simon proposes to build a model based on the available empirical data concerning his behavior. The decision-maker does not seek the optimum or best solution in the absolute sense, which in any case is out of reach, but he does always seek a "rational" solution. Which one will he choose? The first solution consistent with his criteria of rationality. Man is not an optimizing, but a *satisficing* animal.

It should be noted that this is not merely a new practical approximation to the classical model. It was a new type of theoretical model, and the new arguments that derive from it are potentially in contradiction with the standard ones. If one wants to understand why a certain decision was made, the course to follow is not to try first to establish what the best rational solution was and then to identify the obstacles which kept the decision-maker from finding or implementing it. Instead, the sequence of options offered him should be seen in relation to the total context in which he was operating; then, the criteria he used, consciously or unconsciously, in deciding whether to accept or reject these options should be analyzed. From a normative point of view, this means that the scientist will no longer propose the use of scientific models of choice but rather will offer advice on how to improve the criteria of satisfaction. It is, of course, necessary that this advice consider the general framework of the rational model, but this still leaves room to attack the constraints which condition the criteria of satisfaction.

The great interest of this conceptual model derives partly from the fact that it recognizes the considerable importance which rational calculation and, more generally, what might be called the ideology of rationality have acquired. The model makes room for them without accepting the underlying reasoning on which they are based. Although the criteria of satisfaction employed by decision-makers have been influenced by the general quantitative trend and by the ideology of rationality, this does not mean that an optimization argument is actually used. Finally, with this model, one can formulate the problem of the relationship between the rationality of the decision-maker and that of the system in more operational terms, since the decision-maker's criteria of satisfaction are naturally influenced by the characteristics of the system.

Simon did not explore the possibilities for a new analysis of systems, however. He was satisfied to have shown that the model of bounded rationality gave a better *cognitive* account of how choices were actually made. This perhaps explains why his model was understood solely as a neorationalist one.

In fact, this new "paradigm" called for a sociological analysis; but sociologists, at that time little interested in phenomena of decision, were not yet capable of undertaking it. Criteria of satisfaction do not arise adventitiously out of personal idiosyncrasies. They stem more from a learning process than an arbitrary choice and reflect widespread cultural values, games involving decision-makers within the system of action, and personal strategic choices made by individuals in this context.

Consider the first type of constraint. Not only is there clearly no universal optimum, but criteria of rationality vary widely from one culture to the next. What is considered rational in Europe will not be in the Middle East. Even so theoretically universal a phenomenon as a consumer market reveals that when it comes to purchases of consumer goods the criteria of satisfaction in an American household are not the same as in France. Does one ascribe this to erroneous choices, backwardness of the purchasers, or imperfect competition? Isn't it more reasonable and useful to analyze the criteria of satisfaction actually employed and to ask how they came into being?

Individual norms are the result of a cultural learning process, i.e., a socialization, reinforced by sanctions imposed by the environment. At the same time, however, they may be considered as a social construct. It should be noted in passing that norms are essential to the existence of a market. It is also noteworthy that norms are transformed by the combined effect of a variety of influences derived from individual and collective experience. Increasingly, it is education that is important in developing them by diffusing advances in knowledge, together with modes of perception and intellectual paradigms which support these modes and are their product. Within this framework, measurement and the ideology of rationality exert their influence. Just as the spread of double-entry bookkeeping transformed the criteria of satisfaction adopted by merchants in the pre-capitalist era, the development of new conceptions of profitability and their general diffusion through American business schools have raised the general level of criteria of satisfaction in business concerns throughout the Western world.[14]

A social system is based on certain traditional criteria of rationality, such as confidence in promises, rigor in discharging obligations, reciprocity, and a minimum level of speed and efficiency, which one may consider as general constraints. These have been supplemented by increasingly specific criteria corresponding to ever-more-specialized systems and to new forms of rationality—technical, administrative, and financial.

At this point, we turn to a discussion of a second type of constraint which arises from the participation of decision-makers in systems of action. It is possible to identify two influences here. One corresponds to the criteria just cited and derives from the more specialized rules on which the operation of the system is based. The other arises more directly from the strategy which must be adopted by the players in a game if they wish to win.

The influence of rules is ubiquitous. Every system develops specific rules. There is no group or profession, or, rather, professional system (for several professions usually operate in symbiosis), without fairly constraining rules which specifically restrict the range of choice open to a decision-maker. Many decisions, rational in the abstract, are impossible in practice. Even in large companies or administrative organs, rationalized in theory, even in the most open markets which are not controlled by a small club of insiders, rules of the game (which are also norms of rationality) are established. For example, it is clear that the criteria of satisfaction employed by a comptroller in the Finance Ministry or an inspector in the Department of Bridges and Highways will be profoundly influenced by the informal norms that develop within their respective organizations. A similar example is provided by the franchised dealers for major makes of automobiles, whose criteria are quite different from those of wholesalers of perishable goods.[15]

The strategy necessitated by the game, however, also exerts an influence which is widely ignored, even though it is perhaps the more important of the two. This, of course, is where organizational analysis can help put our thinking about decision on a new footing. If we may refer once more to the caricatural example of the Industrial Monopoly, it is clear that, within the limits established by general criteria of technical and fiscal rationality, and the still more general norms of civilized behavior, the criteria of satisfaction are influenced primarily by the necessity to choose from among a small range of possible strategies in order to maintain power—as in the case of the maintenance worker, for instance. With knowledge of these criteria of satisfaction, it becomes possible to predict what choices the decision-maker will make. Certain technically rational solutions are eliminated *a priori*, as are certain organizational solutions. Still others are acceptable. The maintenance worker in the Monopoly will not, of course, go about calculating the costs and benefits of each possibility from the standpoint of maximizing his power; it is no more possible to find an optimum solution here than it was from the standpoint of abstract rationality. Yet the worker will reject every solution that does not satisfy his minimum criterion: to safeguard his influence in the system. The solution he will accept will be the first that appears to offer a reasonable hope of satisfaction and also meets his other criteria.

This caricature is not so far removed from reality in many cases where the pressure of highly constraining games is so strong that it becomes impossible to introduce new or tighter criteria of profitability, for instance. In a good many cases, the complexity of the strategies obscures the theoretical rationality, and to increase the rationality of the system it must first of all be restructured. Rational calculations may lead to such a step but will not contribute a great deal to the actual process.

If the decision-maker is basically oriented toward maximizing his profit, it is conceivable that one might find a relationship between the *a posteriori* rationality emerging from the mutual adjustment of the parties in the system and the *a priori* rationality of each decision-maker. There is an over-all coherence in this situation which is rather difficult to apprehend in a comprehensive way. It is possible, however, to understand elements of the interrelationships involved. In this case, an indirect social control is exercised by the fact that it is possible to measure achieved results against fundamental values. Many decision-makers will feverishly attempt to improve this type of result because they know that success will bring considerable rewards. Yet improvement can certainly not be obtained by the free play of mutual adjustment, which supposedly leads to the best, most "natural" rational solution. It can only be obtained by constant efforts to construct and/or restructure systems of action. That these efforts are mostly ill-conceived and based on false premises does not prevent them from being made or from bringing results.

Here again we encounter the problem of learning. Cost-benefit analysis can be of little use, since it is through experience that the decision-maker learns what was possible and what he had been seeking without really being aware of it. If he were capable of using an adequate, concrete theory of collective learning to guide change, he would certainly be able to improve his ability to make choices. We shall return to this problem in the last part of this book.

11

Two Empirical Analyses
of Decisional Sequences

To understand the practical relevance of the theoretical models we have just examined, we are now going to compare them with concrete cases of decision-making, which have been analyzed in sufficient depth to provide us with the data we need for a serious discussion. To this end, we have chosen two examples of decisional sequences studied by American political scientists.[1]

The Cuban Missile Case

The case of the Cuban Missiles is quite a spectacular one, since it involved a major confrontation—perhaps *the* major confrontation since the Korean War—between the two superpowers, with a real risk of war. It was, moreover, a brief crisis which was unambiguously resolved, concerning which abundant sources, from the American point of view, are available. Finally, there is perhaps no better example of the successful implementation of a well-prepared decision. Thus for its analyst, Graham Allison, conditions were particularly favorable for testing the various theories under discussion.

At this point, it may be useful to remind the reader briefly of the facts of the case. After the American disaster at the Bay of Pigs, the Russians decided to press their advantages by installing missiles on Cuban soil. The Americans belatedly discovered the full scope of the operation. The executive committee of the National Security Council met in emergency session, and, at the conclusion of its deliberations, President Kennedy ordered the naval blockade of Cuba. In the resulting test of strength, Khrushchev was forced to yield and hurriedly withdrew his missiles.

At first sight, Kennedy's decision appears to be a model of rational decision-making, and this is one of the main reasons for studying it. A crucial and urgent problem was studied without passion or haste. A large number of possible solutions were envisaged, and their costs and benefits were compared and openly debated with the maximum use of available information. The final choice was the one that combined the greatest number of benefits and the smallest cost, and the correctness of the choice was clearly demonstrable since the immediate application of the decision taken gave exactly the result hoped for.

Unfortunately, this idyllic view is not in the least confirmed by the analysis, which did not prevent the optimistic version of events from playing a role in the American rationalist euphoria of the early sixties, as well as in the establishment of a new psychological balance of power between America and the USSR.[2] It is true that a number of possible solutions were subjected to reasonably thorough scrutiny, but this number hardly included all of the options, and, what is more, errors in the available information had a profound impact on the ultimate choice. Above all, the deliberations were much more a complex political process than a rational calculation. The execution of the decision, finally, despite the importance of the stakes, only very imperfectly reflected the directives issued by the president.

If, then, we are able to show that, even in so favorable a case (where, of course, the maximum number of resources had been assembled to insure the rationality of the decision) the rational model certainly did not apply; and that, to account for the choice, a model like that of bounded rationality is much more enlightening, then we will have made as powerful a case as we can hope for in favor of our thesis.

The Various Solutions Envisaged

Seven solutions were discussed:

Doing nothing. This prudent solution was seriously considered, but the installations identified were too sizable. They would have increased the Russian nuclear striking force by fifty percent. This would have had a considerable military significance, but no less important was the fact that the political and psychological consequences were difficult to calculate and might have proved disastrous.

A diplomatic offensive. This solution was favored by several members of the executive committee. It offered no risks, put the United States in a favorable posture, and might result in a diplomatic defeat of the Russians. But it contained several major drawbacks, which were essentially due to the fact that the implantation of the missiles was discovered too late. The diplomatic solution involved delays which would have been much too long. The Russians would have had the opportunity to make use of their veto power, and, meanwhile, the balance of power would have been changed definitively.

Negotiation with Castro. This solution, attractive because the United States was in a sufficiently strong position, appeared completely unrealistic upon analysis, for Castro seemed totally to have lost control of the operation. Only the Russians could be dealt with.

Exchange of Soviet installations in Cuba for American installations in Italy and Turkey. Theoretically, this solution was quite advantageous, since it was a diplomatic solution without risks. Moreover, the benefit sought—elimination of the Russian military threat—could have been obtained at very low military cost: the withdrawal of these missiles had long since been accepted as a viable option, since the secretary of defense had shown that nuclear submarines in the Mediterranean were much more effective and less visible than the missiles. On the other hand, this solution involved a high diplomatic cost, for it would have dangerously weakened the credibility of American commitments in Europe. It would have appeared that the United States had agreed to sacrifice the security of its European allies in order to eliminate the threat to itself. It was therefore attractive but very controversial.

Invasion. This was of course the solution favored by the hawks. The Russians' aggressive intentions having been demonstrated, and Castro's total lack of independence from them having been made obvious, it would have afforded an excellent opportunity to get rid of this extremely irritating problem once and for all. There were, however, 200,000 Soviets in Cuba who would certainly have been involved in the battle. The risk of war, or, at the very least, of violent countermoves in Berlin and Turkey, was considerable. This was therefore a very dangerous solution.

A precision air strike. This solution was very attractive, because it was immediate and radical but at the same time limited and specific. There would have been no interference in Cuba's internal affairs. Only non-Cuban military installations of a proven offensive character would have been targeted. The risk was certainly considerable, but the United States found itself in a sufficiently favorable moral situation. The essential problem was one of the surgical precision of the air strike. Could it be done in such a way that it would not appear to be a massive attack against Cuba? Could loss of Russian lives be limited sufficiently? The military experts did not think that a genuinely "surgical" strike was possible. They favored a massive attack as the only entirely sure bet.

Naval blockade. This, too, presented numerous drawbacks. It was quite as illegal as the air strike, and less effective. The delay was longer. There was risk of confrontation between Soviet and American ships. But it did offer benefits: it left Khrushchev time to think, since it did not have the finality of certain other solutions. It put the ball in the other court, leaving the Russians the initiative of entering into direct combat if that was what they were bent on. It spared them the deep humiliation of allowing Soviet soliders to be killed without reacting. All things considered, it was therefore the most acceptable solution, once the global objective had been defined: how to compel the Russians to withdraw their missiles without bringing on world war.

The Flaws in the Rational Model

The subsequent analysis of the costs and benefits of the various solutions envisaged gives the impression that the classical rational model best describes the process. It was really the optimum solution, selected after research into all the possible alternatives and calculation of their outcomes. If, however, we extend the discussion to the actual decision-making process and its implications, we find a good many flaws in the standard interpretation.

In the first place, the process by which solutions were sought was not one of optimization; it was in fact a procedure similar to what Simon describes. The first solution which satisfied the president's minimum criteria was the one chosen. The naval-blockade solution was in fact not put forward until late in the deliberations. When all other solutions had been eliminated because they did not meet the criteria, the search was resumed, and it was then that the naval-blockade solution was hit upon.

The solutions actually advanced were not abstract inventions of the group of decision-makers, but rather programs previously elaborated in the context of comprehensive planning by the various administrative organs involved. The range of possible solutions was therefore a relatively limited one, and each option was itself structured in advance, depending on the capacities and objectives of the organization that elaborated it. The decision-maker's range of choice was thus restricted by the very rigid structure imparted to it by the characteristics of the systems of action which were responsible for elaborating and implementing the decision. Since it was generally the same organization which fulfilled both these functions, it is evident that the routine procedures and constraints prevalent in the executive apparatus were of considerable influence in determining the range of options.[3]

Information, too, had a high degree of structure. Though obviously well-monitored and rigorously controlled in a problem of such importance, it was clearly not unaffected by the procedures of the organizations which produced it. The reason for the elimination of the diplomatic solution was that it was already too late to adopt this course. If the time available was too short, however, this was because the information had not arrived soon enough. If we ask why this was the case, we find that the bureaucratic information-processing procedures inevitably slowed down its preparation in usable form. From the time an agent was first able to identify the profile of a missile to the time the directors of the CIA could obtain a reliable confirmation, thirteen days elapsed. Five more days were needed to declare the western portion of Cuba a suspect zone, and it took two additional days to decide to send a U-2 spy plane on a reconnaissance mission over this zone. Two more days were needed to make the flight and process the photographs that could provide the confirmation needed before action could be taken.

The considerable delay of nearly a month was due to the necessary precautions involved in classifying and verifying intelligence data. Contributing factors included many that were characteristic of the internal policy of intelligence organizations and their troubled relations with the outside world: a variety of internal CIA problems, rivalries between the agency and the air force, unpleasant memories left by the incident when the U-2 was shot down over the Soviet Union, etc. Here again, the organizational problems posed by intelligence handling are not questions of cost but rather problems of systems of action which cannot be avoided by merely adopting rational procedures. Finally, to forestall critiques of bureaucratic confusion, it should be noted that, although the division of responsibilities among a variety of services and agencies is one cause of delay and sluggishness, this is the price which must be paid in order to maintain an open system which does not imprison the president. Having only one intelligence agency, like one police force, may simplify operations but presents both a political risk—the power of the agency becomes too great—and a professional risk—its information becomes less reliable.

It is furthermore untrue that the point of view of the specialists is neutral. A crucial point in the deliberations was whether or not a "clean" operation, a limited (surgical) air strike, was possible. The negative opinion of the military experts was given at the moment the president appeared to be leaning toward this option.[4] Subsequent studies have demonstrated, however, that this opinion was completely erroneous. The experts' fears were exaggerated. Why was such an opinion given? Essentially because the air force preferred the massive strike that it had carefully studied and prepared. This was the action for which it was ready. No other option had been studied by its experts, and they were prejudiced against the one ultimately suggested to them.

Thus the range of choice of the decision-makers is inevitably limited by the support services which they cannot do without, but whose prisoners they become. These supporting agencies bias the available information and determine the range of possible options. It is therefore impossible to understand the deliberations, much less the ultimate choice, solely as the outcome of a rational calculation; a political game is also involved, through which contradictory pressures are integrated. It will be useful to have another look at the behavior of the air force in this case. Had they favored a surgical strike, they would have "won." Their declaration that such a strike was impossible was due in part to a question of technical preparedness, but also to considerations of political strategy. At that particular juncture in the deliberations, they were so certain of winning that they took the risk of locking themselves into the "hardest" position by declaring all the intermediate positions technically impossible.[5] But they had made a poor diagnosis of the nature of the game in which they were operating: this game was more open that they thought in terms of the feasible range of options, and much tighter than they thought in terms of those that were really applicable. Because they wanted to win too much, they ultimately lost everything. The result, in any case, seems to have been determined as much by the quality of the prior analysis of the nature of the game as by the skill of the participants in playing it.

One additional vicissitude of the politics of the deliberative process was equally significant, if less decisive. Though apparently quite committed already to the naval blockade, the president wanted in any case to maintain a degree of neutrality and thought he had to appease the hawks. So he put forward the solution favored by Stevenson, the exchange of bases. The hawks were quite vehement in their criticism of this option. Kennedy rallied to their side and gave them a symbolic victory, which subsequently made it possible to paint the solution he favored as a middle-of-the-road course. The hawks' ability to keep up a strong opposition had been weakened, because they had, in a sense, exhausted their arguments in the struggle against the Stevenson solution.

Graham Allison's Interpretations

Graham Allison examines three different interpretations of the facts in question: the rational interpretation, which approximately corresponds to our exposé of the costs and benefits of the various solutions; the organizational interpretation, which shows how these solutions were determined by the characteristics of the organizations which produced them; and the political interpretation, which explains how the "political" operators negotiated over what option to choose. For Allison, each of these interpretations is valid, but corresponds to a different level of reality, especially in the case of the last two. The president and the other major figures were involved in a political game, whereas the lower echelons were caught up in bureaucratic machinery.

Allison presents his views in a very suggestive and convincing manner, reminiscent of the narrative technique that made the Japanese film *Rashomon* such a success.[6] In our view, however, his work has several drawbacks. First, too sharp a distinction is made between organizational and political constraints; the actual situation is not very well described by the separate treatment of organizational and political games, each of which is supposed to take place on a different level. In fact, there is always some degree of intermixing. Though politics may play a more significant role at the top, this does not mean that the difference is qualitative. The president is obliged to respect the rules of the system of action in which he operates, even if he has put it together himself. There was no qualitative difference between this system of action and, say, the Defense Department (regarded as a system). Last, but not least in importance, is the fact that Allison's presentation, in separating the three modes of argument,[7] conceals the relationship among them and hence the actual role played by the rational model and organizational constraints.

The Sociological Contribution

Based on Simon's concepts, we have put forward a sociological model which leads to a rather similar interpretation. It is structured quite differently, however.

1. Each player sufficiently independent to warrant analysis of his behavior will behave in a way consistent with a model of bounded rationality. In other words, he will formulate and accept options on the basis of a rationality determined by his personal criteria of satisfaction. These criteria depend on the norms he observes (both general norms and more special ones determined by his group environment) and on game conditions.

2. His success, in terms of influence over the final decision, depends on his margin of liberty within the organization and on his correct judgment of the nature of the central game.

3. The principal actor, in this case the president, can exert a great influence on the nature and rules of the games. He is capable of imposing his own criteria of satisfaction as a model of rationality. It is not within the president's power, however, to choose the optimum solution. But he can organize the game in such a way that there will surely be sufficient number of alternative options to insure that at least one of them will meet his criteria of satisfaction. In establishing these criteria, he is making a more or less conscious choice of a mode of rationality. This choice is inseparable from the problems he faces. Kennedy, for example, found that he faced the simultaneous constraints of an electoral campaign, which required an extremely firm attitude (given his public commitments, based on his confidence in Khrushchev's good faith), of the necessity to avoid taking too dangerous a chance, given the risk of war, and of the nature of his personal relationship with Khrushchev. At the same time, he was nonetheless the most willing of all the players to accept a broader definition of a rational method. Such concepts as progressive retaliation or the strategy of détente did not fail to play a role in the empirical process of defining his criteria of rationality. It should be noted that these concepts were themselves shaped by experiences in crises similar to the one we are analyzing. The choice of the naval blockade accorded rather well with the new theories of progressive retaliation and communication. Its success gave these theories a new vitality.

4. It is never sufficient to define criteria of rationality even in a rigorous

way, and there are risks in doing so. The system must still be able to generate acceptable options within the criteria determined by any given mode of rationality. If one hopes to improve the quality of decision-making, it is not enough to develop new concepts and techniques. The primary necessity is to transform the system's bureaucratic pattern of operation—what Allison calls the organizational level—along with its broader and more intractable aspects—the political level.

The Case of the Conglomerate

It is particularly interesting to compare the case study of the conglomerate conducted by Joseph L. Bower with the case of the Cuban missile crisis. Unlike the latter, Bower's case involves not a crisis decision but rather a sequence of decisions which, though important, were relatively routine. These were decisions of the sort which must constantly be faced by the management of a large corporation.

Bower studies private concerns operating in highly competitive markets, i.e., he deals with an area in which the logic taught by the American business schools—*their rationality*—has been most concretely and effectively implemented.[8] In theory, this means that there can be no ambiguity about goals, since it is possible to reduce all indexes of results to one single measure—profit, the yardstick of success.

Conditions are thus presumably ideal for the rational model. Yet the model does not seem to describe very well what happens in practice, even if, from the standpoint of classical theory, the degree of rationality is relatively high. What is more, it is possible to draw conclusions from this study which are surprisingly similar to those drawn from Allison's.[9]

Bower's point of departure was the planning system used by the firm in question. This was an extremely well-developed system quite earnestly used by corporate management, which put a good deal of time and effort into the project. Plans and goals were coordinated through a participative process involving personnel at all levels. All were allowed to express their opinions. In return, all were expected to make themselves aware of their relationship to the over-all picture, which was supposed to insure that the firm's general interest would take precedence over particular interests; so ran the argument, at least. Thus planning was designed to facilitate the maximum possible circulation of information and to put top management in a position to identify the optimal solutions and facilitate their execution.

To everyone's surprise, however, the study of the plan's impact on actual decisions showed that in practice the plan had no influence on the choice of investments.[10]

How, then, were decisions made? Joseph Bower limited his study to the influence of the three highest echelons of management. The first was known as the *corporate* echelon: this consisted of management staff detached from corporate headquarters and assigned to general management roles without operational responsibility. Second was the intermediate or *divisional* echelon, which corresponded to a grouping of subsidiary companies on the basis of a similarity in technology or markets. Finally, the operational level, there was the *product-market* echelon, which consisted of management units integrated around a product or series of products sold on a sufficiently unified market. According to the planning model, and, more generally, the rational model, it was the corporate echelon which set general objectives on the basis of information received from the subunits. Then each subunit could set its own objectives by applying more detailed suboptimization procedures.

It turned out, however, that decisions were in fact made by managers on the product-market level. Their procedure was to use an economic calculation which was strongly influenced by the necessity to arbitrate among various associated groups, all of which were seeking to maintain or increase their influence.

The influence of the divisional echelon was exercised on the "organizational" level, in defining personnel policy. This affected the career prospects of the higher-level managers and consequently encouraged them to make decisions which they believed would fit in with the wishes of divisional-level management.

What remained then for the corporate echelon, which is often thought of as consisting of superpowerful individuals? Its role was to establish the rules of the game by structuring and restructuring the complex collection of companies. It also established the criteria of rationality which the operational decision-makers were then required to internalize, since it was on this basis that their efficiency would be judged.

Strategic analysis interprets these functions as follows. The corporate level wields the weapon of total dissausion, by controlling the survival of the organization. This weapon is hard to use, even if its power is subdivided by the creation of distinct subunits, which makes its use more manageable. In the operational sense, however, it is more feasible to intervene by controlling the criteria of rationality. This does not mean that the corporate echelon makes decisions in place of its subordinate managers. But it can exert power by raising or lowering some minimum standard of performance or by changing the rate of return used in calculating the profitability of investments. It is by suspending over their managers this Sword of Damocles—in the form of sanctions against "bad management"—that American business leaders succeed in imposing a much more rigorous and rational policy than their European counterparts are able to do.

If we compare this model, for instance, with common practice in a large

French industrial group, we find that the leaders in the French case are involved in a great many operational decisions. This seemingly makes them much more powerful, since they exert a more direct control over a chain of subordinates. Besides being less liberal, this practice also has other serious drawbacks. Since they take part themselves in the decisions made, it is less easy for the leaders to dissociate themselves from the consequences. Nor can they impose overly rigorous criteria of judgment, for this would expose them to the risk of failing to meet these criteria themselves. This means that the subordinate managers are more hampered in taking initiatives. In return, they are much better protected than their American counterparts. Their affairs may be interfered with, but they can in turn interfere in the affairs of others. The more top management has a hold on them, the more they have a hold on top management.

A few remarks by way of conclusion:

First, the similarities between the two examples are quite striking, in spite of the differences between the institutions, the problems, and the mechanisms of decision. The analysis of the conglomerate disclosed a system which was held in equilibrium in a way totally different from what might have been expected:[11] at the grass-roots operational level, the most important political act, it seems, was decision-making initiative; in the intermediate echelon, it was management of men and organization of the game; in the upper echelon, elaboration of criteria of rationality. President Kennedy's system of decision-making in Cuban missile crisis was less clearly delineated, of course. It is nevertheless quite clear that Kennedy derived his influence from his ability to define the criteria which had to be satisfied by the ultimate decision. His role, in other words, was not to order a certain action, but to impose criteria of rationality corresponding to his estimate of the actual constraints. In the lower echelons, these distinctions are somewhat blurred, since on this level initiatives are only proposals for action. Still, as we have seen, the political and the organizational are fundamentally intertwined.

In this respect, the example of the missile crisis allows us to put matters in perspective. It is not true that there is one mode of argument or explanation corresponding to each level. Clearly, the leaders of the conglomerate are involved in politics when they modify the dominant mode of rationality, just as President Kennedy was when he defined his criteria of satisfaction. The system of action constrains all the actors. They have no choice but to manipulate the system by working with the organizational realities.[12] It is also clear that we find in the conglomerate as well the same sorts of interrelationships between the political and the organizational that we have pointed out in Allison's example, despite Allison's own interpretation. The difference comes not from the separation of hierarchical levels within a system of action, but rather from control of particular sources of uncertainty at each level. What the two systems have in common is a largely analogous empirical distribution pattern of control and sources of influence.

Our second remark is that the model we have borrowed from Herbert Simon has not only been useful in interpreting two decision-making systems, but also has normative consequences, which we have already pointed out in demonstrating that a system may be governed by manipulating its internal criteria of rationality. President Kennedy and the leaders of the conglomerate understood this intuitively and used this device as their primary source of influence.

There is a lesson to be learned from these two examples which may be put to use in order to interpret certain aspects of everyday experience. Many of the battles in which the leaders and high-level staff of an organization become involved are the results of attempts by an actor to structure the range of options open to the other actors in the system. His purpose in doing this is to influence their criteria of satisfaction in such a way as to make his own wishes a factor in their decisions. In both the conglomerate's institutional pattern and Kennedy's informal group of decision-makers, there was a conscious intention to structure these battles so as to permit the highest echelon to identify and assert its responsibility.

A third and final remark is that both the patterns we have looked at represent interesting compromises aimed at resolving the contradiction alluded to above between *a priori* and *a posteriori* rationality. It is possible to interpret our two examples as reflecting the dominance of an *a posteriori* rationality, since all proposals for action originate at the grass-roots level, and it is the play of the market and the mutual adjustment that takes place which order the final result. It is equally possible, however, to assert that an *a priori* rationality dominates, since the definition of the "law of the market" and the mechanism of mutual adjustment which will prevail is *decided a priori* by the leaders of the organization. This definition may be sufficiently precise to control the criteria of satisfaction which the actors will internalize, and hence to set limits on the range of possible actions.

12

Decision as Change and as Systems Phenomenon

Now that we have put Simon's model of bounded rationality to the test in two examples, we would like to go on to explore its sociological implications by showing how organizations and systems fashion the criteria of rationality used by the decision-makers. Since sociologists and decision theorists have yet to identify what ideas they share, we shall try in particular to formulate basic problems and suggest the most promising directions for research within this new paradigm.

The System Constituted by the Decision-Makers

The executive committee of the National Security Council, which made the decision on the Cuban missiles, may be regarded as a system. Indeed, several of Allison's remarks reveal interrelationships among the members sufficiently stable to be thought of as a game with constraining rules, which had a strong influence on the outcome. It is clear, for instance, that this outcome would not have been the same if the president or the chairman of the Joint Chiefs of Staff had engaged in separate dialogues with each member of the group concerning his particular area of expertise. One aspect of this problem relates to social psychology and group dynamics, and we shall not examine this here.[1] But there is also a sociological question involved. Not only do interpersonal relationships among the members of the decision-making group enter into the problem; the political and systems phenomenon which these relations represent is important as well. The influence of each member is only partially determined by his personal qualities. It also depends on his possession of certain resources which are his by virtue of his relation to the system, and on his capacity to use them.

How is the group's decision influenced by its composition, size, open or closed character, and relations with the complex system with which it deals?

Catherine Grémion has brought out the importance of these questions in a most intensive study of a case relating to an important administrative reform. The decisions she has studied were connected with the drafting of the decrees of March 1964, concerning the organization of the *départements* and *régions* in France.[2]

In appearance, the problem facing the decision-makers was relatively simple. It was a question of reforming and rationalizing the French internal administration, which had become (and has remained) so cumbersome and complex that action, in the opinion of all experts, is paralyzed. Each ministry and agency conducted its affairs on the local level through its own subordinate bodies and according to its own criteria and objectives. Theoretically, it is the prefect who provides the necessary coordination and imposes respect for the public interest on the various feudal strongholds. In practice, however, his efforts consumed vast amounts of energy, relied on indirect means of pressure, and inevitably failed to accelerate the decision-making process.

At the top (which ultimately meant at the level of the president of the Republic, at that time General de Gaulle), the criteria of satisfaction lacked specificity. What was ostensibly desired was the most profound possible reform, modernizing and rationalizing to the utmost; but the political sphere was not to be tampered with. Two interdependent avenues of reform were suggested: (a) decentralize decision-making in favor of the prefect; and (b) restore the prefect's power over the *départemental* directors representing the central administrative agencies.

With this end in mind, an informal decision-making group was set up, with a series of committees assigned the task of investigating these problems and reporting the results to the government. This group was to assume responsibility for the reform. We may regard it as a system. For two years, it debated the reforms and negotiated their provisions with the interested parties in detail.

What characteristics did this system have? Because it included representatives of a good many authorities and decision-makers who would be affected by the ultimate reform, it was *open;* at the same time, it was *closed* to politicians and representatives of the individuals and organizations under its administrative jurisdiction. It consisted exclusively of civil servants. No national political figure, no local political representative, no delegate from the various constituencies of the administrative bodies was admitted to the panel or even heard in its deliberations. It was, therefore, a system whose members were quite splendidly representative of the status quo—or perhaps it would be better to say, representative of the administrative apparatus in charge of this status quo. Such a system offered the advantage of embodying a very high level of technical competence. It may even have been thought that its deliberations would facilitate implementation of the reform, since all the officials responsible for this would have been heard and would thus—it may have been hoped— have been more deeply committed to the outcome.

In fact, we find when we analyze how the system operated and developed that in time the objectives of the reform were progressively diluted in the complexity of technical decisions. The system, it seems, used its mastery of technique to protect itself against both interference from the summit and pressure from the base. Only information derived from the administrative apparatus was used in the system's deliberations. As comprehensive and pertinent as such information may have been, it was interpreted according to a rational framework determined by each segment of that apparatus. Thus we find reproduced in the decision-making system the very same obstructions which were the cause for complaint in the first place. There was an instinctive denial of the political and practical significance of reform.

Thus the scope of the reform was limited in a way which actually ran counter to the objectives outlined by the summit. These objectives, as we mentioned above, were unspecific. In particular, practical hindsight revealed that the criteria of satisfaction embodied in them were contradictory. On the one hand, a thorough reform was desired. On the other, the existing administrative framework was to be preserved. The system was so constituted that it was quite well-equipped to meet the second criterion, which corresponded to the common interest of the various organizations represented. But it was scarcely capable of finding an acceptable way to rationalize administrative processes.

It should be noted that we find here another characteristic of the system quite typical of the highest levels of the French administrative apparatus. It included, along with representatives of the various "feudal baronies," members of the several "*Grands Corps.*" The latter, of course, have connections with the different baronies, but nevertheless enjoy a relative independence. Traditionally, members of these corps have been involved in change and synthesis. They have been capable of finding "technical" compromises, i.e., solutions which would not require recourse to the political sphere for arbitration between the contradictory requirements of different agencies. Their presence in the system prevented a complete stalemate, which would have brought failure into the open.

In spite of all this, there were relatively sharp debates in which quite different conceptions of administration opposed one another. Splits appeared, and it might have been thought that open conflict was imminent. In the end, however, the closed structure of the system was to prove strong enough to contain these differences.[3]

Catherine Grémion also studied the parallel decision which related to the problem of organizing the *régions*.[4] This decision, allowing for its limitations, was a good deal more innovative in its consequences. It was drafted in a far shorter period (six months) by a decision-making system which was partially identical with that involved in the *départements,* but which had a structure flexible enough to make room, in particular, for political officials.

With this second example, it becomes possible to conduct a sort of check on the results in the previous case. It should be noted that though the objectives of both reforms were similar, that of the latter examples was more ambiguous and seemed to make progress just as the other marked time. It attempted to break new ground in areas where technical habits and notions of rationality were not already entrenched.

Nevertheless, the decision was still administrative, and the legislature was never involved. Politicians were brought into the process, however, and the high-level civil servants who dominated the group did not fail to consider the political consequences of their decisions. It was natural that there should be an appeal to the summit for the needed arbitration. Certain administrative categories (called at the time the "active forces") had to be negotiated with, because their participation was necessary. Behind these mechanisms and the formal structure of committees, we can make out a small group within the larger group of decision-makers. This former group was a coherent alliance of active reformers. Ultimately, it would take charge of the reform, draft the final compromise, and see it through to adoption by lining up support from both the top echelon and the organized forces which wielded sufficient political clout.

There is nothing to prevent one from speculating as to the wishes of the politicians involved—in this case, General de Gaulle in particular; it is possible, if one chooses, to attribute the outcome of the reform effort to his genuine intentions. We find such an interpretation in this case rather inconsequential. All things considered, the formal and informal structure of the decision-making system and reform group had more influence on the outcome than the general's intentions, which, in any event, this group represented rather poorly.[5]

Though the general, as chief executive, was in theory free to do as he pleased, he did not think it was wise to put together a decision-making system which would not be representative of high-level civil servants, for whom he had great respect. In the abstract, there was nothing to prevent him from creating such a system, but the political cost would have been high. His natural inclination was to follow custom. It is conceivable that this tendency was reinforced by a lack of sensitivity to the problem's importance and an insufficient appreciation of the consequences of the choices he was making. His criteria of satisfaction were, of course, conditioned by his personal conception of the state, which depended on cultural tradition, certain preferences in the style and manner of exercising power, an idiosyncratic notion of human relationships, and a particular mode of reasoning. On each of these levels, we find, with the aid of our analysis, how powerfully influential the central paradigm derived from organizational analysis is in practice: man is prisoner of the organization, without which he cannot act. Yet, the organization itself has a great inertia, which man cannot control insofar as its causes elude his understanding and respect.

The Relationship between the Decision-Makers' System and the System Affected by Their Decisions

It is of course quite difficult to distinguish the problem of the group of decision-makers, regarded as a system, from the problem of the larger system inside which it operates. The reform group's characteristics are influenced by the constraints of the system its members are attempting to reform (which may be wholly or partially identical with the system to which the reformers belong). These characteristics are also determined by the gambles made by the reformers in trying to achieve their goals. What emerged from our study of the preparation of *départemental* and *régional* reforms in 1964 was that the constitution of the "decision-making system" is an important, though largely unconscious, element of the reform strategy. If we hope to gain a better understanding of this strategy and clarify the significance of this choice of a system, it is important that we consider the structures, regulations, and problems of the systems which the reform aims to transform.

With the aid of two recent research efforts, we can assemble enough data to make a comparative study possible, in order to accomplish this task in somewhat more concrete form. The two cases we have in mind relate to two different reforms in rather similar areas: the 1959 hospital reform in France, which was also a reform of medical education and indirectly of the whole medical profession;[6] and the reform of mental-health institutions and legislation in California in 1967, which was also a reform of the related medical and paramedical professions.[7]

At stake in these reforms were not only significant interests but also values, habits, conceptions of the world, and ways of reasoning. Both were set in motion by small groups of determined reformers who had one particular trait in common: they were marginal in the old system, yet had access to what might be considered its "establishment," and they were located at the interstices of several key subsystems. To use Jamous's expression, they were *boundary-spanners*. This similarity is still more significant in that the two systems differ profoundly in other respects. The two groups of decision-makers employed quite disparate strategies, and the systems they formed had very little characteristics.

We will turn first to a discussion of the French case, which involved hospitals and universities. The system in question was complex and immense, but very highly structured, quite coherent, and remarkably isolated both from the society it was designed to serve and from the public authorities responsible for regulating it and, at least indirectly, financing it. It was thus a system protected from both its clients and the legislature. It was dominated by a relatively strict hierarchy in the hospitals, whose legitimacy the public authorities assured by means of competitive examinations for hospital posts. Though poorly paid, those who occupied them enjoyed status and prestige, and, more prosaically, they were insured a large income from private clientele and decisive influence in the informal organization which controlled the medical profession.

This quite stable and protected system had, up until the time of reform, displayed an absolutely remarkable imperviousness to outside pressure. Among other things, it had been capable of absorbing the seemingly revolutionary reform of the Social Security laws without change in its structures or system of power. Of course it favored dialogue between doctor and patient, but one in which the doctor remained comfortably in the dominant position.[8] It was a system which protected the whole profession from excessive legislative interference and from politics in general. It also guarded against the chaotic upheaval which might have resulted from a hasty application of scientific discoveries without proper precautions. Such discoveries could ultimately be accepted and implemented competently, but only in a manner in keeping with the structure of the system, and on terms designed to insure its survival.

The mental-health system of the State of California shared some of these characteristics of isolation and protection. It is conceivable, in fact, that these features are inherent in the sort of problems associated with the practice of medicine. The California system was not, however, a coherently structured one. For one thing, its hospitals were managed to a much greater degree than its French counterparts by a relatively aggressive and pervasive administration. Secondly, there was a strong, independent psychiatric profession which benefited from the absence of inexpensive public treatment centers accessible to all. This group was jealous of its independence and quite hostile to a hospital system from which it anticipated no benefits.[9] Between these two camps there was virtually no contact. But the system as a whole was much more subject to political influence than was the French hospital system.

Though different, both systems were severely criticized and exposed to vigorous attack by the reformers.

In the French case, there were an increasing number of complaints about the system's major dysfunctions, whose effects, it seemed, were becoming intensified.

1. Dominated by hospitals modeled on the lines of the clinical tradition,

the system appeared increasingly unsuited to make first rate contributions to modern scientific research, whose outlook was more "fundamentalist."[10] Furthermore, since Social Security had eliminated the old modes of financial regulation, it was likely that cost inflation would force the public authorities to intervene in the affairs of the medical profession.

2. A bastion of stability in a changing world, the hierarchical social system of the profession appeared anachronistic and conservative; it was also becoming increasingly difficult to manage, given the increasing pressure of competition for so coveted a career.

In the American case, the criticism was aimed primarily at the profession's methods and philosophy. There were complaints about the repressive character of the hospital and, more generally, about mental-health legislation. The absence of some form of social assistance was criticized, as was the lack of community commitment, which was said to be the only kind of support that would enable the patient to enter or reenter society and play a useful role. The prohibitive cost of private psychiatry was also deplored.

If we proceed to analyze the two reforms, we find that quite contrasting strategies can be rewarded with similar success, depending precisely on the characteristics of the system to which they are applied.

The strategy of the French reformers was to break with the past, which they did through a long sequence of tactical moves:

1. An action group was formed, consisting of marginal figures who were known to be hostile to the system by reason of their fundamentalism, yet successful enough in competing for recognition to be taken seriously by the traditional "establishment," whose "boundary" they "spanned";

2. This group sought out political support; it established a bridgehead into the reformist circles in the upper reaches of the bureaucracy during the Mendès-France experiment.

3. In view of its relative failure, it then sought and found a spokesman in the person of Professor Robert Debré, one of the most prestigious figures of the medical establishment, whose commitment reflected, beyond his own personal convictions, his freedom vis-à-vis the system; he was one of its chiefs, and his very success afforded him a certain measure of aloofness.

4. It profited, finally, from an exceptionally favorable combination of political circumstances: the arrival of General de Gaulle in power, which put the restored government in a position to intervene actively in the reform effort, and the nomination as prime minister of Robert Debré's son, Michel Debré.

5. The reform, which required full-time work in the hospital, transformed medical education, disrupted the old balance of power in favor of the fundamentalists, and emphasized basic research. It was drafted in

secret and imposed on the various factions with a minimum of discussion and negotiation and without prior public debate.

One is justified in calling this a strategy of rupture, insofar as its conscious aim was to break down with force, if necessary, some of the old system's basic mechanisms, without undue concern for the consequences. In particular, there was little worry about how the reform, once formulated, would be implemented. Underlying this strategy was the argument that the system did not lend itself to evolutionary change. It was assumed that if the various factions were consulted in advance, they would do their utmost to block the reform. It was also widely believed that the existing establishment had such great influence over the political system that it could have turned public debate in its favor.

The break with the past was in fact made successfully, but the actors who had dominated the old system were able to recover some of what they had lost, thanks to the extraordinary difficulties which accompanied the implementation of such sweeping changes. Furthermore, events actually followed a course which differed considerably from what the reformers had intended. Totally unforeseen new dysfunctions emerged. There was an increase in internal tensions within the system, which ultimately led to new explosions.[11]

The American reform group's strategy was quite different. Though it, too, spanned boundaries, the American group was from the beginning far more highly politicized, and its strategy was guided by the constraints of the political context as much as those of the medical and hospital system. It was a pressure-group strategy aimed at mobilizing public opinion in order to put pressure on the legislature and to neutralize the reactions of the powerful professionals, whose unity and credibility were seriously damaged by the public debate.

After eighteen months of legislative battles and negotiations marked by the twists and turns of a very lively public debate, a complex law was passed. In spite of numerous compromises necessitated by the negotiations, this law did succeed in working a basic transformation of the system by which the mentally ill were treated in California. This reform was both legal, changing the patient's juridical status, and institutional, in that community treatment centers were established. The action group's determination, perseverance, and skill were crowned with success, despite the very unfavorable prognosis which had been issued at the outset by specialists in California politics. The new law did, of course, raise a good many problems, but thanks to collaboration with the professionals, the reform got off to a much better start than in France. Many of the practical problems of implementation had been solved in the course of negotiations. The process of change had already begun in the drafting of the reforms. The gap between intention and achievement was smaller than in the French case, and the cumulative results of the reform have been much more positive.

If one compares these two reforms, similar in so many respects, the conclusions one will draw will depend on whether the accent is placed on the cultural differences between France and the United States or, instead, on the particular strategies adopted and their consequences. A third alternative might emphasize the relationship between each of the strategies and the concrete system of action within which it operated.

Perhaps the simplest approach is to compare the consequences of the two strategies. A superficial examination seems to indicate that the greatest differences lie here.

Because the French group adopted a strategy of rupture, it underestimated the difficulties of implementing the reform and forgot that it was attacking a very complex system of action. What is more, it erroneously believed that it could impose a new structure simply because in theory it ought to have been more effective. The Californians, by contrast, had the courage to accept the constraints and risks of legislative and public debate. This meant that they had to reformulate their proposals under continual pressure from the professional community, taking the reactions of public opinion into account. By accepting the risks, they gained invaluable understanding of the problems, which ultimately helped make their reform more effective. They discovered, moreover, that public opinion could be used to pressure the professionals. More generally, they learned to use the weapon of public debate to apply social pressure to the system, which contributed to its evolution.

If we interpret the two cases in this way, we arrive at conclusions analogous to those of Lindblom: a model of negotiation is superior to a model of rupture.

Yet each of the above cases belongs to a particular cultural setting, and the two exhibit marked differences. It should be noted that each of the reform groups shows certain features (in its modes of argument, relations with the institutional apparatus, and response evoked on the part of the institutions) which have frequently been observed and ascribed to cultural differences between France and the United States. To be specific, Americans are supposed to be a pragmatic people given to negotiation, while Frenchmen are held to be dogmatic and given to dramatic breaks with the past.

If each strategy does indeed reflect a cultural model, the preceding conclusion may be relativized: the model of negotiation is superior only in certain cultures.[12] At this point, one is faced with contradictory alternatives. Either one can suggest to the French that they change their cultural model, in the belief that negotiation is without doubt the better strategy.[13] Or, one might counsel the French to adopt a French-style strategy if they hope to succeed in the French context.

Quite clearly, such "advice" is at best banal, absurd, or both. This is because the would-be advisors ignore those facts which are less clear-cut. Wildavsky has demonstrated the utter ineffectiveness of certain American decision-making systems which chose poorly prepared strategies of rupture (for instance, the War on Poverty, which was based on the model of the great union "rupture" during the New Deal); he also shows how certain negotiating mechanisms were totally stalemated (the case studied by Wildavsky and Pressman is a good example of this).[14]

In the French case examined in the preceding section (regionalization reforms), we saw the relative failure of a reform based on a strategy of compromise (albeit without recourse to politics and public opinion). On the other hand, a strategy of compromise and negotiation with appeal to public opinion was recently successful in France in the case of the passage of the law on adult education associated with the name of Jacques Delors.

It is possible even to find a French counterpart for the specific problem attacked by the Californians. We have in mind the administrative reform known as "sectorization," which has some points in common with the organization of the California community treatment centers. The French reform, which was not a legislative act, was unable to associate elected officials with the new institutions or to provide local financing. It nevertheless did lead to substantial change, thanks to the reformers' judicious use of their know-how and their reliance on a certain strain of public opinion.[15]

To avoid making the kinds of mistakes alluded to above, we believe that comparative study must be pressed further. It is important to analyze more closely the relationship between a strategy and the system of which it is a part. If a strategy of rupture is superior, or at least inevitable, this is due not to the cultural context (in any case, not primarily) but to the characteristics of a particular concrete system. If the French reform group chose a strategy of rupture in the case of the medical system, this was because it faced a very large and well-integrated system which exercised as powerful an influence over the political system as does public opinion.[16] Where the French reformers were remiss was in not understanding in time the unavoidable consequences of an otherwise entirely reasonable strategy, and in not having tried to create more open and flexible subunits. Conditioned by the system to which they belonged, they were more concerned with changing the balance of power than with the system's model of regulation.[17]

If, on the other hand, the Californians succeeded in spite of what was actually a rather adventurous strategy, it was because they benefited from a very favorable balance of power which they were able to recognize intuitively. The psychiatric system was poorly integrated and actually polarized in two camps: the public sector of the large hospitals, solid but highly bureaucratized, riven by many antagonistic currents, and weak in relation to the State of California; and the private sector, highly independent but wholly dispersed and without great influence over public opinion. The state legislature enjoyed a much wider margin of liberty in this relatively unstructured situation than had been thought. On the other hand, it was quite vulnerable to the pressure of public opinion. Over a long period of time, this opinion was sensitized by liberal publicity to the anachronism represented by the asylum system.

If one wishes to draw normative conclusions from the foregoing, it should be noted that the important factors are not only the consequences of strategic choice and the compatibility of the strategy with the cultural context, but also the quality of the diagnosis of the situation and the degree to which the potential evolution of the system is accurately predicted. Attention should also be called to the institutional and systemic characteristics which facilitate strategies of negotiation. This may help in determining what kinds of institutional and systemic reforms would usefully contribute to the development and implementation of such strategies.[18]

The Existence of Conflicting Rationalities and the Possibility of Improving the Rationality of Decisions

Decision-makers are constrained by the nature and rules of the decision-making system in which they take part. There is a certain intrinsic structure to the problems they face, and this structure conditions their strategic choices and influences the chance that a given strategy will succeed. The structure in question is not apparent, however, and it is essential that the decision-makers be capable of diagnosing it correctly. The "problems" are only distorted reflections of the requirements of the system affected by the decision. Neither requirements nor problems are objective at this level. It is up to the decision-makers, in fact, to choose—one would like to say invent—the problem(s) they will treat. Once a choice is made, the constraint may be quite strong, but the actors are free at least to choose what set of constraints they wish to accept. The capacities to make a "good diagnosis" and to choose a "good problem" are personal qualities. But these qualities are acquired through an experience and a learning process which are strongly influenced by the culture. They reflect *rationalities of action* whose particular properties structure the field. These properties may be identified with the various microcultures in which the decision-makers and their colleagues and subordinates participate.[19] Other constraints are imposed by the fund of existing methods, intellectual tools, and concepts (which is quite relative), without which it is impossible to make a good diagnosis, choose a good problem, or predict the consequences of a strategic choice.

Once again, it is useful to refer to Herbert Simon's model of bounded rationality. If it is true that man cannot make optimal choices in terms of an absolute rationality because he lacks the means to obtain and reason with the necessary information, then it is easy to understand the following finding, which experience confirms: due to indolence, time pressure, and a knack for capitalizing on experience, in conjunction with conditioned criteria of satisfaction, man will in general define and solve his problems with the aid of preestablished programs which he learns because they are well-known in his microculture. These fashion his criteria of satisfaction. This does not mean that a simple determinism operates on this level, any more than elsewhere. The decision-maker remains free, of course, to invent another program which would offer a better solution; in many microcultures, moreover, this is precisely what he must do in order to establish his independence. Some microcultures are very constraining, whereas others are relatively lax. With this point of view, one may embark on new avenues of research. First, the facts must be established— what is the degree of openness or constraint? Next, one should proceed to analyze the origin of these particular properties, and to ask how they come to be structured in more or less coherent models of rationality. Finally, one may study the evolution and transformation of these systems. In any case, it seems futile to expect to find explanations by means of the (multivariate) techniques of the social sciences. Instead, the universal structures must be investigated. There is no other way to understand what is certainly one of the greatest constraints on the content and genesis of decisions.

We are persuaded that organizational and systems analysis can be useful here as elsewhere. Indeed, cultural and systemic data, as we have previously pointed out,[20] are consistent and mutually structure one another. The establishment of models of rationality will structure a problem or field of action. These models are necessarily contingent; they develop through the interaction of the intellectual tools that are available and within the constraints imposed by the structure of these fields, i.e., in conformity with the game requirements imposed on the actors in a system. It would be exciting and, we believe, fruitful to adopt this point of view in explaining the relationship between dominant modes of rationality (i.e., particular structures of rationality corresponding to each microculture, including their analytical schemata, theories, and solutions) and the characteristics of the systems within these modes are used. Ultimately, one would like to be able to relate both of these to the objective results of action (i.e., to the measurements which it is possible to make of these results).

Lacking such research, we must be satisfied for the moment with the empirical knowledge obtained from organizational analysis. Since organizations are particular modes of structuration, organizational analysis yields knowledge of their special brand of rationality. Without prejudging the relative part played by social and cultural, as opposed to organizational, sources in these structures of rationality, this first approximation discloses the logic involved and makes it possible to interpret its influence. It enables us to predict results. In other words, we can evaluate the constraints which limit the decision-makers' options. We can also judge how stable these constraints are.

In a sense, it may be that the most direct contribution which organizational analysis can make at present to pragmatic problems of decision is to set forth a list of conflicting modes of rationality (which become concrete as they are integrated into various organizational games), along with the microcultures which support each of them.

For example, we may consider the problem of public-policy choices in France. To understand such choices, we must analyze the manner in which the problems to which they are intended to respond were defined The process of definition, of course, involves one of the several financial, technical, administrative, and juridical modes of rationality which may be operational in the given area at the moment of policy formulation. Each of these modes is identified with one of the major administrative or technical organs of the government (e.g., Inspectorate of Finance, Bridges and Highways, Mines, Council of State, Prefectoral Corps, etc.). To analyze the actual choices, empirical knowledge of these modes is more fruitful than application of the rational theory of choice. The modes of question depend on administrative structures, and on the relations between administrators and administered that they reflect and crystallize (which explains why they are so difficult to transform).

A good description of these mechanisms was provided by Jean-Claude Thoenig in his book on the *Ponts et Chaussées*.[21] The same phenomenon was studied by Erhard Friedberg in connection with the influence of the Corps of Mines and the Inspectorate of Finance on decisions relative to industrial policy.[22] In work on the end of the republican administration, Pierre Grémion explained the opposition between the rationality of the general interest, embodied by the prefect, and the local rationalities, embodied by the mayors.[23] The same problem was then analyzed by Crozier and Thoenig.[24]

In the business world, the existence of such contrasting rationalities may be less apparent, but it is nevertheless a very real phenomenon behind the apparent domination of the rationality of profit. Engineers, sales people, fiscal managers, and research workers all employ quite different modes of rationality. These groups engage in a complex struggle, which may be said to be due to structural causes. As we have shown, this struggle takes the form of highly organized games, but one may also think of these games at representing at conflict of rationalities. A problem's solution depends on how it has been defined. It is almost impossible to predict which solution will be chosen, for this depends on which rationality is applied. In general, the struggles center not so much on costs and benefits but on the definition of the problem, i.e., on the question of which rationality is to apply. The partners are only too well aware that once this definition has been established, the orientation of the eventual decision will already have been tightly structured. This explains why the actors regard it as extremely important that areas of authority be clearly delineated and devote so much energy to the wording of problems. This behavior would otherwise be absurd and incomprehensible.

How can these diverse rationalities be integrated? The difficulty is increased as each becomes more firmly established. Empirical analysis suggests that it is the specific characteristics of the game that will determine which rationality will dominate at each turn. In many cases, existing patterns and structures will bring about accommodation and integration. This explains why structural change is so important. It also explains why such change will be resisted by groups that have established a "monopoly" over a certain field of action or class of problems, thanks to their particular "expertise" and cohesiveness. This means that they will feel directly threatened by any change which risks breaking their monopoly by introducing a new rationality.

We are thus in a position to give a description of the actual field in which decisions are made. This does not mean that we aim to predict the outcome of the class struggle after the fact by adding just the right dose of ideology and false consciousness. Nor do we aim to disguise the uncertainties of rationalism by introducing such human and social variables as functionalist analysis provides. Our intention is rather to determine the precise limits of the ultimate range of options which enter into a decision. We seek to identify the key points of the process by which a structure is given to the problem which the decision in question must "resolve." We also aim to foresee what conflicts will be unavoidable, as well how conciliation and integration can be brought about.

The foregoing discussion allows us to begin reaching some conclusions as to how the rationality of decisions might be improved.

The empirical viewpoint we have adopted may at first sight appear difficult to reconcile with the normative objectives of a science—or an art—of management. We have stated that the rationality of decisions can no longer be measured as a function of an absolute *a priori* or even *a posteriori* rationality. Furthermore, we have explained why we do not think it possible to substitute for one absolute rationality a whole range of possibly conflicting rationalities which would be integrated *a posteriori* in a manner consistent with the respective influence of the groups which represent them. If these two points are accepted, then it is difficult to see how a normative theory can be justified.

Intuitively, however, our feeling is that the rational theory of decisions is extremely useful as long as certain limits are observed. Secondly, analyses such as those we have given should enable the sociologist to contribute a limited but positive knowledge which may be put to normative use.

We have learned from empirical study that an absolute rationality is impossible to achieve, nor may it even be taken as a point of reference. On the other hand, we can show that some solutions (or decisions) are *more rational* than others with respect to a bounded rationality determined by a game with well-defined parameters.

Once again, we believe that one can generalize by transposing Simon's mode of argument: although the idea of the rational in itself is not tenable, it is possible to work according to a relativistic model; although it may not be possible to distinguish the rational from the nonrational, once the problem has been limited, one may argue in terms of the *most rational*. Such a methodology may be shocking. How can we speak of the "most rational" if we do not know what is "rational"? Yet it is this methodology which is in fact in common use, and it is relatively effective. By trial and error, it has led to fairly substantial progress in improving our capacity to formulate and solve problems. Though this methodology is frequently justified by theories of absolute rationality, these are ultimately only generalizations which make dubious extrapolations from successful results obtained in restricted settings. Useful as such theories may be, they are not necessary.

The advantage of such a mode of argument is that it makes it possible to include problems of organization and systems in rational discussion. No organization or system is rational in itself; there is no such thing as a sick or healthy organization. With a given framework and goal, however, there are systems and organizations which are *more* rational from the point of view of efficiency, adaptability, and potentially—why not?—their particular conception of justice.[25]

Similarly, we may derive normative insights of some consequence, though limited in scope, as to the means for improving the capacity of an organization or system to process information and solve complex problems. Finally, using the systems point of view, it is possible to discuss how a greater range of rationalities might be integrated within a given organization or system. We believe that the justification for this line of argument lies in the fact that organizations and systems actually have improved and are improving, albeit with some reverses and regressions, their capacities to make more rational decisions, and they are doing so in spite of their many and repeated errors, thus challenging the psychoses of panic and pessimism with which society at times seem to be afflicted.

Can analysis of concrete systems of action shed light on these developments? We believe so, and we are further persuaded that this is a crucial test of the significance of the scientific contribution of systems analysis.

Analysis of decisions is useful for bringing to light the relevant system(s) within a complex entity. Similarly, analysis of concrete systems of action helps make clear what the broader significance of a particular strategy is. It clarifies the problems associated with change, especially those changes in rationality associated with a particular strategy. One of the major weaknesses of most normative theories is that they draw their conclusions directly from analysis of decisions without considering the systems of action involved. Yet is imperative that we improve our understanding of these systems in order to treat decisions associated with change in a scientific way.

We will defer discussion of these problems until the next and last part of this work, which will be devoted to change. To conclude our discussion of decision, however, we would like to make a few observations concerning the problems associated with the introduction and refinement of new rationalities and intellectual tools. Our treatment of these problems, it is hoped, may be among the most important contributions which organizational analysis has to make to normative decision theory.

We have suggested that there is a relationship between (1) a mode of rationality; (2) the strategy of the group(s) which represent it; and (3) the structure, system of power, and mode of regulation within the encompassing organization or system. To understand how a new rationality can come into being, develop, and win success, it is important to comprehend this relationship. If a new intellectual tool is to be applied and bring with it a new mode of reasoning—i.e., a new rationality—it must find a group to represent it, and the encompassing system must be transformed in order to accommodate its application. Every new development faces resistance from the established system. Its success will be determined by the degree of openness of the system. Not only can the system hinder the spread of the new rationality, but it may even impede the discovery of new arguments. Once again, we find that the organization may structure the field in such a way as to preclude learning and discovery. Conversely, in the long run, models of human relationships will be greatly influenced by the introduction of new modes of reasoning.

The fundamental problem associated with the development of rationality is how to understand this triple-input relationship, whose mechanisms of feedback and, more generally, cultural and systemic determinants have yet to be studied in detail.[26]

To treat this problem, we believe research should focus on two areas: (1) historical analysis of situations in which substantial change has occurred; and (2) current instances where new intellectual methods and models are being introduced. The significance of the latter will be less clear; it impels us to recognize the uncertainties inherent in the process and to examine the possibility of failure.

It should be possible, moreover, to shed some light on this problem by analyzing others which are closely related but more readily accessible. For example, one might study the problem of transposing models of rationality which have been tested under favorable conditions into new situations which do not seem well adapted to their application. The traditional administrative sectors of health, education, and welfare are currently particularly fruitful areas for research into the effects of the introduction of models of rationality derived from business experience, like the American PPBS or the French RCB. As negative as the results of such experiments may prove in practice, they are extremely fruitful from our point of view. We must look to such situations with an eye to determining how far structures and modes of relation can evolve after the introduction of a new mode of reasoning. The research should examine to what extent discord and tension between old and new forms can exist; when, and by what processes, the new mode of reasoning loses its influence; and what conditions must jointly be present if, on the other hand, it is to succeed in maintaining itself and developing.

There is similar interest in a related type of problem. This is the question of how a new rationality develops from a technical tool which improves the collection and application of information, in particular making it possible to calculate the consequences of various options more precisely. Of course, we are speaking of computers. They embody a potentially new rationality, but in general the implicit possibilities are either not exploited or are exploited poorly. This is because they run up against existing rationalities which defend their entrenched positions with the aid of very rigid structures.[27] The consequence of this is the phenomenon the Americans have called GIGO, *Garbage in, garbage out:* if worthless information is fed into the computer, what comes out will be of no greater value.

New relations must develop among partners if a new technical tool is to respond effectively to the demands placed on it. This requires a change in the system itself—that is, in the games played and in the manner of their regulation.[28] The computer cannot be relied upon to invent solutions or to impose them automatically, nor should management use it in such a way.

A stimulus as well as a problem, a new technical tool can be a valuable instrument. It may, indeed, be fruitful for new tools to pose problems somewhat beyond our capacities to solve them.[29] Ultimately, however, what is necessary is that man learn new practices, and that he learn them collectively, as part of a system.

Five   **Reflections on Change**

13

Change as a Systems Phenomenon

Change as Problem

Most theories of change on which current political and social discourse is based—whether Marxist or liberal—seem to us to be seriously compromised by the confusion they engender between two series of propositions that are not easily reconcilable. On the one hand, we have a set of functionalist propositions which are relatively complex and rigorous, but which are applicable only to conditions of stability. On the other hand, we have a set of dynamic propositions relating to development. While they are more vague, they are much more useful for purposes of polemic and essentially derive their power to persuade from the fact that they seem to be linked to the first set. In truth, however, there is no logical link between them.

It will be useful to examine the reasoning underlying both of these propositions. The first step is to establish the laws of coherence of a given society. This involves a difficult but realizable exercise in functional analysis. Secondly, by extrapolating the tendencies of various key factors in these laws, it is, presumably, possible to show that contradictions will increase (a dubious proposition) and that rupture is inevitable (a proposition which is absolutely unfounded). Finally, a second logical fallacy leads to the conclusion that by a radical transformation of the basic parameter, the system may be reconstructed at a higher stage of development. Once the rupture has made it possible, this reconstruction will follow automatically, since all other parameters will be obliged by the coherence principle to follow the change in the basic parameter.[1]

It is unnecessary to insist on the totally arbitrary and illusory character of this last proposition. It emerges, however, only in perspective, and can be demonstrated by emphasizing the logical linkage of the several propositions. Each of them is undoubtedly interesting and even exciting intellectually. Nevertheless, their combination produces something more akin to rhetoric than to scientific logic. Even if each of the propositions were valid, it would be so only partially and tendentially The probability

211

that these tendencies would coincide in such a way as to yield the final proposition with logical certitude is almost nil.

In the typical philosophical discussion, the determinist and voluntarist positions on change are contrasted in a wholly artificial way. Our view is that this opposition raises a false problem. All explicit theories of change are in fact both voluntarist and determinist. In our schema, sacrificing some of the rigor of the functionalist argument would be enough to change the theory's character from determinism to voluntarism or, if you will, adventurism.[2] If one assumes that the mechanisms analyzed are perfectly coherent and that they comprehensively embody the interaction of all useful social forces (which would seem to be the height of determinism), then the temptation is great, if not irresistible, to act on the key variable[3] of this coherent system. This basic manipulation is of course supposed to lead to systemic change and to transition to a higher, or at least a crucial, stage of evolution.

The voluntarist activist assumes from the outset that the functionalist mechanisms are coherent (and possibly continuous), which enables him to forestall any doubt as to the possibility of achieving the desired change. It bears repeating that for such an activist, determinism requires both rupture (since coherence is indispensable, contradictions will bring this on) and reconstruction (coherence remaining the law of the system, change in the key term will necessarily entail changes in all other terms).[4]

Although the opposition between the two positions appears complete at first glance, the confusion of the problem is such that most writers have adopted both of them successively, if not simultaneously. Determinism is used as a defense against arguments which challenge the difficulties or human costs of a particular strategy, or which attempt to propose possible alternatives. Voluntarism, on the other hand, is used to justify the choice of a particular strategy and to obtain the support needed to put it into practice.

In this respect, Marxists and many liberals seem to face the same problem. There is a curious parallelism between writers like Althusser and Poulantzas and the American liberals who are anathema to them. A theorist as conservative as Skinner draws from his basic behaviorist model of learning[5]—which for him is as rigorous as the capitalist mode of production is for Althusser—the conclusion that this one factor should suffice to transform society completely. He justifies his belief that this is the model of regulation which underpins all societies with a functionalist argument as weak as the argument of the Marxists.[6] Similarly, American economists and political scientists in the fifties thought they had found the source of the *take-off*, the key variable of their system, in mass consumption.[7] Even a functionalist concerned with the problem of values like McClelland went as far as to base all hope for development on manipulation of the "need for achievement" value.

The weakness of all these positions is that they are based on the same generally unconscious refusal to consider change as a problem. Change is supposed to be a consequence of a supraindividual logic, which may be of an economic, ecological, biological, cultural, or moral order. We do not mean to challenge the idea that each of these factors may influence change, and a constraining combination of some of them will certainly be influential. To say, however, that change is a problem for man does not determine his response to that problem, nor, for that matter, does it imply that he will respond in any way at all.

When we say that change should be considered as a sociological problem, we mean that it is men who change, that they do not change passively, and, moreover, that they change in their collectivity and as a collectivity: not individually, but in their relations with one another and in their social organization. Though change may be a response to nonsociological problems, this response is necessarily a sociological innovation and must be studied as such.

All current theories rely on three types of assumptions which are weakened or invalidated by what we know, if not of societies as a whole, at least of organizations and systems of action: these are (1) the postulate of coherence; (2) the postulate of hierarchy; and (3) the postulate of the homogeneity of the social field.

It will be convenient to consider the postulate of coherence first. We said previously that both determinism and voluntarism rely on two postulates of coherence: coherence of organizations and coherence of social mechanisms. The study of systems, however, seems to show that coherence of the organization is always quite relative. While there are always mechanisms of integration, the various subsystems are never coherent over-all. Every system incorporates contradictions, and it is difficult to see how a society or social organization would have fewer of them than a more integrated group. Even a highly integrated organization is never governed by a single principle. If we are correct in this, then it hardly makes sense to argue that the development of contradictions inevitably casts doubt on a system's capacity to survive, since no human system has ever existed without contradiction.[8] If there is a problem, it is perhaps one of determining a certain threshold of contradiction beyond which a system's capacity to effect integration would be called into question, and thus would cast doubt on its ability to maintain itself.

The second postulate, that of the interdependence and stratification of the elements and social mechanisms, poses other problems. One may in fact uncover powerful mechanisms which appear to recur quite frequently; these nevertheless remain approximate laws concerning the developmental tendencies of a system, and are never unambiguous in their application. Their effect is always masked by the existence of other mechanisms with which they are inevitably coupled. Furthermore, there is no empirical basis for the assumption that an implicit or explicit hierarchy exists which would make it possible to demonstrate that the problem incorporates some key variable. What is the point of discussing the priority of values or economics, when experience teaches that every system may be thought of as having multiple inputs, which means that an effect can be obtained by manipulating a variable which is neither the most basic nor the most crucial according to theoretical principles? Nor is one obliged to await change in the most basic variable in order to attack less fundamental ones. With an appropriate strategy for influencing the system, one variable may serve as well as another. If certain approaches are better than others, this is not due to some hypothetical priority among the variables, but rather to certain characteristics of the system and to the availability of certain resources.

There is therefore no reason to believe that merely by touching the right levers one can set a mechanism in motion or cause a system to change course. There is no primary lever. At a given moment, some course of action (and *not* one single course) may be preferable to others. This choice can be made only if the characteristics of the entire system are taken into consideration.

The final postulate, that of the homogeneity of the field, is no less vulnerable than the other two: it is perfectly possible for two contradictory mechanisms to coexist in different sectors or at different levels of a system, as we have shown.[9] Of course, the relationship between such disparate phenomena is not random; adjustment and, if not equilibrium, at least over-all integration are effected through game strategies. There is no reason, however, to assume that an action aimed at one mechanism, even in several sectors and at several levels, will trigger a general rearrangement. A system can accommodate not only inconsistencies, but even symbioses of apparently contradictory mechanisms. If we wish to go further, we must try to understand how different games may coexist, and what substitutes develop for mechanisms that are eliminated or weakened. To this end, organizational and systems analysis is, in our view, irreplaceable. Through such analysis, we may broaden the range of comparison, learn more practical ways to intervene, and understand the ordinary processes of change which are encountered every day. Furthermore, we can learn how to conduct controlled experiments on processes of change.

When change is analyzed as a sociological problem, the questions that arise have a pragmatic character. This pragmatism should not be frightening. It does not eliminate our political and social responsibilities; quite the contrary; it deflates the ideological illusions and rodomontade behind which even scientists love take shelter.

The point is not to gain knowledge which would pinpoint which type of rupture is presumably inevitable as a consequence of the present state of development. We cannot predict the course of evolution or the inevitability of rupture, much less its form.

We can, however, state, and begin to outline a solution to, the following important empirical problem of sociology: under what conditions do tensions which have hitherto served to reinforce the existing system reach a level at which they begin to provoke its disintegration?

Secondly, it is more useful to consider the consequences, rather than the nature, of an eventual rupture. Although we do learn from analysis that real change always presupposes rupture and crisis (we shall return to this point below), crisis by itself is neither a solution to the problem of change nor even the key event from which change would almost magically emerge. Many crises have done no more than trigger adaptive mechanisms; often they have led only to temporary regression. Only in a minority of cases have crises triggered innovative mechanisms. The sociological problem is thus not the avoidance of crises and ruptures or their replacement with gradual evolutionary processes. It is rather to understand how and under what conditions a crisis may bring about innovation rather than regression.

Finally, the very substance of change is also a problem for sociology. It demands a prudent approach, but it must not be avoided.

To identify which changes best correspond to man's aspirations to move to a higher level of perfection and satisfaction, the terms of the discussion must be changed. We have criticized simplistic, mechanistic, overly deterministic and rigid formulas which try to compress a whole economic or social system into a phrase; this does not mean that there are no differences among systems and societies. Nor does it mean that we see no problems in moving from less diverse and abundant systems which find themselves unable to achieve their goals to others which embody the opposite qualities.[10]

What really differentiates these systems, to which, for the moment, we have given very vague attributes? The answer lies neither in the arrangement of the components nor in the basic variable. Isn't it rather the capacity to tolerate a greater diversity, incoherence, and degree of openness? Of course, this implies that there must also be a capacity to manage the inevitable tensions which result from such tolerance. On the systems level, this leads us to consider the problem of systemic or organizational collective capacities and how they develop or, if you prefer, how they are learned.

Thus we are led to ask if the foregoing does not imply that the view which would limit history to a play of special interests is too simplistic. If new capacities had not been developed when a change in the model of rationality was needed, the logic of interests would have always led to an impasse. With a change in the model of rationality, it becomes possible to redefine these interests and to confront the problems they present. New constructs of collective action and new games can then be elaborated in order to treat the new problems.

Change as a Systems Phenomenon

It is wrong to think of change either as an inevitable stage in the logical unfolding of human progress or as the result of the implementation of a model of social organization which is thought to be more rational than some prior model. Nor is it the outcome of power struggles. What it is, in the first place, is the transformation of a system of action.

What this expression means is that for change to occur, a whole system of action must be transformed—i.e., men must put new human relations and new forms of social control into practice. More precisely, it is the games that guide social relations and form the fabric of social institutions, as we have tried to show, which are in question. It is not the rules of these games which must change (as is sometimes hastily assumed) but rather their very nature. The transition from the feudal to the capitalist system[11] was not accomplished by a change in the rules of the feudal game to allow the vassal more freedom relative to his lord or to reverse their roles. It was brought about by the learning of a new, completely different type of game. The capitalist game is not an improvement of the feudal; it is another kind of game. Change may also affect the system of regulation whereby the contradictions inherent in cooperative enterprises are integrated. Finally, the various forms of social control, which both make regulation possible and at the same time complicate its task, must also undergo change.

For such changes to occur, the balance of power must be favorable. Even more important, sufficient capacities must at least potentially be available: e.g., cognitive capacities,[12] relational capacities, models of government.

Thus to define the problem does not necessarily facilitate its solution. We do not possess sufficient analytical knowledge of actual change in the systemic context. Though in many instances we do know the sequence of events, the usefulness of such knowledge is limited, because we are unable to interpret the significance of these events as reflections of development and change. We therefore find ourselves incapable of participating in discussions at the highly sophisticated level of general theoretical debate. On the other hand, we are in a position to make some preliminary contributions, not to a theory of change, but rather to our understanding of the lessons taught by changes which actually do occur in concrete systems.

Thus it is easy to see that the heart of the debate concerns the existence of systems effects, which we took for our point of departure. These effects are inevitable and reveal the nonnatural, artificial character of the games and modes of regulation. Every system of action relies on regulatory mechanisms to impose limitations on the range of acceptable strategies; and hence these affect every initiative for change and directly influence the problem which must be solved.[13] To some extent, they *are* the problem, for the simple reason that their existence implies "dysfunctional" consequences for the organization. In other words, change, like decision, is *systemic*, and depends on the system of action within which strategy is evolved and to which it applies.

To make the foregoing concrete, it will be useful to give a brief analysis of the difficulties usually encountered whenever one tries deliberately to change an organization or organized group. In pragmatic terms, there are two inevitable problems: how to elaborate a program for change, and how to implement it once it has been decided upon.[14]

It is convenient to begin the discussion by looking at the apparently simpler problem of how to implement a fixed program. One usually thinks of the problems encountered in attempting such an implementation in terms of resistance to change. In order to overcome the natural resistance of men whose habits or interests have been disturbed, it is supposed to be necessary to undertake a tireless program of persuasion, training, and education. If necessary, the letter of the reform has to be sacrificed in order to save the spirit. The anachronistic behavior and selfishness of the last holdouts will then be exposed by clever tactics. But this model is utterly inadequate. It takes no account of the way in which organizations and systems of action actually operate, as illustrated by our earlier strategic analyses. In reality, the members of an organization are not passive, routine-bound, or limited by habit. They are fully prepared to make rapid changes if the game proposed to them is in their interest, and if this interest can be demonstrated to them. Habit is of much less importance than is commonly assumed. On the other hand, there is a very reasonable and almost instinctive awareness of the potential risks that change entails.

We believe that we have shown that, even in the humblest context, the decisive factor in determining behavior is the game of power and influence in which the individual participates and through which, despite the constraints, he asserts his existence as a social being. Change is dangerous because it inevitably calls the conditions of an actor's game into question and modifies or eliminates the zones of certainty under his control.

It is therefore of great importance whether or not the participants are partisans of a given reform. They may accept its goals in all sincerity, and yet it would be asking too much, even then, to require them to give up what they must if they are to retain at least partial control over their own actions. Without this minimum capacity, there would even be a danger that they would no longer possess the means necessary to accomplish the task assigned them by the reform. In an unconscious but nonetheless legitimate way, they will obstruct any move that threatens their autonomy and will seek to manipulate the change so that they can maintain or even reinforce the zone of uncertainty under their control. This sort of opposition can easily take on quite serious propositions, since change imposed from above often takes the guise of rationalization, which may give the illusion that these zones of uncertainty are to be reduced or eliminated. In any event, regardless of whether such opposition surfaces, the unconscious actions of participants at a subordinate level are enough to undermine the spirit of a reform completely, even when such action is well-intentioned and aims only to maintain the individual's autonomy.

It is a fact of experience that every human group has an extraordinary capacity to absorb formal change of any kind and still preserve its essential characteristics.[15] This is revealed, and in part explained, by strategic analysis of organizations and systems of action. This capacity is a consequence of the use (even if it is unconscious) of the margin of liberty which each player enjoys in the organizational games, a consequence which is not only legitimate but also inevitable. Thus it is not difficult to see that any approach to the problem based on the usual sorts of argument, according to which reform efforts fail because of lack of information, inertia, routine, special interests—in short, because of the "irrationality" or "alienation" of the subordinates, clients, etc.—will totally fail to achieve its aim.[16]

The above strictures are reinforced by the fact that any program of change is susceptible to a no less vigorous critique from a second point of view. The reader will recall that this relates to the question of how the program in question is elaborated.

We have argued thus far as though neither the rationality nor the quality of a proposed program of change depended on its organizational or systems context. In reality, this context is most important, since, as we saw in the preceding section, the information which is fed into the decision-making process is obtained under conditions established by the organization or system.

As we have previously pointed out, the most serious of the problems associated with the elaboration of a decision is not the cost of seeking information (a factor with which economists too readily content themselves), but rather the impossibility of obtaining unbiased information.[17]

Information is always an important element in the game of power and influence. Its exchange is not neutral. The informational and executive structures, if not actually identical, do overlap considerably. Thus the organized system profoundly influences the orientation of a decision. The system does not determine this orientation, but structures, limits, and constrains it. If reformers opt for a strategy that seeks to evade these constraints, their play may be more courageous but will certainly be less adequate; if, on the other hand, the strategy attempts to use these constraints, it risks decreasing its potential influence.

The dilemma is a practical one. Every administrator, politician, and company manager encounters it when he commits himself to a reform effort. Should he consult the "inside" experts, whose instinct will be to thwart the impulse toward change precisely because they are also the key men in the executive system? Or should he draw up his plans for reform on the basis of an *a priori* analysis and on information obtained from an "outside" source?

In the first case, he will at least in part be adopting the logic of *a posteriori* rationality, relying on the willingness and flexibility of the parties to come up with a course of action which will appear rational after the fact. In the second, his choice favors the synoptic model of a rationality elaborated *a priori*.

There is no reason to examine the synoptic model again; we have discussed its defects at length in connection with Lindblom's theses. But it is worth returning to the logic of the *a posteriori* model, even if this logic is quite clearly applicable to the case of planned change only in a very special sense.

Organizations and organized systems evolve. For one thing, in order to survive, they must adapt to the changing demands of the environment; for another, they must take account of the fact that they are comprised of human beings who also change. One might suppose that a mutual adjustment of groups and individuals which is based on the principle of self-interest would be the best procedure discovering the right solution, the one which would be most pragmatic and equitable as a result of extensive negotiation. We have already criticized this hypothesis in examining Lindblom's arguments. In an organizational setting, the problem is particularly concrete. If the organization were completely transparent, and if its members and the various groups they participate in operated within a perfectly fluid and homogeneous system in which relations of dependence were impossible, then the superiority of incremental logic would be evident. Such is not the case, however. Although it is possible to conceive of more transparent systems, the establishment of a system so transparent that the logic of mutual adjustment would be enough to eliminate inequalities, injustices, and dysfunctions cannot even be dreamed of.[18]

In reality, what we face in the context of concrete systems of action, as we know and even as we might imagine them, is a collection of unequal games, structured around nodes of power related to the control exercised by individuals and groups over key zones of uncertainty important for the satisfactory operation or survival of the whole. In these games mutual adjustment does take place, but the optimal solution that results may be considered rational only with respect to the subsystem operating on the level where it comes into being. It will therefore do no more than reinforce the dysfunctional vicious circles of dependency, noncommunication, and control which every structured organization harbors.

Mutual adjustment among actors thus turns out to be not only a blind process, but above all a profoundly conservative one, which tends to reinforce the equilibrium or disequilibriums implicit in existing power relations. Of course, it is possible that a certain number of adaptations will take place in this setting. A realistic and/or cynical leader might even allow the inequalities and dysfunctions produced by mutual adjustment to be exacerbated to the point where they became plainly visible to all, in order to justify his own intervention. In any case, he cannot rely on mutual adjustment to bring change about. Thus it is inevitable that any initiative he takes which aims at transforming not merely the formal but also the underlying structure of such systems will arouse resistance. Even if a majority of individuals favor such change *qua* individuals, the sum of their games within the framework of the system will constitute a natural obstacle to real reform, which can only be a transformation of the nature of the games played in the system.

It is clear that any approach which reduces planned change to a choice between a synoptic and an incremental logic, or even to a more or less lame compromise between the two, will in reality neglect its primary relationship to the structure of the system and the perverse effects which it induces. With such an approach, there is a great risk that ultimately one will end in an impasse, a pseudo-change, or both. It is therefore impossible to conceive of, and, *a fortiori,* to justify, the implementation of a program of change outside of the particular system to which it would apply, and whose characteristics and mode of regulation would in turn profoundly condition its development. Change is a systems phenomenon, and, like the construct it aims at, it is contingent.

Change as the Learning of New Forms of Collective Action
Change as the Discovery and Acquisition of New Capacities

Thanks to the foregoing discussion, we believe that we have achieved a more realistic, as well as a more collective, view of the nature of directed change. Change is not a question of deciding on a new structure, technique, or method, but rather of beginning a process in which actions and reactions, negotiations, and cooperation are implicit. It is not a matter of implementing the will of one individual, but rather of using the capacities of the various groups associated with a complex system to cooperate in a new way on some common project.

Successful change is therefore not achieved by replacing an old model with a new one conceived in advance by supposedly wise heads. It is the result of a collective process which makes possible the mobilization and even the creation of resources. This leads to the institution of new games. When this takes place under conditions of freedom rather than constraint, it becomes possible for the human, as opposed to machinelike, character of the system to emerge. It should be noted that planned change always has two aspects. It is first of all change of an activity, a function, an operational mode, or a technique directed toward an economic, social, or financial end. Simultaneously, however, it is also a transformation of the characteristics and modes of regulation of a system. In its extreme, it may even involve transformation of the mechanisms of change themselves.

If we redefine the problems of planned change in this way, it becomes possible to bring out a dimension which seems to us fundamental to every process of change, whether planned or "natural": we are speaking of *learning–i.e., the discovery, creation, and acquisition by the actors concerned–of new relational models, new modes of reasoning, and similar collective capacities.*

It may be objected that it is not possible to reduce social change to a simple learning process, even if it is a collective one. It is common to assume that change refers primarily to a certain set of material and social conditions: it is supposed to manifest itself by an upheaval in the relative power of the various forces within the economic and social structures of a society. It is true, of course, that no change or collective learning can take place without rupture. This is certainly the gist of our conclusions. Yet, ultimately, it appears that the balance of power changes only when a new capacity for resolving the problems of collective organizations has been established. Transformation comes when an improved capacity begins to show its worth through a new form of organization. A change in the balance of power, however, does not *necessarily* entail the development of a new capacity or a change in the nature and rules of the game: one elite group may simply replace another.

We beg the reader's indulgence if we illustrate this statement with a somewhat superficial historical speculation. It would appear that every important social change has been preceded by the establishment of new organizational or systemic capacities. Furthermore, it would seem that once these capacities were established, the ensuing mutation took place much more quickly than is often thought, because the image of an immutable past blinds us to the truth.

This has been brilliantly demonstrated, in our view, by Georges Duby in his study of the early Middle Ages in the West.[19] Western peasantry was constituted on the basis of a mutation in the modes of human relations and reasoning which attended the transition from a model of offering and pillage to a model of contract and calculation. This made possible an acceleration in development whose importance can be compared only with the Industrial Revolution of the eighteenth and nineteenth centuries. Collective capacities, which one might even call organizational, were developed, capacities of which the conventional static or deterministic analysis of feudal society took absolutely no account.

A similar point could be made in connection with the enormous mutation in the Arab world during the eighth and ninth centuries. The messianic religious and bellicose aspects of this change do not account for its success. What actually came into being at that time was a new mode of organization of which the Koran was only the sacralized expression. The superiority of this new mode as a means of action and an instrument of development immediately proved substantial. It would be possible to say the same of all the great human adventures, whether national in scope, as in Spain during the fifteenth and sixteenth centuries, or in Sweden and Holland during the sixteenth and seventeenth centuries; or confined to a particular class rather than identified with one particular society, as in the case of mercantile capitalism or the Industrial Revolution.

All major changes of this kind have been rapid and have relied on the discovery and acquisition of new capacities, e.g., for communication, exchange, or reason. These, in turn, make possible new form of collective action.[20]

If, then, we agree to consider change as *collective learning,* we thereby commit ourselves to putting the accent on indeterminacy in history and social existence, and accordingly on the impossibility of laying down laws of evolution or predicting the courses of events. Change is a problem because it is not a natural process but a process of creation, invention, discovery, and fabrication. The very fact that constructs of collective action are indispensable means that, once established, they become obstacles to learning, i.e., to the invention of new constructs.

Constructs of Collective Action as Obstacles to Learning

It will be useful to return first to the notion of collective action which underlies this discussion in order to make its meaning more precise. The notion is borrowed from the vocabulary of psychology, and the transposition lends itself to misunderstanding. When it was used in sociology for the first time, it was very poorly understood.[21] To those, familar with the French educational tradition, in fact, the term learning immediately suggests the idea of assimilating a preexisting model, which may be taken (in advanced societies) from the environment, or developed intellectually by innovative thinkers. This, of course, was not our intention. What we had in mind was the process of trial and error whereby a new behavior could be worked out and developed into a system. The fruitfulness of the learning concept in psychology had pointed the way. Psychologists, we believed, had begun to make progress from the moment they abandoned typology and causal analysis of character and relations and began to formulate problems like that of learning in experimental terms. This made it possible to investigate in a fresh light the processes of invention and innovation that enable individuals to learn (i.e., discover and acquire) new ways of solving the problems facing them. We saw no reason why sociology should not profit from a similar change of paradigm,[22] if sociologists could agree to focus on the processes by which human systems are restructured and modes of regulation changed, rather than persist in their habit of combining typology and causality in deterministic accounts of the sociological regularities in individual behavior.

We shall call collective learning the process by which a collection of actors learn (i.e., invent and institute) new game models, together with their affective, cognitive, and relational components. These games, or, if you prefer, this new social praxis, reflect and at the same time induce a new organizational structure. This implies that the system will now embody new methods, problems, and results, as well as a new mode of regulation.[23]

Though still vague, this formulation immediately makes clear that one must abandon any hope that this problem might be assimilated to that of individual learning. It is clear that the procedure by which an individual learns a game already in operation is quite different from the *collective learning* of this game. An individual can learn very quickly once others have learned before him. A problem arises only when all the actors must learn *together*, which is a requirement if a new game is to establish itself successfully.

In this connection, we face a problem of collective creation or innovation which, by its very nature, is largely *indeterminate*.[24] There must be a realignment not only of interests, power relations, and habits, but also of ego defenses and intellectual models, if a new game is to be conceived and established, or if the actors are to acquire the collective capacities implicit in its adoption. As a rule, problems are perceived only if solutions to them are known. Furthermore, solutions are known only for those problems which fit the framework of existing organized games and which are consistent with the relational and intellectual capacities developed in connection with these games. Thus the old games cannot be expected automatically to engender the new. On the contrary, if we examine the situation carefully, we see that the old is likely to impede the genesis of the new.

This is the major contribution that a discussion of organizations and concrete systems of action can make to the study and understanding of collective learning. We previously alluded to this when we were analyzing the game constructs that underlie an organization. The existence of an organizational collective capacity imposes a certain rationality and certain instruments of action and eliminates others. It allows the resolution of certain problems but as a result impedes collective learning by structuring experience, thus conditioning the capacity to invent new relational modes or game rules. In an earlier discussion, we identified this state of affairs as both consequence and cause of the vicious circles that characterize the organizational process. These contribute to the organization's inertia, but at the same time increase stability of its processes.

It is possible to extend this argument further. If one assumes that every field is in one way or another structured (as we believe we have demonstrated), and that this structure, by defining what might be called the "matrix of wins and losses" in social existence, affects the manner in which the actors organize their games and systems of action, then it becomes possible to see that a sort of systemic collective capacity does exist. As a mode of rationality and of social control, this capacity underlies the game constructs and integrative processes which *permit* such a system of action to exist. The "perverse" effects of social action, as well as the vicious circles which accompany it, may then be considered as components of every collective enterprise. Vicious circles will inevitably be found in every system of action; according to the abstract logic of the systems phenomenon, moreover, they will tend to reproduce themselves indefinitely.

This, of course, is not the case; human undertakings do fail, undergo transformation, and rehabilitate themselves constantly. But the facts are at variance with the conventional image of them. The very mechanisms which support the organization of a collection of actors into a system of action[25] are intimately related to the self-reproductive capacity of the system and hence to its characteristic vicious circles.[26] Change is difficult because actors are prisoners of systems of action and hence are caught in existing vicious circles. And apart from these systems, they have neither the know-how nor the capability to act.[27]

Change as Rupture

Because we are all fascinated by a long tradition of sophisticated discussions as to the meaning of history, these initial remarks may seem far too vague.[28] Yet they may well prove useful in helping us to escape the traditional impasses.

Learning new games is a matter of conquering institutions as well as acquiring new capacities. Such learning is difficult because it presupposes the rupture of existing vicious circles and the establishment of new ones. It is, of course, conceivable that the new vicious circles will prove less costly and inhibiting. Still, from an abstract point of view, they are open to criticism since, no less than the old, they are constructs and hence contingent.

This fact is often concealed by a religious or intellectual model that is edifying or at least soothing. The past is depreciated, and the phenomenon of rupture is transposed. When it comes to a rupture in modes of relation, games, and models of regulation, it is common to situate the problem in the domain of state power, force, and violence. Not that learning new games does not often give rise to conflicts and even to subversion of the established order. Yet all in all, it does not seem to us that force is the midwife of history, certainly not of that part of historical development which represents a genuine conquest by mankind. It is true that during periods of rapid change—i.e., at times when new games were being learned—conflicts have often been exacerbated and violence has reigned for a time in the midst of the general turmoil. There is no reason, however, to assume that this means that learning took place only because of struggles for power, much less that this will be so in the future. We are persuaded that the contrary is true: it was the emergence of new models of relation and new games that transformed the field of power. The eventual winners were those who perceived this intuitively. Mass learning of a new model was not due to a change in the cast of the powerful, or to a victory of the forces of good, or to the exponents of some new logic.[29]

From this perspective, two further remarks may be constructive:

First, the capacity of a society or any human group to change is determined not by the extent of its material wealth and surplus,[30] but rather by the relative affluence it enjoys. Perhaps we should explain what we mean. A social group that is poorly endowed is, of course, also a rigid one, because it is totally dependent on such well-worn institutions as it has managed to establish. The system of action that has developed is fundamental and indispensable, and its disappearance would immediately provoke regression. A richly endowed, and consequently more diversified, group, on the other hand, subsumes a great many "vicious circles" which work to assure its integration. We may therefore assume that some of these vicious circles are redundant, so that any particular one is less rigidly constraining. Such a group can more readily accommodate the rupture of one or more of these vicious circles without damage. In contrast to what is conventionally thought, in fact, a modern, complex society or group is, up to a point, less fragile than one that is organized on traditional lines and relatively poorly endowed.

Generally, but not necessarily, wealth and surplus are coupled with what appears to be a relatively lesser degree of coherence. A poorly endowed group is integrated by such "poor" forms of constraint as coercion, religion, or a crude ideology. It is characterized by rigid and deceptively coherent systems of action. It is therefore not easy for the members of such a group to risk change.

Change is facilitiated by the existence of *slack* in the system.[31] If history is cynical, it is because progress requires not violence but wealth. To a certain extent, it is the most advanced societies which are most likely to be inventive.[32] The more complex and less tightly integrated a society is, the more resources it possesses, the more readily it can transform itself.[33]

This explains the attraction of decentralization and various forms of self-management as accelerators of change. It also makes it easy to see why any model of planning or government which is too highly integrated, coherent, and rational is risky.

It is important that we add a second remark as a caveat to the first.

All learning requires *rupture*, all real change means *crisis* for those who are experiencing it. Learning is impossible in a context of gradual and harmonious evolution. The idea that gradualism is superior, a notion which we encountered and criticized earlier in our discussion of the theory of mutual adjustment, is really quite superficial. The relatively greater success of England, and later America, during particular periods of the collective learning process was due to their superior endowment, which in turn allowed for relatively loose and less-constraining integrative processes. In their systems of action, consequently, there was a relatively greater slack, as well as a greater abundance of resources. This meant that they could more readily pay the price, often quite high, of change, without bringing on regression. If we look beyond the development curves, however, we see a less tranquil picture which reveals at least as many crises and ruptures as in the nonevolutionist countries.[34]

Mutual adjustment is not sufficient to cause a new model to emerge, because human initiative and leadership are indispensable. The model underlying positive change and collective learning is one of nonregressive crisis, crisis overcome by learning. Every rupture may bring on regression. If a rupture is to have a chance of leading to positive learning experiences, it is necessary that individuals take responsibility for the process at some point. If change is truly desired, the inevitability of crises must be accepted. But free choice is equally indispensable, for without it crises could not be dominated and overcome.

We are acutely aware that such general propositions are virtually impossible to verify. We think, nevertheless, that there are two important reasons for stating them clearly. First, there is no other way to escape the deterministic impasses and implications of the typical discussion in which change is reduced to an effect of a logical process which man does not control and which is independent of his action. Second, we think that they offer a more realistic view of man's own responsibility for change.

That we all have such responsibility explains and justifies the passion we bring to the discussion of the problems of change. As actors with a certain amount of freedom to act within a world which is in other respects an unalterable given, change represents our major moral problem.

14

Reflections on Intervention in Processes of Change

Up to this point we have tried to understand change from the point of view of the system within which it appears and which it affects. In this perspective, we have shown that change must necessarily imply the development of new collective constructs. Stating the problem in this way, however, makes it impossible to avoid a fundamental contradiction, which cannot be resolved as long as one remains on the level of the system and its regulation: the only basis for elaborating a new collective construct is an old one, since it embodies the only available experience; yet, at the same time, the change represents a rupture of this construct, hence can only be elaborated in opposition to it.

A resolution of this contradiction is possible only because the actors can, by their action, contribute an "additional value"; in other words, because invention and choice play decisive roles in collective affairs. Were action conditioned solely by societal and systemic determinants, change would never have taken place. But systemic and, to an even greater degree, societal regulation are not determinants but merely constraints, which afford the actors a certain independence and margin of liberty. Thus it becomes possible for these actors to intervene in the operation of the system.

To pursue this line of argument, it will be necessary first to return to our discussion of strategy and strategic analysis. In other words, it will again be important to look at the problem from the actor's point of view, since he is the author of change, rather than persist in analyzing the systemic context, which is both the object of action and the fundamental constraint on it.

What form will the problem then take? In reality, the actor is not in a position first to choose an objective, then to decide on the basis of the goal he has selected what strategy would be best for attaining it. He is faced with a system of action which, though it is, to be sure, a human construct and not a necessity, was constituted before his arrival on the scene and independently of his influence; he is also confronted with the results of changes in the system due to the prior efforts of others. In order to develop a strategy for overcoming the limitations imposed on him, he must understand both these constraints and his remaining freedom to make use of the available resources. This means that his first order of business must be to determine what his actual margin of liberty is; eventually he must try to broaden it. Adjustments, reactions, and corrections of errors are prerequisites to innovation.[1]

At this point it will be useful to discuss the theoretical problem of a simple choice that occasions no hesitation. Suppose that an actor confronts the following alternative: he can use his margin of liberty either to hasten a regressive process which will lead to the system's becoming stuck in a vicious circle, or to set in motion a learning process which will lead to the acquisition of new collective capacities. In a pragmatic sense, his problem is not what choice to make once the alternatives have been put in such terms. It is rather how to bring this alternative to light and accept its implications. If rationality of the goals is given first priority, then he will be led to subordinate his immediate responsibility to principles or to a policy which may not be suited to his situation and problem. If he does not see the concrete alternative, he may even fail to perceive the extent of his individual responsibility.

If it is true that the form that an actor's involvement in a process of change takes is, in a very basic sense, associated with his ability to see the actual alternatives (which, in fact, it may even be up to him to create), then there is no longer any point to beginning a discussion of intervention with a description of the system.

If we hope to go further, it will not help to simplify. Instead, we are going to concentrate on the most classical problems of intervention. As our example, and, for the time being at least, as our hero, we shall take the leader whom society has authorized to act as a guide for the system of action he heads. What advice can experts offer him as to a choice of strategy?

In contrast with our earlier analyses, we shall develop this discussion in a normative sense. Even if a discussion of strategy does not immediately enforce a choice of goals,[2] it cannot pretend to remain entirely within an analytic framework. It is incumbent upon the analyst to put himself in the actor's place, adopt his perspective, and propose models of choice.

The Priority Which Must be Given to Knowledge

When the sociologist becomes involved in the above sense, the first normative problem to arise is that of knowledge. On the basis of what information are the necessary choices to be made? What, in reality, is known about the system to be acted upon and about the problems to be attacked?

As an example, let us look at the case of a typical public or private organization in France, with the following characteristics: a high degree of stratification, a limited number of exchanges among strata, egalitarian pressure within each particular stratum, and a strong negative solidarity which makes it difficult for the leadership to intervene—much less to impose its view—except by issuing specific formal rules and establishing cumbersome centralizing mechanisms.

In such a system, there is a great deal of compartmentalization; outside pressure is rejected; the structure is little influenced by the environment. Adaptation is still possible. At each level of the organization, it will take place when a responsible individual (even one in a rather humble role) is free enough to experiment with a new solution to the problem with which his job confronts him or which is raised by relations with the organization's clients.

The sort of change we envisage would be associated with local solutions to problems of this type. It may be that these solutions, taken together, are contradictory and would produce dysfunctional effects at the organizational level. From the point of view of the individual responsible for implementing them, however, they are rational, and the experience gained in this process represents invaluable knowledge. If it were possible to mobilize this kind of knowledge, the process of change, as well as the definition of a program for action, could be considerably facilitated.

The problem is that the content of local solutions of this kind is virtually unknown at the top levels of the organization. Why? The fact is that while an individual may have an interest in finding a solution to his local problems, he stands to gain little or nothing if he communicates what he learns from this experience. In fact, too much candor may even entail serious risks. Reward may be precluded, for instance, by the fact that a promotion may be difficult to obtain, because the organization is too highly stratified, or because rigid job specification will not permit individuals without exam credits or a university degree to rise to a position of responsibility. If it were to become known that an individual had presumed to interpret organizational rules in his own way, he might be at some risk. Furthermore, by publicizing what he knows, an employee is liable to contribute to the reduction of his own margin of liberty, if such publicity allows certain problems to be rationalized. Not least important is the fact that an employee would thereby sacrifice the advantage he enjoys over his colleagues, subordinates, and others by sharing his knowledge of how to solve a certain problem.

Such an example brings home all the complexity of the relationship between the individual and the organization, a complexity which is commonly underestimated, if not ignored. This relationship is not limited to a simple contract for the execution of a particular task; it transcends the domain of individual or collective negotiation. Because the assertion of freedom within organizational constraints is involved, the relationship in question has an effect on the system of power and responsibility and influences the potential for communication and for mobilizing one's constituency. Once we recognize the complexity and ambivalence of this relationship, it becomes possible to discover the fundamental dilemma in all administrative change: on the one hand, we see how important the resources contributed by each participant are and how necessary it is to mobilize them; on the other hand, it becomes clear that it is difficult, if not impossible, to achieve this mobilization, due to the characteristics and rules of the games prevailing in the organization. In terms of our example: the more rigid and bureaucratic the organization is—the more difficult communication becomes—the more likely it is that adaptations and innovations will run counter to the system, and hence the more difficult it will be to bring about the mobilization of resources which has become all the more necessary as a result.

At this point, one could backtrack a bit and draw the rather superficial conclusion that all change is futile so long as the "system" has not been changed. Unfortunately, the problem is not a question of choosing between black and white. As we noted above, a totally or even largely transparent problem is inconceivable. We cannot imagine a world in which a system of action could exist through time without a minimum necessary structure, i.e., rigidity; hence, there must also be vicious circles and dysfunctions. Thus to mobilize the knowledge, experience, and cooperation of the participants is bound to be difficult.

For this reason, it is essential to have knowledge of how the systems in question really operate. Such knowledge is the first step in rupturing the vicious circle, and it is the one on which all subsequent steps depend.

It is true that men have not waited for knowledge of systems before changing them—whether they are responsible reformers or revolutionaries, empire builders or entrepreneurs. But our response to this objection would be that such knowledge need not be purely theoretical: it might have been, and frequently still can be, intuitive and empirical. It is always possible for a leader to test the reactions of the group he heads in the course of action. He will always regard action as an experiment, to be conducted within the limits of the margin of liberty left him by more general societal and organizational constraints. Even though such experiments may sidestep the issue and even produce quite erroneous results, it is still possible that they will contribute to over-all knowledge of the system.

At present, however, we face an increased need for knowledge, because intuition is no longer sufficient. The complexity of problems and interactions has increased to the point where it is no longer possible to picture an organization in its entirety in order to isolate the sensitive spots in its regulatory mechanisms.

Change makes sense only in relation to the system that is being brought into question. Ends and means can be understood and judged only in relation to the characteristics of this system. Furthermore, key resources are not always rationally measurable; more frequently they are what might be called "virtual resources," which must first be liberated in order to be used. Once we understand all this, it becomes evident that the knowledge of systems is fundamental. More generally, once we are aware of the counter-intuitive effect of all systemic development, we see once again that such knowledge plays a critical role.

One point needs to be clarified at once. When we speak of knowledge, we do not mean theoretical knowledge, at least not in the form of the universal substantive propositions which too often pass for theory. The attractive but superficial hypotheses of Daniel Bell concerning the critical influence of knowledge in "post-industrial society" have lent credence to the simplistic notion that we are now embarking on a new age of theory.[3] The specious novelty of this idea only comforts the system-builders in their traditional blindness.[4]

In reality, it is not knowledge of this sort which is growing ever more crucial to planning for progressive change, but rather knowledge of a system's capacities and resources. What is important on the theoretical level is the research methodology which can help to unlock the answers. It is a mistaken belief—though a common one—that modern societies do not abound in theoretical speculations; we also have enormous masses of information relating to contexts and problems. Yet there remains a curious ignorance as to how practical systems actually operate.

When sufficient knowledge of a system is lacking, reform typically gets bogged down in an interplay of action and reaction which gradually suffocates all desire for change. In the absence of a reasonable judgment as to the nature of the games and regulatory mechanisms which govern the system, it is inevitable that defensive reactions will be provoked. The "system" adapts, while making a series of compensatory adjustments which preserve its identity and more or less totally transform the direction of the reform. This disparity between intention and effect obliges the reformer to extend his reform so as to bring recalcitrant elements under control. The cost of such interference is high and leads in turn to other dysfunctions. Ultimately, a compromise will be reached, whose success will depend on how well the difficulties have been intuitively judged. In many cases, the achievement of what was thought to be a simple reform requires such constant investment of new resources, and such continuous widening of the effort to control an ever-vaster range of elements in an overly complex bureaucracy, that in the end no choice will remain but to abandon the project in failure. No matter how well endowed, all organizations and societies are part of a world in which resources are limited; consequently, the desire to change is all the more easily dampened.

If, on the other hand, action is based an adequate knowledge of the context, it can go *with the system* rather than against it, thus economizing on resources which are inevitably scarce and improving the outcome.

We insist on this apparently obvious point because detailed study of how decisions are made in France and other Western countries reveals the crying lack of concrete knowledge of the systems to be acted upon. The time devoted by planners to analyzing the context of the decisions they intend to implement is never adequate. It is indeed rare that the problem is even recognized. A great deal of energy and money are invested in the study, analysis, and processing of the technical and economic aspects of the problems. But the planners fail to bear in mind that the problems in question exist only through the systems of action designed to deal with them. These systems cannot be reduced to an aggregate of tangible problems. As human constructs, they are never mechanically or automatically responsive to injunctions or decisions handed down from above or relayed through a central regulatory mechanism. In the absence of any concrete knowledge, the future must be decided on the basis of a commitment to specific positions of principle.

What Strategic Analysis Can Contribute

In order to understand the concrete contribution that might be offered by strategic analysis of systems of action, it is useful to consider an actual example. Rather than use it illustratively, we will treat it as a case study for research.

We shall be looking at the conclusions of an in-depth study carried out in 1958–59 on the administration of one of the largest French banking chains. Three major conclusions were reached in a preliminary wide-ranging survey of the problems faced by clerical and lower-level supervisory personnel in this bureaucracy.[5]

First, the clerks and supervisors were relatively well adapted to their task and to the organization, and were relatively satisfied with general policy. Comparatively speaking, the supervisors were the less satisfied of the two groups, however.[6]

Second, clerical personnel and supervisors were at odds over questions of productivity and job standardization. The supervisors were accused of both pettiness and duplicity.

Finally, relations between management and the lower-level supervisors seemed to be characterized by an utter lack of understanding. Not only was there a complete failure on the part of the supervisors to comprehend management's stated objectives in the area of "human relations," but in addition they were convinced of its insincerity. Management, for its part, could not admit that its clearly defined goals were not being implemented, let alone that their validity was being contested.[7] This lack of understanding was indicative of the enormous inertia of the organization, of which there were a good many other signs as well—in particular the consistent points of view which existed for the most part within each stratum and the huge differences in point of view between one stratum and another.[8]

Discussion of these results with members of management aroused vigorous reactions, particularly with regard to the last point. To make sure that the apparent lack of understanding was genuine and to understand its significance, we then proposed to organize sessions during which we would discuss the results in detail with all the relevant supervisory personnel.[9]

This was a rather drawn-out operation, because it was necessary to form twenty groups of ten persons, each of which met three times. But in the process we discovered several factors which added to our understanding of the behavioral strategy and which we think are crucial for making a diagnosis of such a system from the standpoint of change.

First, it should be noted that the participants in our experiments were profoundly traumatized when they learned what severe judgments their subordinates had brought against them.[10]

During the second meeting they read the findings which dealt with their own behavior. When they learned that these responses fell into a sort of general deterministic pattern, which showed that each individual's point of view and mode of behavior depended on his role in the system, they were immediately excited, expressed themselves at length and intelligently, asked a great many questions, and suggested supplementary analyses.[11] They had instinctively understood that the opportunity to put their difficulties into perspective made possible an interpretation which relieved them of responsibility for these problems. Where after the first session they had been crushed with guilt, they could now feel absolved, since the guilt did not fall on each individual but, rather, implicated the system. They had all been required to play the nit-picking role of supervision, in some sense against their will. They also found comforting the implication that in their place their subordinates would have behaved even worse: it was not unusual for the latter to respond that "a subordinate's work has to be watched closely because you can't trust him."

It is worth pausing for a moment to consider this reaction. We have here an excellent example of a phenomenon which to some degree is dominant in the current political and intellectual climate: as far as possible, society is held responsible for all problems. There is a natural tendency for modern man, overwhelmed by impossible choices and threatened with having to shoulder responsibility for problems which surpass his understanding, to try to persuade himself that he is an insignificant factor in his difficulties.

In our view, however, it is essential that each individual recognize that he has some freedom to adopt strategies other than the routine and familiar ones, if new games are to be learned. And in point of fact, in our study it turned out to be easier than we had supposed to win recognition of this fact. Contrary to expectation, during the course of our three sessions, each of the twenty discussion groups underwent a complete turnabout from its original position. There were no exceptions, in spite of differences in personalities, origins, and group climates.

Once assured that their responsibility for the problems was less grave than they had at first believed, the participants in our discussions implicitly but very clearly rejected the determinism to which they had resigned themselves in the second session. They set about trying to determine what freedom they in fact had, and what they might do with it. Without the least interference from us,[12] they invariably insisted on their autonomy and questioned what use they were making of it. Many discovered, in certain instances to their own surprise, that they were quite well aware of how to cope with the system, and therefore that they were not helpless cogs in the machine.

The logical force of this argument was even more potent in our eyes since it was repeated twenty times in various, yet similar, terms by individuals who could not have discussed their feelings in concert and over whom we exercised no influence. We thought there was a general lesson in this. Because of the nature of this large and highly constraining system, the lower-level supervisory personnel had been held responsible for the system's dysfunctions at their level. They therefore had no alternative but to reject in toto the demands made on them to remedy this situation, because they had no means of taking action and thus had to refuse a responsibility that they were incapable of discharging. In this light, it is altogether natural that they should have rejected management's instructions, as we have seen. If, however, they could be given reassurance and be absolved of their general sense of guilt, as we managed to do, then they were quite ready to accept specific responsibilities. In this connection they were even prepared, if need be, to reveal secret tactics and techniques which had hitherto been kept concealed from others and even from themselves.

Their desire for participation and commitment took a very concrete form. During the second session, they had reiterated that they did not believe in good intentions of management, because of obvious contradictions in management's behavior toward them. But, in the next session, they returned to this problem indirectly, as they looked for areas in which change was possible and discussed the concrete problems inherent in their jobs. They also suggested that management be apprised of what modifications were necessary in its rules and policies if such changes were to be implemented.[13]

Of course, one might continue to argue that they were still willing to change only if the system changed. But negotiation had taken a concrete form, and it now appeared possible to mobilize the necessary forces for change. Indeed, such a mobilization had already been partially achieved, insofar as this group of employees was concerned.[14]

Convergent Action on Men and Structures

Knowledge makes it easier to achieve a rupture of the vicious circles inherent in existing regulation. It allows the process of mobilizing resources and individual and collective capacities to begin. It does not, however, obviate action itself. It is impossible to take refuge within the protected universe of discourse, as the social sciences, since psychoanalysis, have too often tended to do.

A strategy of action based on knowledge of the regulation of the relevant system(s) is, nevertheless, quite different from the sort of strategy which the classical reformer would have adopted. The first priority is not to make a precise analytical découpage of the problem. One does not try to enumerate the component problems in accordance with a classification based on functional categories, in order later to reassemble the pieces in line with a model of mechanical coherence. Instead, the concrete units are to be attacked as a whole. A system is a human organism whose actors are not conveniently divided up into theoretical problems and subsystems. It is possible, for instance, for a personnel department to promulgate rules that would correspond to a logical system of relationships abstracted from reality. But these rules must apply to employees who also fit into a technical system of organization on the shop floor and into a system of production management distinct from the abstraction imagined by the personnel managers. Such employees do not reason in a fragmented manner. They use their position in one system in order to act on another. Whereas the rules are incoherent and complex, because individuals are whole they are able to maintain a certain autonomy and capacity for action. For instance, it is possible for an employee to exploit a career advantage in his strategy of communication, or a good position in the information network in order to gain an advantage in the game of responsibilities, etc.

Instinctively, an individual will make use of the formal structure in this manner. Often, if he is to avoid becoming a cog in the mechanism, he has no other alternative. In view of this perfectly legitimate state of affairs, it is impossible and futile to think of reconstructing a comprehensive managerial unity. The point is to focus on the reality rather than the appearance. For this, it is essential to understand the many different varieties of logic. In view of their diversity, any attempt to impose a specious analytical order on the actual complexity of things is condemned to failure.

It may be useful to simplify the problem. An action that aims to bring about change may follow one of two paths: one can act on men, using education and technical training, recruitment policy, promotion, and personnel management (which, from the scientific point of view, is supported by psychology); or one can act on structures, guided by rational models elaborated on the basis of data drawn from technology, from the scientific organization of labor, and from the firm's economic situation.

If either of these two avenues is followed exclusively, one is condemned to unanticipated consequences and the maximum possible counterintuitive effect. If both approaches are used separately, the situation is improved, but only as chance dictates. The only reasonable way to develop and implement a program of change is to coordinate both approaches closely within a single strategy.

If it is done in isolation, without coordinated action on structures, action on men is dangerous. It all too readily takes the form of manipulation, and even if, as is usually the case, it is inspired by men respectful of the freedom of others, uneasiness and suspicion are naturally aroused. There is reason to think that any action of this nature will be regarded as a form of "brainwashing," since the fear of manipulation is so strong in a country like France (and in other countries as well).[15] This means not only that failure will be inevitable but also that any possible impact of the effort will be negative. In addition, in the absence of clear goals or genuine links with work experience, an insensitive implementation of a program of training and education also runs the risk of being counterproductive. There is strong collective pressure to adopt options of this type. It is common to avoid training that is too closely related to work requirements in order to avoid controversy, and the result (in the French context, at least) is a tendency to reproduce the model of the national educational system.[16] Although manipulation becomes less likely, the fear of it, curiously enough, remains, while the interest of the participants declines steadily and the real potential impact vanishes.

If action on structures neglects human problems, it can be just as blind. For the benefit of those exclusively concerned with the dangers of the human-relations approach and psychological control, however, it should be noted that this second form of action is much more common, and, due to the power of the apparatus that it can set in motion, much more dangerous in a pragmatic sense. As crude as it is, the manipulation to which it subjects the individual is even more injurious. It can bring on a series of chain reactions—development of parallel power relationships, perversion of objectives, withdrawals, vicious circles of noncommunication—which over the long run will be equally deleterious to the organization.

To guide structural reforms, it is not enough to utilize knowledge of the human system in question. Such knowledge must be backed by shrewd speculation as to how men will react, what their current individual and collective capacities are, and what potential exists for developing these capacities. Fortunately, human behavior need not rely on the limited predictions that can be made on the basis of a static analysis of the status quo. Latent capacities exist which are quite ready to be mobilized. The development of potential resources must be encouraged and relied upon.

It should be noted that it is only through action that such implicit potentialties can be exploited. Action on structures is calculated to develop possibilities for transforming systems: all available means must be used to increase the players' capacities to take advantage of the opportunities that arise. For instance, such action might include the creation of special training courses designed with the desired changes in mind. It is important that some effort be made to adapt existing support policies (management, promotion, training) to the objectives of the reform, to which they are frequently in opposition.

A general discussion of this nature, which deals with parallel action on men and structures, may appear rather simplistic. It would seem that common sense ought to show well enough the correct path that obviously should be followed. Yet experience shows that this is rarely sufficient, because in practice this extremely simple strategy runs into obstacles which are not easily overcome. This is due to bureaucratic habits of specialization which make it almost impossible, for instance, for a personnel department to cooperate with budget controllers or management information systems. Government agencies do not have a monopoly on such bureaucratic misunderstanding. Large private organizations are also severely afflicted.

It has been possible to demonstrate the importance of this argument in practical cases. Perhaps the most convincing was our analysis of the effects of a long-range program of training in human relations carried out by the large public-utility monopoly EDF-GDF, which is responsible for supplying electricity and gas in France. In a study comparing regions and districts in which such training was offered with others where it was not, we reached the following conclusions:[17]

1. First, training did have a real impact on the attitudes of the personnel, but no influence on their practical behavior. Attitudes invariably became more liberal, but behavior remained unchanged, with all its attendant difficulties and frustrations, except in a minority of specific cases.

2. These exceptional cases all corresponded to a fortuitous coupling of

the training program with a change of structure or work demands which necessitated an improvement in communication; where it was possible to apply the improved capacity to communicate which the training program had brought about, there were basic changes in behavior.

3. By contrast, it should be noted that where this convergence was absent (change of structure or job without training, or training unaccompanied by change of structure of job), results were unfavorable (operational problems in the first situation, increased frustration in the second).

These findings are supported by other studies, particularly those made by Renaud Sainsaulieu.[18] This is a very broad area which we believe is crucial in questions of change, and yet it remains almost unexplored. It would be extremely useful for sociological and psychosociological research to focus on this realm, which we believe is the most vulnerable target for reform.

Lastly, the reader will have noticed that we have adopted a point of view in our discussion rather close to that of "organizational development," which has enjoyed remarkable success in the United States in years past and which is now beginning to take root in France.[19] The OD specialists, as they are called, often remain prisoners, however, of a normative model, the permissive psychological model, even if they do make this explicit and recognize the model's contingency.[20] Furthermore, because they take the pragmatic point of view of the consultant, we believe that they are too often confined by the *a priori* schemas of management, which often lead them to neglect underlying problems of power in an organization. This has important consequences on the options they propose.

We are far from underestimating the contribution of pioneers like Harold Leavitt, Paul Lawrence, Russel Ackoff, or Chris Argyris, who have introduced a more human, more prudent, and "more systemic" outlook into management. What we are warning against is the tendency to generalize the OD model as a collection of recipes—sophisticated, to be sure, but also supposedly universal in scope—which would do away with the necessity to understand actual systems and their inherent conflicts.[21]

Instead, we propose that choices be based on analysis of the actual experience of the actors. We want an approach that integrates the problems of power and potential crises. Our priorities thus preclude such simple recipes, at least in the initial phase. Our alternative is to develop strategies aimed not at avoiding crises but at insuring that the necessary ruptures do not bring on regression. Our strategies are intended to make durable innovations, through experimentation and learning of new games and new modes of government.

The Importance of Implicit Negotiation

Does the approach that we have just outlined, like the organizational-development outlook which we were criticizing, coincide too closely with the viewpoint of the leadership? Is there a risk of second-order manipulation? Leaders and followers are not equally capable of using knowledge and adopting a "systems" strategy. Does this not ultimately mean that the leaders enjoy an undue advantage over other members of the organization? Won't they inevitably take advantage of this situation to strengthen their positions?

The objection is entirely pertinent, and it is impossible to dispose of it. Of course, any strategic approach will be more readily usable by the established powers than by their opponents. To some degree such a recognition may reduce the force and amplitude of the objection. No social situation can be symmetric because, as we have frequently noted, every social organization is structured. It is thus clear that regardless of the mode of argument or type of knowledge proposed, it will first be utilized by those whose social and cultural situation makes them more likely to profit from it. In this respect, the differences between models of action are not differences of kind, but of degree. Thus the question is no longer one of distinguishing between good and evil; yet there are nonetheless decisive differences between models. The technocratic model, for example, is quite different from more open approaches which aim at extending participation to a wider range of people.

It is just such an approach that we are proposing—one which makes it essential to acknowledge the freedom of the actors. This openness can in fact be increased, by taking into account the relationships between the reformer and his partners.

These are not relationships of active agent to passive object; they are relationships of negotiation. Using his knowledge of the system, the reformer proposes changes in regulation intended to permit the development of new games. The interested parties will respond to such a proposal by taking advantage of the "opportunities" offered them, but by doing so, of course, from their own points of view. What will the reformer then do? Will he seek to impose his model because he believes that he alone is in possession of the truth? Certainly not, if he really means to adopt the approach we are recommending. Indeed, it will not be possible for him to uphold his vision of what is correct against the judgment of the actors actually involved in the change. His first response must therefore be to extend and modify his interpretation. His first analysis was imperfect. By taking account of the reaction of the other interested parties, he can improve it and thus rework his proposals.

From the systems point of view, this cycle of actions and reactions should be understood as a kind of negotiation between an initiator and those who react to his initiatives. This negotiation transforms the "objects" of reform into "subjects," and cooperation develops more openly and broadly.

Negotiation is an ambiguous word, however, and it should be made more precise. The negotiation in question here is not and cannot be an open one. In most cases, explicit discussion would commit the participants to a certain course of action and restrict their freedom, which would constitute an intolerable risk.[22] What will take place instead might be called an *implicit negotiation*. In this case the actual behavior and its interpretation become elements of mediation which insulate the freedom of all parties involved. The reform initiative provokes a reaction in the members of the affected organization or system which is not only a response but also an appeal. This appeal is not very explicit, insofar as the interested parties are vulnerable and accustomed to adopting a defensive posture. If, however, the reformer is able to understand the significance of this appeal and respond to it, a cycle of negotiation may begin to develop which will be able to break out of the round of action-reaction and reach a level of genuine learning. Ultimately, this may make it possible to institute more open negotiations.

The risk and principal constraint implicit in open negotiation come from the likelihood of becoming enmeshed in previously established institutional channels, whose power may be so strong as to make all change impossible. Whether initiated by management, union, state, or third party, therefore, directed change must remain, at least initially, in the domain of implicit negotiation, given the present state of our institutions.

Of course, the ambiguity has not yet been removed, as we are the first to recognize. There is certainly a risk of manipulation. But if we may be permitted to take the offensive in our turn, what action, whoever its author, does not involve such a risk? Can there be action without an author? Can one take refuge behind the masses or the direction of history? Any action, any human initiative, is dangerous. No transcendental purpose can so sanctify it as to place it beyond criticism.

For a Methodology of Action Based on the Capacities of the Actors

Through all our discussions we have emphasized a common theme: that a plan of action will have an impact only if it is based on the actors' capacities to take advantage of opportunities to broaden their contingent freedom within the system.

The positive significance of such a formulation is that it allows us to take a different and, we believe, more fruitful and realistic view of the thorny problem of the goals of change. We will return to this question in our final chapter. Such an approach also has a negative, critical significance insofar as we are able to contrast it with a methodology of action which, in spite of its shortcomings, continues to be used. This methodology grants an enormous intellectual and moral importance to the goals and motives of the actors, which almost inevitably leads to the sort of impasses to which we have referred time and time again in connection with the logic of the *one best way*.

It is quite common to argue as though the real measure of all action were the actor's intention. To sacrifice this postulate seemingly challenges the common conception of what a person is, and attacks certain of our essential ego defenses. The psychology of the actor, therefore, becomes the crux of a controversy. The man in the street will ask, "What exactly did he want?" The judge or moralist will seek to ferret out his deeper motivations. Implicitly, one assumes that everything is ordered, comprehensible, and justified in relation to the desired goal. It would then follow that the actor does, or should, function according to the mental image he has of that goal. Thus his act can and should be understood and judged in relation to this image.

This morality has its grandeur. It was to some extent the basis of our culture's notion of responsibility and individuality, and as such represented a huge advance.[23] But it faced increasingly insuperable difficulties from the time the complexity of human relationships destroyed the fiction that the actor-author was uniquely and individually responsible for his act.[24] Earlier we showed how the actor shunned a responsibility that transcended him, a phenomenon which is quite widespread.

The actor, then, may try to hide behind the system, and modern moralists, both lay and religious, may lay sin and error at the feet of society. There is nevertheless a general willingness to continue the old theoretical line of argument, and to accept the claim that there is an ideal actor entirely free in his motivations. If man acts badly, the guilt is no longer his but that of the society from which he is alienated. In that case it would suffice to replace the given society with one which was nonrepressive, so that, finally rid of his alienation, man might turn to the achievement of his desires. Stripped of this idealistic cant, however, the basis of all action remains the actor's motivation; his goal is still to achieve what his motive compels him to.

This logic, which, for the sake of simplicity, we propose to call the logic of motivations, is incomplete and inadequate. It will not withstand serious analysis. Its shortcomings derive from the fact that it takes no account of the circumstance that man discovers his desires in relation to the opportunities he perceives.[25] It is a logic which reduces man to the decision through which he expresses himself; but his choice, always forced, is always limited to one of several possibilities. Man does, indeed, frequently make such choices; this does not mean that they are necessary. The simplification is unjustified because it neglects man's right not to know what he wants, as well as his right to change his desires in view of what is possible or what he believes to be in his interest. In practice, every individual proceeds in this way, and it is no cause for criticism. Any explanation of behavior must be based on recognition of these facts and their legitimacy, rather than on an ideal model never encountered in practice.

There is something apparently simple and "moral" about the argument in terms of intentions and motivations, on the one hand, and satisfactions of needs, on the other. It invokes such popular notions as democracy and equality. One man is worth as much as another; satisfaction is the measure of everyone's pursuit of happiness. It is an argument that can be used to indict the narrow-mindedness of the engineers and economists who are the proponents of technocratic rationality, as well as the selfishness of the capitalists who refuse to accept the democratic verdict.

This is a dangerous argument, however. It takes no account of the uncertainty as to what the actor's desire really is. It leads directly to the impossible debate over the potential perversion of that desire by manipulation, alienation, and repression. What is more, it lends itself to manipulative application: if one can ascertain what man's deep psychological needs are and what laws govern satisfaction of those needs, then how is one to resist the temptation to satisfy them—manipulatively, if need be—in order to induce people to recognize their own needs and accept the gifts benevolently bestowed upon them?

We feel that it is from this point of view that the scientific debate which has dominated American and European psychosociology for two decades is best approached.

The "mangerial" simplifications introduced by the human-relations school in the fifties led to considerable advances in American psychology. Strongly influenced by the hierarchy established by Maslow,[26] this psychology recognized the existence of higher-level needs and began to attach more importance to the problem of "self-actualization" than to the problem of belonging. Consequently, it began to view man as less "affective" and "social" and much more "complex," i.e., more free and less determined. The contingent and dynamic character of needs began to emerge. The mainstays of this school, however, were preoccupied with narrow normative and prescriptive concerns,[27] which led to static, one-dimensional, and mechanistic explanations of "self-actualizing" man, just as before. In spite of the further nuances that have developed in such theoretical positions, there remains a tendency to give more and more priority to man's psychological needs—in this case, needs of personality (search for dignity, self-actualization, etc.) which are considered of preeminent importance in normal individuals.[28] From these needs, one deduces a series of prescriptions as to desirable organizational structures. In short, these authors are seeking an optimal "fit" between individual psychological needs and the requirements of the organization as embodied in its structure and formal rules, which leads them to argue as though there were relatively stable and universal psychological needs in individuals which only work can satisfy. Once known, it is presumably possible to predict behavior and, potentially, to direct it by making appropriate structural changes.[29]

In our view, it was this paradoxical employment of a logic of motivations and psychological needs which made these authors relatively vulnerable to the movement of protest in the late sixties, which partially put an end to their influence, at least among the rising intellectual generation.

In France, where the intellectual foundation was much more solid, one has the impression that, initially at least, the great majority of psychosociologists became involved in the protest. The vogue among French "radicals" in 1968 and in the years following the student revolution was to embrace a psychosociological philosophy which comes straight out of the human-relations movement; the fact that this philosophy was so violently abhorred by all the intellectual left of the preceding years is not the least puzzling paradox of our time. The various small groups which led this movement, usually known as "institutional analysis," all share the same one-dimensional, fundamentally psychological view of human relations.[30] These writers were eager to enjoy unequivocally clear consciences, which they managed by inverting the problem in order to state that the organization had to be adapted to the man, and not the man to the organization.

We anticipate the objection that while there really was a risk of manipulation by the established powers in the fifties, these new movements represent no such risk. Their logic may not be flawless, but they are involved in a sincere struggle against the most pernicious form of oppression there is: bureaucratic organization.

We must say that, all things considered, we are not persuaded. The illusions sustained by these theorists represent a mental confusion that is actually a regression toward the naïve illusions of scientism and Taylorism; it should be noted that Lenin was particularly attached to these. They dream of the anti-organization, a would-be universe of transparency, of total communication, of festival, of close relationships, of nonconstraint—in short, a universe from which, just as in Taylor's vision, conflict between individual and collective ends is excluded. There is thus no further occasion for power and manipulation to appear in human interaction. According to this "philosophy," change is ultimately nothing more than the victory of good over evil. Only self-interest and backwardness prevent passage through the needle's eye into this paradise.

It is not difficult, if one is willing to allow a little perspective and to eliminate the rhetoric, to see what thin analyses underpin these illusions of harmony. If they are so hardy, it is because they are reflected and echoed in the world—and what a "serious" world it is—of real responsibility, which continues to base its action on a logic of the *one best way*.

According to this methodology, only one act counts—the decision—and only one problem is important—that of goals. Everything must be coordinated and logically integrated in view of the objectives. The decision codifies and makes concrete the one best solution, which is elaborated during the preparatory–study phase.

Directed change cannot merely impose a preestablished model, but must deal with the vagueness and confusion which are inevitable in guiding a system which must be made to evolve in spite of paralyzing blockages. But this is an idea that remains wholly foreign to most of our responsible officials in both the public and private sectors. They persist in the belief that a decision or reform, because it is good in itself—because it is the one best way—should be applied as is, without modification.[32]

The belief that insofar as an objective is correct, or good, or is based on a sound theory and rigorous analyses, its implementation requires only energy and rigor; the radicals' belief that if the tactic has been well-chosen, the spirit of the masses or the scientific model of socialism will not fail to come up with the needed solutions; and the belief that the necessary administrative apparatus will simply fall into place once the decision has been made—all these beliefs reflect the same myopia. Not only must implementation not be neglected, it should in fact be regarded as the primary problem. In change, as in war or love, all the art is in the execution. When expressed in so many words, this may seem obvious. And yet it is ignored by countless theories, from variants on Rostow's "take-off" to primitive or advanced Marxisms and leftist dreams of the spontaneity of the masses. All such theories are ultimately no more than rationalizations useful for giving clear consciences to those who thus commit themselves to blindness.

If one wishes to explain why a good objective should produce such *bad* results, it seems to us that it is too easy to incriminate for the thousandth time technocracy, alienation, or irrationality, only to propose doing away with these evils by invoking what amount to the same procedures. That the same apparently inevitably process should be repeated time and time again cannot fail to be striking. First objective: suppression of bureaucracy, liberation of human potential. First effort to achieve this goal:

increase in bureaucratic vicious circles. New objective: correction of errors, increase of rigor and energy, huge educational effort, explanation of objectives, even indoctrination. Final result: admission of failure, or, more frequently, emendation of all information and substitution for actual experience of an "official" reality more in conformity with the requirement of consistency which takes on an ideological meaning.

In fact, it is the priority accorded to ends in the domain of *political* options which accounts for the fact that means are of primary importance in the only arena that counts—the practical. Insofar as the goal is given so high a value that it becomes absolutely restricting, no freedom of choice remains. As we have already noted on several occasions, the paradoxical result of contempt for the means employed is thus the reign of the technocrats,[33] who alone are in possession of the technical secrets through which the indispensable *one best way* may be discovered.[34]

If we accept the notion that action on or for men makes practical sense only on the level of their abilities, we can escape the traditional moral trap, which is to attempt to do good for others without consulting them. Whatever ideological trappings cloak the attempt to influence motivations, manipulation is the result. It is more difficult to help others develop new capacities if you accept the possibility that such capacities may be used against you. But the risk is a reasonable one, and it is all the more reasonable because it is morally less dangerous. Such a methodology of action relates to our earlier proposals, in which we recommended the incorporation of bounded rationality, acceptance of the impossibility of cooperation without conflict, and acknowledgment of the inevitability of universal relations of power.

15

The Ends of Change

Throughout this work, we have tried to isolate the problem of ends as much as possible from the main themes of our discussion. This was not because we think that means ought to dictate ends or that tactics should take precedence over politics, but rather because from a research standpoint, it is indispensable to know the constraints created by the context, and the resources and opportunities available to the actors, before we approach the problems of the goals of action. To conclude, we would now like to turn to the question of what our analyses can contribute to the debate over the possible and desirable ends of change.

Power Relationships as Obstacles to Change and as Ends of Change

The first problem we would like to raise in connection with the ends of change is the problem of power. This is not only because power is an indispensable prerequisite to action—the only possible ends are those for which capacities for action, i.e., sufficient power, can be mobilized. No less important, perhaps, is the fact that no change is possible without transformation of the system of power. This transformation thus becomes an essential stage, if not the primary aim, of every effort at change. Yet power remains an even more difficult taboo to break down than sex. For a time, power was deemed legitimate to the extent that it was considered sacred. Now that all authority has rightly been stripped of transcendental trappings, power has yet to be humanized. It is still deemed dangerous and disquieting. In emergencies, or for suitably noble purposes, it may acquire a temporary justification. But it is generally held to be suspect for even intrinsically evil. Ideally, all power would be suppressed. Every utopia of our day happily does away with it, and it would seem that the inclination to get rid of power, together with guilt and death, is irresistible.

Our research, on the contrary, shows that relations of power are inevitably bound up with human action. Such relations are directly asso ciated with the zones of liberty which are the basis of man's existence, the basis of the existence of the individual as actor. The use of power in strategy and conflict is woven into the very fabric of all social life. Precisely because this freedom exists, there is no determinism; history and society must be understood as a creation, a human invention, and our social constructs are, and can be, nothing other than contingent. Our findings, therefore, have led us to the novel proposition that neither social action nor collective structure exists unless there is freedom for the actors, and, consequently, unless there are relations of power. It should be noted that in this perspective power is neither a desire nor a need which is to be satisfied or repressed in view of some moral judgment. It is a vital, irreducible fact, which we must incorporate into our reasoning.[1]

If relations of power are inevitable, then, in concrete terms, this means that we must continue to live in a world of conflict, manipulation, and ambiguity. It means also that no *society can rely on its supposed virtuousness to insure harmony*. A final consequence is that certain goals make no concrete sense, which means that we ought to revise our way of thinking about goals so as to relativize them and divest them of their sacredness. Contingency is inevitable.

It may be painful to accept that the world is one in which relations of power cannot be avoided. This should not prevent us from seeking to change it, however.

Our analyses have shown that it is possible to analyze and regularize the relations in question in very different ways. To learn about new collective capacities and the way in which they are crystallized in a social construct is to effect the necessary transformation in out thinking. Relations of power impose constraints on our action which we are obliged to accept. As such, they can and must become primary goals of this action.

Our research, however, suggests that to be successful in this, a radically different mode of argument is needed. It is impossible to contain power by attempting to suppress it, refusing to recognize its existence, or simply rejecting it. On the contrary, it is necessary to accept the existence of the phenomenon. A greater number of persons must be allowed to join in the game. They must be granted a greater autonomy, freedom, and range of options. Only power can fight power. The greater threat of abuse comes not from allowing the actor to take initiatives, but rather from suppressing his freedom to do so in order to restrict all initiative to a monopoly of certain actors or higher authorities.

Just as our thinking about power has changed, similar reasoning shows that we must also change our perspective in discussing problems of leadership. It is impossible to resolve the problem of elitism, for instance, by negation of the phenomenon of leadership or by waging an indis-

criminate battle against elites. Only the development of leadership capabilities can counter the abuses of leadership.

If there is a problem, it is because the characteristics of our social
construct make it possible for certain individuals or restrictive groups to
monopolize leadership functions by making access to such positions quite
difficult. These functions are then exercised so as to create relations of
dependence around them which block all change. To fight such practices,
there is no alternative but to develop greater leadership capabilities. It is
not enough merely to try to limit their impact or to refuse to face the
problem. If one does no more than this, the outcome will be maintenance
of the status quo or accentuation of the need to rely on charisma or
bureaucracy in case difficulties are encountered. If, instead, as wide a
range of individuals as possible are encouraged to take initiatives and
assume formal or informal leadership functions; and if these roles are
exposed to public view, valued highly, and rewarded; then social existence can be made more dynamic, the risk of elitism diminished, and the
society made more fluid.

To those who think that power relationships are only one aspect of
broader structures of political, economic, and cultural domination, we
reply that structures of domination can only be implemented by means of
relations of power; transformation of such relations is therefore the only
concrete way to attack them.

It is not solely, or even primarily, in a negative form that the problem of
human emancipation arises. New relations of power will not come into existence "naturally" following the disappearance of general structures of
domination. If we may return for a moment to the simplistic example of the
so-called "prisoner's dilemma," in a manner of speaking we are all prisoners who, in order to escape the dilemma in which we find ourselves and
the vicious circles in which we are caught, must conspire to act in concert,
and hence must organize so as to inspire mutual confidence. We can do
this by accepting the charisma of a person who is universally regarded as
superior, or by submitting to the constraint of an authority structure
which must be obeyed because of its threats of punishment. In our view,
such alternatives correspond to an old model of the social construct.
Another option is to try to build up games in which we can have confidence without recourse to such polarization. The elaboration of such a
construct is a concrete problem of development which involves power
relationships among the actors.

Thus, since existing relations of power are obstacles to change, they
must become primary targets of any effort to achieve it. The development
of new relations of power is inseparable from the development of collective capacities. We may consider it not only as the common denominator,

but also, in a more fundamental sense, as the implicit goal, of a great many apparently divergent objectives.

Ends Derived from Experience Versus Ends Derived from Abstract Choice

If we are correct in asserting that it is actually on the level of concrete relations of power that change takes place, then it is at the base of the social pyramid that the real potential for change can best be appreciated, and ends can be most clearly perceived. This is because it is at the base that the opportunities in question are part of actual experience.

Such an assertion may readily win the intuitive support of the vast majority, as it is consistent with ideas currently in fashion. Yet it goes against all our mental habits and our understanding of the way in which society is structured. The usual assumption, in fact, is that responsible choice can only be made at the top of any integrated group, organization, system of action, or even society, because that is where rationality can emerge.

In fact, it is customary to make a relatively unconscious distinction between ends which are part of everyday experience and those which are actively chosen. There is no problem in saying of the former that they are felt most clearly at the grass-roots level. The latter must reflect and embody them, of course, but owing to the inherent mechanisms of collective choice, they become clear options only at the highest echelons.

Our view, however, is that this dichotomy is neither useful nor desirable, a conclusion which we think is justified by the results obtained in our strategic analyses and by the discovery of new modes of argument concerning systems of action and decision. It is not true that the meaning of a particular goal is discovered at the top. On the contrary, it is discovered on the level where this goal is a part of actual experience. Choices are, of course, necessary at the top, but they do not automatically dictate the choices made at the operational level.

This paradox needs to be stressed. There is a tendency to view the bottom echelon solely in terms of problems of application or technique. Our research, however, leads us to hypothesize that the margin of liberty and consciousness of practical experience are such that change can be most clearly perceived there, rather than at the top.

Were we operating on the basis of a simple logic according to which a single peremptory goal had to be implemented rigorously, this conclusion would be false. Such is rarely the case in human affairs, however. No one goal can be given priority and enforced above all others. Even if we wished to give absolute priority to the establishment of equality, for instance, there would remain implicit requirements to conserve some degree of initiative, expression, and human emotional relationships. Each of these signifies the recognition of another goal which at a certain stage of its implementation might strongly contradict the egalitarian aim.

If this is correct, it is clear that one of the essential problems in every policy of change is that of choosing among contradictory goals. All are presumably worth striving for, and no metatheory, science of history, or metarationality can aid in making a definitive choice. Experience has shown repeatedly that the "least bad" resolutions of these contradictions can be discovered only at the grass roots, with goals which are inherent in everyday experience. The scientific approach, as we have tried to show, especially in the section above which treated the problems of decision, makes it possible to justify this empirical finding, since it demonstrates that there cannot be any absolute rationality and introduces the notion, in connection with the model of bounded rationality, that goal choices can be based on the actual experience of those involved.

Goals imposed from above, no matter how magnanimous they are, necessarily result in bureaucratic dictatorship. Intuition is wrong in suggesting that idealism and bureaucracy are opposed in this respect. The opposite is true. One infallibly entails the other. There is a simple reason for this. If the actors for whom contradictory goals are embodied in actual experience are deprived of the opportunity to make the necessary compromises among them, then this task necessarily falls to the bureaucrats responsible for the program of change. The more rigorous the program is, the greater are the contradictions on the level of experience, and the more bureaucratic arbitrariness there will be.

In order to make the discussion more concrete, it may be useful to discuss for a moment the fundamental problem of transforming power relationships in a society like the French. At the top, there is no difficulty in finding vehement ideological oppositions and conflicts of interest that are quite difficult to overcome, involving such contrasting principles as "participation," "self-management," "management by objectives," and "delegation of responsibilities," which are all code words in the vocabularies of natural adversaries, both labor and management. Yet the translation of such ideals into practical projects does not give rise to the same conflicts if pragmatic constraints are taken into account. For the same simple option is implicit in each of them: it is moral and desirable to emancipate men, to make them masters of their own lives, more autonomous, and more capable of deciding for themselves. Of course, the proponents of each of these doctrines harbor certain implicit reservations and provisos, which means that they recognize the necessity to take other values into account as well.[2] The only real discord, however, relates to problems of implementation; there is no opposition of values. Insofar as analysis reveals the freedom of the responsible individuals at the various levels, these reservations are no longer preconditions but rather constraints which merely have to be taken into account. We move from the plane of the moral categorical imperative, which is impossible to transcribe in reality and useful only in polemic, to problems which are thornier because they are more fundamentally rooted in experience. But light can be shed on these problems through trial and error, knowledge, and experience. If action is commenced, it may be possible to find at least an implicit consensus.[3]

There are many other problems to which attention is drawn by a deliberate exploration of practical solutions at the grass-roots level which would otherwise have gone unnoticed. These solutions are based on the idea that actors have a margin of liberty and should assume responsibility. This allows common-sense compromises to be struck. It becomes possible to formulate goals in a more pragmatic manner. Furthermore, new modes of relating may be discovered or learned, which may be useful in eliminating or transforming the initial contradiction. This is the fundamental rationale for reform.

It may, of course, be possible to obtain a similar outcome with a reform set in motion from above. In many circumstances there may be no other way. Typically, however, the leadership will be incapable of predicting what this outcome will be and how it will develop. No scientific analysis, no theory of change or management can eliminate this uncertainty. It may be reduced by a diagnosis of the situation and of the capacities of the actors involved. But change is inevitably a gamble, a calculated rupture. The gamble will be successful if conditions can be arranged in such a way as to permit the actual "implementers" to take charge of the reform on their own level, after they have been adequately prepared. It will fail if the situation and the strategies and capacities of the "participants" have been misjudged.

When the problem is one of transforming relations of power, the learning and discovery of new relational modes at the operational level are particularly important. The participants must accept[4] new constraints if a closed, hierarchical type of game is to be replaced with one which is more egalitarian and open.[5] These constraints do not necessarily compromise the undertaking, if the participants actually take responsibility for them. This is part of the learning process in which they are engaged. But if the constraint is perceived as imposed from above, it may cause the reform to fail, since it is commonly thought that reforms decreed from above entail no constraint on those who impose them, but only gratification.[6]

Self-management Is a Problem and Not a Solution

At this point, two clear conclusions may be stated: first, the indispensable choices among the various ends which are concurrently pursued in every society are best made at the bottom; and, second, one goal is fundamental to both top and bottom echelons: to contribute to human emancipation. Under the circumstances, is there any reason not to regard self-management as the necessary and sufficient solution to all problems of change?

It is no doubt unnecessary to point out that, unfortunately, the problem is not one of choosing values or adopting a universal model of society, even if it is a decentralized model. Of course, the partisans of self-management base their arguments on the idea that a greater likelihood exists that there will be unanimity concerning values at the operational level, an idea for which we have already noted the supporting evidence. Furthermore, they do articulate and successfully reconcile the imperative that intervention come from above (the necessity of which we have recognized ourselves) and that implementation be carried out at the grassroots level. There can be no doubt that they marshal these ideas and the evidence for them in a very convincing and coherent way, which is supported by a strong ideological commitment. Nevertheless, they run into two difficulties, which in our opinion are insurmountable.

First, their manner of proceeding is too ambitious. Their project is excessively rational, for it tries to integrate the goal of giving power to the greatest number with a method which is based on an *a priori* model employing a synoptic logic. But these two orientations are profoundly contradictory.

It is quite possible that, at the concrete operational level, one may find, if not consensus on goals, at least an openness to experience and a capacity to invent solutions which can be exploited in order to learn new pragmatic techniques, without this implying that, at the level of society as a whole, there need be any agreement as to ends, means, or strategies. A politically enthusiastic movement represents a force, but the pressure it exerts may be particularly dangerous, for it provokes fears, arouses enormous expectations, and perpetuates illusions. If the movement is successful and actually implements some of its ideas, the very magnitude of the ideological commitment it has aroused introduces rigidities; and thus all the obstacles—including those related to the existence of opposition and those related to the need to respect different values simultaneously—increase the pressure for bureaucratic solutions. As we noted a short while ago, it is not correct to infer that idealism and bureaucracy are irreconcilably opposed in a practical situation of this kind. On the contrary, one infallibly brings out the other.

Self-management cannot be decreed from above any more than any other goal. It is in fact less likely than other goals to be achieved by constraint or indoctrination, even if the latter is referred to more politely as education. A closer look at the matter reveals that self-management is not a solution but a problem to be considered in relation to the society as a whole. To us, it seems that this problem is still rather poorly formulated by the "self-management movement," as it is generally known.

In the current state of thinking about self-management, we do not believe that the problems associated with change can be well formulated, because the crucial character of power is still largely ignored. Even self-management's most sophisticated advocates, who are beginning to glimpse the importance of power, are often mistaken as to its significance.

The hidden goal that underlies the self-management movement is generous but impossible to achieve, and to attempt to do so is idle, if not dangerous: we are referring to the idea that all power can be suppressed. Here, we touch on a second, deeper difficulty, whose implicit logic is at least partially responsible for the first.

Power is impossible to eradicate, and relations of power are an essential component of cooperation and human relations in general; as long as self-management's partisans refuse to admit this, any action they undertake will run the risk of producing an effect opposite to what they wish to achieve. Power can be regularized and moralized only by flushing it out into the open, in order to prevent the consolidation of positions of strength and the crystallization of dependency relationships around these positions. On the other hand, the intention may be to establish self-management on a model which is too "democratic," i.e., egalitarian. In this case, the risk is that respect for the intentions will be no more than perfunctory, and that it will prove impossible to halt the spread of a variety of manipulative practices, which will crystallize around key points in the system. If tight controls are adopted in order to prevent this, it may be possible to establish a model for decision-making and enforcement. Such a model may appear to be collective, but the relations of power will then reintroduce themselves into all the interstices of the machine, thus reproducing the traditional dysfunctions of bureaucracy. Access to the system's critical points[7] cannot fail to create problems, and around these will crystallize new structures of dependence which will lead to development of the classic vicious circles.[8]

Even the most sophisticated French and Italian advocates of self-management[9] commit the same error when they speak of collective appropriation of the means of power, a slogan presumably broader in scope and more effective than the classic collective appropriation of the means of production. Though they are well aware that problems of power are central, they do not understand that, because power is a relation and cannot therefore be possessed, it can no more be appropriated and distributed collectively than confidence or love. It is, of course, possible to appropriate authority insofar as it is a legitimate and formalized function or role. Yet appropriation of authority and its "distribution" among the actors does not make it possible to eliminate relations of power. Even after such a revolution, the situation would be exactly the same as if such relations had been ignored and schemes of formal democracy had been accepted as satisfactory.

At bottom, what is in question here is still the possibility of creating a *virtuous society*. In our view, the danger in the myth of self-management is that its proponents misappropriate—in very good faith, it goes without saying—deeply felt values from daily experience in order to integrate them into a new Christian heresy similar to those that have shaken the West since the Middle Ages.

Self-management does remain a problem. Perhaps the point will be conceded that any reform which aims to bring about, through controlled action, the broadest conceivable liberation will encounter difficulties which might be called difficulties of self-management. In this sense, self-management is an essential problem, perhaps the most important of our time. But, we repeat, it is a problem and not a solution.

A so-called "experimental society formula" has been proposed which might seem to offer a way out of these difficulties, insofar as it accentuates the notion of a world unfinished and in constant development. Such a formulation clearly gives a certain perspective with respect to the overly coherent model of a preestablished society, as well as the constraining tradition of the revolutionary dream. As a formula, it seems to us more felicitous and promising than, for instance, the competing slogans of the relational, informational, or anti-organizational society.

Yet there is reason to ask if even this formula is not based on illusions concerning the limits of man's capacity to support experimentation, which are narrower than is usually thought. No one hitherto seems to have been aware of the human cost of experimentation. The greater the number of initiatives taken by participants in a system, the more relations of power grow and diversify—and in turn, the greater the freedom of the individual. But the problem of over-all management then becomes more complicated. It is too facile to reply that the participants in this system can assume the responsibility themselves; this will be possible only after the development of a huge social construct, which at present hardly seems possible without a long period of learning. One has only to imagine, for instance, the considerable increase in management and organizational capacity required to transform a conventional school into an experimental one which would permit, among other things, the students to choose freely among several programs of instruction, organization of teaching teams by subject and level, creation of effective counseling services, alternative individual and collective activities, and a modicum of democratic participation by students and their families.[10]

We would agree that as much experimentation as possible is needed. Yet this must not be taken to mean that a totally or even largely experimental society is desirable. If we must choose a slogan, we would instead propose the "learning society," meaning that man is engaged in constant experiment on himself and is never entirely "grown up." By itself, however, this formula does not account for another element of the problem, the freedom of the individual and his need for protection.[11] Not everybody can, wants to, or should be continually involved in experimentation. A system certainly can and should always be in motion, but that doesn't mean that all the individuals who compose it ought to be. It is man's glory that he is an animal capable of solving problems, but this is not his sole activity, particularly not in the area of social learning.

If this distinction is kept in mind, it is possible, we think, to draw certain conclusions regarding the problem of the respective responsibilities of base and apex of the social pyramid. The apex cannot impose a comprehensive model, nor can it dictate an unambiguous hierarchy of goals. Insofar as the virtuous society will never be a reality, such a model or hierarchy will remain impossible to attain. No matter how noble the intentions, the practical effect will be bureaucratic arbitrariness and the reconstitution of a hierarchy of dependence on a new basis, instead of the desired suppression of these phenomena. Leaders do, nevertheless, bear an essential responsibility—but a less spectacular one. It is not a question of defining the good for people who have the right to make definitions of their own, but rather of making it possible to discover what contradictory values and goals exist on subordinate levels and of showing how the means to resolve these inherent contradictions may be found. This implies that those at the top must develop a clearer understanding of the system and of appropriate strategies than those at the bottom, but this does not necessarily mean that their goals are different. It is perhaps worth noting that leadership at this level is increasingly inseparable from knowledge; from this standpoint, intellectual growth and personal renewal are more important than the abstract choice of goal. It may be that at present the necessary perspective and capacity for experimentation are frequently lacking at the bottom; on the other hand, what seems to be lacking at the top is the barest familiarity with, much less knowledge of, the complexity and wealth of practical experience at the operational level. The attitude of "there's no more to it than . . ." is more widespread, it seems, at the top than at the bottom in France—and not only in France.

Thus we come back, at the end of our analyses, to the actor and his freedom, as well to as his responsibility in using that freedom. Neither scientific analysis nor ideological bias makes possible a determination of the best choice in an absolute sense. Even with knowledge of all pertinent data, it would be impossible, as we have seen, to establish the best objective; nor would it be any more possible to determine the best means for attaining that objective once it was fixed. Why? Because it is only the actor who, by trial and error, can make a satisfactory choice of goals consistent with his individual freedom. Whatever illusions of total freedom he may have had are eliminated by scientific analysis, which helps him to discover the constraints and limitations on his action. In return, it offers the possibility of revealing new resources and opportunities and of increasing the actor's effective margin for maneuver. His responsibility is to discover his freedom and independence and to make use of them.

Since it is not up to us whether or not to get involved with others, this responsibility is even greater. We *are* involved, like it or not, though we may not always be aware of it. When we take advantages of opportunities which arise within our zone of liberty, our actions structure the field in which others operate. To try to control the effects, to estimate accurately the costs and consequences, and to take full responsibility for the confrontation we cannot avoid with our partners is our duty and our contribution to social progress.

The virtuous society is impossible. Goals cannot be stratified and integrated into a model of an ideal society. Man himself must bear the primary responsibility for change. Not abstract man or universal man. But concrete man, finite man, who acts for himself in his own context. Scientific analysis does not confirm the convenient sociological determinism which would allow the actor to look to the system to excuse his failures, and therefore invites him to discover in his margin of liberty his real responsibility.

Appendix

The Theory and Practice of the Research Method

Strategic analysis and systems analysis are not merely abstract theories. They are above all modes of research. This has been the general thrust of this book, and in treating a good many examples we think we have given a concrete demonstration of the character of these types of analysis. It may be useful to provide a more complete description of the research procedure as it is actually practiced. We propose to do so in this appendix. We will also give a brief theoretical justification of the principal assumptions on which it is based.

The Investigator and His Area of Research
Inductive Logic

It will be useful to return for a moment to the point of departure for strategic analysis. This form of analysis rejects all determinism of context, environment, "objective structures" of the problems, etc; as we have shown, it does so by relativizing such determinisms. In their stead, it raises a question which belongs to another analytic level: what constraints are placed on the capacity of an organization and each of its members to act, develop, and change by the conditions, modalities, and constructs of the games through which they have managed to achieve cooperation?[1] This question has no general answer. The constraints it envisages are always linked to concrete and specific problems and solutions, situations, and actors.

To understand and explain the origin and nature of these constraints, we have proposed the strategic method, which cannot study a field of action in the abstract, on the basis of some *a priori rationality*. Instead, we must adopt a restricted phenomenological viewpoint in order to reconstruct the intrinsic logic and rationality of the relations and interactions which operate within the group; this is the only procedure which makes it possible to discover the weight of the constraints on the actors and on the organization they comprise. In each given instance, the contingent nature and rules of the games which structure the relations among actors, and consequently condition their strategies, are sought by the investigator. Once this has been done, it then becomes possible to go back to the modes of regulation which assure the integrated interdependence of these games within a system of action.

In approaching his area of study with such a project in mind, the investigator does not, of course, begin at absolute zero. Apart from his *problematic*, of which we have just given a summary sketch, and his *mode of argument*, which arms him with an analytical instrument, built around such concepts as strategy, capacity, zone of uncertainty, the game and its rules, and suited to the treatment of this problematic, he is in possession of certain preliminaries from which he constructs in a more or less formal way an initial framework for his study.

For one thing, he has "experience." He will himself have previously studied this field or others that are more or less similar. He will be familiar with research done by others in related areas. Consequently, his attention will naturally be drawn to certain situations which "experience," in some sense, will have equipped him to presume will be critical zones or areas of conflict. By giving priority to the analysis of these situations, it will be possible to make more rapid progress in understanding the special features of the field. He may know of certain particular structural features and "objective" constraints characteristic of his field of study; in any event, in his first concern will naturally be to obtain such knowledge if he does not already have it.[2]

Once this initial orientation is achieved, however, the job has just begun. The investigator may be aware that every system of action is constituted through power relations among actors seeking to control zones of uncertainty relevant to the problems to be solved. But this general formulation reveals neither the particular and contingent dynamic of such confrontations, nor the specific configuration of the actors concerned, nor the extent of their strategic fields, nor the limits of the system whose existence must be demonstrated and whose workings must be analyzed. More concretely, if he knows, for example, that every formal rule constitutes an artificial source of uncertainty which may be used by the actors in their strategies, this will suggest leads to follow up. Only after investigating them, however, will he be able to specify the relevance of such and such a category of actors, or measure their general importance.

The problem is the same with knowledge of the particular structural features of the field considered, and with the "objective" constraints that characterize it. Though analysis of such factors is indispensable, it can do no more than indicate a series of limits circumscribing the participants' strategic fields and channeling the possibilities of action—excluding some, creating others. In themselves they are insufficient to enable the investigator to answer the only interesting question: namely, *which* of the potential alternatives is actually chosen by the participants? By the same token, the investigator will not yet be in a position to understand *how* and *why one strategy is pursued rather than another*, or what the significance of each strategy is.

The answers to these questions can be found only by clinical (and necessarily contingent) analysis of the effective relations which grow up among actors in the specific field under study. At this point, the investigator may proceed to study the games and modes of regulation characteristic of the particular system of action.

Strategic analysis is designed to study phenomena which are irreducibly contingent. Once this is acknowledged, it is clear that there is no choice but to adopt a *hypothetico-inductive method* in order to define, in successive stages, an object of study, through observation, comparison, and interpretation of the manifold processes of interaction and exchange which compromise the life of the system under analysis. The method uses the *actual experience* of the participants in order to formulate and verify increasingly general hypotheses concerning the characteristics of the ensemble.

The Path of the Research toward Its Goal

To illustrate how the investigator's thought progresses toward its goal, it is perhaps best to take an example from the field of organizations. We have deliberately chosen a crude one.

An investigator walks into an office where lower-echelon employees are performing extremely monotonous and routine tasks. Contrary to his expectation, however, all, or almost all, find their work interesting, maintain that they are able to take a fair amount of initiative, and seem to be quite satisfied. The investigator's common sense, outside experience, tastes, and knowledge of the formal prerogatives of these employees would lead him to say to himself that they were dulled by their work to the point where they were no longer even capable of recognizing its real nature, and consequently he might be tempted to discount their testimony. As a sociologist, however, he must say: "These people find work interesting which apparently is not. If they say it is, there must be a reason. What is it?" Following this lead, he has to begin searching for possible explanations. This raises problems of comprehension, for he is outside the game. He will first compare this testimony with that of other groups in similar situations, or with what the same group has to say about other problems. Next, he will use these comparisons to formulate hypotheses concerning the *strategy* on which the statement of the employees is based, and the *game* in relation to which such a strategy might appear rational. In attaching a significance to their expressed "interest" in their work, he will be led to discover certain key elements of the situation, e.g., the nature and characteristics of the game within which members of this group develop their strategies. It will be useful to review and comment rapidly on the principal steps in this process.

In order to be in a position to observe, compare, analyze, and interpret observed behavior, the investigator first has to be skeptical of the appearance of this behavior as perceived and described by the actors themselves. He must obtain a certain critical perspective on sense experience and common-sense categories (the actors' as well as his own). The observed facts must be stripped of their "evident" character, which is the way in which the participants ordinarily regard them.

This is a well-known epistemological requirement. Bachelard,[3] among others, has devoted some luminous pages to the question; it is no doubt useless to treat it again here. We have neither the desire nor the capability to engage in the traditional endless and intractable discussion as to the status and role of the social scientist in society; it should be noted that this often revolves around a requirement which it is clear is never completely fulfilled and which, moreover, does not depend solely on an "intellectual attitude" of the sociologist. Indeed, the whole problem of the investigator's autonomy—his institutional and financial as well as his personal and intellectual, if not cultural, independence—is involved.

Initially, the investigator is in the position of an outsider generally skeptical about the nature of the reality he observes. But this position offers no criteria for judgment, no normative base, which would allow him to "evaluate" what he sees. He must avoid "ethnocentrism." There is no *one best way*, and, *a fortiori*, no rationality exterior to the field that he can take for granted as evident. His problem is not to evaluate or even criticize the observed practices, but to understand them. The basic heuristic assumption which guides the whole approach is this: no matter how anomalous, contradictory, or senseless the observed phenomena may appear at first sight, *they all make sense and correspond to some rationality from the moment they come into existence.* It is precisely the search for this "deep sense," often hidden behind the apparent "sense" or "nonsense," which is the essential part of the investigator's work. To accomplish his task, he must find the particular constraints in relation to which apparently irrational conduct is irrational no longer.

This means that he must abandon the position of detached observer standing outside the field of inquiry in order to take a "detour" through the "inside" of the actors' own situations. It is only by reconstructing *from within* the inherent logic of the situation as perceived and experienced by the actors themselves that he will reach a position where it becomes possible to discover the *implicit factors* in relation to which apparently aberrant conduct takes on sense and meaning. In a manner analogous to that which he saw in the above example, the "objective" structure of the field can be elucidated by identifying its key elements, not all of which will necessarily be evident at the outset. This is accomplished by explaining the "subjective" significance of the behavior of the actors.

Thus the research method involves two complementary but contrasting orientations, and constant interchange between them. Initially, the investigator must gain some perspective to preserve his autonomy and his unjaundiced view. But he then has to move right to the heart of the matter, as it were, to "put himself in the place" of the various actors in order to reconstruct the logic of the diverse situations they face. Finally, having taken this "plunge," he will in one way or another have to recover his own exteriority and compare the many contingent rationalities or strategies he may have observed; then, little by little, he can gain access to the implicit characteristics and rules of the game which structure the field in which he is interested.

What really interests the investigator are the relations of power among the actors and the implicit rules that govern their interactions. In order to get at this underlying reality, he must be able to separate from the mass of available observational data the information useful to his argument.

The criteria that govern this sifting of data are elaborated by the investigator himself, who uses what might be called the *method of anomalies.* Its principle is simple. In a more or less formalized manner (depending on the phase of the research), the investigator will use the available descriptive data relative to his field in order to formulate a series of hypotheses as to what ought to be observed if everything went "normally," i.e., in a way consistent with the logic and "rationality" used in elaborating the hypotheses. By then comparing these predictions with what actually occurs in practice, he will discover a whole series of "anomalies" or processes and conducts which do not seem to obey the rational "norms" embodied in his hypotheses.

These anomalies are invaluable. They indicate the areas where the hypotheses are in contradiction with the actual behavior of the actors. It is thus possible to pinpoint those places where a rationality different from the one known to the investigator is guiding the relations among individuals and groups. These anomalies thus indicate parts of the argument which need to be developed, and this in turn leads to the discovery of further characteristics of the organization.

The Importance of the Actors' "Experience"

It is apparent from the foregoing that the logic of the strategic-analytic method accords a primary importance to the *experience of the participants*. This means that *interviews* must be regarded as a prime source of information.

The usefulness of the interview depends on its ability to provide the investigator with the insight into the actor's inner experience which he is seeking. Interviews are a technique for rapidly acquiring a significant amount of concrete information regarding the actors' experience and the *implicit* factors associated with the field under study. Using this information, the investigator may ask how each actor confronts his situation and its inherent constraints, *what objectives* he sets for himself, and how he perceives his potential for attaining these objectives within the given structure. In other words, he seeks to know what *resources* the actor possesses, what his *margin of liberty* is, and *in what way, under what conditions, and within what limits* he can make use of them.

This means that the tension between the two poles identified above—the exterior and the interior—is reproduced in each individual interview. This is characteristic of the method. The investigator who wants to explore largely unfamiliar terrain must display a particularly open attitude in order to demonstrate to his subject that he is an interested and understanding partner whose role is limited to asking open questions which allow the other person to talk of his work, describe his situation as he sees it, etc. By definition, the interviewees are always "right," since it is they who experience the situation, not the investigator.

For all these reasons, the investigator's attitude toward his subject must be respectful and open; but obviously this does not man that it should be passive, as a completely nondirective approach would require.[4] The interviews have a precise goal: they must bring out the opportunities and capacities to act that are characteristic of the various actors in the specific field under study. The investigator's problem in other words, is to lead his subject to reveal the sources of his action and to explain the characteristics of the strategic field in which he must act as he sees them. Each interview, then, is a strategic situation, in which the researcher's problem is to use the "spontaneous" dynamic of the session in order to achieve his own objectives.

It will be said that the testimony gathered in this way by the sociologist will not in general reflect "objective" reality, but rather the way the actor perceives and experiences it from his point of view: *it is inevitably "subjective."* This is not a valid objection to strategic analysis. The essential point of this method is precisely to surpass the artificial dichotomy between "objective" and "subjective" reality. The strategic analyst regards the subjectivity of others, their manner of choosing strategies according to their perception of the constraints binding them, as an important element—quite as "objective" as the technical or economic constraints—in defining the situation in relation to which each individual elaborates his particular strategy and conduct.[5]

It is perhaps worth noting that from our viewpoint this recourse to the "experience" of the actors is much more than a kind of symbolic tip of the hat to "the importance of the human factor." By the same token it is much more than a perfunctory complement to knowledge of the formal characteristics of the field. It is the *primary condition for a genuine understanding of the field in question.* "Objective" knowledge can be constructed only through analysis of "subjective" experience, and this is the only procedure that allows the investigator to discover and set out in detail the effective significance, importance, and range of some supposedly objective constraint which was not at all obvious at the outset.

The problem, therefore, lies not in the subjective character of the testimony, but rather in the use to which strategic analysis puts the data thus gathered. In effect, we are treating the information obtained from interviews as a sort of primary indicator, ultimately the only one, of the subjective choices made by the actors among the opportunities offered by their respective situations. The actor's testimony is taken as an *expression of his strategy.* It is not self-evident why this should be justified. The point is worth considering at greater length.

The Problem of Materials

Implicit in what appears at first as a choice of method is, as we have indicated, a different conceptualization of attitudes, a conceptualization which touches on both the links between attitudes and behavior and the processes by which these links are formed. From the standpoint of strategic analysis, individuals develop attitudes not as a function of the past (their socialization, their past experience), but as a function of the future, of the present and future opportunities that they see in the games they are playing and in relation to which they orient their strategies. For the sake of simplicity, it might be said that here attitudes are explained not so much by the individual's past insofar as it conditions present behavior, but rather by the present behavior itself. Through it, we come to understand the nature and rules of the games which direct it, and whose characteristics are at the heart of the organizational phenomenon. This is what the investigator tries to grasp in examining individual attitudes.

Before we turn to setting out in detail the premises and consequences associated with such a reversal of perspective, and to giving some illustrations, we must describe very succinctly how social psychology has used attitudes, what evolution the notion has undergone, and what theoretical premises are implicit in this evolution.[6]

Attitudes in Social Psychology

When it made its appearance in the vocabulary of German *experimental* psychology toward the end of the last century, the notion of attitude was assimilated to *a neuropsychic state which preceded and facilitated an action.* In this first restrictive usage, it designated primarily a mental process, a sort of "mental adjustment,"[7] a provoked and therefore conscious "attention" of individuals in an experimental situation which facilitated and accelerated their response to a stimulus given them.[8]

The discussion of the concept in social psychology and its introduction into situations of a less experimental nature greatly extended and broadened its range of application and essentially modified its status. Through various stages about which there is no need to go into detail here, the term *attitudes* came to designate *relatively permanent normative orientations* of individuals with respect to certain privileged social objects, selected according to the central interests and specific needs of the research: unemployment, women's suffrage, religion, political parties, work, the company, etc.[9]

Discernible behind this extension of the concept's usage is a significant shift in the burden of research, on both methodological and substantive levels. On the methodological level, first, the technique of observation and measurement changed. Attitudes were no longer observed directly, but rather *indirectly* through a series of more or less complex measurements of the degree of satisfactions felt by individuals with regard to the various dimensions of such and such an object of the social reality under study.[10] As a result, attitude became the *inferred basis*, constructed after the fact, for the judgments and opinions collected from the subjects. It was the stable element, the psychological structure underlying the opinions and giving them sense and coherence. Opinion—which came to mean instantaneous evaluation of a social object—depended in some way on a more stable evaluation of this same object, which was the attitude.

On the substantive level, this implied a movement toward an increasingly abstract object of research, from opinions to attitudes and finally to the value systems to which individuals were supposed to subscribe. Attitude was the bridge between observable individual conduct and the value structure which was supposed to orient this conduct but which was unobservable. *Values were sought through attitudes.*[11]

This explains why the study of attitudes came progressively to focus not so much on the attitudes themselves but rather on the processes by which they are *formed and transformed.*[12] From this standpoint, the problem for research was one of identifying social situations, structures, and roles in which individuals undergo significant experiences of social learning, and of defining the social objects concerning which they acquire attitudes. Consistencies in the constitution and acquisition of attitudes were sought through study of the mechanisms by which these attitudes were formed and transformed, and attitude itself was conceptualized as reflecting the motivations which oriented and explained behavior.[13]

With a little perspective, it becomes clear that this use of the notion of attitude is based on certain theoretical premises which are not always very explicit. It will be useful at this point to bring them out clearly.

First, regardless of how the concept is extended, *attitude* is always considered an *individual attribute.* It refers to what is individual as opposed to what is "situational." In a given situation, several types of behavior are possible. Attitude makes it possible to understand the individual's choice of one of them. It thus tells us something about him.[14] It implicates the features of his personality and even his system of values.[15]

It is of course true that the concept of the individual varies and can be more or less complex. Initially, the individual was defined wholly in terms of the attitudes he adopted through meaningful experiences of social learning. Later, an attempt was made to incorporate the individual's analytical capacities into the argument, but an irrational component remained, that was irreducible to an instrumental calculation: this was the "attitude," which was based on the individual's prior experience.

Regardless of which point of view as adopted, attitude was defined with reference to the individual, his personality, his system of values, and its formation. Here we encounter a second more or less implicit theoretical assumption: when attitudes are used to explain behavior, they come to be based, intentionally or not, on a *theory of social learning in the matrix of society.* In other words, one implicitly refers to a theory that incorporates the following chain of deductions: first comes society with a certain social structure; then the personality is formed within this structured universe through meaningful social experiences which lead to the adoption of certain values and personality traits; these in turn induce certain types of opinions and behavior.[16]

Explanations for the acquisition of values through meaningful social experiences vary. For the behaviorists, as is well known, this is a process of instrumental learning in which attitudes form and are reinforced, little by little, in response to punishments and rewards coming from the environment. Other approaches, such as the *theory of cognitive dissonance,* deduce learning and transformation of attitudes from a principle of internal coherence.[17] Still others use methods inspired by psychoanalysis to look for the origin of attitudes in the needs, anxieties, inhibitions, motivations, and defense mechanisms of individuals, i.e., in the *functions* the attitudes fulfill in relation to the subject's experience and subconscious.[18]

This explains the *retrospective character* of most analyses. From such a vintage as we have been describing, attitudes can only be understood in relation to the subject's past experience, of which they are in some sense the reflection. This also explains the interest in and justification for *studying attitudes in themselves.* Once acquired and established, they are relatively stable, hence measurable. They have a life and logic of their own, which is precisely what needs to be brought to light in order to understand the subjects' reactions. This, finally, accounts for the *predictive use* which has often been made of attitudes. Since they may be regarded as relatively stable, if we know what they are we can predict the reactions and behavior of subjects in different circumstances, and even direct them by controlling their learning experiences.

An Example

Attitudes have been studied in industrial sociology and in the sociology of work. Very simply summarized, the personality of the individual on the job is analyzed in these disciplines as a set of attitudes which govern his responses to organizational requirements. In order to understand these responses, and eventually to change them so as to make improvements in the operation of the organization, the attitudes in question must be measured and explained.

Though strategic analysis belongs to this current of thought, it has gradually evolved another use of the concept. We would like to illustrate this with the following example, taken from a study made between 1956 and 1958 in six Parisian insurance companies.[19] A questionnaire was used to obtain information concerning individual perceptions, feelings, and opinions relative to various aspects of work experience. Consistent with the "classical" outlook of the sociology of work, one of the aims of this study was to measure and understand how individual attitudes toward work were structured. The study produced disconcerting results which led to a change in our point of view. We would like to call attention to these results before we go on to discuss their implications in greater detail.

Two major dimensions were incorporated: first, the manner in which individuals evaluated the interest of their *work,* and, second, the *satisfaction* they felt with regard to their *situation.* At the top of the hierarchy, the policy writers exhibited interest in their work with the greatest frequency, but at the same time they were the most likely to declare themselves dissatisfied with their situations. Conversely, the individuals at the bottom of the hierarchical ladder were most likely both to find their work uninteresting and to say they were satisfied with their situations.

This pattern in the results was disconcerting: it was difficult to accept the fact that satisfaction with the situation is more pronounced at the bottom than at the top of the hierarchy, especially since these results contradicted the "objective" analysis, which found very low salaries but relatively tranquil working conditions at the bottom of the scale and higher salaries but poorer working conditions at the top.

To move our interpretation forward, it was necessary to change our view of attitudes. No longer were these seen as mere reactions to a passively evaluated reality, but rather as signs of the strategic perception of each actor. At the lower level, the employees felt too threatened to complain about their situation. But there were fewer risks in expressing dissatisfaction with their work. This even enabled them to move the implicit negotiation with the company onto ground where they felt more secure; they were able to assert their superiority to their station and thus demand better working conditions as a reward for their loyalty. On the other hand, a high-level position in the hierarchy conferred certain advantages which reduced the risks involved in criticizing one's situation. At this level, the function was accompanied by a certain undeniable prestige which was an advantage in the implicit negotiation, insofar as the importance of the work could be used to justify an improvement in the situation.

To sum up, the policy writer complained about the conditions to which he was subjected by his company in the name of the importance and dignity of his job, while the secretary tended to use her loyalty to the company as justification for asking for more interesting work.

Attitude in the Strategic Procedure: Premises and Consequences

Although the foregoing example is limited and incomplete,[20] it is a good illustration of the change of perspective in the treatment of attitudes. For strategic analysis, these are no longer reflections of a reaction or a summation of past experience, but rather correspond to the strategic *orientations* adopted by the social actors, taking into account their possibilities and resources, as well as the constraints that bind them. They therefore reflect the actors' choice of an orientation for their action in the face of the risks and opportunities offered by the games in which they participate. In simple terms, for strategic analysis the attitudes of the actors do not depend on the past but rather on the future, as the actors, with their present resources and expectations, see it; more precisely, attitudes depend on opportunities discovered in the games in play, to which behavior must be adjusted. In short, it is opportunity that makes the thief, not his past history.[21]

Thus we may say that the analysis of attitudes in this perspective is *prospective* rather than *retrospective* in character. Certain opportunities emerge from the actors' situations and games. Depending on their resources and capacities, some of these will be taken advantage of, and corresponding strategies will be adopted. The actors will adjust their behavior to these choices. According to a schema which extends and develops the approach to social learning in terms of a cognitive dissonance that requires an effort to restore coherence,[22] these choices will in turn represent a strong pressure on the orientation of the actors' attitudes. Attitudes thus express a kind of choice:[23] they are indicative of the effective use which actors can and wish to make of the available resources in view of the opportunities offered by the game.

Thus the retrospective aspect of attitude is supplemented by a prospective dimension. The attitudes of the actors express a *strategic orientation* that comes out of an evaluation of their potential for action, a sort of anticipatory computation of wins and losses, and in which the present situation is analyzed in terms of advantages and resources which may be mobilized in the future. To return to our previous example, it is clear that neither the policy writers' nor the secretaries' attitudes can be explained by a simple accounting of profits and losses. Another kind of calculation is involved. Both policy writers and secretaries seek to determine the strong and weak points of their situation, together with potential means for taking offensive or defensive action.

Of course, the past experience of the actors, their values and attitudes in the social-psychological sense, do not disappear in such an analysis: they largely condition the way the actors will perceive their game opportunities and structure their capacities so as to take advantage of these opportunities. As we showed above,[24] an individual will adopt a particular strategy not only because he sees an opportunity, but also because he has the necessary capacities—material, affective, cognitive, relational—for accepting its risks and difficulties. Similarly, if a group adopts a certain game, it does so not only because of its goals and resources, but also because of the constraints which limits its margin for maneuver and range of options. These constraints come from the mechanisms of integration (including values) and constructs which the group has no choice but to rely on for its very existence as coherent entity. The past experience of individuals, their "socialization," and the resulting values therefore do not disappear from the analysis; they are merely relativized. Here, these factors become nothing more than the elements which structure the capacities of individuals and groups, thereby indirectly conditioning individual strategies and collective games.

For the strategic method, attitudes indicate not the characteristic or "personalities" of individuals as determinants of their behavior, but rather the subjective *relationship* that individuals establish between their situation and the game in the light of their resources and capacities, or, in short, the *strategies* they have adopted or will adopt. It is possible, therefore, to take attitudes as signs which reveal these strategies and consequently the characteristics and rules of the games that define the range of possible strategies and keep the system of action operating.

Attitudes thus provide access to "inside" knowledge of the way in which members of a system of action intend to use the margin of liberty, hence of power, available to them within a given framework of games. Similarly, they indicate what resources and opportunities are distributed by the system among its members. Attitudes will apply to individuals, then, but in this view what is of explanatory value is their situation within a game to be discovered. In other words, at the risk of giving a somewhat caricatural description, it would be possible to characterize the reversal of perspective sketched above in the following way. In social psychology, the explanatory value of attitudes lies in the fact that they are supposed to reveal permanent individual dispositions to act, and hence intrinsic individual values as these define and differentiate a given personality. In strategic analysis, on the other hand, the explanatory value of attitudes lies in the state of a system of action which they reveal. The characteristics and mode of regulation associated with this system state structure the games in which the members must play, which is the basis of the explanation of their behavior.

It follows that strategic analysis is not interested in observing attitudes outside of a specific situation and its associated structure. Attitudes have no other structure. *The attitude no longer has any value in itself; it ceases to be an "in-itself"* (en-soi). There is no longer any point to collecting attitudes for the purposes of abstract measurement; they are only a tool for inferring the strategic orientations of the actors.

If it were possible to have direct access to knowledge of games, which could be described as ranges of options aimed at certain individual capacities; and if, moreover, it were possible to identify and measure these capacities; it would then be possible to dispense with the notion of attitude. That such a procedure is difficult if not impossible underscores the interest in an analysis of attitudes. We may think of them as tools permitting rapid access to the essential point: the various choices effectively made by the members of a system of action from a range of options.

Attitudes, then, are convenient, yet imperfect, research devices or tools which strategic analysis uses to observe the subjective aspect of a game which remains to be discovered. They are useful in a *heuristic procedure* whose purpose is to facilitate the observation and comprehension of the way the members of a system of action put together their situational potential in order to exploit the opportunities offered by the game. This is the primary goal of the research. The important point is to understand the interdependence of the subjective combinations of the potential in various situations. To put it another way, one wants to understand the interdependence of the various strategies in a system. This will make it possible to understand the structure and regulation of the system of action under study

Interpretation: From Feelings to Games, From Games to Structures

The investigator's first order of business is to familiarize himself with the terrain and to make a quick inspection tour to determine its objective characteristics.[25] He will then have to devote a fairly extensive amount of time to gathering information by interviewing actors belonging to the various categories which he identifies with the aid of his formal, and inevitably rough, knowledge of the field.

From these interviews, the investigator will collect a variety of data providing quite concrete information as to the perceptions and feelings of individuals and groups regarding their respective situations. In particular, his data will include: detailed information regarding perception and behavior, constraints and ensuing difficulties; information on relationships among the actors, the importance placed on them, associated expectations, nature of frequent conflicts and of solutions generally attempted; information concerning the actors' evaluations of their activities, situations, relations, areas of satisfaction and/or dissatisfaction, hopes and disappointments; finally, the actors' estimates of their own and others' action potential in view of the foregoing.

Whether these data are qualitative in nature, deriving from relatively unstructured interviews, or the result of a statistical treatment of quantified answers to a formal questionnaire, in the strategic method the problems of interpretation are always the same. The descriptive data regarding opinions, perceptions, sentiments, and attitudes must be used to reconstruct the power structure, together with the games and their rules, which regulates the interaction and conduct of the actors.

To this end, the investigator's first priority will be to establish what different strategies are involved. This is the object of the intensive analysis that he will make of the explicit and implicit[26] contents of the interviews or statistical studies.[27] Inevitably, there will be at least indirect and implicit indications of the power element involved in each actor's relations with the others, and of their respective evaluations of the chance for profit and loss. The data collected will be studied as evidence of the actors' perceptions, feelings, and attitudes, their comments on certains problems, their explanations and rationalizations for certain behavior, and their satisfactions and dissatisfactions. This is true even though these data always reflect certain "official" aspects of their situation. Nevertheless, the investigator gains access to the *strategic perceptions* each actor makes of his situation, and to the *adjustment* he makes to a more or less conscious system or relations with the properties revealed by the research.

By a continual effort to reconcile the convergent and/or discordant data derived from the interviews, the investigator will attempt to discover the internal logic that implicitly structures the set of perceptions, feelings, and attitudes of each category of actors. The goal is to identify and detail the various strategies involved.[28]

If quantified data are available and the field of investigation is suitable,[29] the investigator may use a supplementary technique to "test" directly the validity of the strategies he thinks he has found. He can communicate the raw results of the investigation to the parties involved, without any commentary, but after making certain hypotheses concerning their probable reactions. For instance, when the results were presented to the workers in the Industrial Monopoly, the reactions of the maintenance workers were extremely revealing as to their particular strategic situation. The members of this group denied and challenged all the results which did not correspond to the majority strategy of aggressive domination. There was one noteworthy exception: the union officials from this group made comments which clearly were worded so as to minimize the sharpness of the prior attack. This is easily comprehensible: it was important that the power of the maintenance workers and the accompanying conflicts remain hidden. Too much publicity would have threatened the status quo, which gave these individuals the upper hand in the union as well as the shop. so they tried to confuse the issue.

Once the strategies have been identified, it remains to *explain* them. Our fundamental hypothesis, according to which the strategies are rational, has been amply justified by its heuristic usefulness.[30] If a strategy appears to be irrational, a closer look must be taken at the situation(s) which enter into the definition of rationalities. Technical, juridical, social, and economic constraints have to be considered, along with the "rules of the game" which reflect the relations of power which structure the organization's system of action. Comparison of the strategies identified with the "objective" constraints will show that the latter are only partially adequate to explain the former. As long as the power structure has not been brought into the picture, a zone of "rationally" inexplicable strategic behavior remains. The nature and "rules of the games" which provide regulation of the underlying system of action must also be taken into account.

In other words, to *explain* the strategies pursued by the various actors, the investigator will seek to *make explicit* the relationship, or, better, the *implicit mediation* which exists between a collection of constraints inherent in the field being studied (technical and economic constraints, official regulations, etc.), which *define the critical zones of uncertainty;* and a *set of strategies* which can be reconstructed from the responses collected during the investigation, reflecting the strategic perception of their respective possibilities by the various actors, in the light of the over-all constraints.

To reconstruct this mediation, the investigator will formulate increasingly general hypotheses concerning the characteristics and rules of the implicit games within which several strategies can be rational simultaneously. He will begin with a simple hypothesis regarding the implicit game between two groups. In order to verify this hypothesis, he will first ask what consequences the characteristics and rules of this first game should have on the strategies of a third group; then he will check to see if the responses given by this group are compatible with his analysis. Depending on the outcome, he may have to reformulate the initial hypothesis, or broaden it, before submitting it to another test against attitudes and feelings, and so on. Using such an iterative procedure—going from feelings to strategies, strategies to games, and then back to feelings, etc.—the investigator will be able to discover, from the experience of the various actors (individuals or groups), the power structure in the field under study and the games that condition the behavior of the actors.

To make this somewhat abstract schema concrete, it may be useful to apply it to a simplified concrete example, taken from the Industrial Monopoly. When his investigation is complete, the researcher will have amassed information concerning the attitudes of production and maintenance workers. From this the undercurrent of conflict between these two groups will emerge clearly, along with the caustic comments each group is bound to make about the other. To explain this undercurrent, the first step is to try to reconstruct the strategies of the two groups. If a crude way, the strategy of the maintenance workers might be characterized as one of attempting to assert a peremptory, if not aggressive, superiority over the production workers. The production workers' attitudes, on the other hand, indicate a strategy of official submission coupled with what amounts to indirect resistance. The next step is to ask what type of game such strategies might correspond to. An obvious hypothesis would be that the two groups confront one another, with highly unequal resources, over a stake of great importance: the extent and control of the arbitrary margin of power possessed by the maintenance workers because of their dominance over a crucial source of uncertainty: the breakdown of machines. Thanks to this dominance, they are the real "bosses" of the shop. If this hypothesis is correct, it will affect relations between production workers and shop foremen. When one examines the attitudes of these two groups toward each other, one finds, contrary to what might be expected in relations between superiors and subordinates, that there is a virtual absence of emotional content. In a similar way, if one analyzes the attitudes of the maintenance workers and shop foremen toward each other, one can support and complete the initial hypothesis, and so on. We have done no more than note the high points of the procedure the investigator will follow. It will lead him to discover the particular importance of the breakdown of machines, which is far from obvious *a priori*, but specific to the system of action within the Industrial Monopoly. He will gain an understanding of the maintenance workers' consistent strategy of defending their expert role by hiding the machine plans and maintenance bulletins, and he will grasp the significance of these strategies for the underlying system of action.

The key to the method of strategic analysis is thus to use the data gathered in interviews in order to define the strategies pursued by the actors and ultimately to have access to the games which correspond to these strategies. These games indicate the structure of the power relations which link the various actors. It is this structure which must be clarified if the over-all regulation of the system of action is to be understood.

Notes

1. Despite differences of context and objectives, the same conclusions on this point can be found in numerous studies of industrial firms since Hawthorne's celebrated pioneering effort, as well as in subsequent studies of administrative organizations and even of prisons and asylums. From this rich literature, the reader may wish to consult, for industrial organizations, F. J. Roethlisberger, W. J. Dickson, et al., *Management and the Worker* (Cambridge, Mass.: Harvard University Press, 1939); C. J. Walker and R. H. Guest, *The Man on the Assembly Line,* (Cambridge, Mass.: Harvard University Press, 1952); E. Jacques, *The Changing Culture of the Factory* (New York: Wiley, 1952); A. W. Gouldner, *Patterns of Industrial Bureaucracy* (New York: Free Press, 1954); T. Lupton, *On the Shop Floor* (Oxford: Pergamon Press, 1962). For administrative organizations, see P. Selznick, *TVA and the Grass Roots* (Berkeley: University of California Press, 1949); P. M. Blau, *The Dynamics of Bureaucracy* (Chicago: University of Chicago Press, 1955); M. Crozier, *The Bureaucratic Phenomenon* (Chicago: University of Chicago Press, 1964). And for prisons and mental hospitals: D. R. Cressey, "Prison Organizations," in J. G. March, ed., *Handbook of Organizations* (Chicago: Rand McNally, 1965), pp. 1023–70; E. Goffman, *Asylums* (Chicago: Aldine, 1961); and A. Lévy, *Les paradoxes de la liberté dans un hôpital psychiatrique* (Paris: Editions de l'Epi, 1969).

2. Goffman gives numerous examples of this in his analysis of life in mental hospitals. Earlier accounts by inmates of concentration camps showed that even extreme terror did not entirely halt the development of autonomous human relationships.

3. Crozier, *The Bureaucratic Phenomenon*, p. 150.

4. It is impossible to understand the real life and dynamic of an organization without admitting the existence of a very strong, and sometimes passionate, attachment of its poorest members, or, if you prefer, of its most "exploited" members, to a liberty which, when viewed hastily from outside, does not seem particularly beneficial to them. We will return to this point. See our remarks on change in part 5.

5. This fact, which ought to be a result of common sense, is not always very readily accepted in the present context. Nevertheless, it provides the only explanatory and interpretative scheme really capable of accounting for the variety and plasticity of human conduct, which always manages to confound even the cleverest a priori "motivational" or "structural" constructions. Nothing else can explain the integration of the wide range of behavior empirically observable in a given "objective" situation, including the extreme case of entirely passive behavior.

6. These constraints may eventually be overcome, but not without a certain cost.

7. Contingent in the radical sense of the term, i.e., *both* dependent on a context, on opportunities and constraints (material and human), *and* indeterminate, hence free.

8. Argyris's thought on this point has undergone continual evolution. Here we are dealing

with the implications of his arguments in works such as *Integrating the Individual and the Organization* (New York: Wiley, 1964) and *Organization and Innovation* (Homewood, Ill.: Irwin, 1965). In his recent books, particularly those written with Donald Shon, he takes a totally different point of view. See below, p. 243.

9. Maslow conceptualizes man's psychological needs as a hierarchy. At the bottom are those psychological needs which dominate all the rest so long as they are not satisfied (food, clothing, etc.). Next are needs of security (those deriving from employment, etc.) followed by social needs (need to feel accepted by others, etc.), which the interactionist school has particularly stressed, and finally by the needs of personality (dignity, self-actualization, etc.). For Maslow, the only important needs are the ones which have yet to be satisfied. Thus in a society of utter poverty, if the physiological needs are not yet satisfied, social needs are not relevant for explaining human behavior. In such a society, the Taylorist assumption of *homo economicus* would therefore be applicable. It is easy to see how such an anlaysis could be—and in fact has been—exploited to advance a mechanistic view. See A. H. Maslow, *Motivation and Personality* (New York: Harper, 1954).

10. We are not really very far from the Taylorist *one best way*, which in some sense has been inverted. The material, economic rationality has merely been replaced by a psychological one. We will have occasion to return to the problems raised by this argument in a much more explicit and caricatural form in what is usually called the "new organizational psychology." See chap. 14, which is devoted to problems of intervention in social action.

11. It is symptomatic of this sort of dilemma that, for instance, in regard to the apathetic behavior he observes, Argyris is reduced to practicing a sort of backward Marxism and to talking of "repressed" or "suppressed" needs. See Argyris, *Integrating the Individual and the Organization*, esp. p. 73.

12. For a good exposition of this model in a research context, see A. Zaleznik et al., *The Motivation, Productivity and Satisfaction of Workers* (Boston: Harvard Business School, 1958). For an application in France, see also L. Karpik, "Trois concepts sociologiques: le projet de référence, le statut social et le bilan individuel," *Archives européennes de sociologie*, 2 (1965):191–222, and "Attentes et satisfactions au travail," *Sociologie du travail*, 4 (1966):389–416. We should add that Karpik seems subsequently to have abandoned this type of analysis.

13. Or, in any case, there is no reason to say a priori that they constitute crucial sources of cleavage. Only empirical analysis of organizational processes makes it possible to answer this question, or, in other words, to take account precisely of the organizational constraints.

14. This remarkable study is to this day the best in-depth analysis of the phenomenon, which is too often accepted as self-evident, of the existence of concrete groups within an organization. The reader should refer to the work from which it was taken: L. R. Sayles, *Behavior of Industrial Work Groups* (New York: Wiley, 1958).

15. Strategic groups are groups which have opportunities on which they can capitalize and which are therefore primarily offensive, and conservative groups are groups which at least temporarily have obtained the maximum and are mainly interested in defending their situation.

16. Note in passing that this type of consideration makes it possible to understand a very common phenomenon which is contradictory to conventional wisdom: in most circumstances within organized groups, the advantage is not with the huge batallions but rather with the small groups which are alone capable of mounting sustained actions and which are eventually capable of mobilizing the huge batallions.

17. For a very fine and suggestive analysis of such processes, see D. Kergoat, *Bulle d'or ou l'histoire d'une mobilisation ourvrière* (Paris: Editions du Seuil, 1973); and, by the same author, "Emergence et création d'un système d'action collective à travers une expérience d'autogestion en mai 68," *Sociologie du travail*, 3 (1970):274–92.

18. These preliminary remarks must necessarily be rather sketchy. They will assume their full significance when we have examined the game mechanisms—the fundamental instrument of organized action—within which such constructs can be elaborated. See chap. 14.

19. The model of the sovereign and rational actor is deeply rooted in our culture and plays an essential role in our thinking. We will return to this point at greater length in the last two parts of this work, which are devoted to problems of decision and change.

20. Working with the results of a whole series of studies of decisions within large organizations, March and Simon have shown, first, that problems were solved sequentially and not synoptically, and that, secondly, various constraints (cognitive, affective, organizational) prevented the actors from seeking the optimal solution and led them instead to settle for the first solution attaining a minimum threshold of satisfaction. See J. G. March and H. A. Simon, *Organizations* (New York: Wiley, 1958); and H. A. Simon, *Administrative Behavior* (New York: Macmillan, 1957). In the chapters devoted to the problems of decision, we will return to all the implications of such a proposition. See chap. 10.

21. This point was strongly and rightly stressed by K. E. Weick in his rich and stimulating analysis of organizational processes, in which he speaks of an "enacted environment." See K. E. Weick, *The Social Psychology of Organizing* (Reading, Mass.: Addison-Wesley, 1969), esp. pp. 63–71.

22. Note in passing the evident kinship of this approach with that of the "interpretive sociology" (*verstehende Soziologie*) of Max Weber, *Wirtschaft und Gesellschaft* (Cologne, Berlin: Kiepenheuer & Witsch, 1964), esp. pp. 1–42, and of A. Schutz, *Der sinnhafte Aufbau der sozialen Welt: Eine Einleitung in die verstehende Soziologie* (Vienna, 1932), which is an attempt to synthesize Weber's views with the phenomenological philosophy of E. Husserl. Schutz's work (see also M. Natanson, ed., *Collected Papers* [The Hague: Nijhoff, 1964]) has recently aroused renewed interest in the United States as well as in Germany and England, where the "ethnomethodological" and "Goffmannian" schools have taken inspiration from it. See esp. P. L. Berger and T. H. Luckmann, *The Social Construction of Reality: A Treatise in the Sociology of Knowledge* (New York: Doubleday, 1966); H. Garfinkel, *Studies in Ethnomethodology* (Englewood Cliffs, N.J.: Prentice-Hall, 1967); E. Goffman, *The Presentation of Self in Everyday Life* (New York: Doubleday, 1959), and *Asylums*.

23. See R. D. Laing, *The Divided Self* (London: Tavistock, 1959), whose works are ample demonstration of the fruitfulness of this method, which is directly inspired by existentialist phenomenonology.

24. See Jean-Paul Sartre, *Esquisse d'une théorie des émotions* (Paris: Hermann, 1960), rev. ed.

25. For a discussion in greater depth of the repercussions of such an approach on research methodology, see our remarks in the Appendix.

26. We only review the highlights of this case here. For a detailed analysis, see Crozier, *The Bureaucratic Phenomenon*, pp. 58–111.

27. For example, a very strict seniority rule codifies in detail the solutions to be applied to the problem of distributing job assignments among the production workers and of moving them from one job to another. Thus it is specified that in case of vacancy (illness, termination, machine breakdown, etc.), the job must go to the most senior person among those available and willing. If no one volunteers, then the person with the least seniority will get the assignment.

28. Since, however, the production workers elect the union leaders, they recover a certain amount of power which they can exploit against the maintenance workers. Of course, the latter answers this extortion by threatening periodically to quit the single union to which they belong and found one of their own. Still, on this level, the maintenance workers are vulnerable. They cannot, therefore, go too far.

29. Only the analysis of relations of power is able to explain why this tense atmosphere

does not degenerate into open conflict. The production workers' dependency is too great. There is in fact a division of roles within the production workers' group. Only those not in direct contact with the maintenance workers allow themselves to make open criticisms. The others (the drivers) focus their criticisms on other points.

30. To avoid misunderstanding, it should be strongly emphasized that the particular importance of breakdowns in the shops of the monopoly is not inherent in the technology utilized. Surveys in other plants in different countries using the same machines demonstrated, in fact, that there were less frequent breakdowns, and that the ones that did occur were repaired more quickly. Thus, while the importance of breakdowns depends, of course, on technological factors, it is nevertheless manipulated by the strategy of the maintenance workers, who derive their power from it. This is confirmed in a recent study by an English sociologist concerning cigarette factories in his country. See P. Clark, "The Cultural Context of Bureaucratic Pathologies and Routine Organizations," in C. J. Lammers, *Organizations Unlike and Alike: Towards a Comparative Sociology of Organizations*, to appear.

Chapter 2

1. Consideration of the actor's experience is indispensable to the understanding of relations which make no sense apart from that experience. On the other hand, the meaning of that experience derives from aspects of power inseparable from the organizational context.

2. The theses developed in this chapter are the fruit of a series of efforts to extend the original notions of Michel Crozier. A preliminary exposition can be found in "Power and Organization," *Archives européennes de sociologie* 5, no. 1 (1964):52–64, and in *The Stalled Society* (New York: Viking, 1973). In addition, we have made use of ideas from the talks given by Jean-Pierre Worms in the course of a series of seminars at the Centre de Sociologie des Organisations (Paris).

3. This is what the American political scientist Robert A. Dahl meant in defining power as the "capacity of person A to make person B do something that he would not have done without A's intervention." See R. A. Dahl, "The Concept of Power," *Behavioral Sciences* 2 (1957):201–15; and "Power," *Encyclopedia of the Social Sciences*, vol. 12 (New York, 1968), pp. 405–15. The attractive simplicity of such a definition should not, however, hide its obvious gaps, and particularly the following: the impossibility with such a definition to distinguish between intentional power and influence without the knowledge of one of the parties, the lack of recognition of the specific dependence of A's power on the action requested, and, finally, the very clear bias toward a viewpoint predicated on the "holding" of power, which is still regarded as an attribute of the actors.

4. The proposition could also be reversed to say that to enter into a relation with someone is—in a more or less explicit way, depending on the case—to put a relation of power into effect.

5. We will return to this point. For the moment, it should be noted that it is of course not a question of an abstract relation, but rather of a relation in situation, therefore one which is contingent on the actors and on the structure in which they act.

6. This aspect of "dependence," indeed of interdependence, which is part and parcel of every relation of power, has rightly been stressed by R. E. Emerson, "Power-Dependence Relations," *American Sociological Review* 27 (1962):31–41.

7. The capacity to experience relations of power is one of the central aspects of an individual's relational capacity. We will return to this point in chap. 6, which is devoted to the relations between organization and culture.

8. See D. Wrong, "Some Problems in Defining Social Power," *American Journal of Sociology* 73 (1968):673–81.

9. That is, one of the actors adjusts his behavior in advance to the perceived or merely anticipated desires of the other.

10. These effects of domination are also what Bachrach and Baratz are working toward with their concept of "non-decisions." Contributing to the *community power debate*, a controversy which grew up in the United States at the beginning of the sixties, notably involving the books of Robert Dahl, *Who Governs?* (New Haven: Yale University Press, 1961), and C. Wright Mills, *The Power Elite* (New York: Oxford University Press, 1956), these two authors argue that the power structure of a collectivity cannot be seriously studied merely by analyzing the decisions actually taken. Account must also be taken of "non-decisions," since the power of certain groups manifests itself not in what they are able to accomplish, but rather in what they are able to block—i.e., in their capacity to produce or obtain "non-decisions" on certain themes or in certain areas of public action. See P. Bachrach and M. S. Baratz, "Two Faces of Power," *American Political Science Review* 56 (1962):947–52, and "Decisions and Non-Decisions: An Analytical Framework," *American Political Science Review* 57 (1963):632–42. As interesting as this distinction is, its contribution to a new comprehension of the phenomenon of power seems to us limited by its noticeable tendency—which underlies, moreover, the whole controversy around community—to regard power as something "held," essentially an attribute of the actors. Paradoxically, such a point of view prevents the problem of the *structural overdetermination* of the exercise of power from being posed in a meaningful way—i.e., the problem of *power as relation*. It is precisely this overdetermination that the authors mean to emphasize with the concept of "non-decision."

11. To exist thus comes down to entering a field of power, since I cannot exist except by bargaining with others over my willingness to do what they want of me or by not responding to the "expectations" they have of me. Thus access to sources of power—i.e., to possible alternatives for behavior—and the *actual utilization* of such possibilities become preconditions not only of all relationships to others, but also of all processes of personalization, of access to identity.

12. The study of power as relation makes it necessary to go back to the situational and structural overdeterminations which alone are capable of explaining the development of observed relations of power. Power conceptualized as a relation thus becomes an instrument of research which makes possible the exploration and analysis of the respective situations of the actors, as well as the structural rules which govern their transactions. We will return below to the structural contingency of relations of power; for the methodological aspects of our procedure, we refer the reader to the methodological appendix at the end of the work.

13. This point is emphasized and forcefully argued by T. C. Schelling when he pleads for abandoning the assumption of symmetry in the theory of games. See his *The Strategy of Conflict* (Cambridge, Mass.: Harvard University Press, 1960), esp. Appendix B, pp. 267–90 (1973 ed., Oxford University Paperback).

14. Ibid.

15. It is a matter of attempting to extend the theory of games to "mixed" (conflict/negotiation) games of nonzero sum.

16. By reintroducing into his analyses strategies which include and make use of chance—i.e., strategies in which promises and threats made are attenuated by their conditional character—Schelling makes his argument more subtle by once again giving a central place to the manipulation, by each of the partners/adversaries, of their own margin of liberty as well as that of the other. See Schelling, *Strategy,* esp. pt. 3, "Strategy with a Random Ingredient," pp. 173–203.

17. True, they are predominant in the problems on which Schelling particularly works. In fact, he is interested in the dynamics of international relations in a context of a balance of terror between *two* superpowers.

18. This is the real object of Schelling's analyses. He is interested in the means and strategies (promises, threats, extortions) which allow an actor to use the structural constraints of a situation for moving the game/negotiation/conflict which opposes him to the

other party onto a terrain favorable to his own interest. He shows that tying one's hands is actually a possible strategy—without, however, sufficiently specifying the structural conditions which circumscribe the validity and effectiveness of such a strategy.

19. Clearly, such transactions are established within the constraints imposed by a market for such services, whose existence we certainly do not want to question. Our empirical reasoning deals with the margin of liberty left by the market, and leads to more general considerations concerning the very development of such markets.

20. The example discussed at length by Schelling is particularly enlightening in this respect.

21. It can even become an actor's principal advantage. Indeed, in a situation in which he has absolutely nothing else, he will have nothing left to lose: time itself leaves him indifferent. Against another actor "in a hurry," this indifference to time may become the advantage which allows him to regain power though he begins from a situation of weakness.

22. The less one can measure one's commitments, the less prepared one is to commit oneself: this is the origin of the well-known protective strategies which are expressed through "withdrawal" or "apathetic" behavior.

23. Similarly, the same resource does not increase the actors' "strategic capacities" in the same way. As in other respects, in this connection cumulative processes exist which allow certain actors to make use of resources which would be of no value to others. "Only the rich get loans," as Talleyrand said. What is more, the same "objective" resource will be noted and actually pressed into service by certain actors, while others will not be able to use it.

24. A capacity susceptible, this time, to empirical analysis.

25. Note that the completely egalitarian market of economic theory is only a limiting case—largely theoretical, moreover—in which the transaction involves only the exchange of measurable goods, making no allowance for the possibility that the unequal resources and action potentials of the various actors may be used to "rig the market." For such a game to be set up and perpetuated, it is easy to see that very complex constraints must be imposed. *The market is a construct.*

26. This does not mean that an actor can establish power relations only inside an organization; the contrary is true, as we have amply demonstrated. It means simply that, whatever the degree of formalization of an "organized group," the existence of relations of power is synonymous with the existence of a minimum of "organization" of the relationships between men.

27 This is what Hickson et al. hoped to formalize in their strategic contingency model of intraorganizational power, in which the power of a subunit in a given organization depends on (1) its capacity to cope with a source of uncertainty for the organization; (2) the degrees of substitutability of this capacity; and (3) its degree of centrality to the organization in question. See D. J. Hickson et al., "A Strategic Continuity Theory of Intra-organizational Power," *Administrative Science Quarterly* 16 (1971):216–29. Such a formulation is certainly useful, especially for describing and measuring the distribution of power within an organization at time *t*. But this is also where its limitations lie. By treating such sources of uncertainty as givens or as "objective" resources, such an approach neglects to investigate the negotiating conditions which define a subunit's potential for using the power it obtains from its ability to cope with a source of uncertainty, and scarcely permits an explanation of the functioning of an organization in terms of the dynamics of the underlying system of power.

28. In other words, their "participation" in the organization will depend on the stakes they perceive.

29. The stake can thus be redefined as a *means* which several actors need at the same time for the purposes of their own strategies and which therefore there will be competition to control.

30. See S. R. Clegg, *Power, Rule, and Domination* (London: Routledge & Kegan Paul, 1975).

31. What is generally referred to in sociological theory as "expertise."

32. Of course, this distinction has an analytic value only. In reality, types of power and types of zones of uncertainty are usually mixed together, sometimes inextricably intertwined.

33. This explains why, in such a perspective, qualitative analysis will always precede quantification. This is why the approach of David Hickson and his colleagues is open to such serious criticism. See Hickson, "A Strategic Contingency Theory."

34. We will return to this problem in greater depth (pt. 2, chaps. 4 and 5).

35. This concept was put forward by Henri Jamous in his study of the decision-making processes leading to the reform of medical education. See *Contribution à une sociologie de la décision: la réforme des études medicales et des structures hospitalières* (Paris: Copedith, 1968). See below, chap. 12, pp. 195 ff.

36. This objectivity is actually only superficial, for all tasks, all techniques are also human constructs.

37. Or merely by transmitting passively and without any elaboration on their part *all* the data in their possession. The recipient of such information, incapable himself of distinguishing what is important from what is not, and equally incapable, very often, of perceiving the real significance of information which comes in in such disarray, will ultimately be as paralyzed as if the information had deliberately been withheld.

38. Only from such a viewpoint is it possible to understand the strategy of management, or, more generally, of the superior officials in any organization, who use the information available to them in order to secure an additional margin of maneuver for themselves by mixing secrecy and candor in a calculated way.

39. See Crozier, *The Bureaucratic Phenomenon*, pp. 13–55.

40. In a very fine analysis, H. Popitz has shown the importance and the positive functions fulfilled by ignorance of legal rules, infractions of which, he shows, are not punished. See H. Popitz, *Ueber die Präventivwirkung des Nichtwissens* (Tubingen: Mohr, 1968). See also the analyses of A. W. Gouldner devoted to the functions of bureaucratic rules, for example, *Patterns of Industrial Bureaucracy*.

Chapter 3

1. In certain cases, the appropriate strategy for a player wishing to impose constraints on his partner may be to eliminate his own margin for maneuver, as we showed in our discussion of Schelling's analyses.

2. March and Simon have demonstrated this quite well by analyzing the quasi-structural limitations that parcelization of objectives imposes on the cognitive capacities of the other actors. See *Organizations*.

3. Their interest will actually be served if they can win acceptance for the notion that the contribution of their group is crucial to the survival and growth of the overall unit. For this strategy to succeed, the partners must accept their partisan and incomplete arguments.

4. This leads to certain well-known types of situation; to take just one example, sales and production departments may quarrel because the technical improvements that the engineers would like to make in the products of the firm would increase their price and make them difficult to sell. Some would argue that a middle course is correct, because a superior product will eventually stimulate demand; others would reply that a market-share must be seized at once and not relinquished. All the participants will attempt to insure that their own particular contribution is crucial to the survival of the firm.

5. In an important article, A. W. Gouldner has stressed the autonomy of certain components of an organization and the *lack of reciprocity* that sometimes characterizes their relations. See A. W. Gouldner, "Reciprocity and Autonomy in Functional Theory," in N.J. Demerath and R A Peterson, *System, Change, and Conflict* (New York: Free Press, 1967).

6. The March and Simon model can thus be extended. They have already stressed the

bounded rationality aspect, of which it may be added that power relations are no less important than individual/structural cognitive limitations in determining the bound. The context in which every organization must operate is characterized not only by the aforementioned feature, but also by *bounded legitimacy* (related to the stability of the actors' normative integration) and *bounded interdependence* (related to reduced functional integration of the strategies, whose validity may even be called into question).

7. Since our world is one of bounded rationality. The implications of such a proposition will be seen in chap. 9.

8. See Goffman, *The Presentation of Self;* Garfinkel, *Studies in Ethnomethodology;* A. V. Cicourel, *Method and Measurement in Sociology* (New York: Free Press, 1964).

9. This is also the viewpoint implicit in D. Silverman, *The Theory of Organizations* (London: Heinemann, 1970), which gives a good presentation of this type of analysis.

10. This model seems to be gaining currency among sociologist with a phenomenologico-structuralist orientation; Clegg, *Power, Rule, and Domination,* is a good example.

11. We will return to this point at greater length in chap. 7.

12. See esp. T. Parsons, "A Sociological Approach to the Theory of Organizations," in *Structure and Process in Modern Societies* (New York: Free Press, 1964); R. K. Merton, "The Role-Set: Problems in Sociological Theory," *British Journal of Sociology* 8 (1957):106–20; R. K. Merton, *Social Theory and Social Structure* (New York: Free Press, 1964); A. W. Gouldner, "Organizational Analysis," in R. K. Merton et al., eds., *Sociology Today* (New York: Basic Books, 1959), among many others.

13. Inconsistencies and contradictions with which the actors do not merely put up passively, but which they provoke or create if the occasion arises.

14. It should be noted that the structuro-functionalist approach itself is not focused on the organization, an artificial phenomenon, but rather on society, a natural phenomenon. Without lingering over this point, which is itself debatable, we should like to point out that for Parsons the theory of organizations is merely an application of the general theory. The usual critiques of functionalism are therefore quite different from ours with respect to this concrete, directly perceptible phenomenon. In part 3 of this work, we will again take up and reformulate our critique. The work of R. Kahn et al., *Organizational Stress* (New York: Wiley, 1964), provides an excellent illustration of the conceptual and methodological hypertrophy, as well as the modesty, not to say banality, of the results produced by a certain type of role analysis—not merely in the organizational domain, but as regards the theory in general.

15. Constraint is certainly not missing from an argument of this kind. But upon closer examination it turns out inevitably to be a matter of internalized constraint. For an old but still suggestive and pertinent critique of such a conception, see D. Wrong, "The Over-Socialized Conception of Man in Modern Sociology," *American Sociological Review* 26 (April 1961):180–93, reprinted in Demerath and Peterson, *System, Change, and Conflict.* We ourselves have criticized Robert K. Merton's analyses of bureaucratic behavior from this standpoint; see *The Bureaucratic Phenomenon,* pp. 179–80.

16. See Silverman, *The Theory of Organizations.*

17. A. Etzioni, *A Comparative Analysis of Complex Organizations* (New York: Free Press, 1961).

18. We beg the reader's indulgence for our scanty discussion here of the highly interesting work of these writers. We have postponed examination of their contributions until the next chapter.

19. For a good introduction to Luhmann's functionalo-structuralist theory, see N. Luhmann, "Soziologie als Theorie sozialer Systeme," in *Soziologische Aufklärung* (Cologne, Opladen: Westdeutscher Verlag, 1970), pp. 113–36. For a more complete exposition of the conceptual framework used by Luhmann, the reader will also want to consult N. Luhmann, *Zweckbegriff und Systemrationalität* (Frankfurt: Suhrkamp, 1973), in which the

Luhmannian concept of "systemic rationality" is presented. For a very suggestive and pertinent over-all critique, see K. Grimm, *Niklas Luhmanns "soziologische" Aufklärung* (Hamburg: Hoffmann & Campe, 1974); and G. Schmid, *Funktionsanalyse und politische Theorie* (Düsseldorf: Bertelsmann Universitätsverlag, 1974), esp. chap. 7, pp. 108–45.

20. Note that structures, processes, and systems do not have an ontological status here. As strategies, they are always susceptible to treatment as problems, and are always replaceable by other strategies. In this connection, see Luhmann, *Zweckbegriff*, pp. 166–257, and *"Soziologie als Theorie,"* pp. 113–36. One must ask, however: Whose strategy? That of the system, of a meta-actor, of the world? Clearly, the deus ex machina of structuro-functionalism, exorcised in one place, has surreptitiously crept back into another.

21. For the formulation of the concept of member role, see Niklas Luhmann, *Funktion und Folgen formaler Organisation* (Berlin: Duncker & Humblot, 1964).

22. In this connection, Luhmann says that the role of member can be understood as a sort of "capitalized loyalty" which insures that when the individual "freely" accepts the member role, he not only accepts the formalized expectations associated with it, but also the changes that may ultimately affect those expectations, such changes being made in accordance with anticipated procedures. See Luhmann, *Zweckbegriff*, p. 340.

23. In reading *Funktion und Folgen formaler Organisation,* and in particular the analysis of the functions of formalization, one often has the feeling that one is reading a recasting of the theses of Max Weber on the advantages of bureaucracy in functionalist language.

24. To avoid any possible misunderstanding, we want to make clear that we do not assume any kind of equilibrium. Power relations are always intrinsically imbalanced, even if reciprocity is an essential component thereof.

25. In other words, and contrary to what Luhmann has maintained in a recent work, the realization of the "alternative to be avoided" (the breakdown of the machine) does not destroy the power of the maintenance workers; their power in fact depends in one sense on the fact that this "alternative" cannot be avoided on occasion. See N. Luhmann, *Macht* (Stuttgart: Ferdinand Enke, 1975), p. 23.

26. Foremost among these other factors is that they must live side by side with the production workers, inside the plant and out. The reserved, if not hostile, attitudes of the latter are thus a weapon for controlling the maintenance workers; as we have shown, this consideration makes it possible to regard these attitudes as "rational." Also important is the fact that the respective situations of the two groups are interdependent. The maintenance workers are aware that abuse of their power might provoke so much discontent that management would come into the picture. This is turn might lead to an attempt to rationalize maintenance, thereby reducing the zone of uncertainty controlled by the maintenance workers. Finally, the two groups share certain values in common: "worker solidarity" and the notion of what constitutes a "fair day's work" prevent the maintenance workers from capitalizing on their advantages to the extent they might wish.

27. Since unpredictable behavior is the only way I have of preventing my adversary from treating me as a mere object, as a means; in other words, I must exert power. Thus no unequivocal and clear formula for describing human behavior exists; it is always ambivalent. Each actor will seek to "reduce the complexity" due to the unpredictable behavior of his partners, while at the same time trying to make his own behavior appear more complex.

28. Here we come once more upon the indissoluble bonds between power and organization, the subject of the preceding chapter.

29. The rules of the organizational game—like other formalities, which, we repeat, are by no means identical—are not spelled out directly. *They are not role expectations.* Unlike rules of polite behavior, they do not prescribe directly what conduct ought to be in different situations. Their extent and effect are indirect: by structuring the stakes and delimiting the possible winning strategies, they limit the freedom of action of the participants.

30. Of course, the various organizational actors will respond in different ways to this

central source of uncertainty. The differences constitute an essential parameter of the margin of maneuver—hence indirectly of the power—of each actor. An actor to whom alternative solutions are available can adopt much "riskier" strategies than one who is "cornered" in the game.

31. To the extent that laws or customs (results of negotiation and bargaining of a more complex sort, which operates at a higher level, in part societal) limit the possibility of capitalizing on structures and rules, certain ruling groups—for instance, capitalists—lose power.

32. It is probably unnecessary to point out that institutionalization is not equivalent to formalization.

33. Here the word "cooperation" is used in the most neutral sense, implying no more than temporary, provisional acceptance of a certain interdependence.

34. This makes it easier to understand the difficulties that arise whenever organizational change is the goal. From this standpoint, organizational change invariably involves a great deal more than moving boxes around on an organization chart or "adapting" workers to a new technology. It actually means restructuring a system of action by redistributing the crucial zones of uncertainty, and, consequently, reshuffling many of the advantages and resources available to the various bargaining groups within the organization. Far more important than the much-bruited "psychological cost" of change, this has a very direct effect on the negotiating capacities of the members of the organization and, accordingly, on their ability to play the role expected of them. It justifies and legitimates the notorious "resistance to change." See part 5 for our views on change.

35. This existence must be demonstrated by showing the presence of power relations.

36. As we shall show below, the formal contours of an organization rarely coincide with those of the underlying system. See chap. 5, as well as our discussion in part 3, which is devoted to systems of action.

37. For the methodological implications of this procedure, see the Appendix.

38. This explains why organizational crises are always opportune for *analyzing* organizations.

39. We have seen the central place occupied by the theory of roles in the structuro-functionalist analysis of Luhmann. Katz and Kahn, for their part, define "role" explicitly as the key concept which allows them to tie together the individual and organizational levels of analysis. See D. Katz and R. L. Kahn, *The Social Psychology of Organizations* (New York: Wiley, 1966), p. 197.

40. As we have said, this is the main reproach which can be brought against the analyses developed by Luhmann in his sketch of a general theory of formalized systems (*Funktion und Folgen*).

41. R. K. Merton's analysis of the emergence of the bureaucratic personality is a good example of such a theory of conditioning.

42. Within limits, it is due also to a sort of "systems ruse" which insures that the system will "tolerate" and indeed "provoke" certain deviations for the sake of its own reproduction.

43. To the extent that the organization, or rather its leaders, will have understood their dependence on the structures, i.e., on the games already in progress, and been capable of controlling them.

44. These games are not identical at all levels of the organization. To consider only one aspect, rather considerable differences may exist between games at the bottom and games at the top of an organizational hierarchy. This does not, however, imply that these games are independent, but rather that they are linked in nonrandom fashion by a series of more broadly based mechanisms of regulation. See chap. 9 for our treatment of this subject.

45. The exact opposite is the case, since preexisting rules of the game define disparate

potential wins and losses. See Schelling, *The Strategy of Conflict*, pp. 99–118, for an analysis of the inegalitarian structures and outcomes of nonzero-sum games. Schelling pleads for abandonment of the unrealistic assumption of equality among the players.

46. Cohen, particularly—and, in our opinion, unduly—ascribes such an assumption to game interpretation. See P. S. Cohen, *Modern Social Theory* (London: Heinemann, 1968).

47. At least this will do as a first approximation, if one is willing to accept the interpretation of the Industrial Monopoly as a closed system. In this connection, see the formalization due to J.-L. Peaucelle, "Théorie des jeux et sociologie des organisations," *Sociologie du travail*, vol. 1 (1969). More generally, we must warn against any attempt, in our opinion premature, to impose formal models inspired by game theory on organizational analysis. Our empirical knowledge is still too limited for these models to be anything but rather crude simplifications (hence quickly sterile) of the reality that one must understand before proceeding to formalization.

48. In this sense, the criteria of rationality and satisfaction available to the actors are themselves conditioned by the structure and type of game in which they are taking part. We will return to this point in treating problems of decision in part 4.

49. Make no mistake about the apparently neutral character of this expression. In fact, it illustrates the basic constraining mechanism. It is possible to "get out of the game with a minimum of damage" in quite different ways; strategies either more or less defensive may be chosen. But unless one quits the game altogether, the consequences of these strategies must be faced, and these are themselves structured by the prevailing "rules of the game."

50. Let us add quickly that the constraint is tighter because the game will be crucial to the actors, who will therefore be less able to risk loss. The analysis must, accordingly, always consider the *centrality* of a particular game within the actor's overall strategic field. In more general terms, the problem is again that of nonconformism, invariably the privilege of the "rich" in the broadest possible, least monetary sense of the term—i.e., the privilege of actors with many alternatives, whereby they are able to diversify their commitments to the greatest possible degree.

51. At the same time, such an example shows that there are other possible strategies open to actors who have other resources whereby they can take greater risks. We shall return to this later.

52. This has repercussions for the notion of attitudes. In the present context, these are almost rationalizations by the actors of their present and future behavior in the game. Accordingly, they may be taken as indicative of the choices made by individuals among the available alternatives. For a treatment of this question in greater depth, see the Appendix.

53. It is this point in particular that Schelling analyzed in *The Strategy of Conflict*.

54. Precisely because the capacities required by the one possible strategy are not possessed by all the actors in equal measure. The Industrial Monopoly furnishes a good illustration. In fifteen of the eighteen factories visited, the behavior of the technical engineers (supervisory personnel responsible for maintenance operations) was remarkably similar. This was because only one strategy was possible in the game they were forced to play with the managers, assistant managers, and quality controllers. There were only three exceptions. The first was the result of a temporary shift in the balance of power within the management group, brought on by heavy capital investments that temporarily strengthened the hand of the manager vis-à-vis his technical engineers. The other two situations were really consequences of individuals being "unfit" for their roles: nervous depression and illness were signs that the situation was pathological (in the true sense of the word).

55. This explains why the study of attitudes is interesting: they reveal the *subjective choices* made by the actors to the investigator.

56. Which are of course personal and social, a nonstructured field being something which does not exist. See chap. 6, in which we discuss organization and culture.

57. We should say, rather, that it is more fruitful to think of them as the only possible ones, unless the contrary is empirically demonstrated. As in the case throughout this book, the burden of proof is reversed, owing to the way we have chosen to define the research: now the exception to the rule needing explanation is not the existence of a margin for maneuver, but rather the *absence* of such freedom.

58. Bear in mind that it is also always possible to play *against* the game, as we showed above.

59. In this respect, however, care should be taken not to adopt too "diffusionistic" a hypothesis. For it may at times be a crucial advantage to an actor to refuse to adopt a strategy chosen by the majority, and he will defend that advantage as long as he can. It follows that in such cases the members of the minority will have no interest in joining the majority, but will encourage the members of the majority to pursue their strategy—i.e., they will support the majority strategy of which their own behavior is implicitly critical.

60. Or, rather, total constraint of actual behavior is an extreme case that must be analyzed and explained.

61. Although not exclusively, as we have already shown.

62. With the exception that in this case it is not chance, incarnate in the form of a rolling ball, that determines the wins and losses, but rather rules of the game produced by a broader power structure (that of society at large), in part laid down by the croupier himself, and, in any case, subject to alteration.

63. We will return to these points in subsequent chapters.

64. Let us stress at once that this criterion of survival is a supple one, applicable to very different realities. Thus, in an economy where growth is widespread, the "necessity" to grow—to increase sales figures, for instance, by a certain percentage each quarter—can become a constraint as crucial as survival, even though survival per se is not in question, at least in the short run.

65. How often one hears the cry, "It's a problem of communication; it's a problem of information" (the implication being that if only people were "correctly informed" and really wanted to communicate, such problems would not exist). We are far from thinking that there is not a good deal of progress to be made in this area. This should not, however, induce us to ignore the limitations inherent in any policy for managing information. These limitations are due to the fact that information is a rare commodity, and that its communication and exchange are not neutral and free processes. To inform another person, to communicate to him elements of information which he does not possess, is to expose oneself, to give up advantages that might have entered into a negotiation as bargaining chips, and to make oneself vulnerable to the other's attempts to seize control of the situation. Moreover, there may well be an advantage in ignoring a piece of information that may tend to reduce the available margin of liberty. Thus it is perhaps not surprising that *all* actors *behave strategically* in this respect—perhaps more than in any other—and commit themselves to give and receive information only in return for guarantees and compensation. We will return to this problem in part 5.

Chapter 4

1. This point deserves to be discussed in greater depth, especially as it concerns the genesis and nature of such "givens" and "requirements" as are imposed on organizations. We will return to it in the course of this section. Here, let us say simply that such "givens" and "requirements" quite clearly do not fall from heaven. They are themselves products of social structures reflecting relations and balances of power among individuals, groups, and social categories, whose interests are divergent if not contradictory. This obvious point needs to be made explicit, for otherwise it is impossible to explain, first, that such "re-

quirements" and "givens" are not univocal but rather changeable, frequently ambiguous, and sometimes even contradictory, and, second, as we shall show below (cnap. 9), that organizations sometimes play a role in defining and formulating them.

2. This school is most prominent, moreover, in the English-speaking world, with its principal center in the journal *Administrative Science Quarterly,* published at Cornell University. Its leading figures are Blau, Hage and Aiken, Hall, Lawrence and Lorsch, and Perrow in the United States; Tom Burns, Derek Pugh, D. Hickson, Joan Woodward in Great Britain.

3. Consider the work of W. F. Whyte, L. Sayles, A. Zaleznik, Walker and Guest, and others in the human-relations school, as well as the early studies on bureaucracy of Bendix, Gouldner, Selznick, and also Blau. Curiously, the latter subsequently abandoned this approach to become one of the leading figures in the "structural" orientation of the sixties.

4. See P. M. Blau, "The Comparative Study of Organizations," *Industrial and Labor Relations Review* 18 (April 1965):323–38.

5. Whence the emergence of a new field of sociology and, indeed, a new sociological concept—that of the formal or complex organization—which, by contrast to more diffuse social organizations (the family, the community, etc.), is characterized by the existence of explicit objectives or goals, of a formalized structure, and of a body of rules designed to shape behavior in view of the objectives to be accomplished. In this respect, there is an abundant literature; see especially P. M. Blau and W. R. Scott, *Formal Organizations: A Comparative Approach* (London: Routledge & Kegan Paul, 1963). As obvious as such a distinction may appear at first sight, it does not withstand serious analysis. Looked at more closely, it is seen to rest on nothing more than an uncritical introduction of categories from common sense into scientific language and procedure. Not that there are not differences between an industrial firm and a family. But by accepting straightaway and as given a certain classification of the reality which ought to be the object of investigation, such a conceptualization merely assumes the difference rather than making it an object of research. All other things being equal, the study of formal organizations is to the sociology of organizations what administrative science is to the sociology of the state: in both cases, an object of study is reified instead of being constituted through the research itself. It follows that in each case the study of the *ought to be* (the formal and juridical) takes precedence over research into what *is* and into the *meaning* of what is.

6. In the sense in which every political phenomenon is cultural and not a natural fact.

7. In order to keep readable a chapter devoted to a critique of the assumptions and methods of structural contingency theory, we have deliberately restricted our discussion to extremely succinct résumés of the theses and main results of the work analyzed. For further knowledge of this research, we refer the interested reader to the articles and books cited in the footnotes.

8. See J. Woodward, *Management and Technology* (London: HMSO, 1958), and *Industrial Organisation: Theory and Practice* (London: Oxford University Press, 1965).

9. The implications of technology for interpersonal relations and for the norms and attitudes of workers was of course studied very early on, and often in great detail, by writers belonging to the interactionist school previously mentioned, as well as in numerous works of industrial sociology devoted to problems of *technological change.* Among others, see W. F. Whyte, "An Interaction Approach to the Theory of Organizations," in M. Haire, ed., *Modern Organization Theory* (New York: Wiley, 1959); C. J. Walker and R. H. Guest, *The Man on the Assembly Line* (Cambridge, Mass.: Harvard University Press, 1952); Sayles, *Behavior;* R. Blauner, *Alienation and Freedom: The Factory Worker and His Industry* (Chicago: University of Chicago Press, 1964); and, for the French view, R. Sainsaulieu and W. Ackermann, "L'étude sociologique du changement technique: pour une analyse strategique," *Bulletin du CERP* 19 (1970): 1–22; A. Touraine et al., *Les travailleurs et les*

changements techniques (Paris: Organization for Economic Cooperation and Development, 1965). The originality of Woodward's research—and in this she is quite representative of the structural school of which she is, moreover, one of the founders—lies in her attempt to study the influence of technology in terms of the structural characteristics of the *organization as an entity*.

10. Obviously, within a given firm, several categories can coexist.

11. As Harvey has rightly emphasized, she neglects the content of jobs, as well as changes in products which do not entail a change of technology. See E. Harvey, "Technology and the Structure of Organizations," *American Sociological Review* 33 (1968):247–59. Woodward and the members of her group have themselves recently proposed other conceptualizations. For instance, they have looked into the question of whether the number of production stages and the range of products are not more useful criteria of organizational differentiation. See J. Rackman and J. Woodward, "The Measurement of Technical Variables," in J. Woodward, ed., *Industrial Organization: Behavior and Control* (New York, Oxford University Press, 1970).

12. It is the users of Woodward's work who have been most apt to succumb to this temptation. But Woodward herself has not always resisted it.

13. After all, structural variations within a given technological category are relatively important. The reproach of technological imperialism has been formulated by D. J. Hickson et al., "Operations Technology and Organization Structure: An Empirical Reappraisal," *Administrative Science Quarterly* 14 (1969): 378–97.

14. Or at least that the fitness to survive, to extend the image, cannot be measured merely by a few economic indicators. Note in passing that we touch here on the theme of *performance constraints*, which we will have occasion to come back to, as it is quite central to all the work that has been done from this structural perspective.

15. Woodward and the members of her team have become aware of this, moreover. In their recent work, these researchers have moved toward a conceptualization of technology in terms of *variety* in the production processes (degrees of uncertainty and unpredictability attached to them), which has led them to focus more and more on *systems of production control*, which are deemed to determine structure and behavior much more directly. See Woodward, *Industrial Organization*.

16. In looking at the work done by Perrow, whose outlook and theoretical affiliations fluctuated somewhat during the sixties, we are mainly interested in the theoretical studies intended to set out a framework for comparative organizational analysis. See C. Perrow, "A Framework for the Comparative Analysis of Organizations," *American Sociological Review* 32 (1967):194–208, and *Organizational Analysis: A Sociological View* (London: Tavistock, 1970), esp. pp. 75–85. In a more recent book, we should add, Perrow seems once again to have moved away from his own comparative framework as well as from the structuralist thinking that informed it. See C. Perrow, *Complex Organizations* (Glenview, Ill.: Scott Foresman, 1972), esp. pp. 163–70 and 177–204.

17. This is what Perrow calls "search behavior," which is aimed at finding a solution to the problem of how to treat a given raw material.

18. This largely coincides with the more classical distinction between programmable manufacturing procedures, which are accordingly routinizable, and others which are not programmable.

19. See especially P. Clark, "The Cultural Contexts," for an analysis of the cigarette industry in Great Britain.

20. On this subject, Perrow has written that "we must assume here that, in the interest of efficiency, organizations, wittingly, or *unwittingly, attempt to maximize* the congruence between their technology and their structure . . . let us assume that they have all studied the sociology of complex organizations and have adapted their structures to fit their technology" (*Organizational Analysis*, p. 80 [italics added]).

21. Perhaps more than Woodward, and certainly more explicitly, Perrow here exhibits what has been called a technological imperialism. As Argyris has stressed (*The Applicability of Organizational Sociology*, p. 37), this *hypothesis is tautological:* technology is a key variable in systems which seek to adjust their structures to technology as much as possible.

22. Just as Woodward does, Perrow seems to overestimate the performance constraint and the influence of structure on performance. We will return to this point.

23. See P. M. Blau, *The Dynamics of Bureaucracy* (Chicago: University of Chicago Press, 1955).

24. See R. H. Hall, "Intraorganizational Structural Variation: Application of the Bureaucratic Model," *Administrative Science Quarterly* 7 (1962):295–308, "The Concept of Bureaucracy: An Empirical Assessment," *American Journal of Sociology* 69 (1963):32–40; and R. H. Hall, J. E. Haas, and J. N. Johnson, "Organizational Size, Complexity, and Formalization," *American Sociological Review* 32 (1967):903–12.

25. See P. M. Blau, "The Formal Theory of Differentiation in Organizations," *American Sociological Review* 35 (1970):201–18; P. M. Blau and R. A. Schoenherr, *The Structure of Organizations* (New York: Basic Books, 1971).

26. Blau strongly emphasizes that he is concerned only with the formal aspects of the organizations he is studying, leaving aside all informal phenomena and everything that pertains to member behavior. See Blau and Scott, *Formal Organizations.*

27. See Argyris, *Applicability of Organizational Sociology*, especially pp. 1–20.

28. Blau's research was one of the largest and also one of the most expensive projects ever undertaken in the field of organizational sociology.

29. Argyris regard Blau's research more as a test of the effectiveness of the rules of public administrations than an original contribution to a new theory—even a formal one—of organizations. See Argyris, *Applicability of Organizational Sociology*, pp. 16–17.

30. Attention should be called in particular to the fact that Blau attributes truly imperious power to the criterion of organizational size; furthermore, he seems to have excessive confidence in the official organization charts, in spite of the fact that numerous studies have stressed their purely theoretical or even downright *false* character.

31. For a critique of the unitary approach, see esp. C. R. Hinings et al., "An Approach to the Study of Bureaucracy," *Sociology* 1 (1967):61–72. For an exposition of their own conceptual framework, see D. S. Pugh et al., "A Conceptual Scheme for Organizational Analysis," *Administrative Science Quarterly* 8 (1963):289–315.

32. Meaning the official objectives, the manifest "social function" of the organization.

33. This is essentially a question of the dependence on the parent organization, and secondarily on certain important suppliers or clients as well. The treatment of this dependence in the work of Aston's group has been the object of a critique by H. Aldrich, which seems to us, however, to miss the essential point, insofar as this critique in reality bears only on the *incomplete treatment* of the dependence and not on its basic conceptualization.

34. This is basically an analytic axis laid out between the two poles of personal control, on the one hand, and impersonal procedures or control mechanisms on the other. For further details concerning this analytic dimension and the relevant parameters, see D. S. Pugh et al., "Dimensions of Organization Structure," *Administrative Science Quarterly* 13 (1968):65–105. For the results of the multivariate analysis, see D. S. Pugh et al., "The Context of Organization Structures," *Administrative Science Quarterly* 14 (1969):91–114.

35. See Pugh, "Dimensions"; also Hinings, "An Approach to the Study of Bureaucracy"; and the similar results obtained by Hall, "The Concept of Bureaucracy."

36. See Hickson, "Operations Technology," esp. pp. 391–96. Note that in this respect their view is close to the analysis by J. D. Thompson of the technological core, some of whose results contradict their own assertions. See J. D. Thompson, *Organizations in Action* (New York: McGraw Hill, 1967).

37. Although it seems that the disagreement between Woodward and Pugh is based on a

misunderstanding. Indeed, as shown by the analysis of Hickson et al. ("Operations Technology and Organizational Structure"), these two authors are not examining the same thing. Thus Woodward's results underestimate the effects of organizational size because they reflect structures directly related to technical processes. Conversely, Pugh underestimates the effects of technology because the activities whose structure he examines are insulated from the technical processes.

38. Of course, the theories on which the research is based are often much more elaborate and subtle, particularly in Pugh's case. In our view, it is the (premature) insistence on quantification at any price which gradually forces the authors in question into reductionism, since insuperable difficulties preclude the operationalization and quantification of more complex models.

39. We should add that these data were obtained by structured interviews with the heads of the firm and with other high-ranking supervisory personnel (to the extent necessary to supplement the other data). See D. J. Hickson et al., "The Culture-Free Context of Organization Structure: a Tri-National Comparison," *Sociology* 8 (1974): 59–81, and "Grounds for Comparative Organization Theory: Quicksand or Hard-Core?" in Lammers, *Organizations Unlike and Alike.*

42. See D. S. Pugh et al., "An Empirical Taxonomy of Structures of Work Organizations," *Administrative Science Quarterly* 14 (1969):115–26.

43. Pugh et al. are actually ambiguous in this respect: on the one hand, they propose a series of causal hypotheses based on their correlations; on the other, however, they insist on the fact that their results show only a statistical correlation and nothing more. See also Pugh et al., "The Context of Organization Structures."

44. As J. Child has remarked, in what amounts virtually to a witticism, the size and the degree of "bureaucratization" of organizations may well be connected because large organizations boast a greater number of "professional" administrators influenced by "management" training courses, in which the accent at present falls on measures whose application entails every likelihood of increasing the degree of bureaucratization. See "Organization: A Choice for Man," in J. Child, ed., *Man and Organization* (London: Allen & Unwin, 1973). For all its wittiness this remark is nonetheless illustrative of the complexity of the processes involved, which in the methodology under analysis is oversimplified.

45. This determinism is always incomplete, moreover, since it is impossible to measure and analyze all the relevant variables. Though in practice under-determining, the approach is nonetheless deterministic in conception.

46. A further ambiguity adds to the confusion here. It is always unclear whether such a judgment specifies the reality (such *is* the case) or is merely prescriptive and normative (such *ought to be* the case).

47. Among the many works devoted to these problems, we think the following particularly worthy of note: T. Burns and G. M. Stalker, *The Management of Innovation* (London: Tavistock, 1961); F. E. Emery and E. L. Trist, "The Causal Texture of Organizational Environment," *Human Relations* 18 (1965):21–32; J. Hage and M. Aiken, *Social Change in Complex Organizations* (New York: Random House, 1970); P. R. Lawrence and J. W. Lorsch, *Organization and Environment: Managing Differentiation and Integration* (Boston: Harvard Business School, 1967); and J. D. Thompson, *Organizations in Action.*

48. See Burns and Stalker, *The Management of Innovation.*

49. These are, of course, ideal types in the sense of Weber, i.e., abstractions not found as such in reality. Real organizations may more nearly resemble one extreme or the other.

50. See also the work of Stinchcombe, who arrives at similar results: A. L. Stinchcombe, "Bureaucratic and Craft Administration of Production: A Comparative Study," *Administrative Science Quarterly* 4 (1959):168–87.

51. See Emery and Trist, "The Causal Texture."

52. We will need to return to this point, but for the present we may say that it is not clear why such an "organizational matrix" should emerge only at the term of an evolutionary process. Is it not true that certain basic regulations govern interactions between organizations? Is it not possible that what makes the difference is not so much the presence or absence of "rules of the game" as the degree to which the actors are consciously aware of them? If this logic seems reasonable, then it becomes apparent that the interorganizational field has always existed; if it has not attracted as much attention as it deserves, the fault lies especially with myopic outlook of writers who study organizations without questioning the processes that constitute them.

53. See Lawrence and Lorsch, *Organization and Environment*.

54. That is, from the standpoint of the organizational structures as much as the orientations and preferences of the actors.

55. Lawrence and Lorsch, *Organization and Environment*, pp. 156–7.

56. The term *structural contingency theory* is due to Lawrence and Lorsch. It has since become commonplace.

57. See J. Child, "Organizational Structure, Environment, and Performance: The Role of Strategic Choice," *Sociology* 6 (1972):1–12 and especially 3–5.

58. It is in this sense that K. E. Weick speaks of an *enacted environment*. We accept his analysis, with slight differences over his insistence on mechanisms of perception and significance, which in our view is too narrowly focused. The extreme radicalism of the phenomenological view taken here entails neglect of the psychological realization of the objective facts; the question is not solely one of perception, but above all of the conditioning of the capacity and the will to perceive through mechanisms associated with power. See Weick, *The Social Psychology of Organizing*, especially pp. 63–72.

59. See A. D. Chandler, Jr., *Strategy and Structure* (Cambridge, Mass.: MIT Press, 1962).

60. This very succinct summary hardly does justice to the wealth of Chandler's analyses, where the accent is on the open, experimental, and relatively unpredetermined nature of processes of structural and organizational change.

61. See R. M. Cyert and J. G. March, *A Behavioral Theory of the Firm* (Englewood Cliffs, N.J.: Prentice-Hall, 1963).

62. Burns very quickly abandoned the mode of argument paramount in this school to center to his work subsequently on the political aspects of organized action. See "Micropolitics: Mechanisms of Institutional Change," *Administrative Science Quarterly* 6 (1961): 257–81; "On the Plurality of Social Systems," in J. R. Lawrence, ed., *Operational Research and the Social Sciences* (Oxford: Pergamon Press, 1966).

63. Similarly, the Swede R. Normann shows in a comparative study of thirteen companies that the power structures and value systems prevailing therein play a critical role in determining their reactions to new ideas and information received from external sources. See "Organizational Innovativeness: Product Variation and Reorientation," *Administrative Science Quarterly* 16 (1971):203–15.

64. By dispelling the illusions associated with the notion of a universal *one best way,* this approach demonstrated the need for spelling out clearly and in detail the precepts of the organizational art, and at the same time provided the first tools for doing so. The pragmatic usefulness of the most suggestive works of this school (and especially of Woodward, Burns and Stalker, and Lawrence and Lorsch) has rightly been stressed by T. Lupton, *Management and the Social Sciences* (Harmondsworth: Penguin Books, 1971).

65. This is the sense of the general criticism which C. Argyris has levelled at this methodology. See *The Applicability of Organizational Sociology* (Cambridge, Mass.: Harvard University Press, 1972).

66. An autonomy implicit in the "anomalous" results of Burns and Stalker cited previously.

67. Largely implicit, moreover, except in Perrow, who deserves credit for bringing this assumption out clearly. See *Organizational Analysis*, p. 80.

68. While the Darwinian notion of survival of the fittest in the hostile marketplace may be applicable to a scant few industrial sectors in the United States—that paradise of free enterprise—it seems completely unrealistic in the context of the more tightly controlled European economies.

69. See the treatment of bounded rationality in Simon, *Administration Behavior;* March and Simon, *Organizations;* and the work on the firm done by Cyert and March, *A Behavioral Theory of the Firm*, especially their treatment of organizational slack. It is also worth emphasizing that norms and objectives are themselves the fruit of transactions with the environment, as is recalled in J. D. Thompson and W. J. McEwen, "Organizational Goals and Environment: Goal-Setting as an Interaction-Process," *American Sociological Review* 23 (1958):23–31. Organizations can, in turn, organize and shape their environment through the same process, as we shall show later. In a two-fold sense the problem of *measurability of performance* also arises here: first, from the point of view of the existence of a *measuring technique,* and, second, in terms of the existence of a *collective and cultural capacity* to accept and tolerate measurement of performance. We will come back to this point.

70. R. E. Caves et al., *Britain's Economic Prospects* (London: Allen & Unwin, 1968), cited in Child, "Organizational Structure," p. 12.

71. See P. R. Lawrence and J. W. Lorsch, *Developing Organizations: Diagnosis and Action* (Reading, Mass.: Addison-Wesley, 1969).

72. J. Pennings, "Environment, Structure, and Peformance of Complex Organizations," *VIIIth Congress of the International Association of Sociology* (Toronto, 1974).

73. This was the direction and intention of work carried out at the Tavistock Institute in England, which centered on the concept of "socio-technical system." It attempted to show that while the technological constraint was important, it nevertheless left a relatively large margin for maneuver and, hence, experimentation. See, among others, E. L. Trist et al., *Organisational Choice* (London: Tavistock, 1963); and E. J. Miller and A. K. Rice, *Systems of Organisations:* The Control of Task and Sentient Boundaries (London: Tavistock, 1967). The pioneering role of the Tavistock Institute during the fifties can be seen much more clearly today.

74. For instance, the area of technology, studies carried out under the auspices of the Centre de sociologie des organisations (Paris) have shown that the "imperatives" of a given technology (computerized management) were absorbed and deflected differently by the systems of action associated with the various firms in which it was implemented. In this connection, see C. Ballé and J.-L. Peaucelle, *Le pouvoir informatique dans L'Entreprise* (Paris: Editions d'Organisation, 1972), and the reports of C. Ballé, *La définition d'une politique informatique* (Paris: C. S. O., 1975).

75. The point has been emphasized by many who work in the interorganizational area. See especially S. Levine and P. White, "Exchange and Interorganizational Relationships," *Administrative Science Quarterly* 10 (1961):583–601, which stresses the dependence of the organization on the environment for needed resources; see E. Litwak and L. F. Hylton, "Interorganizational Analysis: A Hypothesis on Coordinating Agencies," *Administrative Science Quarterly* (1962):395–420, which shows the reciprocal character of this dependence.

75. In this respect, J. Child is open to criticism for too closely identifying the problems of strategic decision making with the environmental relationship or technological constraints. The way an organization "manages" its relationships to the environment, for instance, is not simply the result of the evaluation made by the dominant coalition of decision makers of the interactions which it considers crucial and of the structural choices that are thereby offered.

It also reflects the collective capacity of the organization to foster exchange with the outside world. Moreover, as we will attempt to show in part 4, which concerns the problems of decision making, it is impossible to understand or analyze a decision apart from the system of action within which it is taken.

77. We will return later to the implications of such a shift in emphasis, which in fact amounts to the recognition of a new object of inquiry—concrete systems of action. See below, part 3.

Chapter 5

1. To avoid misunderstanding, we want to make clear at the outset the organizations do not act as though they were autonomous actors.they are mere structures, which impose constraints on the actors, but which also enable them to act. Our personification of the organizations here should not, therefore, give rise to the impression that we regard them as unified actors with their own "needs," "objectives," etc. It is merely a stylistic fillip, a convenient shorthand, which, however, must not be allowed to hide, the reality of the complex processes for which it stands.

2. Rather than argue ambiguously about the "environment" in general, it would seem useful to introduce a preliminary *découpage* made in the light of the *tasks and objectives* of the organization under consideration. The *relevant environment* of the organization does not coincide with what is usually denoted by the word "environment." Its extent is more limited: it includes all social actors whose behavior influences the organization's capacity to function satisfactorily and attain its objectives. These goals, of course, are not objective data, but are rather the product of power relations and bargaining, whereby the underlying system of action is structured, along with exchange between its actors and the relevant environment. For a similar distinction between "general" and "specific" environment, see R. Hall, *Organizations, Structures, and Processes* (Englewood Cliffs, N.J.: Prentice-Hall, 1972); and Thompson, *Organizations in Action*. See also more general treatments from an interorganizational perspective, especially the work of W. Evan, "The Organization-Set," in J. D. Thompson, ed., *Approaches to Organizational Design* (Pittsburgh: University of Pittsburgh Press, 1966); R. Warren, "The Interorganizational Field as a Focus of Investigation," *Administrative Science Quarterly* 12 (1967):396–419; and H. Turk, "Interorganizational Networks in Urban Society," *American Sociological Review* 35 (1970):1–19. We will return to this subject in the chapters devoted to concrete systems of action.

3. See Lawrence and Lorsch, *Organization and Environment*.

4. There is nothing automatic about this structural differentiation, as the work of Lawrence and Lorsch shows clearly. In this they contradict the overly mechanistic assumptions of certain theoreticians concerned primarily with organizational size, such as Blau.

5. These observations are based on the research and reflection carried out during the sixties by members of the Centre de sociologie des organisations who studied the French government bureaucracy, and in particular on the work of Pierre Grémion, who initially worked out a methodological approach for the analysis of local administration in France. See Pierre Grémion, "Introduction à une étude du systéme politico-administratif local" *Sociologie du travail* 1 (1970):51–73; and *Pouvoir local, pouvoir central: essai sur la fin de l'administration républicaine* (doctoral thesis, Université René Descartes, Paris, 1975), published under the title *Le pouvoir périphérique* (Paris: Editions du Seuil, 1976).

6. *Mutatis mutandis*, the mechanisms involved here are the same as those involved in the relation between an organization and its members, and, in a more general way, in every power relation. The members of an organization can "manipulate" only by allowing themselves to be manipulated in return. The same finding is applicable to be manipulated in

return. The same finding is applicable to the gatekeepers. In this way, we encounter the broader problem of representation. In fact, as a representative, the gatekeeper is structurally a traitor to the extent that he can satisfy the requirements of his role only by securing at least partial independence for himself with respect to the "legitimate interests" of his constituents; he may even have to sacrifice some of those interests. Increasingly, it seems to us that awareness of the fundamental contradiction between loyalty and treason to the interests of the constituency lies at the root of the present crisis of representation as a basic mechanism for the articulation of collective interests. See the treatment of these problems in Grémion, *Le pouvoir périphérique*.

7. Is it necessary to point out that not all gatekeepers are equivalent in this respect? Their power over organization will vary as a function of the *relvance* and *degree of centrality* (relative to survival of the organization) of the environment source of uncertainty under their jurisdiction, as well as in proportion to the relative *ease of replacement* characteristic of their role. We shall come back to this last factor below, for its manipulation is basic to the strategies of all parties.

8. For themselves and for their constituents: these two aspects are actually interdependent. If the gatekeeper obtains advantages for his constituents, he increases his hold over them, and, consequently, his capacity of action as their representative.

9. With the important caveat that the liberty of each partner/adversary emerging from such a relation is here greater *a priori*. We will return to this point.

10. Since what is essential he is not the "objective" resources available to the actors, but their *actual utilization* in a given relation of power, it is easy to see that such a procedure is difficult to quantify, usually requiring a searching clinical examination just to identify the phenomena to be explained. The failure to recognize this difficulty is to our mind the major weakness of the resource-dependence model, in particular in the work of Aldrich. As a result of factoring phenomena to make them susceptible to statistical analysis, Aldrich ends by losing sight altogether of the significance of what he is measuring. See H. Aldrich, "The Environment as a Network of Organizations: Theoretical and Methodological Implications," (paper presented to the Eighth Congress of the International Association of Sociology, Toronto, 1974).

11. The personalized gatekeeper is indispensable as long as there are no other means for the organization to reach its relevant environment—its market, for instance. Recourse to the personalized gatekeeper, however, implies channeling of communications, hierarchical relations, dependence and counter-dependence. It is, however, possible to bypass the usual personal gatekeepers—the notables, the merchants, agents, and various other intermediaries—by organizing impersonal gatekeepers, for instance, by using the media as an information organ or by using statistical techniques of market analysis. The opinion survey, the professional analyst, and the consultant may then supplant the privileged informant who represents and shapes demand. Once the market has developed to a certain level, new regulatory functions totally different from the roles played by the traditional intermediaries can be envisaged. Looked at in this way, it might prove profitable to restudy many different professions and business sectors, from insurance to politics. In general, wherever knowledge of and interaction with a specialized clientele are involved, this methodology may prove useful.

12. This change in the nature of the game brings out the organization's unique characteristics as a special case in the general category of "organized systems." We shall have more to say about this in part 3, particularly in chap. 9.

13. To avoid misunderstanding, we want to make clear at once that such a monopoly can exist at different levels, and empirical analysis must carefully distinguish among them. Thus, for instance, many theoretically possible personnel changes will never occur if a certain gatekeeper manages to make himself unique and irreplaceable during a specific period of time, with regard to specific problems, etc.

14. Again, the situation is one of fairly complete integration of the gatekeeper. Furthermore, this integration will diminish contact between the organization and the environment; this can be counteracted only by creating *new* gatekeepers, who will always have to face the resistance of those already in place. We shall return to this point.

15. Of course, such examples can only be rough approximations.

16. Such systems of relation must always be analyzed from a diachronic standpoint. Indeed, because they are less formalized, games between segments of the organization and gatekeepers are more sensitive to *fluctuations* in available resources and opportunities. Colonized by its gatekeepers at time t, an organizational segment can gain in autonomy by time $t+1$, and vice versa.

17. It follows that control of such relations is always a major stake in intraorganizational conflict. Here again the relation to the environment appears as a source of uncertainty. See above, chap. 2.

18. Convenient, because already in existence.

19. Of course, the nuances previously indicated are still valid here.

20. Such an analysis throws a different light on the well-known difficulties that government bureaucracies face in coordinating their various competing, but often highly compartmentalized centers of decision making. The multiplicity of such centers does not merely reflect the tendency of administrative structures to perpetuate themselves; it may also be interpreted as a sign that the government's monopoly on certain administrative functions cannot be attenuated and counterbalanced by the gatekeepers in any other way. Similarly, compartmentalization might be interpreted as an attempt by the various components of the administration to limit interagency competition and to reestablish their monopoly on a higher plane.

21. The importance of the evaluation of performance deserves treatment at greater length. For the moment, we shall content ourselves with saying merely that its essential function would appear to be to impose a constraint on political choices via feedback of the outcome thereof, and in so doing to clarify and rationalize those choices. Measurement is a reality principle whose existence allows, if not the regulation of power relations, then at least their delineation and clarification of their scope.

22. In such a state of affairs, the benefit for one party or another is clear, as is the temptation for each to create such situations.

23. Without reflecting such an ideal-typical situation in every detail, of course, the system of relations between the French public administration and the social groups under its tutelage may profitably be compared with a model of this kind, as is shown by the analysis of Jean-Pierre Worms, "Le préfet et ses notables, " *Sociologie du travail* 3 (1966):249–76. We come back to this point in the following case study and again in part 3, chap. 8.

24. Numerous empirical analyses attest to the reality and importance of these constraints. The case study of the Ministry of Industry which we present below is one illustration. Another example is the well-known dilemma faced by many police forces which, in their battle against crime, often depend heavily on a network of informers which has been built up with great difficulty and whose preservation sometimes greatly restricts their freedom of action.

25. It thus becomes easier to understand how an organization can "ignore" over long periods often important changes affecting its environment, especially since segments of the organization will frequently be accomplices in such strategies.

26. In his analysis of cooptation mechanisms implemented by the Tennessee Valley Authority, P. Selznick offers a striking example of such a selective integration of the environment. See *TVA and the Grass Roots*.

27. And not only for research: manipulation—intuitive or conscious, it matters little—of the contours of the relevant system of action by the actors may be their most important means of changing the situation and "rules of the game" governing their interactions. We

have already illustrated the importance of such manipulation in our analysis of some of Schelling's examples in *The Strategy of Conflict*. Proof is also afforded by numerous empirical cases. For instance, we have shown how certain actors strengthened their hand in intraorganizational negotiations by mobilizing their gatekeepers. See J. C. Thoenig and E. Friedberg, "The Power of the Field Staff," in A. F. Leemans, *Managing Administrative Change* (The Hague: Nijhoff, 1976); for another striking example, see Grémion, *Le pouvoir périphérique*.

28. These very useful concepts were worked out by R. Pages on the basis of a diachronic study of a staff crisis in a Parisian private school. See his "L' inélasticité d'une organisation en crise de direction," *Sociologie du travail* 4 (1965); and *L'égalité des systèmes d'emprise à différents niveaux et leur interaction* (mimeo; Paris: Laboratoire de Psychologie Sociale), February–June 1967.

29. From all of this it emerges clearly that periods of organizational *crisis* are always of paramount importance for the analyst. During crises the underlying balance of power within the organization is most clearly revealed. "Jurisdictional" conflicts will also be intensified at such times, because "outside" actors will attempt to impose constraints on the organization in order to influence its evolution and the outcome of internal disputes.

30. The replaceability of gatekeepers may be an invaluable index in this area. As we have shown, the more difficult it is to get rid of a gatekeeper, the more he will be part of the relevant system of action on which the analysis is focused.

31. Without prejudging the organization's degree of centrality in the larger system of action. As we shall show below with the aid of the example of the Ministry of Industry, it is important not to confuse the starting point of the research with the center of the system under investigation. Sometimes the organization will turn out to have been only a relatively insignificant component of a system whose actual centers of power lie elsewhere.

32. We merely mention this change in the analytic perspective, about which we shall have more to say in part 3, which is devoted to "concrete systems of action."

33. But we offer the hypothesis that the phenomena brought to light here are found in all organizations, in varying degrees to be determined empirically in each case.

34. This investigation was carried out at the end of 1969, and its results were published in a mimeographed report: Erhard Friedberg, *Le ministère de l'industrie et son environment*, CSO (Paris: Hachette, 1970), microfiches AUDIR. See also Friedberg, "Verwaltungsreform, Organisationssoziologie und Politikwissenschaft," *Österreichische Zeitschrift für Politikwissenschaft* 2 (1973):145–59. For an overview of the development of the state's system of action in industrial policy, see Friedberg, "Administration et Entreprises," in Michel Crozier et al., *Où va l'administration française?* (Paris: Editions d'Organisation, 1974). In spite of changes in the formal structure since the time of the investigation, the bulk of our results remain valid.

35. Such as the directorate of chemical industries, iron and stell, mechanical-electrical-electronic industries, textile, etc. Several industrial sectors do not, however, fall under the ministry's jurisdiction, including construction, shipbuilding, weapons manufacture, etc., these being the province of other concerned ministries.

36. One of their essential missions in this regard was to examine applications for subsidies filed by industries in their sector, and to prepare *technical evaluations* of these requests.

37. Knowledge of great importance for the ministry. Its formal decision making prerogatives were often quite weak, as we shall see.

38. In addition, a functional directorate was responsible for personnel management and budget. Its role, however, was quite limited, since it played no part in formulating personnel policy, and since the vertical directorates were independent in budgetary matters. Moreover, its weakness offers a good index of the vertical fragmentation of the ministry, as we shall show.

39. The diversification was first of all *sectorial,* as we have alaady indicated: "sectorial responsibility" for the various industrial sectors was divided among a great many ministries, including, in addition to the Industry Ministry, those of Transportation, Defense, Public Works, Post and Telecommunications, etc. It was also *functional:* the various directorates of the Ministry of Finance divided responsibility for fiscal and financial stimulation, price policy, and promotion of exports, and certain governmental or paragovernmental bodies, like le Crédit national, le Crédit hôtelier, and other sources of loans or assistance to industry, were given strictly circumscribed responsibility in corporate financing. For further details, see Friedberg, "Administration et entreprises."

40. Particularly the various directorates of the Ministry of Finance, a major actor in the system, though itself fragmented.

41. We should add that things were not always so. During the immediate postwar period of scarcity, the ministry played a major role as rationer of raw materials. Simiarly, it subsequently dominated the regulation of foreign trade, which declined in importance only in the middle sixties. It is from this period that the real decline of the ministry dates; what is more, the loss in power was unequal in the various directorates.

42. The "horizontal directorate," a "new formula" coming out of the 1970 reforms, experienced the same failure, as the reform of 1974 attests.

43. The Corps des mines is roughly comparable to the Army Corps of Engineers in the U.S., yet it exercises much broader functions, exerts greater influence over the career trajectories of its members, and enjoys a relative budgetary autonomy for reasons which the text makes clear.—Trans.

44. By Grands corps de l'état de France one generally means Foreign Affairs, the Council of State, la Cour des comptes, and l'Inspection générale des finances. The latter two incorporate various functions analogous to the Bureau of Internal Revenue, the Treasury and Commerce Departments, and diverse regulatory agencies in the U.S.—Trans.

45. The Corps des mines is one of the most prestigious of the "corps" which form the elite of the French civil service. It includes nearly 350 members, recruited from the Ecole polytechnique and distributed more or less in equal parts in the administration, the public sector, the parapublic sector, and the private sector. For further details, see E. Friedberg and D. Desjeux, "Fonctions de l'état et rôle des grands corps: le cas du corps des mines," *Annuaire international de la fonction publique* (Paris, 1972).

46. Its financial resources are used in a variety of ways. A good portion still goes to supplement the salaries of the "corpsmen" in public offices and of the other agents working in the corps' sphere of influence. The advantage is obvious: such resources enable corps-managed agencies to retain and indeed to attract highly qualified civil servants.

47. The real nature of this personnel policy was divulged in many of our interviews. The interviewees described how each member of the corps was scrutinized early in his career, and how they were discouraged from tarnishing the image of the corps by choosing employment with a relatively unprestigious private firm. They also told how the particular talents of various members would be used to stake out new zones of competence. Statistical analysis of their careers, moreover, demonstrates strong regularities in the patterns of their development. See Friedberg and Desjeux, "Fonctions de l'état."

48. The reader should take care lest he take too conspiratorial a view of the corps' action. It is by no means a system in which a few behind-the-scenes figures pull all the strings, taking decisions to which the other members respond as puppets. Within limits, such phenomena may exist from time to time in relatively mild forms. The real power of the corps, however, lies elsewhere. It is based on a much simpler and more prosaic phenomenon. In a world where both government and industry are hamstrung by compartmentalization, stratification, privilege, and *a prioris*, the mere possibility of communication—and, what is more, communication in the midst of conflict (for conflict is almost invariably implicated)—may repre-

sent an enormous advantage, considerably more powerful than any sort of emotional manipulation.

49. Our interviewees left no doubt in this respect, explaining that even if their ministry were eliminated, their services and their activities would remain and would be integrated into the administration in some other location.

50. One of these limits, the constraint of small numbers, deserves mention. The Malthusianism in the recruitment of the Grands corps is striking, in fact. Looked at in the context of systemic regulation, it is clearly "functional." Without it, the corps would not be able to operate according to its peculiar management model—based wholly on interpersonal relations and mutual adjustment, and on a high level of internal cohesiveness owing to common values and experiences.

51. Thus the horizontal services within each of the vertical directorates usually had no impact on their day-to-day operation.

52. Many trade associations, moreover, set up research groups or other bodies subsidized by the state, in which the "responsible directorate" was of course represented. Outside activities of this kind brought prestige and sometimes even additional remuneration to the officials involved.

53. When the 1970 reforms were made, the strength of these ties was underscored by the intense involvement of the trade associations, lobbying on behalf of "their" services. The gatekeepers mobilized all their resources in order to limit the organization's will to change.

54. Here we describe only the *consequences* of the persistence of such systems. To understand the *reasons* why they persisted, we would need to determine the origin and especially the mechanisms. In other words, we would need to analyze the over-all regulation of interactions between industry and government—i.e., the strategies of the actors involved in this expanded system, the balance of power prevailing in it, and the structure-determining "rules of the game." For the outline of such an analysis, see Friedberg, "Administration et Entreprises."

55. Not to mention manipulation and, indeed, the conscious withholding of information.

56. Essentially, the procedures connected with the technical evaluation of applications for industrial subsidies, whereby the weak directorates could, if not initiate grants, at least impede their issuance, though this power was rarely used.

57. It is not possible to describe this evolution here. We will say only that the increasing importance of financial leverage for intervening in industry led to an increasing stratification of these systems under a dominant actor: the Ministry of Finance, in relation to which the services of the Ministry of Industry take on more and more the role of mere gatekeepers.

Chapter 6

1. In the sense in which "cultural" is opposed to "natural."

2. These game constructs may themselves be analyzed as capacities, as we shall have occasion to show later.

3. See Crozier, *The Bureaucratic Phenomon,* especially pp. 187–94 and 213–36. The hypotheses suggested in this work have been further explored by various researchers at the Center for Sociology of Organizations. See R. Sainsaulieu, *Les relations de travail à l'usine* (Paris: Editions d'Organisation, 1973); J. C. Thoenig and E. Friedberg, "Politiques urbaines et stratégies corporatives," *Sociologie du travail* 4 (1969); J. C. Thoenig, *l'ere des technocrates* (Paris: Editions d'Organisation, 1973); and J.-P. Worms, *Une préfecture comme organisation* (Paris: Copedith, 1968), reproduced in microfiches AUDIR (Paris: Hachette, 1973).

4. In this connection the reader should recall the example of the shops of the Industrial Monopoly.

5. A study of the reform of the Ministry of Equipment and Housing has made it possible to analyze in greater detail the mechanisms and the almost inexorable logic of stratification, thereby throwing light on their effects on the operation and capacity for change of this administration, showing in particular how the confrontational logic prevailing in interagency relationships ultimately assumed greater importance than the objectives of the reform itself. See J. C. Thoenig and E. Friedberg, "Politiques urbaines;" and "The Power of the Field Staff," Thoenig, "La stratification," in Crozier et al., *Où va l'adminstration française?* pp. 29–53.

6. Here we have given just a brief summary of the model, which is well known. For further details, see Crozier, *The Bureaucratic Phenomenon,* especially pp. 187–236.

7. This game is particularly important, albeit not the only one in play. Other— exceptional—games coexist in the same structure and at other levels are paramount. We will return to this point in the next part of this book, especially chaps. 7 and 8.

8. And, secondarily, to the rules governing authority relations, corollaries of the first.

9. In this connection, recall the technical engineers in the Industrial Monopoly. Dispersed throughout the factories of the Monopoly, they barely knew one another.

10. Peer group pressure in such a system is the functional equivalent of hierarchical pressure; both are instruments for insuring the indispensable minimum degree of conformity among the individuals involved.

11. This point will be discussed in greater detail below.

12. See A. Gouldner, *Patterns of Industrial Bureaucracy;* and P. Selznick, *TVA and the Grass Roots.*

13. The results of a comparative study of work organization, interpersonal relations, and authority systems aboard a British and an American freighter confirm this argument. They show that in contrast with the British vessel, the system of action aboard the American freighter was characterized by a proliferation of impersonal rules resulting in extensive division of authority according to functional areas. See S. A. Richardson, "Organizational Contrasts on British and American Ships," *Administrative Science Quarterly* 1 (1956):189–207.

14. The importance of informal groups in American organizations is attested to by numerous descriptions of the climate, both at the shop level (see the studies of the interactionist school) and the supervisory level (see, among others, M. Dalton, *Men who Manage* [New York: Wiley, 1959]).

15. See, among others, C. Nakane, *Japanese Society* (Berkeley: University of California Press, 1974); J. C. Abegglen, *The Japanese Factory* (New York: Free Press, 1958); *Management and Worker: The Japanese Solution* (Tokyo-New York: Kodansha International, Inc., 1973); and R. P. Dore, *City Life in Japan* (Berkeley: University of California Press, 1958).

16. For particular mention we should like to single out lifetime tenure of employees, promotion by seniority, nondifferentiation of roles, consensus-style decision making, and pay scales keyed to the group and scarcely discriminating between individuals as to their effort or performance. In this connection, see Abegglen, *Management and Worker.*

17. Involvement which may verge on total identification.

18. Vertical as opposed to horizontal, seemingly characteristic of Western societies—but not only these.

19. This is what emerges from Abegglen's analysis of the development of Japanese management practices between 1956 and 1966: see *Management and Worker.* He emphasizes the extraordinary stability of these practices, which have tended on the whole to strengthen their hold. Moreover, other studies show that the Japanese have been successful in exporting their model to their foreign subsidiaries. See R. T. Johnson, *Made in America,* Stanford University manuscript, 1973. However, there is room to wonder how well such a system will

weather a cataclysmic shock like the latest worldwide recession and the ensuing period of slowed growth. Abegglen raises this same question in his book without providing an answer.

20. Two points emphasized by Nakane and Abegglen come to mind. The first relates to the extreme emotional toll taken by constant immersion in group life. The second concerns the serious difficulties that strongly vertically integrated groups face in merger situations, particularly evident in strong resistance to mergers in Japanese firms. See Nakane, *Japanese Society;* and Abegglen, *Management and Worker.*

21. For example, the paradoxical (to Western eyes) combination of an intensely individualistic style with lifetime tenure and seniority promotion is striking, since in the West we tend—perhaps simplistically, but not entirely wrongly—to associate the latter two characteristics with a model of avoidance and ritualism.

22. Such as the comparison undertaken by W. F. Whyte between modes of organization in the United States and Peru, wherein the author compares Peruvian organizational models with a model based on notions of authority and interpersonal relations along the lines laid down by studies in organization theory, anthropology, and linguistics. See W. F. Whyte, "An Intercultural Context for Organizational Research," in Whyte, ed., *Organizational Behavior: Theory and Application* (Homewood, Ill.: Irwin, 1969), pp. 719–42; as well as the study of the British cigarette industry by Clark, "The Cultural Contexts of Bureaucratic Pathologies and Routine Organizations;" or the comparison between British and German firms by J. Child and A. Okieser, "Organization and Mangerial Roles in British and West German Companies: An Examination of the Culture Free Thesis," both in Lammers, *Organizations Unlike and Alike* (to be published).

23. Such differences were key to our own comparisons above, largely speculative in nature.

24. From an abundant literature, see, among others, T. Parsons and E. A. Shils, "Values, Motives and Systems of Action," in Parsons and Shils, eds., *Toward a General Theory of Action* (Cambridge, Mass.: Harvard University Press, 1951); Clifford Geertz, "Ideology as a Cultural System," in D. Apter, ed., *Ideology and Discontent* (New York: Free Press, 1964); F. R. Kluckhohn and F. L. Strodtbeck, *Variations in Value Orientations* (New York: Row, Peterson & Co., 1961); and H. C. Triandis, *The Analysis of Subjective Culture* (New York: Wiley, 1972).

25. In a remarkable article, J. G. March has developed an argument on analogous premises, pleading in particular for a "technology" or, if you prefer, a "rationalization" of foolishness which would make it possible to understand when and how individuals might discover new solutions—and, in so doing, new values. See J. G. March, "For a Technology of Foolishness," in H. Leavitt et al., eds., *Organizations of the Future* (New York: Praeger Publishers, 1974).

26. See W. R. Schonfeld, *Obedience and Revolt: French Behavior toward Authority* (Beverly Hills: Sage Publications, 1976).

27. In common parlance, *chahut* means an uproar, specifically in the classroom, for which, curiously enough, there seems to be no precise equivalent in English. The word is used here in a more restrictive sense as well, which is explained in n. 29 below.—Trans.

28. Schonfeld defines this term as a personal legitimacy recognized in superiors perceived as "powerful, strong, imposing" characters. Clearly, this is something rather close to Weber's charismatic leader. The teachers so endowed need not impose exemplary punishments. The students submit to their personalities (whether perceived or real), not to shows of power on their part.

29. To avoid any possible misunderstanding, let us make clear that Schonfeld defines *chahut* more restrictively than does common parlance (see n. 27 above). In this category he places only situations in which the teacher really has lost control of his class, involving

serious and systematic insubordination by the students. The figure of twenty to twenty-five per cent refers to these cases only, and not to situations where slight departures from the "orderly classroom" are tolerated by teachers who in other respects are in control of their classes.

30. This did not occur in the vocational classes at the senior level, where the influence of the baccalaureate was absent.

31. The authority-laden syndrome is most prevalent in relations between students and teachers afforded a Caesaristic type of legitimacy.

32. What is involved, however, is not really an internalization of norms, since as far as the students are concerned, the rules are still imposed from without. Thus the quotation marks.

33. We are so intimately familiar with relations of avoidance that we have a hard time conceiving of them as deriving from a capacity. And yet in many situations, the mastery of avoidance is a real advantage, which makes it possible to capitalize on opportunities, to escape from difficult situations—in short, to act, where others, without this capacity, would be paralyzed. Similarly, the Japanese hierarchy and its underlying sense of loyalty are also indicative of a capacity, a technique for "managing" the emotional burden of interpersonal relations—a burden which, if not channeled and bridled, might at any moment split the group apart. Essential in this connection is the development of a tolerance for ambiguity. This tolerance is not merely a psychological trait, it is a cultural capacity acquired through action.

34. Carrying on with the analysis, we may say that values, norms, and attitudes are as much, if not more, rationalizations ex post facto of strategies and behaviors actually adopted, than they are expressions of preferences motivating the action. This viewpoint, closely related to the line of thought developed by L. A. Festinger, *A Theory of Cognitive Dissonance* (New York: Harper, 1957), will arise several more times in the present work. See in part 4, devoted to problems of decision and in chap. 14 of part 5, the discussion of problems of intervention and controlled change. Finally, the methodological repercussions for the treatment of attitudes are discussed in the Appendix.

35. Here we can do no more than scratch the surface of a subject which is central to work in many respects revolutionary, and surely pioneering: that of R. D. Laing and his group. In particular, by analyzing the role of the family in the origin of mental illness and especially of schizophrenia, they have brought to light the real importance and seriousness of this phenomenon. See Laing, *The Divided Self; The Self and Others* (London: Tavistock, 1961); Laing and Esterson, *Sanity, Madness and the Family;* and Laing, *The Politics of Experience.* In work he did at the CSO on cultural learning processes in the workplace, R. Sainsaulieu took a similar approach. See *L'identité au travail* (Paris: Presses de la fondation nationale des sciences politiques, 1977).

36. Broadly speaking, this is the same situation as in Sartre's *No Exit.*

37. This is even more true if the situations are more stable and less readily escapable. Another variable must also be taken into account: the nature of the job. In fact, the less the job places technical factors between the individual and these relations, the more they must be "personal," and so the more likely they will be to trigger the emotional mechanisms described above, along with their corollary protective strategies. In this sense, Michael Pusey is certainly right in regarding educational organizations as one of the best places to observe the impact of culture on organizational game models. See his excellent study of the Australian secondary schools: M. R. Pusey, *Dynamics of Bureaucracy* (New York: Wiley, 1976).

38. On this point see R. Sainsaulieu, "Pouvoir et stratégie de groupes ouvriers dan l'atelier," *Sociologie du travail* 2 (1965); R. Sainsaulieu and D. Kergoat, "Milieu de travail et modèle d'action," *Analyse et prévision* 4, no. 6 (1968); Sainsaulieu, *Les relations de travail à l'usine, L'identité au travail.*

39. See above, pp. 17–18.

40. For a detailed description of this strike, we refer the reader to Kergoat, *Bulle d'or;* and "Emergence et création."

41. Very schematically, the assembly line workers, the maintenance workers, the laborers, the drivers, and even the supervisors.

42. Essentially consisting of workers of foreign origin.

43. Burns and Stalker, *The Management of Innovation.*

44. This is of course only a shorthand description of a far more complex process. The "organization" does not react consciously in a planned fashion. However, the structure-determining rules of the game indirectly imposed constraints on the actors, forcing them, if they wish to avoid losing, to use certain strategies and to respond in certain ways to external threats, thereby reinforcing the existing organizational mode.

45. See chap. 4 above, which is devoted to a critique of structural contingency theories.

46. In light of this reasoning, one may well wonder whether it would not be useful in general to turn the question of learning upside down, asking not how individuals learn, but rather what *prevents them from learning.* In other words, we may ask how structures and rules, essential instruments of action, learning, understanding, and problem solving, become obstacles to learning owing to the fact that they impose a certain structure on individual experience. We will return to this inversion of the learning question in the chapter devoted to problems of change. For views close in certain respects to ours, see J. G. March and J. P. Olson, "The Uncertainty of the Past: Organizational Learning under Ambiguity," *European Journal of Political Research* 3 (1975):147–71.

47. In fact, there is no natural or spontaneous "tendency." There is no certainty that actors in such a favorable situation would want to engage in an experiment of this kind. And even if they did, there is no reason to think they would want, or be able, to help others "profit" from their experience. As we indicated above, the opposite may well be anticipated.

48. Here we only scratch the surface of one aspect of a series of extremely complex and as yet little explored sociological problems dealing with processes of innovation and learning in systems of action. We will return to this subject at greater length in the last part of this work.

49. Because to flout the rule is still to use it.

50. Which, the reader will recall, are only ideal-typical models.

51. In a twofold sense. No relation of power can be established without cultural underpinnings; every political deed is a cultural deed in the strong sense of the term.

52. Especially to the extent that one can "make do" with one technology more easily than another, depending both on the strengths of the benefited groups and on the power to resist of the victimized groups, depending also on the capacity of individuals, groups, and organizations to make use of the technological innovation—i.e., to organize along the lines of the relational models implicit in the technology.

53. This, of course, is the main criticism to which the "structural contingency" approach is open, as we saw above.

Chapter 7

1. We will have occasion to reformulate our definition of the term *system* several times in the course of this chapter. We beg the reader's indulgence if the meaning of the term is not very clear at the outset. We think that a good definition can be understood only after the phenomenon to which it applies has been analyzed.

2. "Formalization" from such a standpoint appears as *one* possible repertoire of solutions.

3. On this view, what is important is not the characteristics of the phenomenon in itself, but rather the problem posed by its existence, which we can understand more readily by

examining the machinery designed to cope with it. On this point, see H. A. Simon, *The Science of the Artificial* (Cambridge, Mass.: MIT Press, 1970).

4. See the methodological Appendix, where this point is discussed in greater depth.

5. We are not suggesting, of course, that Goffman's work be assimilated to Homans'. In many respects the two are radically different, but from the standpoint we have adopted here, they have in common the ambition to reconstruct the social game on the basis of a direct analysis of individual interactions—simple and adaptive for Homans, unpredictable and strategic for Goffman. Explicitly aiming to reconstruct modes of sociability and domination through analysis of everyday interactions and, if need be, of agitated situations, the ethnomethodologists push this tendency to its extreme limits.

6. Let us make clear immediately that this mode of argument has nothing to do with the permissive view according to which behavior is an artifact of the system, whereby both guilt and freedom are eradicated in one fell swoop. Nor is it intended to justify existing practices. We shall return to these points at greater length in our final chapters.

7. A detailed analysis of this case may be found in Ballé and J.-L. Peaucelle, *Le pouvoir informatique*.

8. Without strategic analysis and the detour by way of the actor's "experience" that it requires, this game would never have been discovered.

9. The clerical agency examined at length in *The Bureaucratic Phenomenon* was the first attempt to formulate a systems argument of this type. The reader may familiarize himself with this case by referring to that work, pp. 13–50.

10. For a long time the abuses of suboptimization in microeconomic theory and of the cost benefit model in decision theory prevented consideration of the much more central and limitative phenomena of power relations, interdependence, and systematic symbiosis—the universal determinants of structure. The leading American specialist in operations research, Russel Ackoff, was the most eloquent critic of this sad state of affairs, advocating—well before James Forrester, precursor of the Club of Rome—a thoroughgoing change of perspective. See R. Ackoff, "The Systems Revolution," *Long Range Planning*, December 1974.

11. Of course, structuration implies inequality, communications bottlenecks, and necessary deviations from the direct course of action. As we have been at pains to show in the first part of this work, structuration above all implies the existence of power relations.

12. Theodore Caplow, *Two against One: Coalitions in Triads* (Englewood Cliffs, N.J.: Prentice-Hall, 1969).

13. The family is as a rule studied as an institution or as a primary group. But it might prove fruitful to study it also as a system whose members must be integrated if a minimum number of common objectives are to be achieved. Taking the family system as a problem rather than a precondition, such an approach will examine the zones of uncertainty controlled by the various family members, as well as the alliances they may form. The family will thus be looked upon as characterized not by ethnological features, but rather by the game or games played within it, by their rules and structures, and by the systemic features it exhibits.

14. See Talcott Parsons, *The Social System* (New York: Free Press, 1951); D. Easton, *A System of Political Life* (New York: Wiley, 1965).

15. For a typical and explicit example of such a mode of argument in organizational studies, see Perrow, *Organizational Analysis*.

16. See Berger and Luckmann, *The Social Construction of Reality*, which defines reification as the conceptualization of human constructs or artifacts as something other than human constructs or artifacts. Applied to the notion of system, this definition clearly aims to *naturalize* what is only a human construct, rather than recognize that such constructs are concrete and impose constraints. After all, while they are human constructs, organizations are nonetheless also concrete objects. To paraphase these two authors, we might say that

the paradox is that man can produce constructs which he experiences as something other than constructs.

17. To be precise, we should add "when this system exists," for the actual situation may involve several systems or a multi-branched system, or possibly—in the case of complete anomie—a system structured by an alien system.

18. Moreover, its existence is what contaminates, in large part, the various versions of functionalism à la Parsons or à la Luhmann, thereby leading them into the errors of naturalism and reification.

19. See Norbert Wiener, "Cybernetics or Control and Communication," *The Animal and the Machine* (New York: Wiley, 1948). True, W. R. Ashby does attempt to develop a more complex model for biological phenomena. But we do not think that our distinction is altered fundamentally by his contribution, which would be interesting to discuss at greater length. See W. R. Ashby, *Design for a Brain* (London: Chapman & Hall, 1952); and *Introduction to Cybernetics* (London: Chapman & Hall, 1956).

20. And not just the cybernetic analogy, which in this respect deserves neither too much praise nor too much blame. As we have said, the several analogies that we would be tempted to call "scientistic" (biological, thermodynamical, linguistic, etc.) share with the cybernetic analogy its neglect of the strategic dimension of human behavior, and its obfuscation of the corollary thereof: power is the basic regulatory mechanism in all collective action and hence in every system.

21. The widely current attempts in France to construct a systems theory based on cybernetic axioms, and to deduce from it normative precepts, is no different. The outcome is invariably formalization, sometimes interesting, but always open to debate. Most important, the normative precepts are based exclusively on deductive logic, impermeable to experience, and accordingly the results are as useless and cumbersome as were the earliest theories of administrative science. See in this connection the already dated work of L. Mehl on cybernetics and administration. See also B. Lussato, *Modèles cybernétiques, hommes, entreprises,* vol. 1, *Introduction critique aux théories d'organisation* (Paris: Dunod, 1972).

22. We will discuss the notion of regulation at greater length below, in chap. 9.

23. We first advanced this viewpoint in a paper presented to the World Congress of Sociology at Varna, 1970, subsequently published in a revised French version: M. Crozier, "Sentiments, organisations et systèmes," *Revue francaise de sociologie* 120 (1971):141–54.

24. Temporary phenomena continue to cause us problems; by this we mean encounters in which power relations can exist without regulation—i.e., without a containing game or system. We will return to this point later.

25. See in this connection the analysis of R. Pagès concerning the temporary institution of an autonomous system of action during a crisis in a school. See Pagès, "L'élasticité d'une organisation en crise." We shall have occasion to mention this point again in connection with a study of Catherine Grémion related to a temporary system of action (in this case more official in nature, however), in part 4.

26. This obsession with measurement, alas, marks a large number of English-language works on "interorganizational systems or networks." A researcher such as H. Aldrich is encouraged thereby to factor phenomena in a manner adapted to a methodology supposed "rigorous" because statistical, albeit wholly unsuited to the complexity of the matter. See H. Aldrich "The Environment as a Network of Organizations: Theoretical and Methodological Implications," (paper presented to IAS, Toronto, 1974).

Chapter 8

1. See Worms, "le préfet et ses notables."

2. For a thorough consideration of all these aspects, the reader should consult the very exhaustive study of Pierre Grémion, *Le pouvoir périphérique.*

3. See M. Crozier and J. C. Thoenig, "La régulation des systèmes organisés complexes," *Revue française de sociologie* 16, 1 (1975):3–32.

4. The Corps des ponts et chaussées is another of the corps of civil servants similar to the Corps des mines (cf. chap. 5, n. 43). Similar remarks apply in both cases.—Trans.

5. Moreover, they control its execution.

6. While the *percepteur* is the local tax collector, he has broader functions than his American counterpart would have. He is also in some sense a comptroller or budgetary supervisor, and it is principally in this capacity that he figures here.—Trans.

7. A system peculiar to France, in which 1 to 2 percent of a project's budget is paid out by the municipality to the Corps which provides technical services and material.—Trans.

8. All these assertions are based on analysis of answers given by the mayors.

9. It is widely believed that the administration is an enormous machine, all of whose cogs are blindly obedient to the driving engine, the formidable power of Paris. Nothing could be farther from the truth, even if, as we shall see later, centralization does in fact exist.

10. Qualitative analysis of the interviews reveals that communication is poor among operational officials on the local level, *départemental* officials, and Parisian functionaries, and that there is a much better understanding among notables and "onsite" bureaucrats.

11. Except where the Communist Party is concerned, but in that case the game involved is different, because their party activities tend to isolate the Communist notables.

12. See Crozier and Thoenig, "La régulation des systèmes organisès complexes," (table, p. 12).

13. See Pierre Grémion, *La structuration du pouvoir départemental* (Paris: Centre de sociologie des organisations, 1969).

14. A large majority of the notables responded candidly that too many people participate in decision making and that citizens are incapable of rising above their private interests.

15. See Crozier and Thoenig, "La régulation des systèmes organisés complexes," (tables, pp. 13–14).

16. We made this observation previously in Crozier, *The Bureaucratic Phenomenon*.

17. See Crozier and Thoenig, "La régulation des systèmes organisés complexes."

18. See Pierre Grémion and J.-P. Worms, *Les institutions régionales et la société locale* (Paris: Centre de sociologie des organisations, 1968).

19. See Crozier and Thoenig, "La régulation des systèmes organisés complexes," (table, p. 15).

20. Ibid.

21. Here, a very serious error is frequently made in identifying the present French notable (and, moreover, his predecessors of the last hundred years) with the traditional notable and with the Spanish or Latin American cacique. The contemporary French notable does have a monopoly, but it is a monopoly in a narrow domain which does not bring him much in the way of negotiating stature. Furthermore, he is tightly controlled by the honeycomb system and by the relative ease of replacement which gives the system its strength and stability.

22. One of the most curious recent examples of this has been the proliferation of public swimming pools. See Crozier and Thoenig, "La régulation des systèmes organisés complexes," (table, p. 17).

23. Ibid.

24. For a complete presentation of the results of this investigation, consult the research report: "Décentraliser les responsabilités. Pourquoi, comment?," *La documentation française* (Paris, 1975).

25. This is why, in our judgment, the *département* is not a suitable entity around which to organize a decentralization that would result in a genuine transformation of the system. See the conclusion of the report cited above, pp. 17–24.

26. See Olgierd Kuty, *Le pouvoir du malade: analyse sociologique des unités de rein artificiel,* doctoral thesis, (Paris: Université René, Descartes, 1973); and "Orientation cul-

turelle et profession medicale: la relation thérapeutique dans les unités de rein artificiel,''
Revue française de sociologie 16, 2 (1975).

27. To simplify the problem we did not look at the choice of objectives, which is very closely related to the choice of the limits of the system. To choose a selective system is to give priority to the organ transplant, which implies close cooperation with the surgical unit reponsible for the operation.

28. The comparison may be challenged, and the critic may claim that we are not dealing with the same problem and the same technique, since, in the case of the "bureaucratic" services, it is a matter of doing dialysis for survival, while in the "democratic" services, dialysis is supposed to lead to an eventual transplant. Still, it is the same illness and the same machine involved in both cases.

29. It is difficult to distinguish between the two objectives, or, rather, the two reasons for the choices made, but Kuty's analysis shows that at the outset the concern for democratic cooperation and team spirit was foremost for one group, while, in the other, achieving the required performance was the primary concern.

30. In the larger system of action, the doctor's free choice (based on the patient's free choice and on the ideology of individual consultation) continues to be paramount.

31. Which, moreover, is in conflict with the values professed by the doctors prominent in this "democratic" mode of organization.

Chapter 9

1. Lawrence Wylie, *Chanzeaux, a Village in Anjou* (Cambridge, Mass.: Harvard University Press, 1966).

2. Essentially—without going as far as the general systems problem of reducing complexity—such approaches are concerned with the maintenance of a differentiation between an inside and an outside, with the ensuing problems, well known since Parsons, of integration and adaptation. For a description and critical evaluation of such a "system of systems references" in Luhmann's work, see G. Schmid, *Funktionsanalyse und Politische Theorie,* especially pp. 112–14.

3. The two quite different notions of games and functions reflect the contrasting approaches and research orientations.

4. We will return to the links between the concrete system of action and social control.

5. This makes it possible to gauge more accurately the famous "sociological weights" constantly invoked by journalists. As distinct from the current usage of the term, these are not externally imposed preconditions. On the contrary, they are artificial constraints, human artifacts.

6. The implications of this particular point will appear later.

7. As we have shown for organizations, this inequality and the structuration which translates it into operational terms are consequences of the varying degrees of control that actors may exert over the relevant sources of uncertainty within their operating domain.

8. This is the main result of the French system of industrial relations and even the *dé-*partemental political-administrative system.

9. In our view, this argument throws a good deal of light on the many logical contradictions that arise in connection with the interpretation of problems associated with the government of large groups or societies. For instance, with it one can understand how it is possible for the Japanese system of hierarchy to be coupled with loyalty to function. If—as Chie Nakane, for example, supposes—this system tolerated no exceptions, no shifting alliances, then no innovation would be possible; the system would be fragile and its power to integrate would be minimal. But history shows that such exceptions do in fact occur constantly, and that they become the centers of the regulatory mechanisms that exert the most influence within Japanese society. To be sure, because they are based on apparent exceptions to the rules, these mechanisms are often troublesome and secretive. That does not

diminish their importance, quite the contrary. See Nakane, *La société japonaise* (preface by M. Crozier).

10. See F. H. Goldner, "The Division of Labor: Process and Power," in M. N. Zald, ed., *Power in Organizations* (Nashville: Vanderbilt University Press, 1970), pp. 97–143.

11. This is no accident, because the discoveries of social psychology were generalized in the light of the predominant deterministic model.

12. See, for instance, the work of R. Likert, in which these modes of argument are laid out relatively clearly, thanks to the author's noteworthy effort to consider practical applications of the group's results. See Likert, *New Patterns of Management* (New York: McGraw Hill, 1961).

13. See George C. Homans, *The Human Group* (New York: Harcourt Brace, 1950).

14. As we have already said, such categories as are determined by socioprofessional or income criteria never, or almost never, constitute groups, organizations, or even concrete systems of action that may be regarded as units capable of acting to achieve a desired goal, or even of provoking an unforeseen result.

15. We have already stressed the contingent character of these categories. See above, our discussions in the chapter on strategy, pp. 18–25.

16. This corresponds to one of our basic criticisms of contingency theory. In this respect, nothing is changed by the use of multivariate procedures or factor analyses. The interpretive schema may be complicated as a result, but the mode of argument is not altered.

17. While experimental work with groups was only a small fraction of the total research effort, the relational paradigm nevertheless dominated sociological thinking, and this paradigm was marked profoundly by research on small groups. The practical application of social science—in our opinion, the best test—was completely determined by this mode of reasoning.

18. The *Grandes ecoles* are institutions unique to France. Highly prestigious and selective, they train students to satisfy the national need for technically competent personnel in a broad range of areas. Perhaps the nearest American analogue would be one of the highly selective technological institutes, such as M. I. T. or Cal Tech, though this comparison gives a rather poor hold on what is meant by *Grande ecole* phenomenon.—Trans.

19. The work published by Pierre Bourdieu and his associates is for the moment completely inadequate from this point of view. It falls under the head of the obsolete deterministic reasoning of which Bourdieu himself, in his most recent book, offered an unwitting caricature. See P. Bourdieu and J.-C. Passeron, *La reproduction* (Paris: Editions de Minuit, 1973). For a good critique, see, among others, Francois Bourricaud, "Contre le sociologisme. Une critique et des propositions," *Revue française de sociologie* (1975 supplement):583–603.

20. For the first steps in such an analysis, see Thoenig, *L'ere des technocrates,* for the case of the *Ponts et chaussées,* and Friedberg and Desjeux, "Fonctions de l'état et rôle des grands corps," for the *Corps des mines.* To avoid any misunderstanding, we should add that we by no means intend to make an apology for the system of the *Grands corps,* of which we have been severely critical in the past. We are simply stressing the possibility of studying such phenomena as concrete systems of action.

21. Except perhaps in Japan, under very different conditions.

22. We will return to these problems in chap. 15.

23. We reiterate that we are not speaking here of any sort whatever of system rationality, but of a rationality *in* the system, i.e., related to the structural conditions of the games that constitute it.

Chapter 10

1. The high valuation placed on the free "decision maker" is one of the most characteristic features of present day management of collective activities.

2. The PPBS, Planning Program Budgeting System, is a method which was perfected at the end of the fifties at the RAND Corporation and introduced by Robert McNamara at the U.S. Department of Defense in order to rationalize budgetary decisions, especially in weapons systems. It was subsequently extended to all Federal budget planning by direct order of President Johnson. Increasingly the object of criticism because of the abuses to which this extension had given rise, it was abandoned upon Richard Nixon's arrival at the White House. The PPBS was first adopted in France by the Ministry of Defense. It was subsequently extended under the name RCB—thanks to the support of Michel Debré, then minister of finance—to cover the whole of the governmental bureaucracy. Its results were, in fact, rather disappointing.

3. See Aaron Wildavsky, *Revolt against the Masses and Other Essays on Politics and Public Policy* (New York: Basic Books, 1971); and Wildavsky and H. Pressman, *Implementation* (Berkeley: University of California Press, 1974).

4. Charles E. Lindblom, "The Science of *Muddling Through,*" *Public Administration Review* 19 (Spring 1959).

5. Charles E. Lindblom, *The Intelligence of Democracy* (New York: Free Press, 1965); see also M. Olson, *The Logic of Collective Action* (Cambridge, Mass.: Harvard University Press, 1965).

6. In the same vein, a number of American authors have developed (more or less humorously) more adventurous paradoxes. For instance, see T. Schelling's demonstration of the usefulness of corruption. Schelling, "On the Ecology of Micromotives," *The Public Interest* 25 (1971):59–99.

7. See Lindblom, *Intelligence of Democracy*.

8. Albert Hirschman, *Development Projects Observed* (Washington: Brookings Institution, 1967), p. 197.

9. The problem and the context are, of course, not matters of indifference. We hope we will not shock any of our readers if we remark that university administration—and not only in France—is certainly one of the areas in which the rationality of decision making is the lowest, whether we reckon with reference to the objectives of the university or the objectives of individuals. Nevertheless, study of the academy yields a rich harvest of valuable lessons for other areas. As always, the analysis of pathological cases—indeed, teratology, the study of monsters—is a useful way of understanding more normal situations.

10. See March, "For a Technology of Foolishness;" and R. M. Cohen and J. G. March, *Leadership and Ambiguity* (New York: McGraw Hill, 1974).

11. We will return to this point in chap. 13.

12. March and Simon, *Organizations*.

13. Simon himself has not exploited the possibilities of his model. He is usually classified as a neorationalist.

14. Certain very simple notions, such as opportunity cost and cash flow, have had profound influence on practical decision making, though this does not necessarily imply that the models used were rational. Indeed, the general procedure has been merely to supplement the usual criteria of decision with certain empirically based factors roughly corresponding to these notions.

Chapter 11

1. See Graham Allison, *The Essence of Decision: Explaining the Cuban Missile Crisis* (Boston: Little Brown, 1971); and Joseph L. Bower, *Managing the Resource Allocation Process* (New York: Irwin, 1972). The reader will have noticed that in the United States few decisions have been studied by sociologists. On the other hand, political scientists, economists, and management specialists have studied a good many. Few studies, however, go beyond descriptive historical or political analysis. The two cases we have chosen are among the few which seriously broach problems of method.

2. The Russians have long been admiring of the high degree of rationality prevalent in the United States. Even now, they are trying desperately to borrow the American methods which insure such extraordinary economic rationality.

3. Obviously, such a link between execution and elaboration of options is indispensable in order to avoid taking unrealizable decisions. It must also be recognized, however, that the bureaucratic logic prevalent in the executive machinery imposes severe limits on the leaders' freedom of choice.

4. President Kennedy was in fact embarking on a difficult campaign for the congressional elections and had publicly expressed his confidence the Russian leaders' sense of fair play.

5. It is interesting to note that this strategy of tying one's hands in advance often succeeds. As we have already noted, T. Schelling, in *Strategy of Conflict,* has admirably demonstrated how this comes about. Unfortunately, he did not specify the conditions under which such a strategy can succeed. They are actually very highly determined by the characteristics of the game. The whole problem for the partners in the present case in to make an adequate diagnosis of the game in which they are involved; the air force generals were incapable of this. See our discussion on pp. 46–47.

6. Allison takes his inspiration rather consciously from *Rashomon,* and the analogy is a happy one, for the film offers fine specimen of the ambiguity of human strategies.

7. This distinction rapidly gained universal acceptance at the Harvard School of Public Policy. It was soon complemented by the addition of a fourth type of interpretation, on a psychohistorical model.

8. The logic of return on investment and cash flow.

9. The two Harvard studies date from the same era. Their results were discussed together and along with several other studies in an exhaustive seminar devoted to the impact of the bureaucracy on decision making, held under the auspices of the Kennedy Institute of Politics (1967–70), and directed by Richard Neustadt and Ernest May.

10. This discovery—corroborated, moreover, by much empirical data—casts doubt on many of Galbraith's premises in his analyses of the technostructure and, in particular, on his model of consumer conditioning associated with planned development. As always, the opponents of the system tend to overestimate its rationality, which perhaps they secretly admire. Even the most sophisticated American firms are hardly as rational as this. Futhermore, progress has long been moving in the direction of diversification (allowing a more flexible adaptive strategy) rather than toward planning (which involves a danger of freezing the resources). See John Kenneth Galbraith, *The New Industrial State* (London: Hamiltoin, 1967).

11. And which was actually assumed at the beginning of the analysis.

12. It is clear, for example, that the corporate echelon cannot vary the criteria of profitability as it pleases. Both the characteristics of the system of action of which it has charge and the characteristics and rules of the game of the wider system of action in which it operates impose constraints. This does not prevent the corporate echelon from manipulating the criteria of profitability (criteria of satisfaction) whereby it can exert and indirect influence on subordinate units.

Chapter 12

1. See I. Janis, *Victims of Groupthink: A Psychological Study of Foreign Policy Decisions and Fiascoes* (Boston: Houghton Mifflin, 1972). In this book on groups of decision makers, Irving Janis greatly overestimates, in our view, the importance of interpersonal relations. He fails to notice the degree to which they are conditioned by the structural preconditions of the problem to be solved and by the preexisting organizational system. Even if the leaders were caught up in the dynamic of the group, the situation would not be changed.

2. Catherine Grémion, *"Décision and indécision dans la haute administration"* (doctoral thesis, Fondation Nationale des Sciences Politiques, Paris, May 1977).

3. The most apparent rift was between innovators who wanted the prefectural staff reorganized—greatly reducing the number of personnel, but augmenting their opportunities to exert influence—and more traditional rationalizers who sought to create a large, centralized public administration around the prefect, which was designed to be more effective than the administration it replaced. Neither social origin nor philosophical outlook affected this split, but it is worth noting that it was influenced by the experience acquired by certain individuals in the overseas *départements* of France and in foreign countries. In any case, the enthusiastic commitment of the participants in the end made little difference.

4. The second decree of March 1964 created the *régions*. These included regional economic development commissions, composed of elected officials, civil servants, and local personalities, and regional administrative councils, composed of members of the prefectoral corps and a few technical specialists drawn from the high ranks of the civil service.

5. General de Gaulle neither expressed his objectives in a clear and unequivocal way nor chose the members of the commissions personally. Yet his interest in the problem, and Louis Joxe's notion of what that interest was, exerted a great influence on their work. His meeting with some of these members and his support for them were crucially important factors in the formation of the "reform" group.

6. See H. Jamous, *Contribution à une sociologie de la décision: La réforme des études médicales et des structures hospitalières* (Paris: CES, Centre National de Recherche Scientifique, 1967).

7. E. Bardach, *The Skill Factor in Politics* (Berkeley: University of California Press, 1972).

8. This must not be taken for a value judgment. This notable inequality, whereby the doctor in *serving* his patient can impose his own conditions, is at least partially justified by the problems facing both parties: the patient's anxiety in the fact of illness and death, which can be relieved by transferring responsibility; and the responsibilities, risks, and tensions that the doctor cannot take on unless he is assured of a minimal degree of protection. Other solutions are possible and desirable, but much less easy to put into practice than it appears.

9. These traits are also characteristic of the mental health professionals in France, who constitute a quite separate enclave within the medical profession as a whole.

10. The very long absence of a Frenchman among the Nobel laureates in medicine played an important psychological role.

11. On this matter, see Jamous, *Contribution à une sociologie de la décision*.

12. See chap. 6, Organization and Culture, and William F. Whyte's findings on models of authority.

13. This is the fairly explicit tendency of many English-language writers. In France, Octave Gelinier adheres to this position, at least in part. Alain Peyrefitte, in *Le mal français*, gives a presentation that is as dazzling as it is unconvincing.

14. Wildavsky and Pressman, *Implementation*.

15. We are not suggesting that the strategy used in this case should, or even can be imitated. Unfortunately, it was not studied closely enough for such a recommendation. We merely want to use the available data to relativize the rather superficial conclusions that one would otherwise be tempted to draw from these examples.

16. Even if doctors don't have a very good press, it is always difficult to mobilize the public against them, especially on such "technical" topics as the relationship among basic research, the curriculum of medical education, and professional supervision. Such is not the case for psychiatry (which, the reader will not need to be reminded, is not medicine), an area in which, in California at least, public opinion has been swamped by a current of thinking hostile to the large bureaucratic hospitals.

17. Which led them, for instance, to give the fundamentalists too great a role in reaching, and to overburden and partially "corporatize" research that they wanted to make influential

18. This is the whole reason for the interest in decentralizing and subdividing overly complex and overly integrated organizations—which are, consequently, not very open to negotiation—into more accessible operational units.

19. Here again, we have to do with the strategic dimension of the analysis, which, starting from the actors and *their* rationalities, show that it is never possible to speak of a rationality of the system. Such a rationality exists only to the extent that it is capable of shaping the strategies of the actors in the system. As such, it is never unique, but merely one among others.

20. See above chap. 6, which is devoted to relations between organizations and culture.

21. See Thoenig, *L'ère des technocrates*.

22. See Friedberg and Desjeux, "Fonctions de l'etat et role des grandes corps."

23. See Grémion, *Le pouvoir périphérique*.

24. See Crozier and Thoenig, "La régulation des systèmes organisés complexes."

25. To avoid any possible misunderstanding: this does not mean that these decisions and these organizations are the most rational possible, given the context (the one best contingent solution), and that there are no others. We reiterate that as always there are several solutions. There is no one best way, even relative to a situation.

26. Of course, there is a certain relationship between this problem and that of the transformation of a scientific paradigms (see Thomas Kuhn); but the resistance of a concrete system of action is of another order entirely. Historians and sociologists of science have not given it the importance it deserves in the matter of changing modes of rationality within an organization. See Thomas Kuhn, *The Copernican Revolution* (Cambridge, Mass.: Harvard University Press, 1957).

27. We have begun to study these problems from this standpoint. See J.-L. Peaucelle, *L'entreprise devant l'informatique* (Paris: Copedith, 1969); C. Ballé and J.-L. Peaucelle, *Le pouvoir informatique dans l'entreprise;* C. Ballé, *L'informatique, facteur de changement dans l'entreprise: Etudie de cas* (Paris: Centre de Sociologie des Organisations, 1975); M. Crozier, "l'influenza dell' informatica sul guverno delle imprese," in F. Rosito, ed., *Razionalita sociale et technologica della informazione* (Milan: Edizioni Communita, 1973), pp. 42–74.

28. This is the lesson of the example we offered above, chap. 7, pp. 115–20.

29. Many other problems—unfortunately, still treated within the confines of the classical model of rationality—should be explored, and we will have the means to do so. To take just one example, consider the problem of trying to determine what system is the most relevant site for the implementation of a new rationality—how to calculate the external factors, for instance. When it becomes impossible to solve a given problem within the context of an existing system of systems, a new system must be created. Or, to take another example, there is the problem of seeking out the intellectual tools necessary for developing a kind of rationality suited to fostering evolution of a preexisting game.

Chapter 13

1. Such a logical evolution of events corresponds best to the Marxist vulgate. Yet there were American liberals in the fifties, and there are certain advanced French liberals even today, who would draw roughly the same conclusions.

2. The very important and very consequential debate in postrevolutionary Russia as to the essence of the proletarian and the kulak—a discussion which, in many respect, is reminiscent of the famous Byzantine debate over the sex of angels—illustrates very well how determinism can veer in the direction of voluntarism, and materialism turn into idealism. See, in this connection, R. Linhart, *Lénine, les paysans, Taylor* (Paris: Editions du Seuil, 1976), which provides useful details, even if its point of view is apologetic.

3. In this type of model, there is generally a hierarachy, hence a key variable, the economic; and subsumed within the economic category, there is property for the Marxists, culture and values for Parsons, etc.

4. This ambivalence is natural. We all get involved in action, fascinated by the extraordinary progress of mankind. As a result, we readily succumb to the voluntarist illusion that to conceive of a rational social model is enough, that in itself that model will enable us to transform society as we might wish and, accordingly, to solve the problems that overwhelm us. At the same time, however, we are tortured by the anguish or responsibility. Aware enough to glimpse the fact that we don't really know what we want, we find it consoling the cling the deterministic theories which would have us willing or not, dragged along by inexorable forces, toward a new system, the inevitable next step in the process of becoming.

5. In fact, training.

6. For example, in his book *Freedom and Dignity,* which enjoyed great success with a very influential public in the United States.

7. Not only Walt Rostow, but also much more subtle men like Almond and even Lipset.

8. Certain Marxists speak of the exacerbation of contradictions, which is already more reasonable. Yet the meaning of this term remains to be seen. We will return to his problem later.

9. See chap. 8, the analysis of the *départemental* politico-administrative system.

10. We dare not say for human development. It is clear that a tribal slave society is less diversified, less wealthy, and less capable of carrying out vast undertakings than a liberal postcapitalist or "advanced" capitalist society. But can one say that men are less happy there? For the time being, cultural relativism, which hold sway over opinion, forbids us to think so.

11. If the reader will allow us this short hand formulation.

12. The invention of double entry bookkeeping, for instance, made possible the development of a capacity indispensable for the establishment of a capitalist game.

13. See above, our remarks on management revisited.

14. Of course, we are aware of the artificiality inherent in distinguishing two phases of the same process which in reality are always inextricably intertwined. Only the purposes of the analysis make this justifiable.

15. This formulation is vague, because the essential characteristics of a system of action (nature of the game, rules and modes of regulation) do not determine a single outcome, but rather a range of outcomes. Changes are therefore possible that do not challenge the essential characteristics of the system of action itself. This raises the problem of how to diagnose the essential characteristics and the limits they impose on the will to change.

16. We have not really discussed the problem of private interest here. They can be much better understood in the framework of the game and the system in which they appear than as interests intrinsic to a person or category. In any case, this approach makes it possible to understand the otherwise inexplicable phenomenon that minority interests are capable of mobilizing majority reactions of resistance, though not by design.

17. A fact that is always forgotten by the cyberneticians and even by as subtle an analyst as Niklas Luhmann.

18. See our discussion pp. 169–75.

19. See Georges Duby, *Guerriers et paysans* (Paris: Gallimard, 1973). English translation: *The Early Growth of the European Economy: Warriors and Peasants from the Seventh to the Twelfth Centuries*, trans. Howard B. Clarke (Cornell: Cornell University Press, 1974).

20. We would be tempted to interpret in this way, somewhat against Foucault himself, the emergence of the disciplinary universe he describes. See Michel Foucault, *Discipline and Punish: The Birth of the Prison,* trans. Alan Sheridan (New York: Pantheon Books, 1978).

21. See M. Crozier, "Le modèle d'action administrative à la française, est-il en voie de

transformation?," in J.-D. Reynaud, eds., *Tendances et volontés de la société françaises* (Paris: SEDEIS, coll. "Futuribles," 1966), pp. 423–444.

22. It was this change of perspective, moreover, that mattered to us, rather than any sort of psychologization of history.

23. One thing must be made clear at once. Such a process is profoundly ambiguous. It always combines old features and new. The difference, the nontrivial innovation in the collective unity, is nonetheless real.

24. Whence the potentially decisive role of the leaders, thinkers, men of action, and other diverse innovators who have the courage to take the risk of opening pathways. Whence the frequent moral commitment and even religious fervor associated with certain innovations.

25. What might be called the "negentropy" of a system of action.

26. Let it be emphasized in passing that the real "test" of the existence of a system of action might be the demonstration and empirical explanation of such vicious circles.

27. The "perverse or dysfunctional effects" of these vicious circles change nothing. There is, moreover, reason to believe that they are not generally recognized as such, and that when they are, one precondition of learning has thereby been fulfilled.

28. This remark is, of course, intended for the French audience, which has been particularly preoccupied with with such a debate in recent years.

29. The revolutionary episodes on which historical research has focused too much seem, from this point of view, not at all conclusive. When they are not purely and simply regressions (i.e., when the regression is not permanent), they may be thought of as temporary regressions which make a new start on learning possible, or else as sanctions taken against learning already accomplished—which may, as a result, be frozen in the state existing at the time of the uprising.

30. Although there is, of course, a close relationship between the two.

31. *Slack* was for a long time the *bête noire* of the economists and, more generally, of all rationalizers. Sociological analysis leads to a change in outlook.

32. At least as long as they remain viable systems of action. More complex systems are also more vulnerable to certain types of threats.

33. Chandler's analysis of the discovery of new organizational models by certain large American corporations is particularly illuminating in this respect. See *Strategy and Structure*.

34. Without going so far as to maintain that learning and violence are connected as cause and effect, we point out that hardly any Western society is more "violent than the American."

Chapter 14

1. If he is immediately forced to take responsibility for a change, he will have to make use of the lessons learned in earlier instances of adaptation, reaction, and correction. This will best enable him to escape the determinism of the system and of his past. Many radical reform efforts are in reality only ill-considered extrapolations of arbitrary reactions to earlier changes.

2. We reserve until the last chapter our discussion of the ends of change.

3. See Daniel Bell, *The Coming of Post-Industrial Society: A Venture in Social Forecasting* (New York: Basic Books, 1973).

4. Such "substantive theories" actually represent a regression, for they are entirely consistent with the old model, based on the logic of the one best way. The idea that the future is indeterminate, that men invent by experimenting with the resources and opportunities offered by "nature," remains foreign to them. What the problem always comes down to for these theories, which begin by analyzing the all encompassing variables which are supposed

to govern social structure and development, is to define the particular historical configuration that determines the best path for men to take. In our opinion, it is this methodology that diminishes the amplitude of a corpus as invariably systematic as that of Alain Touraine, for instance. See his *The Self-Production of Society,* tr. Derek Coltman (Chicago: University of Chicago Press, 1973, and *The Post-Industrial Society,* tr. Leonard Mayhew (New York: Random House, 1971).

5. Which consisted of five thousand persons.

6. Actually, they were almost as satisfied. But this unusual absence of disparity may be looked upon as significant of a malaise. What is very curious, moreover, is that when they heard the results of the survey, the supervisors worried about this point themselves and became indignant upon learning that their subordinates *were as satisfied as they were.*

7. These objectives, concerned with the amount of attention to be paid to personnel and training, and the priority to be given human problems, were relatively vague. As long as these objectives were not discussed, it was possible to believe that they were in part respected. But the interviews forced the issue and revealed that the goals were flatly rejected by the supervisors, who deemed them inapplicable, from which they drew the conclusion that management itself did not take them seriously.

8. The regularity of the curves recording attitude distribution was striking, especially relative to rank in the hierarchy.

9. This experiment in communicating the survey results was inspired by the work of the social psychologists of the Michigan school and in particular that of Floyd Mann, work carried out in the several years preceding our trial. We, ourselves, had made several earlier attempts of similar intention, in particular in connection with the Industrial Monopoly case. Since that time, many other experiments in intervention have been designed and implemented in France. But very few of them have made rigorous use of the method that we perfected, based on the first American experiments. See F. Mann, "Studying and Creating Change, a Means to Understanding Social Organizations," *Human Relations in the Industrial Setting* (New York: Harper, 1957), pp. 146–47. The single good work in French along these lines is that of R. Palm, *Une organisation en analyse ou la réforme de la cour des comptes den Belgique: Rapport d'une recherche-action de changement, 1970–1973,* (doctoral thesis, Catholic University of Louvain, 1974).

10. A certain number of tables, diagrams, and graphs were presented as simply as possible and with a minimum of commentary. We merely answered questions put to us. All the questions on this subject were received in the deepest and most agonizing silence. We did not go back on our decision to remain resolutely reserved and made no remarks that might have relieved the tension. Some time had to pass before certain participants regained their powers of speech, when attention was turned to other tables. Some of them remained silent throughout the meeting.

11. They understood more quickly and more thoroughly than the members of the management committee.

12. Because we were neither looking for nor expecting the least reaction of this sort, we were scarcely capable of intervening.

13. We are passing over the problems of the workers themselves, who at the time were far less sensitive to the constraints imposed by the organization than they are now. They, too, might have made a contribution, and had the means to do so. Had we been able to continue our experiment, it would, of course, have been vital to take account of what they would have said.

14. The experiment yielded no practical result in the end, because of differences within management over the problem.

15. The reader will recall the frequently violent hostility of the American unions toward the human relations movement.

16. As, for instance, was the case with many training programs conceived within the framework of the law of 1972.

17. R. Sainsaulieu and J.-C. Willig, *Les effets de l'expérience de formation menée par le groupe local de Saint-Symphorien à EDF-GDF* (Paris: Copedith, 1967).

18. Sainsaulieu, *L'apprentissage culturel dans le travail.*

19. A French practitioner, Pierre Morin, has given an excellent analysis of the lessons of the American experience and the possibilities of extending it to France. See *Le développement des organisations, management et sciences humaines* (Paris: Dunod, 1971), p. 120.

20. In this connection, see F. E. Fielder, *A Theory of Leadership Effectiveness* (New York: McGraw Hill, 1967).

21. We will return to this problem in the last section of this chapter. See below, pp. 241–47.

22. Without taking account of the fact that a negotiation can be the most subtle of manipulations. First, because whoever defines the agenda for the negotiation can thereby structure the course of the discussions and potentially even their outcome. Second, particularly because verbal skills, negotiating talents, etc., are never equally distributed among the actors. Beyond a shadow of a doubt, formal democracy can be an illusion.

23. You can't have one without the other.

24. The postwar existentialist movement was itself ambiguous in this regard. Implacable destroyer of pharisaical bourgeois morality and its pillories, it was at the same time— particularly with the notion of the "S.O.B." (*salaud*) so dear to Sartre—responsible for focusing our attention to an even greater degree than before on the intentions an motivations of the actor.

25. In fact, it is chasing after chimeras, by the same token as the sort of economic analysis which would take its point of departure in the satisfaction of man's real needs. What is a "real need" apart form the basic physiological necessities? No one has or ever will have an answer.

26. As we have seen (see above chap. 1, p. 20), Maslow has a hierarchical conception of man's psychological needs, where the hierarchy, in a sense, defines the types of satisfaction sought through action. See Maslow, *Motivation and Personality.*

27. Among others, we should single out Chris Argyris, *Integrating the Individual and the Organization; Understanding Organizational Behavior* (Homewood, Ill.: Dorsey Press, 1960); and Intervention Theory and Method (Reading, Mass.: Addison-Wesley, 1970); R. Likert, *The Human Organization: Its Management and Values* (New York: McGraw Hill, 1967); H. J. Leavitt, "Applied Change in Industry: Structural, Technological, and Humanistic Approaches," in J. G. March, *Handbook of Organizations* (Chicago: Rand McNally, 1965); W. Bennis, *Changing Organizations* (New York: McGraw Hill, 1966).

28. In passing, we want to stress the importance for the authors in this school of such ambiguous normative notions as "maturity," "normality" and "health."

29. This is similar to the position adopted by Chris Argyris during the sixties, when he was concerned with laying a philosophical foundation for intervention based on a "model of man." In his latest books, particularly the one written with Donald Schon, he takes a much more pragmatic view. His insistence on the opposition between the "theory preached" and the "theory practiced" by the actor brings him to conclusions very close to our own. See especially Argyris and Schon, *Theory in Practice: Increasing Professional Effectiveness* (San Francisco: Jossy Bass publ., 1974); and Argyris, *Increasing Leadership Effectiveness* (New York: Wiley, 1976).

30. This has given rise to what might well be called a "dysfunctionalist" style of intervention. Placing the accent on the repressive character of all organization, it attempts through intervention to bring about the conditions in which awareness of this repression and of its possible transcendence in a new organization become possible. This new organization is supposed to be liberating for all man's potentialities. For a good introduction to the theory of

institutional analysis, see the collective work: "L'analyse institutionelle et la formation permanente," *Pour,* nos. 32–33, series "Les dossiers pedagogique du formateur"; as well as Georges Lappassade, *Groupes, Organisations, et Institutions* (Paris: Gauthier-Villars, 1967); R. Lourau, *L'instituant contre l'institué* (Paris: Editions Anthropos, 1969); and *L'analyse institutionelle* (Paris: Editions de Minuit, 1970).

31. Jacques Attali, *La parole et l'outil* (Presses Universitaires de France, 1975).

32. Few of them are capable of absorbing the most fundamental lesson of human experience: that the changes which are successful are generally those whose implementation entailed a reexamination of the original objectives.

33. And of their colleagues, the psychosociologists, the public relations men, and all those ideologists whose job it is to induce people to enjoy what has been decided for them.

34. In recent history there are countless cases to prove this claim: for instance, the successive attempts to bring about educational reform, which, though based on grandiose themes of civilization, and theoretically implicating the future of society and politics, have ultimately bogged down, one after another, in technocratic byways.

Chapter 15

1. Relations of power are equally inseparable from the mechanisms whereby personality is formed and asserted (and equally indispensable therein).

2. Obstacles to joint action, these reservations are not—as is too often believed—merely reflections of technical constraints, self-interest, and/or power relationships, but are also indicative of the existence of different kinds of goals: personal protection, respect for equality, respect for the right of independence, of nonparticipation, and of maintaining effectiveness. All these values are, if not shared on a conscious level, at least deeply experienced in the rank and file, which accounts for the fact that it is only at that level that choices can be made among them.

3. This does not mean, however, that all problems can be solved merely by entrusting their solution to personnel on the operational level. For change there to be successful, efforts must first have been made at a higher level to make available new opportunities for unblocking vicious circles. Often, initiative and risk taking must lead the way; this implies recognition of the irreducible and arbitrary nature of human freedom. While innovation is indispensable, the sort of innovation we have in mind is not the rational plan designed to answer all questions beforehand, but rather intuitive dialogue between bottom and top levels of hierarchy.

4. We trust the reader will indulge our use of these subtle distinctions. Choices are never black and white.

5. We will return to this point.

6. This is the classical myth of the poisoned gift.

7. Here it is worth noting that the problem of access, which is the consequences of a human choice, creates an objective problem for collective action aimed at giving direction to the (active) response and at the development of a once again arbitrary construct. There is nothing "natural" about this, except the existence of an insuperable logic which leads from involuntary restriction of access to the pathological development of vicious circles.

8. This is the case with Yugoslavia, which, while not the Soviet Union, nevertheless has encountered anew many bureaucratic difficulties it thought it had disposed of. Thus it, too, flounders amidst insuperable dysfunctions. This is also the case in the People's Republic of China, which may have gone farther than any other modern society toward promoting the model of a virtuous society, from which every vestige of individual power—at least in the formal structure—has been eradicated.

9. Pierre Rosanvallon, *L'age de l'autogestion* (Paris: Editions du Seuil, 1976).

10. Here we list only a few modest reforms, actually tried out in practice, which might

hold out some promise for remodeling our educational system. One should not be misled by the examples of the experimental school run by a charismatic personality and serving a limited number of pupils.

11. This is one of the main conclusions to be drawn from the work of R. D. Laing, in particular his studies on the family as a construct producing madness. The limitations of man's emotional capacities can be seen very clearly there. So, too, can the very serious consequences stemming from the emotional burden of inadequately structured situations which, in extreme cases, no human being can tolerate. This is an important and all too easily forgotten limitation on any plan involving widespread experimentation. See Laing, *The Divided Self.*

Appendix

1. In the broadest and, therefore, most neutral sense of the term, which in no ways rules out (we remind the reader, lest there be any misunderstanding) situations of domination. Of course, the games that prevail among actors will depend on whether cooperation is obtained by force or voluntarily, whether it results from domination by one set of actors rather than another, or, alternatively, from a relatively egalitarian situation. In any case, it is legitimate to speak of cooperation.

2. He has several ways of doing so: organization chart, internal regulations, technology, etc., in the case of an organization; the, in some sense, "objective" logical structure of the problem, the formal prerogatives, and the material resources of the principal actors involved in the case of a more diffuse system of action.

3. See especially Gaston Bachelard, *La formation de l'esprit scientifique* (Paris: Vrin, 1970).

4. Without entering into a discussion of the most general problems raised by nondirective techniques (conditions of their possibility, potential abuses, etc.), we will say that insofar as the procedure attacks a relatively formalized problem, a totally nondirective attitude would be out of place, if not basically aberrant.

5. More generally, shouldn't all the elements of "social reality"—as "objective" and "predetermined" as they may appear at first sight—be regarded as social constructs maintained by social action, i.e., the product of conflicts and power relations between individuals or groups—in short, between social actors. It is the sociologist's research strategy, i.e., his choice of terrain and his level of analysis, which reintroduces the dividing line between that part of social "reality" that he may consider as a given precondition and that which he must explore and explain as a social construct.

6. Such a review must necessarily be brief. For a presentation and discussion of all these questions, we refer the interested reader to G. Lindzey, ed., *The Handbook of Social Psychology* (Reading, Mass.: Addison-Wesley, 1954); S. E. Asch, *Social Psychology* (Englewood Cliffs, N.J.: Prentice-Hall, 1952); A. Levy, *Psychologie sociale* (Paris: Dunod, 1965); G. Summers, *Attitude Measurement* (Chicago: Rand McNally, 1970); M. Jahoda and N. Warren, eds., *Attitudes* (Harmondsworth: Penguin, 1966); and S. Moscovici, "L'attitude: théories et recherches autour d'un concept et d'un phénomène," *Bulletin du CERP* 2 (1062):177–191. In addition, we would like to thank W. Ackermann for the aid and advice he gave us in the writing of this section.

7. The German word *Einstellung* means, first of all, adjustment in the sense that a machine must be "adjusted" for certain operations.

8. This is, in particular, the sense given the word by N. Lange in relating his experiments on the different *reaction times* of individuals, depending on whether or not they were consciously prepared to make a desired gesture after having received the agreed signal. See especially G. Allport, "The Historical Background of Modern Social Psychology," in Lindzey, *Handbook of Social Psychology.*

9. This usage of attitudes is well known in the sociology of elections, psychosociology, industrial sociology, and even commercial market research, etc.

10. Such as satisfaction with regard to various aspects of work, the situation, hierarchical relations, etc., which are dealt with in the studies of industrial psychosociology or the sociology of work.

11. Two utilizations of the study of attitudes must therefore be distinguished. The first focuses on attitudes as way of predicting behavior, by establishing an implicit equivalence between attitude and behavior (such and such an attitude, such and such a behavior). The second focuses on what attitudes reveal of regularities and modes of structuration within individual categorizations of the social world, i.e., the universes of professional, occupational, or national values. We have previously emphasized (see chap. 6) the deterministic reasoning that usually underlies such a utilization of attitudes.

12. This interest in the processes of learning and transforming attitudes reflects the accent placed on the "socialization" processes by functionalist sociology.

13. This is the perspective adopted in countless sociological studies of attitudes. In passing, we point out the implicit normative argument behind this research effort. Its latest avatars are met in the "motivational" approach to organizations, to which we alluded previously. There we can see the temptation to use knowledge of attitudes to give direction to training processes by manipulating their experiential and situational content. In short, the learning of "correct attitudes" can be insured by taking measures to control the places of learning.

14. The claim, of course, is that a hold is also obtained on collective attitudes. But actually these are always derived from aggregate individual attitudes. What may be collective is the conditions under which these attitudes are acquired, as these may be relatively similar from one individual to the next. But the attitudes themselves remain individual.

15. In this respect, the conclusions of a psychometric study by the Swedish psychologist U. Remitz are quite explicit. According to him, only ten percent of the variation in attitudes toward work can be attributed to external social factors, while factors internal to the firm (in this case a bank) could account for at most an additional ten percent. The remaining four-fifths of the variation reflect, in his view, the existence of a *sui generis* factor, the *individual disposition to satisfaction,* which might be isolable and measurable in the same way as intelligence. See U. Remitz, *Professional Satisfaction Among Swedish Bank Employees* (Copenhagen, 1960).

16. This makes more readily comprehensible the accent placed on the formation and transformation of attitudes in the above-mentioned research, as well as the convergence already noted between this research orientation and that of functionalist sociology.

17. See Festinger, *A Theory of Cognitive Dissonance.*

18. See, among others, Theodor W. Adorno et al., *The Authoritarian Personality* (New York: Harper, 1950); D. Katz and E. Stotland, "A Preliminary Statement of a Theory of Attitude Structure and Change," in S. Koch, ed., *Psychology: A Study of Science,* vol. 3 (New York: McGraw Hill, 1959).

19. For further detail concerning this example, which we can summarize only *briefly* here, we refer the reader to M. Crozier, *Le Monde des employés de bureau* (Paris: Editions du Seuil, 1965), especially chap. 5, pp. 80–105.

20. Other examples might be cited. For instance, the "antiurban attitude" which was prevalent among engineers in the State Public Works Ministry at the time of the reform of the Ministry of Equipment. As we have shown elsewhere, this "antiurban and technocratic attitude" can only be understood as the expression of the *dominant strategy* pursued by these middle level functionaries. Its full significance emerges when it is seen in the light of the power struggle which pitted them against their superiors, the engineers of the Ponts et chaussés, over control of the regional offices of the old Ministry of Public Works. See

Thoenig and Friedberg, "Politique urbaine et stratégies corporatives," *Sociologie du travail* 4 (1969).

21. Except insofar as his past history, in part, conditions the "thief's" present and future opportunities, as well as the actor's capacity to act as thief.

22. Festinger, *A Theory of Cognitive Dissonance*.

23. Attitude reflection becomes in this perspective an extreme case which may be interpreted, in turn, as a sign of resignation or impotence.

24. See chap. 6, which is devoted to links between mode of organization and culture.

25. What we generally referred to as the "hard facts." This appellation seems to us to be an abuse of language which perpetuates a misconception that must be dispelled. In fact, these hard facts frequently turn out to be much softer andless resistant to change than the so-called soft "human" factors that are the object of strategic analysis. To consider only the area of organizations, for instance, to change an organization chart is a relatively simple matter; organizational change is often reduced to a mere redefinition of this kind. By contrast, to change the ongoing games within the organization is infinitely more difficult.

26. Quite as important as what is said explicitly is what appears only between the lines or what is, perhaps, even passed over by certain interviewees. For to avoid mentioning a problem or conflict which is commented on at length by others may be as revealing a way of making one's opinion and point of view known as speaking volumes about it.

27. Obviously, many kinds of more sophisticated procedures may be applied in this area, provided they are securely founded, i.e., that the *relevance* and *significance* of what is being measured is known. Indirectly, this points to the basic importance of the *qualitative, exploratory investigation* in such a methodology. Not merely a formal familiarization with the research terrain, this will always be one of the high points, if not the key step, in the whole research enterprise. It is actually an investigation in its own right, and its execution may be fairly time-consuming, but the results should make it possible to formulate a first, relatively precise diagnosis of the specific properties and regulations of the system of action under study.

28. Obviously, with these strategies, the investigator forms an idea of the actors' fields and their real categories, which will usually be little in line with the official analysis or common sense. A typical example in this respect is the complicity between prefects and notables analyzed above, strikingly different prefects and notables analyzed above, strikingly different from the rhetorical antagonism prevailing between these two categories of actors.

29. Which will essentially be the case in organizational studies.

30. That is to say they have a "rationality" which must be uncovered. It should be noted that here the basic assumption of strategic analysis—that individuals make rational and strategic use of their zone of liberty—is divulged in its true colors: it is a *heuristic procedure* which makes it possible to structure and comprehend a social field and its various components, rational and irrational, conscious and unconscious, voluntary and involuntary.

Bibliography

Abegglen, J. C. *The Japanese Factory*. New York: Free Press, 1958.
———. *Management and Worker: The Japanese Solution*. Tokyo-New York Kodansha International, Inc., 1973.
Abel, Peter. Editor. *Organizations as Bargaining and Influence Systems*. New York: Halsted Press, 1966.
Adorno, T. W. et. al. *The Authoritarian Personality*. New York: Harper, 1950.
Allison, G. *The Essence of Decision. Explaining the Cuban Missile Crisis*. Boston: Little Brown, 1971.
Allport, F. H. *Theories of Perception and the Concept of Structure*. New York: Wiley, 1955.
———. *Pattern and Growth in Personality*. New York: Holt, Rinehart and Winston, 1961.
Argyris, Chris. *Understanding Organizational Behavior*. Homewood, Ill.: Dorsey Press, 1960.
———. *Integrating the Individual and the Organization*. New York: Wiley, 1964.
———. *Organization and Innovation*. Homewood, Ill.: Irwin, 1965.
———. *Intervention Theory and Method*. Reading, Mass.: Addison-Wesley, 1970.
———. *The Applicability of Organizational Sociology*. Cambridge, Mass.: Harvard University Press, 1972.
———. *Increasing Leadership Effectiveness*. New York: Wiley, 1976.
Argyris, Chris and Schon, Donald. *Theory in Practice: Increasing Professional Effectiveness*. San Francisco: Jossy Bass Publ., 1974.
———. *Organizational Learning: A Theory of Action Perspective*. Reading, Mass.: Addison-Wesley, 1976.
Asch, S. E. *Social Psychology*. Englewood Cliffs, N.J.: Prentice-Hall, 1952.
Ashby, W. R. *Design for a Brain*. London: Chapman & Hall, 1952.
———. *Introduction to Cybernetics*. London: Chapman & Hall, 1956.
Attali, J. *La parole et l'outil*. Paris: Presses Universitaires de France, 1975.
Bachelard, G. *La formation de l'espirit scientifique*. Paris: Vrin, 1970.
Bachrach P., and Baratz, M. S. *Power and Poverty: Theory and Practice*. London, 1970.
Ballé, C., and Peaucelle, J.-L. *Le pouvoir informatique dans l'entreprise*. Paris: Editions d'Organisation, 1972.
Bardach, E, *The Skill Factor in Politics*. Berkeley: University of California Press, 1972.

Barnard, C. I. *The Functions of the Executive*. Cambridge, Mass.: Harvard University Press, 1938.

Bell, Daniel. *The Coming of Post-Industrial Society. A Venture in Social Forecasting*. New York: Basic Books, 1973.

Bendix, R. *Work and Authority in Industry*. New York: Wiley, 1956.

Bennis, W. G. *Changing Organizations*. New York: McGraw Hill, 1966.

Benveniste, Guy. *Bureaucracy*. San Francisco: Boyd & Fraser, 1977.

Berger, P. L. *Invitation to Sociology*. Harmondsworth: Penguin, 1966.

Berger, P. L., and Luckmann T. H. *The Social Construction of Reality: A Treatise in the Sociology of Knowledge*. New York: Doubleday, 1966.

Bertallanfy, Von. *General Systems Theory, Foundations, Developments, Applications*. New York: G. Braziller, 1968.

Black, M., ed. *The Social Theories of Talcott Parsons*. Englewood Cliffs, N.J.: Prentice-Hall, 1966.

Blau, P. M. *The Dynamics of Bureaucracy*. Chicago: University of Chicago Press, 1955.

Blau, P. M., and Scott, W. R. *Formal Organizations: A Comparative Approach*. London: Routledge & Kegan Paul, 1963.

Blau, P. M., and Schoenherr, R. *The Structure of Organizations*. New York: Basic Books, 1971.

Boudon, Raymond *Education, Opportunity, and Social Inequality. Changing Prospects in Western Society*. New York: Wiley, 1974.

Bourdieu, P., and Passeron, J.-C. *La reproduction*. Paris: Editions de Minuit, 1973.

Bourricaud, François. *Equisse d'une théorie de l'authorité*. Paris: Plon, 1961.

Bower, J.-C. *Managing the Resource Allocation Process*. New York: Irwin, 1972.

Braybrooke, D., and Lindblom, C. *A Strategy of Decision, Policy Evaluation as a Social Process*. New York: Free Press, 1963.

Burns, T. "On the Plurality of Social Systems." In J. R. Lawrence, ed. *Operational Research and the Social Sciences*. Oxford: Pergamon Press, 1966.

Burns, T. "The Comparative Study of Organizations." V. Vroom, ed. *Methods of Organizational Research*. Pittsburgh: University of Pittsburgh Press, 1967.

Burns, T., and Stalker, G. M. *The Management of Innovation*. London: Tavistock, 1961.

Caplow, T. *Principles of Organisation*. New York: Harcourt, Brace, 1964.

———. *Two Against One: Coalitions in Triads*. Englewood Cliffs. N.J.: Prentice-Hall, 1969.

Castoriadis, C. *L'institution imaginaire de la société*. Paris: Editions du Seuil, 1977.

Chandler, A. D., Jr. *Strategy and Structure*. Cambridge, Mass.: MIT Press, 1962.

———. *The Visible Hand: The Managerial Revolution in American Business*. Cambridge, Mass.: Belknap Press, 1977.

Child, J. "Organization: A Choice for Man." *Man and Organization*. Edited by J. Child. London: Allen & Unwin, 1973.

Child J., and Kieser, A. "Organization and Managerial Roles in British and West German Companies: An Examination of the Culture Free Thesis." In *Organizations Unlike and Alike: Towards a Comparative Sociology of Organizations*.

C. Lammers, ed. (to be published).

Cicourel, A. V. *Method and Measurement in Sociology*. New York: Free Press, 1964.

Clastres, P. *Society Against the State*. Translated by Robert Hurley. New York: Urizen, 1977.

Clegg, S. R. *Power, Rule, and Domination*. London: Routledge & Kegan Paul, 1975.

Cohen, P. S. *Modern Social Theory*. London: Heineman, 1968.

Cohen, R. M., and March, J. G. *Leadership and Ambiguity*. New York: McGraw Hill, 1974.

Cooper, W. W., Leavitt, H. J., and Maynard, W. S., ed. *New Perspectives in Organization Research*. New York: Wiley, 1964.

Cressey, D. R. "Prison Organizations." In J. G. March, ed. *Handbook of Organizations*. Chicago: Rand McNally, 1965.

Crozier, Michel. *The Bureaucratic Phenomenon*. Chicago: University of Chicago Press, 1964.

————. *The World of the Office Worker*. Chicago: University of Chicago Press 1971.

————. *The Stalled Society*. New York: Viking, 1973.

————. "Comparing Structures or Comparing Games." In G. Hofsted and M. M. Sami-Kassem ed. *European Contributions to Organization Theory*. Amsterdam: Van Gorkam, 1976.

Crozier, Michel et al. *Où va l'administration française?* Paris: Editions d'Organisation, 1974.

Cyert, R. M., and March, J. G. *A Behavioral Theory of the Firm*. Englewood Cliffs, N.J.: Prentice-Hall, 1963.

Dahl, R. *Who Governs?* New Haven: Yale University Press, 1961.

Dahrendorf, R. *Essays on the Theory of Society*. London: Routledge & Kegan Paul, 1968.

Dalton, M. *Men who Manage*. New York: Wiley, 1959.

Demerath, N. J., and Peterson, R. A., eds. *System, Change, and Conflict*. New York: Free Press, 1967.

Dore, R. P. *City Life in Japan*. Berkeley: University of California Press, 1958.

Dubin, R. *The World of Work*. Englewood Cliffs, N.J.: Prentice-Hall, 1958.

————. "Stability of Human Organizations." In M. Haire, ed. *Modern Organization Theory*. New York: John Wiley & Sons, 1959.

Duby, G. *The Early Growth of the European Economy: Warriors and Peasants From the Seventh to the Twelfth Centuries*. Translated by Howard B. Clarke. Ithaca: Cornell University Press, 1974.

Dunlop, J., et al. *Industrialism and Industrial Man*. Cambridge, Mass.: Harvard University Press, 1960.

Easton, D. *A System of Political Life*. New York: Wiley, 1965.

Emery, F. E. *Systems Thinking*. Harmondsworth: Penguin, 1969.

Etzioni, A. *A Comparative Analysis of Complex Organizations*. New York: Free Press, 1961.

Etzioni, A. ed. *Complex Organizations: A Sociological Reader*. New York: Holt, Rinehart & Winston, 1961.

Evan, W. "The Organization Set." In J. D. Thompson, ed. *Approaches to Or-*

ganizational Design. Pittsburgh: University of Pittsburgh Press, 1966.

――――. *Organization Theory, Structures, Systems, and Environment.* New York: Wiley, 1976.

Festinger, L. A. *A Theory of Cognitive Dissonance.* New York: Harper, 1957.

Fielder, F. E. *A Theory of Leadership Effectiveness.* New York: McGraw Hill, 1967.

Forrester, J. *Urban Dynamics.* Cambridge, Mass.: MIT Press, 1970.

Foucault, M. *Discipline and Punish: The Birth of the Prison.* Translated by Alan Sheridan. New York: Pantheon Books, 1978.

Friedberg, E. *L'analyse sociologique des organisations.* GREP, 1972.

Friedmann, G. *Industrial Society: The Emergence of the Human Problems of Automation.* New York: Free Press, 1964.

Galbraith, J. K. *American Capitalism: The Concept of Countervailing Power.* Boston: Houghton Mifflin, 1958.

――――. *The New Industrial State.* London: Hamilton, 1967.

Garfinkel, H. *Studies in Ethnomethodology.* Englewood Cliffs, N.J.: Prentice-Hall, 1967.

Glaser, B. G., and Strauss, A. L. *The Discovery of Grounded Theory.* London: Weidenfeld & Nicolson, 1968.

Goffman, E. *The Presentation of Self in Everyday Life.* New York: Doubleday, 1959.

――――. *Asylums.* Chicago: Aldine, 1961.

Gouldner, A. W. *Patterns of Industrial Bureaucracy.* New York: Free Press, 1954.

――――. *Wildcat Strike.* New York: Harper, 1963.

――――. "Reciprocity and Autonomy in Functional Theory." In Demerath and Peterson, *System, Change, and Conflict.* New York: Free Press, 1967.

Gouldner, F. H. "The Division of Labor: Process and Power." In M. N. Zald, ed. *Power in Organizations.* Nashville: Vanderbilt University Press, 1970.

Grémion, Pierre. *Le pouvoir périphérique.* Paris: Editions du Seuil, 1976.

Hage, J., and Aiken, M. *Social Change in Complex Organizations.* New York: Random House, 1970.

Haire, M. "Biological Models and Empirical Histories of the Growth of Organizations." In M. Haire, ed. *Modern Organization Theory.* New York: Wiley, 1959.

Harbison, F., and Myers, C. A. *Management in the Industrial World, An International Analysis.* New York: McGraw Hill, 1959.

Herzberg, Frederick. *Work and the Nature of Man.* New York: World Publ. 1971.

Hickson, D. J., et al. "Grounds for Comparative Organization Theory: Quicksand or Hard Core?" In C. J. Lammers, ed. *Organizations Unlike and Alike: Towards a Comparative Sociology of Organizations.* To be published.

Hirschman, A. *Development Projects Observed.* Washington: Brookings Institution, 1967.

――――. *Exit, Voice, and Loyalty. Response to Decline in Firms, Organizations, and States.* Cambridge, Mass.: Harvard University Press, 1970.

Homans, G. C. *The Human Group.* New York: Harcourt Brace, 1950.

――――. *Social Behaviour: Its Elementary Form.* New York: Harcourt Brace 1961.

Jahoda, M., and Warrren, N. eds. *Attitudes*. Harmondsworth: Penguin, 1966.

Janis, I. *Victims of Groupthink: A Psychological Study of Foreign Policy Decisions and Fiascos*. Boston: Houghton Mifflin, 1972.

Kahn, R., et al. *Organizational Stress*. New York: Wiley, 1964.

Katz, E., and Stotland, E. "A Preliminary Statement of a Theory of Attitude Structure and Change." In S. Koch, ed. *Psychology: A Study of Science*. Vol. 3. New York: McGraw Hill, 1959.

Katz, D., and Kahn, R. L. *The Social Psychology of Organizations*. New York: Wiley, 1966.

Kergoat, D. *Bulle d'or ou l'histoire d'une mobilisation ouvrière*. Paris: Editions du Seuil, 1973.

Krupp, S. *Patterns in Organization Analysis: A Critical Examination*. Philadelphia: Chilton, 1961.

Kuhn, T. S. *The Structure of Scientific Revolutions*. Chicago: University of Chicago Press, 1962.

Kuty, O. *Le pouvoir du malade: analyse sociologique des unités de rein artificiel*. Doctoral Thesis. Paris: Université René Descartes, 1973.

Laing, R. D. *The Divided Self*. London: Tavistock, 1959.

———. *The Self and Others*. London: Tavistock, 1961.

———. *The Politics of Experience*. Paris: Stock, 1969.

Laing, R. D., and Esterson, A. *Sanity, Madness, and the Family*. London: Tavistock, 1964.

Lapassade, G. *Groupes, Organisations, et Institutions*. Paris: Gauthier-Villars, 1967.

Lawrence, P. R., and Lorsch, J. W. *Organization and Environment: Managing Differentiation and Integration*. Boston: Harvard Business School, 1967.

———. *Developing Organizations: Diagnosis and Action*. Reading, Mass.: Addison-Wesley, 1969.

Leavitt, H. J. *Psychologie des fonctions de direction dans l'entreprise*. Paris: Editions Hommes et Techniques, 1958.

Leavitt, H. J., ed. *The Social Science of Organizations: Four Perspectives*. Englewood Cliffs, N.J.: Prentice-Hall, 1963.

Leavitt, H. J., Pinfield, L., and Webb, E. eds. *Organizations of the Future*. New York: Praeger Publishers, 1974.

Lévy, A. *Psychologie sociale*. Paris: Dunod, 1965.

———. *Les pardoxes de la liberté dans un hôpital psychiatrique*. Paris: Editions de l'Epi, 1969.

Likert, R. *New Patterns of Management*. New York: McGraw Hill, 1961.

———. *The Human Organization: Its Management and Values*. New York: McGraw Hill, 1967.

Lindblom, C. E. *The Intelligence of Democracy*. New York: Free Press, 1965.

Lindzey, G., ed. *The Handbook of Social Psychology*. Reading, Mass.: Addison-Wesley 1954.

Long, N. E. "The Local Community as an Ecology of Games." In L. Coser, ed. *Political Sociology*. New York: Harper, 1966.

Lourau, *L'instituant contre l'institué*. Paris, Editions Anthropos, 1969.

———. *L'analyse institutionnelle*. Paris. Editions de Minuit, 1970.

Luce, R. D., and Raiffa, H. *Games and Decisions*. New York: Wiley, 1957.

Luhmann, N. *Funktion und Folgen formaler Organisation*. Berlin: Duncker & Humblot, 1964.

———. *Soziologische Aufklärung*. Cologne, Opladen: Westdeutscher Verlag, 1970.

———. *Politische Planung*. Colgone, Opladen: Westdeutscher Verlag, 1971.

———. *Zweckbegriff und Systemrationalität*. Frankfort: Suhrkamp, 1973.

———. *Macht*. Stuttgart: Ferdinand Enke, 1975.

Luhmann, N., and Habermas, J. *Theorie der Gesellschaft oder Sozialtechnologie*. Frankfurt: Suhrkamp, 1971.

Lukes, S. *Power: A Radical View*. London: Macmillan & Co., 1974.

Lupton, T. *On the Shop Floor*. Oxford: Pergamon Press, 1962.

———. *Management and the Social Sciences*. Hardmondsworth, Penguin Books, 1971.

Lussato, B. *Modèles cybernétiques, hommes, entreprsies*. Volume 1. *Introduction critique aux théories d'organisation*. Paris: Dunod, 1972.

McClelland, D. et al. *The Achievement Motive*. New York: Appleton-Century-Crofts, 1953.

McGregor, D. *Leadership and Motivation*. Cambridge, Mass.: MIT Press, 1966.

March, J. G., and Simon, H. A. *Organizations*. New York: Wiley, 1958.

March, J. G., ed. *Handbook of Organizations*. Chicago: Rand McNally, 1965.

———. "For a Technology of Foolishness. In H. Leavitt et. al. ed. *Organizations for the Future*. New York: Praeger Publishers, 1974.

Maslow, A. H. *Motivation and Personality*. New York: Harper, 1954.

Merton, R. K. ed. *Reader in Bureaucracy*. New York: Free Press, 1952.

Merton, R. K. *Social Theory and Social Structure*. New York: Free Press, 1964.

Michels, R. *Political Parties: A Sociological Study of the Oligarchical Tendencies of Modern Democracy*. New York: The Free Press, 1949.

Miller, E. J., and Rice, A. K. *Systems of Organisation: The Control of Task and Sentient Boundaries*. London: Tavistock, 1967.

Mills, C. Wright. *The Power Elite*. New York: Oxford University Press, 1956.

———. *The Sociological Imagination*. London: Oxford University Press, 1959.

Morin, P. *Le Développement des organisations, management et sciences, humaines*. Paris: Dunod, 1971.

Moscovici, S. *Society Against Nature: The Emergence of Human Societies*. Translated by Sacha Rabinovitch. Sussex: The Harvester Press, 1976.

Mottez, B. *La sociologie industrielle*. Paris: Presses Universitaires de France, 1971.

Mouzelis, N. P. *Organisation and Bureaucracy*. London: Routledge & Kegan Paul, 1967.

Nakane, C. *Japanese Society*. Berkeley: University of California Press, 1970.

Olson, M. *The Logic of Collective Action*. Cambridge, Mass.: Harvard University Press, 1965.

Palm, R. *Une organisation en analyse ou la réforme de la cour des comptes en Belgique: Rapport d'une recherche-action de changement 1970–1973*. Doctoral Thesis. Catholic University of Louvain, 1974.

Parsons, T. *The Structure of Social Action*. New York: Free Press, 1949.
——. *The Social System*. New York: Free Press, 1951.
Parson, T. "A Sociological Approach to the Theory of Organisations." In *Structure and Process in Modern Societies*. New York: Free Press, 1964.
Parsons, T., and Shils, E. A., eds. *Toward a General Theory of Action*. Cambridge, Mass.: Harvard University Press, 1951.
Parsons, T., and Smelser, N.J. *Economy and Society*. New York: Free Press, 1956.
Perrow, C. "Hospitals: Technology, Structure, and Goals." In J. G. March, ed. *Handbook of Organizations*. Chicago: Rand McNally, 1965.
——. *Organizational Analysis: A Sociological View*. London: Tavistock, 1970.
——. "Departmental Power and Perspectives of Industrial Firms." In M. N. Zald, ed. *Power in Organizations*. Nashville: Vanderbilt University Press, 1970.
——. *Complex Organizations*. Glenview, Ill.: Scott Foresman, 1972.
Popitz, H. *Der Begriff der sozialen Rolle als Element der soziologischen Theorie*. Tubingen: Mohr, 1967.
——. *Ueber die Präventivwirkung des Nichtwissens*. Tubingen: Mohr, 1968.
——. *Prozesse der Machtbildung*. Tubingen: Mohr, 1969.
Poulantzas, N. *Political Power and Social Classes*. Translated by Timothy O'Hagan. London: New Left Books, 1978.
Roethlisberger, F. J.; Dickson, W. J.; et al., *Management and the Worker*. Cambridge, Mass.: Harvard University Press, 1939.
Rose, A. M., ed. *Human Behavior and Social Processes: An Interactionist Approach*. Boston: Houghton Mifflin, 1962.
Sainsaulieu, R. *Les relations de travail à l'usine*. Paris: Editions d'Organisation, 1973.
Sartre, J. P. *The Emotions: Outline of a Theory*. Translated by Bernard Frechtman. New York: Philosophical Library, 1948.
——. *Questions de méthode*. Paris: Gallimard, 1960.
Sayles, L. R. *Behavior of Industrial Work Groups*. New York: Wiley, 1958.
Schein, E. H. *Organizational Psychology*. Englewood Cliffs, N.J.: Prentice-Hall, 1965.
Schelling T. C. *The Strategy of Conflict*. Cambridge, Mass.: Harvard University Press, 1960.
Schonfeld, W. R. *Obedience and Revolt: French Behavior toward Authority*. Beverly Hills: Sage Publications, 1976.
Schutz, A. *Collected Papers*. M. Natanson, ed. The Hague: Nijhoff, 1964.
Selznick, P. *TVA and the Grass Roots*. Berkeley: University of California Press, 1949.
——. *Leadership in Administration*. New York: Harper & Row, 1957.
Silverman, D. *The Theory of Organizations*. London: Heinemann, 1970.
Simon, H. A. *Administrative Behavior*. New York: Macmillan, 1957.
——. *The Science of the Artificial*. Cambridge, Mass.: MIT Press, 1970.
Skinner, B. F. *Beyond Freedom and Dignity*. New York: Vintage Books, 1971.
Steinert, H. *Die Strategie sozialen Hadelns*. Munich: Juventa Verlag, 1972.
Stinchombe, A. L. "Social Structure and Organisations." In J. G. March, ed.

Handbook of Organizations. Chicago: Rand McNally, 1965.

Summers, G. *Attitude Measurement*. Chicago: Rand McNally, 1970.

Taylor, F. W. *The Principles of Scientific Management*. New York: Harper, 1913.

Thibaut, J. W., and Kelley, H. H. *The Social Psychology of Groups*. New York: Wiley, 1959.

Thoenig, J. C. *L'ere des technocrates*. Paris: Editions d'Organisation, 1973.

Thoenig, J. C., and Friedberg, E. "The Power of the Field Staff." In A. F., Leemans, ed. *Managing Administrative Change*. The Hague: Nijhoff, 1976.

Thompson, J. D. *Organizations in Action*. New York. McGraw Hill. 1967.

Thompson, J. D., ed. *Approaches to Organizational Design*. Pittsburgh, Pa.: University of Pittsburgh Press, 1966.

Touraine, A. *Sociologie de l'action*. Paris: Editions du Seuil, 1966.

——. *La conscience ouvrière*. Paris: Editions du Seuil, 1966.

——. *The Self-Production of Society*. Translated by Derek Coltman. University of Chicago Press, 1973.

——. *The Post-Industrial Society. Tomorrow's Social History: Class, Conflict, and Culture in the Programmed Society*. Translated by Leonard Mayhew. New York: Random House, 1971.

Triandis, H. C. *The Analysis of Subjective Culture*. New York: Wiley, 1972.

Vroom, V. H. *Work and Motivation*. New York: Wiley, 1964.

Walker, C. J., and Guest, R. H. *The Man on the Assembly Line*. Cambridge, Mass.: Harvard University Press, 1952.

Walton, R. E., and McKersie, R. B. *A Behavioral Theory of Labor Negotiations: An Analysis of a Social Interaction System*. New York: McGraw Hill, 1965.

Weber, M. *Wirtschaft und Gesellschaft*. Cologne, Berlin. Kiepenhauer & Witsch. 1964.

Weick, K. E. *The Social Psychology of Organizing*. Reading, Mass.: Addison-Wesley, 1969.

Whyte, W. F. "An Interaction Approach to the Theory of Organizations." In M. Haire, ed., *Modern Organization Theory*. New York: Wiley, 1959.

——. "An Intercultural Context for Organizational Research." In W. F. Whyte, ed. *Organizational Behavior: Theory and Application*. Homewood, Ill.: Irwin, 1969.

Whyte, W. F., ed. *Organizational Behavior*. Homewood, Ill.: Irwin, 1969.

Whyte, W. F. et al. *Money and Motivation*. New York: Harper 1955.

Wiener, N. Cybernetics or Control and Communication. *The Animal and the Machine*. New York: Wiley, 1948.

Wildavsky, A. *Revolt against the Masses and Other Essays on Politics and Public Policy*. New York: Basic Books, 1971.

Woodward, J. *Industrial Organisation: Theory and Practice*. London: Oxford University Press, 1965.

Woodward, J., ed. *Industrial Organisation: Behavior and Control*. New York: Oxford University Press, 1970.

Wrong, D. "The Over-Socialised Conception of Man in Modern Sociology." In Demerath and Peterson, *System, Change, and Conflict*.

Wylie, L. *Chanzeaux, a Village in Anjou*. Cambrdige, Mass.: Harvard University Press, 1966.

Zald, M. N., ed. *Power in Organizations*. Nashville: Vanderbilt University Press, 1970.
Zaleznik, A., and Moment, D. *The Dynamics of Interpersonal Behavior*. New York: Wiley, 1964.

Index